Healing Power:

Ten Steps to Pain Management and Spiritual Evolution

REVISED

Philip Shapiro, M.D.

Introducing the Universal Healing Wheel

authorHOUSE®

AuthorHouse™
1663 Liberty Drive
Bloomington, IN 47403
www.authorhouse.com
Phone: 1-800-839-8640

First published by AuthorHouse 7/16/2010

ISBN: 978-1-4520-4520-7 (e)
ISBN: 978-1-4520-4518-4 (sc)
ISBN: 978-1-4520-4519-1 (hc)

Library of Congress Control Number: 2010909296

Printed in the United States of America
Bloomington, Indiana

This book is printed on acid-free paper.

For my courageous patients who teach me
forbearance, sweetness, and humility every day.

PRAISE FOR THE BOOK

This book is a true gift. Dr. Shapiro has melded his unique perspective as a physician and clinical psychiatrist with his study of the teachings of the great sages. The synthesis of concepts is remarkable. The result is a universal toolkit for managing the physical, psychological and spiritual pain that life brings.

The first part of the book draws a map of how we perpetuate our suffering, big and small. The second part offers an abundance of tools to break the cycle and manage life's pain. This is not an "Instant Karma Reduction" self-help book. It puts you on the path to relief from suffering, and arms you with a boatload of practical tools to deploy when the going gets tough. The rest is up to you.

To be fully effective, at least some of the techniques presented (those most relevant for you) must be integrated into your daily life. The payoff appears to be as big as you want it to be. Beyond relief from pain or anguish, this book also offers the promise of a life that may never look the same to you again. In an amazing way.

Mark Block

In this remarkable book, Dr. Shapiro takes on the world of "Brutal Reality," which he sees as threefold: death, pain and suffering, and the unknown. It is a world we avoid at all costs, but he takes us there and brings us back alive, healed and enlightened. This book is meant for all of us who are helpers or who are seeking help in the recovery process. We can all find something to learn here.

This book is a great blessing to those of us making peace with our lives and the world we live in. Philip Shapiro has crafted a handbook for how to live with less suffering, greater freedom, and love. As a professional in the field spiritual counseling, I deeply appreciate the user-friendly presentation of the great wisdom teachings of the world. I value that an individual on the street, a physician, or a healthcare professional can apply the teachings to their own personal development or use it with clients. I use this book with my clients and find it to be highly effective.

We use this book as a resource in our clinic. What it does exceptionally well is create an architecture for problem-solving. Whatever the source of distress--spiritual, emotional or physical--the methods and qualities presented here help the individual develop peace and eventual mastery over pain.

Both medicine and the world's great religious traditions aim to alleviate human suffering. What Dr. Shapiro has done is distill the underlying spiritual principles and techniques of these traditions and demonstrate how we can use this wisdom to treat life's most painful difficulties.

In a chronically under-funded health care system, we need affordable tools to help people obtain relief from suffering. In *Healing Power*, Dr. Shapiro synthesizes complex concepts and presents them in a way that is exceptionally relevant and useful for health care professionals today.

Meg Kaveny, MSW, Supervisor, Mobile Crisis Team

This book is a profound journey of growth and development. Using a system of steps, the reader/practitioner is able to progress towards a spiritual awakening at their own pace. This inspiring work will shed its light upon the path of any serious student seeking the transformative power of spiritual healing.

Corbett Monica, Founder/Executive Director,
Dual Diagnosis Anonymous of Oregon, Inc.

I really like the idea of being able to replace one's ego with spiritual qualities. Dr. Shapiro shows us how to proceed toward that goal. He teaches us methods that lead to habits of peace, contentment and wellness. His Ten Steps make a wonderful resource for the individual seeker, and an excellent study for a small group.

Anastasia Moret, Manager, Occupational and Physical Therapy

This book found me at a time of great change. Everything in my personal and business worlds had crashed at once, and life kept getting harder. Phil's book opened my eyes, gave me hope, and outlined a way to move forward with a clear, effective plan to become a better and stronger person. Having simple methods to create new habits has helped me more than I could imagine.

David Whitney, President, Progressive Finishes, Inc.

In this book, Dr. Shapiro offers a compelling and practical approach to dealing with humankind's deepest questions, most troubling problems, as well as the challenges of everyday life. Perhaps his greatest contribution is his ability to reveal universal truths and to make these truths accessible and useable for anyone seeking wisdom.

Steve Bearden, PhD, Assistant Professor of Marriage
and Family Counseling, George Fox University

Healing Power brings a compelling message of hope and resilience to healthcare professionals and to consumers. As a gifted teacher and mentor, Dr. Shapiro takes a fresh approach to spirituality as an essential component of healing. True to its title, this book instills a sense of power over one's life and provides tools for a lasting change.

Mona Knapp, LCSW, Director of Clinical
Services, Luke Dorf, Inc.

Philip Shapiro's inspiring and newly revised book, *Healing Power*, has something for almost all of us, whether we identify ourselves as helpers or those needing help, healers or those in pain, spiritually aware or those who seek awakening. Dr. Shapiro compassionately and courageously provides, through a comprehensive, but easily understandable approach, methods for any of us to identify how we get tripped up in our attempts to achieve balance and peace in our lives. He then provides techniques that have proven effective through centuries of practice, taking the most useful advice and guidance (the greatest hits?) from a number of the world's leading spiritual masters. The unique value of this approach is the integration of spiritual understanding into the mix of biological, psychological, and social influences on our wellbeing.

Whether you use this book to develop your own plan for self-care, recovery, or a path to happiness, or simply wish to understand how and why things are the way they are, this is a great resource. I can't recommend it highly enough.

David Pollack, MD, Professor for Public Policy,
Oregon Health Sciences University

Dr. Shapiro has created a rare gift for everyone on this difficult path of life. As a Western trained psychiatrist and a meditator steeped in the wisdom of the East, he distills knowledge from both paths into a guide for dealing with painful issues. People of all faiths and temperaments can use this book. A profound work.

Bill Johnson, Author, "A Story is a Promise"

CONTENTS

PART ONE
TEN STEPS / 1

PART TWO
SPIRITUAL PRACTICE / 95

PART SEVEN
CONCLUSION / 479

ACKNOWLEDGMENTS

I have been blessed with profound support from family, friends, teachers, patients, and editors. I would like to express my deepest gratitude to the following. Without their help, there would be no book. I thank:

My beloved parents, Edward and Dorothy Shapiro. My father teaches goodness. My mother embodies empathy. My sister, Suzanne, who showed me purity of heart. My grandparents, grandchildren, aunts, uncles, and cousins for their continuous love and support.

My patients, who teach me courage, forbearance, sweetness, and humility every day.

All of my teachers.

The lineage of spiritual masters in Self-Realization Fellowship, for their boundless wisdom, particularly Daya Mata, Swami Sri Yukteswar, and Paramahansa Yogananda.

My extraordinary writing coach, Bill Johnson, and deft line editor, Charity Heller. My friend and advisor Salli Slaughter.

My friend Adrianne Brockman, for use of her prize winning photo, *What Joy!*, which she graciously provided for the cover of this book. My friend Sam Tyler for her brilliant artistic contribution in designing the book cover.

The members of my spirituality and healing groups, my students, and all of my colleagues and clients at Central City Concern 12th Avenue Recovery Center for their invaluable commentary on how the ten-step healing model works in their lives; and a special thank you to Erika Armsbury, Ed Blackburn, Megan Chaloupka, Sara Goforth, Shauna Hahn, Colette Romero, Kathleen Roy, and Rachel Solotaroff.

My friends, Steve Bearden, Phil Bolton, Barbara Colleran, Monica

Desmond, Mary Faulkner, Kent Hathaway, Sue Hathaway, Meg Kaveny, Terra Kelsey, Corbett Monica, Stacey Moret, and Teddy Taegder for their kindness and support on spiritual matters.

My sons, Jon and David, and daughter-in-law, Siobhan, for their loving patience while I have been immersed in this project.

My phenomenal wife, Sharon Whitney. She knows things. She is the Goddess of Culture. She is my muse. She protected the space needed to create this book. She makes me laugh.

I bow to you all. May God bless you.

PART ONE
TEN STEPS

CHAPTER ONE

THE IMPORTANCE OF
PERSONAL SPIRITUAL HISTORY

The Birth of a Model

Life is difficult. Our problems are deep, complex, and severe. Often, we find ourselves caught in a web of pain. We don't know how we got there, and we don't know how to get out. Because we manage our pain poorly, we find ourselves in more trouble; poorly handled problems are a source of untold difficulty.

We need help. We need to learn more about the origin of our suffering so we can manage it more skillfully. Then, instead of dragging us down, our problems become a source of strength and peace.

I have a passion for learning how healing power acts as an antidote to pain and devastation. I have studied with the teachers, masters, and gurus of psychology, psychiatry, and spirituality, searching their models with a fine toothcomb, looking for elements that strengthen our ability to heal. The ten-step model described in this book is a composite of healing principles and methods I have extracted from the great wisdom traditions and organized into cognitive-behavioral practices. These techniques are designed to help the reader transform any troubling problem into spiritual power.

In this chapter, I will describe some of the key events in my life that led to the birth of the ten steps. See if you can find yourself—and, if you are a healthcare professional, your patients—in this story.

BRUTAL REALITY AND THE ILLUSION OF SAFETY, SECURITY, AND IMMORTALITY

In May 1943, I was a seven-month-old fetus. Of course, I don't remember what it was like, but I imagine it was a good place to be: warm, quiet, peaceful, safe, and protected. One day, in an instant, the feeling of safety and the quiet vibrations of motherly nurturance were replaced by fright, flight, and freeze.

My parents went out for dinner. A neighbor was babysitting Suzanne, my twenty-month-old sister. The neighbor left Suzanne on a table and walked away. She fell. When my parents came back, they discovered their baby daughter running a fever and convulsing with seizures. They took her to the hospital, where a spinal tap revealed blood in her spinal fluid. She had a type of brain damage that causes muscle spasms, a permanent condition known as cerebral palsy.

Suzanne's life was one of severe and chronic disability. She had difficulty walking and often fell; loud crashes could sound in our house at any time. My parents and I would run to her in fear of what we might find. Would there be a broken leg, a cracked skull, blood? Due to muscle spasms that inhibited her ability to swallow, she would often choke or gag on her food, banishing in a flash the camaraderie of our family supper.

She was a beautiful person, physically and spiritually. I never saw her angry. She was pure love. Despite her beauty, she remained homebound, isolated, and lonely because her disability prevented her from keeping up with her peers.

At age twenty-four, a sudden loss of eyesight compounded her problems. Over a few short weeks, she became blind; no physician could diagnose the cause. She went to a school for the blind, where she learned braille and met the love of her life, a wonderful man who was also blind. It was her lifelong dream to get married, and, at twenty-seven, she did. On the weekend of her honeymoon, she got sick. Six weeks later she was dead. The same mysterious neurological disease that caused her blindness had destroyed her nervous system.

Each of us has to deal with brutal reality—perhaps not as early as the seventh month of fetal life or, in Suzanne's case, at twenty months, but eventually the time comes. Brutal reality is defined in Step 2 of the ten-step model as death, pain and suffering, and the unknown. In this work, we will study how our ability to manage brutal reality determines whether we move forward, slip backward, or stay stuck in this life.

THE CHEESEBURGER EFFECT

I was born on July 14, 1943 to a middle-class family of Conservative Jewish faith. Conservative Judaism lies between the Reform and Orthodox branches of Judaism. The tradition includes a strong sense of tribal identity and solidarity, a profound emphasis on taking care of family, support and encouragement of higher education, a great sense of humor, excellent food, the expectation that you marry in the faith, the discipline to follow certain dietary laws, and more.

I followed the rules and customs faithfully until age twelve, when I was in downtown Chicago at an athletic club my dad belonged to. I was there on Saturday morning to work out. It was time to go home. Back then pharmacies had lunch counters where you could get a sandwich. All of my non-Jewish friends were eating cheeseburgers, but I wasn't supposed to due to the kosher laws. I wanted to see what it would taste like. I ordered a cheeseburger, French fries, and a shake. There are several sins here: the meat was not kosher; you don't mix cheese with meat; the fries may have been made in pig fat; and, I chased it with a shake, which added more milk to the meat.

I ate the whole thing. Then I knew why other people eat cheeseburgers. It was delicious. I loved it, but there was a problem. Since God was watching and didn't approve of my lunch, I thought I would be punished—swiftly and severely.

The mind of a little Jewish boy who breaks the law for the first time works something like this: The Jewish superego says do not eat a cheeseburger. The id, or pleasure principle, says, do it. The result is guilt. I thought, "I am going to get run over by a bus because God is angry with me." But I got home safely. That night, I thought, "This is really cool. If I can eat a cheeseburger and not die, what else can I do?"

I call this seemingly harmless little event the "Cheeseburger Effect." It marks a profoundly important factor in my understanding of how belief systems work. More about this in a moment.

TERROR AT THE ABYSS

Move the clock forward to the University of Michigan. I am nineteen years old and taking courses in preparation for medical school. I am one of forty-five thousand students from all over the world. This was a period of intense study and intellectual conversations. A little white wine on Friday night and all of the big questions are on the table: "Why am I here?" "What is the meaning and purpose of life?" "Why is there so much suffering and evil in the world and what can be done about it?" No idea was immune to examination. Is this complex world of good, evil, joy, and suffering accidental or designed? And the ultimate question for me: "Does God exist?" One night, the answer: "I don't know." Between the cheeseburger as a twelve-year-old boy in Chicago to my loss of God as an undergraduate, I lost the rites and rituals of my belief system of origin one by one. Enter existential anxiety, or "terror at the abyss." I still had my values, but I no longer had a story to tell me what it is all about, a story to help me manage the suffering of brutal reality.

Think of a chess game as a metaphor for belief systems. The cheeseburger is a pawn. Other concepts, images, rites, and rituals are represented by the rook, knight, bishop, and queen, all of which are there to protect the king. I lost a pawn when I ate the cheeseburger. I proceeded to lose one piece after another, until, one day, I wasn't sure of God's existence. There was a meltdown of the entire system. When the king went down, I experienced the unknown, the abyss, the great mystery of life, untempered by my inherited religious story.

This abyss is a difficult place to be. The loss of a belief system can be devastating. Belief systems provide us with meaning and purpose, story and metaphor, inspiration, protection, guidance, truth, healing, community, service, and expansion of spiritual qualities such as love, compassion, understanding, and forgiveness. Whether we stay in our religion of origin or not, belief systems are monumentally important.

HEALING THE PAIN

In my early adult years, my terror at the abyss—combined with my fair share of character defects—left me lost, confused, and overwhelmed much of the time. My relationships weren't working, and I wasn't sure of myself at work. I could not figure it out myself. I knew I needed help, so I sought out psychotherapy. I had several therapists, but none helped until I met Dominick. He looked like Pavarotti. He was a jolly, fabulously brilliant, psychoanalytically oriented psychotherapist. Ours was a direct relationship of face-to-face conversations. I did not lie on his couch. We did not dwell in the past. We looked at problems and solutions in the here and now. I would walk into his office in pain, twisted like a pretzel. I walked out feeling better. Sometimes I went with my wife, Sharon Whitney. We would enter his office frustrated, angry, and stuck, but right after the session, we would be able to eat breakfast in friendship. How does that work? I started to think, "Pain and healing. Pain and healing." I was fascinated with it. What did Dominick do to help us feel better?

My sons were having some trouble with the street and drugs. I went to Alanon, which didn't work, so I tried Alcoholics Anonymous. I would identify myself as Phil and state why I was in the room: "Although I am not an addict or alcoholic, we all have problems, and I have addiction in my family, so I would like to stay and just listen." Since the meetings were open, they would accept me and carry on. Again, I would walk into the meeting in pain and walk out feeling better. What is this healing power? How does it work?

Psychotherapy was good and AA helped, but I needed more. I was still in great pain. My search for solace and healing expanded to the spiritual domain. I mined the great religious field for pearls. My studies included Christianity, Hinduism, Buddhism, Native American spirituality, Judaism, Zen, and others. I reviewed the lives of the saints, sages, teachers, masters, and gurus. I studied Jesus, the Buddha, and Krishna. Sacred texts described heroic and courageous events, gentle acts of quiet, humble service, a promise of healing, and higher states of consciousness. I thought, "What do I know? Maybe I should listen to the masters."

But whom do I follow? What is spiritual truth? In the vast array of spiritual books and teachers, there are a variety of conflicting ideas and beliefs. Where should I place my trust?

THE SCIENTIFIC METHOD IN METAPHYSICS

In my search, I instinctively resisted a "my way or the highway " approach. But if the teaching I was exploring said, "There are many ways to climb the mountain—try this method and see if it works; you can prove it to yourself through direct personal experience," I relaxed because it appealed to my sense of scientific inquiry and respected my needs and individuality.

To verify spiritual truth, I accept no idea on blind faith. I decide for myself via experimentation. My laboratory is human experience. My test tube is the body. My tools are the built-in equipment of the body: consciousness, energy, reason, feeling, intuition, and direct personal experience. I use these tools when I practice any of the spiritual disciplines described in this work, and I recommend you do the same.

We can decipher the difference between spiritual fiction and fact even without test tubes, lab tests, and X-rays. We can take life's profoundly important questions and put them to the test. For example, saints proclaim that compassionate service to humanity gives peace of mind and strength, that meditation works, that higher states of consciousness exist, and that the body harbors the actual God of the universe. Are their claims true or false?

Each of the spiritual methods described in this work gives us an opportunity to test new ideas in the laboratory of personal experience. We can prove or disprove a new idea by developing a spiritual practice. This is the scientific method in metaphysics. It appeals to scientific agnostics. True believers and true non-believers may not be able to use this method.

I practiced a variety of spiritual methods for years. Contemplation, affirmation, progressive muscle relaxation, prayer, meditation, mindfulness, service, yoga, breathwork, and the transformation of emotion proved especially helpful. I started to feel better, became a better person, and experienced a variety of the wonderful superconscious states I had been reading about.

A MODEL EMERGES

In 1980, I worked as a staff psychiatrist at Harlem Hospital, in a fully funded psychiatric rehabilitation program similar to the well-known and highly successful Fountain House in New York City. This was no ordinary psychiatric job. There was so much devastation: racism, poverty, mental illness, substance abuse. A popular street drug at that time was Angel Dust, or PCP. To take this drug is like playing Russian roulette. Experience ranges from euphoria to permanent brain damage and horrible, atrocious acts of violence toward oneself and others.

I decided to call a meeting and focus on substance use. People came. We were just trying to understand what was going on. There was no model. An agency in another part of town heard about this group and thought I knew what I was doing with dual diagnosis: mental illness combined with substance use. They invited me to give a talk and I accepted.

I look back on this incident with wonder. How could I accept this invitation and not have a model? I chalk it up to the male ego, which cannot refuse an invitation. Like a peacock, it wants to show its gorgeous tail and feathers. What feathers! I didn't have any to show. About four days before the talk, I thought, "You'd better get some feathers!"

I took out my trusted clipboard and jotted down some notes. I reviewed with fascination the relationship of pain and healing: Dominick, the analyst; AA meetings; a host of psychotherapy healing models; the lives of saints and sages; spiritual practices. Thanks to this psychospiritual technology, I was feeling better, becoming a better person, and experiencing higher states of consciousness.

On the other side of the coin, I met brutal reality. On the same morning that I experienced a superconscious state in meditation, I walked the streets of Harlem. The devastation of mental illness, substance use, racism, and poverty were in my face.

In my notes, I lined up pain and healing and tried to connect the dots. After about four days, I saw a model in those pages. The day I gave my talk, I presented "Brutal Reality and the Illusion of Safety, Security, and Immortality," a model describing four universal domains where we can work to expand healing power and manage pain more skillfully. It was well received and has lasted all these years as an effective method for understanding the intimate connections between pain and healing. Now, it forms a stand-alone platform for the ten steps described in this book.

Before we get to the model, let me ask you a question. You are in pain. You go to your doctor. The doctor makes an accurate diagnosis and gives you the right medication, diet, and exercise program. You follow the instructions, but you still have pain. You may go back to your doctor or pursue alternative care. Now, assume you have reached maximum benefit from traditional medical and complementary and alternative remedies and still have pain. This can be any pain of body, mind, or soul. What do you do now? How do you try to heal your pain in the psychological, social, and spiritual domains? See Figure 1.

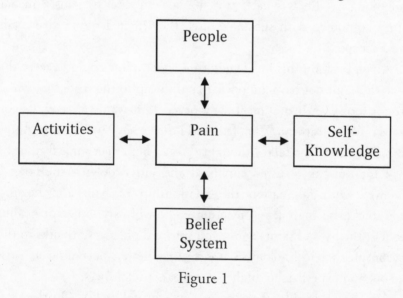

Figure 1

To heal our pain, we work in four domains. Here is an example of how this works.

PEOPLE

I lived in New York City for nine years and Alaska for two years before I came to the polite society of Oregon. New Yorkers and Alaskans are a little more expressive, and I may have been a carrier of that "assertive" vibration. People at work notice. Feeling something different, they might say, "Phil, you are a little too New Yorky." I am sensitive to criticism of any kind and feel bad. Fear, insecurity, worry, and doubt replace my peace of mind. I think, "Relax, these feelings are the natural human reaction to criticism." I ruminate. I can't seem to shake it.

The first thing I do when I get home from work is talk to my wife, Sharon Whitney. She is my best friend, a genius, funny, the goddess of culture, and a muse. She helps me. I tell my story. She might say, "Don't worry. Once they get to know you, they will enjoy you more." This helps, and I feel better. But she could say, "They are right. You are that way." Sharon could be telling me the truth, and I just need to suffer more to see the light.

People may help the pain or make it worse, and, sometimes, they are just wrong. Examine any network closely enough and you will find good, bad, and ugly. Networks heal and create pain. The idea is to have the best possible network. We all need love, compassion, understanding, patience, kindness, and humor.

But no matter how good the network, even if it is perfect—and none of us has that—it is still incomplete. There is no way to eliminate all of our pain in the network. To try to do this creates codependency and more pain.

People are like medication. When we find the right people at the right dose, we get the most pain relief and healing. We can approach the "right people dose" and then turn to the second universal healer: constructive meaningful activities.

ACTIVITIES

Constructive meaningful activities include work, training, volunteering, culture, the arts, hobbies, sports, and recreation. I turn to my activity program for healing and pain management. I get my Walkman and listen to rock and roll as I jog in the city streets. I go to work and serve humanity. I come home and eat dinner while I watch TV or go to the movies and eat popcorn. I run on the track of activities that exist on the physical plane from the beginning of my day until I reach exhaustion and, finally, sleep. Sometimes this works, but not always, and even if my activity program is perfect, there will be residual pain.

Most of us get into trouble with bad habits because we try to eliminate the residual pain with unhealthy painkillers. All too often, people resort to substance, sex, and food abuse, gambling, materialism, power trips, and a host of other activities in an attempt to reduce or eliminate their suffering. This is described in more detail in Step 4 of the ten-step model and in the chapter on habit transformation.

Activities are like medication. When we find the right activities at the right dose, we have more healing power and our ability to manage suffering improves. When we approach the "right activity dose," where the most healing and pain management occur, we can turn to the third universal healer: belief systems.

BELIEF SYSTEMS

I lost my religion of origin, my Judaic belief system. Looking back on that, I came to understand in a deep and personal way what belief systems provide for us. It is staggering that working with belief systems is not part of mental health training. How can we even think about recovery unless we include meaning and purpose? Meaning and purpose are at the heart of the healing process.

Positive thoughts lead to positive feelings and vibrations that promote the healing process. Many people go to church, synagogue, or mosque for positive thought, worship, support of like-minded people, committee and charitable work, and more. I turn to my belief system: yoga, meditation, mindfulness, prayer, affirmations, and contemplation of sacred texts. These powerful tools stimulate healing power and reduce my pain, but it still hurts. Now what? There is one more thing I can do: ride the pain waves.

SELF-KNOWLEDGE

I spend time alone with the pain, without people, activities, or help from organized religion. I just sit with the pain and let it teach me. By going deep into the center of the pain, I discover my issues, problems, solutions, and strategies. This is self-knowledge, that part of my personal story *that can only be discovered if I ride the pain waves alone.*

For complete healing to occur, we need introspection, or self-analysis. To succeed in introspection, we need to learn to successfully navigate our way through painful emotion. Painful emotion is a teacher that bears the gift of self-knowledge.

There is a lot going on inside of us: thoughts, attitudes, emotions, and desires drive our choices, behaviors, and habits. Introspection allows us to see our strengths and our limitations. If we don't review and understand what is going on inside ourselves, we are more likely to make unwise choices that lead to trouble.

All of us experience emotional pain in response to ordinary daily events. Emotions are intelligent—they carry meaningful information about our story. We need to unpack that story, for it is there that we can find our problems and our solutions. Peace and strength live on the other side of every painful problem; you will learn more about how this works in the lesson on Transformation of Emotion.

This completes a brief summary of the four healing universes: people, activities, belief systems, and self-knowledge. These four offer a potent combination of healing and pain management. Pain management and healing are maximized when we get these four universes balanced, at the right dose.

To complete the model, we need to bring back brutal reality and the illusion of safety, security, and immortality. See Figure 2.

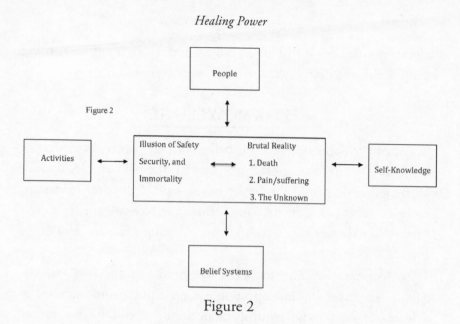

Figure 2

BRUTAL REALITY

Brutal reality is death, pain and suffering, and the unknown. It has ultimate power. No one escapes. It asserts itself in the life of anyone, anytime, in a seemingly endless variety of ways. It manifests as illness, disability, and trauma and includes other kinds of loss as well, both on an individual level, and—in the case of events such as war, earthquakes, and economic depression—at a cataclysmic, global level. Ultimately, brutal reality manifests as the death of both individuals and of large groups of people.

At death, we go somewhere or nowhere. Often, we have trouble with small changes, let alone a radical transformation into the mysterious unknown. We don't like this power arrangement. The ego is about control—we want to be in charge, but we're not. Brutal reality has the ace in life's deck of cards. We can get as many cards as possible, but we can't get the ace.

We try not to think about this part of reality. It is so difficult to understand and accept. But avoidance leads to even more trouble. If we're not prepared, if we don't have a plan or a program, we can easily get overwhelmed when life gets rough. Remember this: *how you man-*

14

age your pain determines whether you move forward, slip backward, or stay stuck in this life. We need an antidote for brutal reality. What can we do?

THE ILLUSION OF SAFETY, SECURITY, AND IMMORTALITY

We have a need for absolute safety in order to function, but this is impossible on the physical plane because brutal reality has ultimate power that transcends the material plane of existence. Safety on the physical plane is temporary and limited, but we often take it for granted or regard it as permanent—this attitude creates what I refer to here as the illusion of safety. We need as much of this illusion as we can get. When we feel safe, we have peace of mind. With peace of mind, we can function at our best.

We get this feeling of safety by thinking we have more time. Immortality, in this case, does not mean life after death; it is the sense that we have more time. If you have an appointment later today, a dinner plan for tonight, and an expectation that you will have a tomorrow, you are most likely living within an illusion of safety. But what happens if a gunman walks into your building at work or if the building shakes from an earthquake? The illusion of safety—and your peace of mind—is replaced by brutal reality and fear.

Safety is everything. We have to have it for our families, our communities, our organizations, and ourselves. It is the drug-elixir of life. And how do we get the illusion of safety? Through people, activities, belief systems, and self-knowledge. We can skillfully manage brutal reality and create the feeling of safety through positive action in the four healing universes. The illusion of safety, security, and immortality is the universal balm we all use to try and cover up our universal phobia: brutal reality. To make our balm, to do the covering up, we use our support network, activities, belief systems, and self-knowledge.

The central theme in this model is that people, activities, belief systems, and self-knowledge offer a four-pronged defense against brutal reality to create the illusion of safety, security, and immortality. The ultimate goal is to utilize the four healing universes to create peace of mind and to hold that peace while facing death, pain and suffering, and the unknown.

There are six components in this model:

1. People
2. Activities
3. Belief systems
4. Self-knowledge
5. Brutal reality
6. The illusion of safety, security, and immortality

I still use this model and continue to teach it to patients, clients and professionals. It can stand on its own, but its components are also the building blocks for the ten-step model described in this book.

MIND-BODY MEDICINE TRAINING

In 2002, I attended a conference on "Spirituality and Healing in Medicine" sponsored by Harvard Medical School and led by Herbert Benson, M.D. This was a professional-life-changing experience. On day one, a variety of speakers focused on the data: there is now ample scientific evidence that people with an active faith system have better outcomes in medicine, surgery, mental health, and addiction. On day two, religious leaders—including a rabbi, a priest, a Hispanic Pentecostal, a Hindu, a Tibetan Buddhist, and an Islamic teacher and professor—described the healing principles of their great faith traditions. Day three focused on integrating the healing principles of Western science with religious healing traditions for the benefit of professionals and their patients.

This was exciting. I had arrived at the same conclusion experientially and intuitively. I knew the importance of belief systems in healing and pain management from direct personal experience and empirical observation. Now, there was proof. In parallel evolution, my little story was a part of something much bigger. My little molecule was part of a big chemistry set.

My theory that belief systems impact disease and healing was confirmed. We can extract and organize healing principles from the great wisdom traditions into cognitive-behavioral or mind-body medicine practices, practice these ourselves, and teach them to our patients.

The stage was set. After the conference, I returned to my work at the community mental health clinic in downtown Portland, Oregon, where a confluence of events ultimately led to the formation of the ten-step healing model described in this work.

SPIRITUALITY GROUP AT MY CLINIC

In public mental health, we are almost always functioning with precious, limited resources, and, sometimes, even those are subject to budget reductions. When I returned from the mind-body medicine training in Boston, the clinic was dangerously underfunded. We had funding for crisis intervention, medication management, and, as needed, case management, but there was no outreach, no groups, no classes, and minimal counseling. Each case manager worked with between one hundred and one hundred and fifty patients, and an additional two hundred patients remained unassigned in a float pool served by the case manager of the day. Most of the case managers were young, relatively inexperienced, and confronted with some of the most complicated problems in mental health. This was a dangerous and frightening time. Eventually, some resources were added. New staff were assigned to the clinic, so we had the opportunity to reinstate some programming, such as a group or two.

We didn't know what the clients wanted, so we sent out a survey offering thirty types of groups and asking clients to give feedback on what additional groups they might want. The number one choice was a group on spirituality and healing. This option was listed along with mental illness education, medication and symptom management, cognitive-behavioral therapy, and other traditional options.

It seemed people wanted more than knowledge of illness and traditional treatment. They wanted to know something about their illnesses, but in a greater context. People want to discuss life's big questions and how those questions related to their personal struggles with disease and disability:

1. Who am I?
2. Why am I here?
3. What is the meaning and purpose of life?
4. Why is there so much suffering and evil in this life?
5. How do I understand suffering?
6. Is there a God, and, if so, what is its nature?
7. How can I find peace, love, and joy in the face of suffering and evil?
8. How do I get through all of this?

I was known as the "meditating doctor" or the "spiritual doctor," so the clinic program manager asked me if I would do the group. I accepted the offer and created a manual of universal healing principles, methods, and qualities from the great faith traditions. Another staff member joined me to facilitate the group.

We formed the group and read the manual. We discussed and practiced affirmations, meditation, mindfulness, breathwork, and other methods. We emphasized universal human and spiritual principles: you are not your illness; your higher self is composed of wonderful qualities such as compassion, love, understanding, and kindness; you are a human being equal to all others. This was manna from heaven, water in the desert. People loved it. They said, "As mental health clients, we have never felt so respected." This was exciting. The success of the group was invigorating and inspired me to write this book. I wanted to share my experience with a wider audience.

THE TEN STEPS

To create the ten steps, I deconstructed each religion into discrete pieces. I took out dogma, ritual, and other nonessentials. I extracted and organized essential healing principles into doable, practical steps and tools designed to help the reader transform any pain or problem into spiritual power.

The first five steps have to do with suffering and the last five steps, healing. Those who follow the ten steps will learn how to expand healing power, become more skillful pain managers, and evolve spiritually. There will be a corresponding shift in the locus of control from without to within, and a new understanding will emerge: that the peace, love, and joy we seek in the outer world can and ultimately must be found within.

That first book, *Healing Power: Ten Steps to Pain Management and Spiritual Evolution*, was published in 2005. This work is the sequel to that book. Here you will find all the information from the original book, as well as some new material. In this work, you will find the material broken down into smaller, bite-size pieces to make it more accessible to the reader.

EXERCISES

1. Following is a quick assessment of the four healing zones:

   a. People: Who is in your life that you can really talk to?
   b. Activities: What is your day like?
   c. Belief systems: Do you have a spiritual activity such as church, prayer, or a personal belief system?
   d. Self-knowledge: How do you handle emotions such as anger, depression, fear, and guilt?

2. Describe how the six components listed below weave the fabric of your life. Focus on how you use people, activities, belief systems, and self-knowledge to shift from brutal reality to a feeling of safety.

   a. People
   b. Activities
   c. Belief systems

   d. Self-knowledge

   e. The illusion of safety, security, and immortality

   f. Brutal reality

3. If you are a healthcare professional, describe how the six components drive the lives of your patients.

4. How do the six components drive the lives of your family, friends, strangers, even enemies?

In the next chapter, you will find a discussion of the ten-step model and its place in the world of traditional, integrative, and mind-body medicine.

CHAPTER TWO

INTRODUCTION

The purpose of this book is to help people accomplish three important goals:

1. Expand healing power: for body, mind, and soul
2. Become more skillful pain managers: for any pain, problem, disease, or disability
3. Evolve spiritually: feel better, become a better person, and experience higher states of consciousness

To guide the reader toward these goals, the book will outline fifteen proven methods—from ancient wisdom and modern science—designed to help the reader transform any painful problem into a source of strength and peace.

I have been a practicing physician and spiritual seeker for forty years. My medical practice has been in community psychiatry, working with people who have profound and complicated problems: major mental illness, substance abuse, physical illness, homelessness, poverty, unemployment, and broken families. As a spiritual seeker, I have studied and practiced a variety of methods from the world's great spiritual traditions. In each of these fields—medicine and spirituality—the goal is to expand healing power and eliminate suffering.

In the beginning of my career, these two tracks remained separate. Bringing any spiritual teaching into the medical realm was impermissible. There was no scientific proof. It would have been considered inappropriate.

This attitude has changed with the advent of mind-body medicine. There is now ample scientific evidence that those with an active spiritual belief system have better outcomes in medicine, surgery, mental health, and addiction.

It is now possible to combine the healing principles of both the medical and spiritual fields. To this end, I have developed a ten-step, self-help model that I use myself and teach to my students and patients.

The book is written for patients, colleagues, and the general public. Specifically, those who may profit from this work are:

1. Healthcare consumers looking for help in managing any painful problem, symptom, disease, or disability
2. Healthcare professionals interested in helping their patients increase their pain management skills and heal (the model supplements the healing practices of all medical specialties, including physical medicine, mental health, substance abuse, and alternative health care)
3. People in crisis struggling with severe problems
4. Beginning or advanced seekers of psychological and spiritual knowledge
5. People who want help with any pain or problem
6. Spiritual counselors and chaplains
7. Yoga teachers and practitioners
8. The intellectually curious

Those who follow the ten steps will learn how to:

1. Expand healing power
2. Become more skillful pain managers
3. Evolve spiritually

We can tap into an expanded reservoir of healing power when we learn how to manage our pain more skillfully. Skillful pain management not only expands our healing power; it also helps us to evolve spiritually. Spiritual qualities such as love, compassion, understanding, and forgiveness grow. We feel better, become better people, and experience higher states of consciousness.

THE INHERENT HEALING WISDOM OF THE BODY

To understand healing, let's start with the intelligent power that operates every cell in the body and see how that relates to current medical practice.

Healing power is unfathomable! To contemplate even a tiny aspect of this Omniscient Power breeds awe and respect. Reflect on its brilliance. A cut heals. In response to bacteria or viruses, the body creates precisely designed antibodies which hunt down and destroy the invaders. The body knows how to transform food into energy and materials for repair of damaged cells. Cells in the body are like construction workers with specialized jobs. Some build. Others tear down. Some transport. Still others eliminate debris.

Every cell in the body forms two thousand proteins per second and sends these proteins where they need to go. The human body has seventy-five trillion such cells working together in near perfect harmony so that we can stand, walk, think, decide, see, hear, touch, taste, feel, love, play, help others, and enjoy beauty. When there is an imbalance disrupting these functions, the intelligent power goes to work to fix it and does so brilliantly. At some point, however, the incomparably wise healing power needs our help.

THE MEDICAL MODEL

The wisdom of the body, however brilliant, cannot fix everything on its own. Some pain or problem gets past the body's inherent protections and breaks through as a symptom that won't go away. A new lump, an unfamiliar pain, or a lingering discomfort disturbs the routine defenses that give us a feeling of safety.

The flicker of a single thought, such as, "This could be serious!" creates anxiety. An alarm goes off. "Am I okay? Am I safe? Or am I going toward what I fear the most—intense suffering, disability, or even death—with its associated fear of the unknown?"

With symptoms and associated fear in hand, we go to the doctor. The doctor makes a diagnosis and treatment plan, which most often involves the use of medication. The medicine in some way helps the healing power do its work. If it works completely, the symptom, pain, and associated fear are gone. Back in our comfort zone, we feel safe and move on.

But what happens when the symptom persists? We go back to the doctor and place the painful problem and fear back on the table.

Doctors do all they can within the constraints of the medical model, but some illness is chronic and there will always be residual symptoms, pain, and fear. Well-intentioned doctors and patients, looking together for pain relief and healing, often get caught up in unhealthy polypharmacy.

Alternatively, the physician knows the limitations of the medical model and does not continue to prescribe medications. In this scenario, the patient is left with unmanageable suffering and may as a result resort to unhealthy painkilling devices such as substance use, codependency, and a variety of other addictions that only lead to more trouble. Enter integrative, mind-body medicine.

INTEGRATIVE MEDICINE

The medical model has great power, but, alone, it can be reductionist, focusing on symptom management without getting to the root cause of disease and healing. Integrative medicine includes biological, psychological, social, and spiritual aspects. We can look for the root cause of disease and healing in each of these four domains.

Integrative medicine looks at the whole person. You still go to your doctor and get your medication but now *you will learn how to heal yourself* in the psychological, social, and spiritual realms.

Integrative medicine defines four evidence-based healing universes:

1. Biological: a healthy body free of pain (this includes traditional, complementary, and alternative medicine)
2. Psychological: a strong, positive, calm, focused, resilient mind ready for solving problems and shaping meaning
3. Social: giving and receiving love and engaging in constructive, meaningful activities
4. Spiritual: finding meaning and purpose, your higher self, and your place in the world

For complete healing and skillful pain management, we need comprehensive treatment planning with interventions in all four zones.

MIND-BODY MEDICINE
THE SPIRITUAL ASPECT OF COGNITIVE-BEHAVIORAL THERAPY

Recent studies in the field of mind-body medicine have shown us that people with an active faith or belief system have better healthcare outcomes in medicine, surgery, mental health, and addiction. These studies have included patients with cancer, heart disease, strokes, high blood pressure, asthma, mental illness, addiction, and other health problems.

The data demonstrates the essential principle that there is no separation between mind and body. The mind is connected to every cell in the body through electromagnetic and chemical waves. In some yet-to-be-determined way, thoughts have leverage in the inner workings of certain cells that effect disease and healing in the body.

Mind-body medicine teaches us how to apply the power of belief to healing. The discipline is emerging as a major force in health care. The burgeoning appeal of mind-body medicine is due to its scientific validity as well as its cost effectiveness; it is ultimately a self-help program. In his book, *Timeless Healing: The Power and Biology of Belief*, Dr. Herbert Benson estimates that mind-body techniques are the treatments of choice in 60–90 percent of all doctor visits and have positive effects no matter the illness.

We can harness the untapped power of the mind to expand healing power, control pain, and cultivate spiritual qualities. This book teaches readers how to do this in the comfort of their own homes, at work, while doing chores, or during leisure time.

EXPAND HEALING POWER

The scientific connection between spirituality and healing has been made; when we activate or intensify our spiritual belief systems, our healing powers expand. A magnificently intelligent healing power operates every cell in the body. We know how to make it grow. We know the leverage is in our very own cells. The key to expanding our healing power is in how we manage our pain.

SKILLFUL PAIN MANAGEMENT

To tap into the expanded reservoir of healing power, we must become more skillful pain managers. Remember: *how we manage our pain determines whether we move forward, slip backward, or stay stuck in this life.*

We cannot control the inevitable suffering of life, but we can control how we respond to it. We are afraid of suffering, disease, disability, the unknown, and death. This mental distress slows down the healing process and makes the pain worse. When disease persists, we can learn how to slow down and relax so we stay in charge and get our lives back.

Often, we cannot take disease away, but we can always help with pain management. Pain is both physical and psychological. All pain is experienced in the mind and can therefore be modulated by the mind. We can contain and reduce or expand and magnify the pain. You can control pain so pain does not control you.

CULTIVATE SPIRITUAL QUALITIES

If we manage our pain skillfully, healing power expands and we evolve spiritually. Spiritual qualities such as compassion, understanding, forgiveness, courage, patience, peace, love, and joy grow. We feel better. We become better people. We experience higher states of consciousness.

SELF-HELP AND SKILLS TRAINING

Much of the healing in the psychosocial and spiritual domain is accomplished via self-help. Self-help can be done through skills training: classes, groups, DVDs, CDs, books, manuals, the Internet. We can teach people how they can increase their healing power, become more skillful pain managers, and evolve spiritually at home or during the day while performing their routine activities. This is very good news, but how can we enter the spiritual domain as healthcare professionals and patients without getting into trouble? There are many barriers to entering the territory of spiritual belief systems.

PROBLEMS ENTERING THE SPIRITUAL DOMAIN

1. We don't work with Spirit.
2. We are not comfortable talking about religion.
3. We have no language or map.
4. We ignore or refer to spiritual counselors.
5. We lack training.
6. Belief systems are personal, intimate, and complex.
7. Many individuals and groups have a traumatic religious history.
8. Belief systems are often protected from changes by defensiveness and fierce feelings.
9. Levels of commitment to working with Spirit vary enormously.

GUIDELINES FOR APPROACHING BELIEF SYSTEMS

Following are the guidelines I used to address these barriers as I developed the ten steps. These guidelines were designed to help patients and professionals work with belief systems to gain the benefits of expanded healing power, skillful pain management, and spiritual evolution:

1. Access: provide safe, efficient, and effective access to the territory of belief systems, including a map on how to properly access these systems
2. Language: provide a common language that enables us to talk to each other about religion and spirituality without getting into trouble
3. Universal and inclusive: include universal or near-universal spiritual principles, methods, and qualities that can work for as many people as possible (atheists, agnostics, spiritual people, and religious people)
4. Individualize: support people to stay in their religion of origin and expand their practice, or to build their own program; there must be a cafeteria of options so people can take what they need and leave the rest
5. Root cause and solution: include the root causes of and solutions to our deepest suffering
6. User-friendly: while looking at our deepest suffering, the model should be as user-friendly as possible
7. Self-healing: design a set of healing methods that can be practiced anywhere, anytime—at home, at work, or at play

Following these guidelines, I created a self-help model in four stages:

1. Deconstruct the religions into discrete pieces
2. Eliminate dogma, ritual, and other nonessentials
3. Extract the healing principles we can use in health care
4. Organize the resulting principles into doable, practical steps and tools

TEN STEPS, FIFTEEN METHODS, ONE HUNDRED QUALITIES

The model has ten steps, fifteen methods, and one hundred qualities. Its purpose is to help readers expand their healing power, improve their pain management skills, and cultivate spiritual qualities.

- TEN STEPS. The first section of the book describes the ten steps. The first five steps describe the evolution of suffering. Here you will see how we mismanage the inevitable suffering of life and make it worse. In the second five steps, you will learn how to transform suffering into spiritual power by developing a spiritual practice.

- FIFTEEN METHODS. The middle section of the book is devoted to spiritual practice. Here you will find a description of spiritually oriented cognitive-behavioral methods proven over the ages to be effective tools for cultivating healing qualities. Detailed instructions explain how these methods help us cultivate love, peace, strength, and courage in response to any pain of the body, mind, or soul. Continued practice of the recommended methods helps us manage any difficulty life brings.

- ONE HUNDRED QUALITIES. The final section of the book describes spiritual qualities. We certainly need to work with our issues, problems, illnesses, and flaws, but these are not who we are. Labels obscure our true selves. Rather than brand ourselves with labels or identify with our problems, we are encouraged to see our true self as a composite of healing qualities adding up to Love. The center of our being is Love. From a list of one hundred qualities, ten are chosen for detailed study. Here we learn how to use our current problems as a springboard for discovering our true identity as Love, compassion, warmth, and kindness. Love is more powerful than any pain or problem. It is the Great Healer. It is a fundamental solution to all of our problems. It is who we really are. I capitalize the word *Love* to emphasize its divine nature.

POINTS TO REMEMBER

- The medical model alone often leaves the patient with unmanageable pain from persisting illness and consequent excessive use of painkilling medications. The healthcare practitioner and the patient need to know how to heal and manage suffering in the psychosocial and spiritual domain. There is evidence that healing takes place in each of these domains.

- The time has come for medicine to embrace four important areas in the study of disease and healing: the biological, psychological, social, and spiritual. We can find the cause and cure of disease in these four areas. Until recently in the West, our focus has been on the biological, with some emphasis on the psychological and social realms. Now, however, the scientific connection between spirituality and healing has been made, giving healthcare professionals, patients—and, indeed, everyone—access to an expanded reservoir of healing power that can be achieved by activating their spiritual belief systems.

- There is no one right way to do this work. The ideas and practices in this book originate from a wide variety of disciplines and teachings. There is no quarrel in the fundamentals of all great faith systems; rather, they complement each other. There is an abundance of inspiration to be found in their myriad expressions. Here you will find the principles of modern science and the pearls of ancient wisdom in a potent combination aimed at healing body, mind, and soul.

- We lack a common language for spiritual discussion. We can do this work together if we solve the problems of language and toxic reactions to religion. This work is not about religion. It is about the healing principle extracted from religion, which we can apply in health care. Here you will find the essential healing principles of the great faith traditions translated into the universal language of mind-body and cognitive-behavioral practices.

- The ten steps are designed for atheists, agnostics, religious, or spiritual persons. Anyone can play in the expanded field of healing power.

- An omniscient healing power operates every cell in the body. The good news is that we know how to make it grow—the healing power can be exercised and increased by choosing a belief system that fits.

- Healing power is brilliant. As part of the inherent wisdom of the body, it does its work humbly and quietly, without our awareness. If we pay attention to it by choosing our thoughts carefully, we can help it do its work. We have more healing power when we find beliefs that work for us. Positive thoughts lead to positive feelings and vibrations that promote the healing process.

- There is no separation between mind and body. The mind is connected to every cell in the body through electromagnetic and chemical waves. Thoughts affect disease and healing in our cells. The connecting link between one's beliefs and the healing power they stimulate is always waiting to be tapped, free of cost.

- There is an intimate relationship between healing power, pain management, and spiritual evolution. These three move forward or backward together depending on how you manage your pain. If you manage your pain skillfully, healing power expands and you evolve spiritually. If you manage your pain unskillfully, healing power shrinks, and you devolve spiritually.

In the next chapter, you will learn how to use this book to expand healing power, become a more skillful pain manager, and evolve spiritually.

CHAPTER 3

HOW TO USE THIS BOOK

HEALING WISDOM FROM
RELIGION APPLIED TO HEALTHCARE

The ten steps do not declare answers to life's big questions, such as why we are born, why there is so much suffering and evil, whether there is a God, and where we go after death. However, we can apply the wealth of healing wisdom in the great faith traditions to help us manage our pain and heal.

To take advantage of the healing principles embedded in the religions, we need to solve the problem of toxic language and traumatic religious history. There is a way to do this. We can design healing models that serve people of all persuasions: Baptists, Sufi mystics, ethical humanists, scientific atheists, true believers, true non-believers—all of us have the same magnificent healing power in every cell of our bodies, and we know how to make it grow.

SPIRITUAL ACTION AND HEALING
WITHIN YOUR PREFERRED SYSTEM

The aim of this book is not to convert readers to a particular faith tradition, but rather to incite them to spiritual action and healing within their preferred system. For those readers building a personal spiritual program, this work offers a variety of ideas and methods to explore and practice. Other readers brought up in one of the world's great traditions, such as Judaism, Christianity, Islam, Hinduism, or Buddhism, may be interested in exploring other universal spiritual principles and methods that will enhance their established belief systems. In either case, whether you are building a program of your own or working from within a particular religion, spiritual practice will augment and intensify your healing power's ability to do its work on your body, mind, and soul.

THE CLIMB

Spiritual work is like climbing a shining mountain. The mountain sparkles with higher states of consciousness and spiritual qualities. Though inviting and attractive, it is not an easy climb. You will need some equipment—some spiritual tools—to help you get a grip and keep your balance. This equipment must fit comfortably. It will vary according to your individual desires and needs.

All too often, people argue about the equipment and the pathway. When the argument starts, climbing stops. The trails of history are populated with tragic stories about confrontations concerning the "one true way." When spiritual seekers become belligerent, or even violent, not only does progress stop, but the combatants slip, slide, and ultimately fall off the mountain.

In this work, you are encouraged to build your own program in the spirit of "take what you need and leave the rest." This stance avoids controversy and debate while honoring individual preference and need. The book offers principles, methods, processes, affirmations, quotes, and homework assignments. If an idea or method is useful, pick it up and work with it. If it is not, modify it or skip it, and move on until you find something that works for you.

GUIDELINES

Before you explore the ten steps, please review the following guidelines. If we follow these suggestions, we can extract the essential healing principle from religion and apply it in healthcare.

a. The model is a composite of universal healing principles from the great wisdom traditions. It does not push religion. It does try to equip persons of all persuasions with the essential healing principle embedded within the religions.

b. The model is for any person: atheist, agnostic, spiritual, or religious.

c. The model is for any problem: physical, mental, emotional, social, spiritual.

d. The methods can be practiced anywhere and anytime: at home, at work, or at play.

e. There is a cafeteria of options. You can add these options to your current belief system or build your own program.

f. Take what you need and leave the rest.

g. One person's traction device is the next person's gag reflex. Don't let language stop you. For some people, even the word spirituality is a problem. Nuke offensive language and substitute your own. For example, you might substitute Higher Power for God, higher self for soul, higher for spiritual, healing qualities for spiritual qualities, or cognitive-behavioral practice for spiritual practice.

h. Some chapters in this book speak to those who believe in a God of Love. Other chapters are more universal. If you don't believe in God, let alone God as Love, substitute with words like spiritual qualities, healing qualities, qualities, The Tao, The Way, The Great Spirit, Creator, compassion, or any other term that gives you traction. The universal goal is to become a more skillful pain manager, expand healing power, and evolve. As you proceed, use whatever term is most acceptable to you.

i. Stay in your own lane.

j. Reform yourself and not others.

k. Do not proselytize.

l. Discuss without debate.

SKILLFUL PAIN MANAGEMENT: 15 METHODS

You may not be able to get rid of all your pain, but you can change your relationship to it. You can become a more skillful pain manager.

Here's how. There are two layers of pain: the inevitable suffering of life, and our reaction to it. We cannot control the former but we can control the latter. When you practice the techniques described in this book, you reduce reactivity, the add-ons to the inevitable suffering of life. You cultivate strength and peace no matter what your body or the world throws at you. You become a more skillful pain manager and your quality of life improves accordingly.

This book describes fifteen methods for healing, pain management, and spiritual evolution.

Horizontal Axis

1. People
2. Activities
3. Belief systems

Vertical Axis

4. Affirmations
5. Habit transformation
6. Progressive muscle relaxation
7. Breathwork
8. Contemplation
9. Meditation
10. Prayer
11. Mindfulness
12. Practicing the Presence of God
13. Service
14. Yoga
15. Transformation of emotion

These are the methods we can turn to when doctors and other healthcare professionals cannot solve our problems or relieve our pain completely. These methods are complementary to physical interventions such as medication, acupuncture, massage, diet, exercise, herbs, vitamins, minerals, and so forth.

These methods help us manage the inevitable suffering of life and our reaction to it. They do not require professional attention. They are self-help, self-healing methods. We practice them on our own.

A comprehensive healing package includes external and internal practices. Methods 1-3 are external. Methods 4-15 are internal.

EXTERNAL WORK:
HORIZONTAL AXIS: OPTIONS 1-3

Options 1-3 describe our work in the external world of people, activities, and belief systems. When you are in pain, you can spend time with family and friends for solace and comfort. You can engage in constructive meaningful activities: work, school, training, volunteering, recreation, sports, culture, hobbies, and so forth. You can go to church, synagogue, or temple for traditional worship, or to a group like Alcoholics Anonymous for support and wisdom. All of this helps and may be enough for some people. Others need to do some additional work on the vertical axis.

INTERNAL WORK:
VERTICAL AXIS: OPTIONS 4-15

Many people make the mistake of trying to solve all of their problems on the horizontal axis of people, activities, and belief systems. Some problems can only be resolved by doing some inner work. If you try to use the horizontal axis to solve problems that must be resolved internally, you will become frustrated, angry, depressed, and anxious. Some people develop codependency, bad habits, and unhealthy attachments. Many become hyperactivity junkies, immersing themselves in activities from morning to night, trying to avoid the work that must be done inside. To avoid adding fuel to your fire, you can practice methods 4-15.

Methods 4-15 describe the work we can do internally. These are the methods of the vertical axis. When you have done everything you can in the world of people, activities, and belief systems, and you are still in pain, there are twelve additional methods you can use to help you with your painful problem. You can practice these methods for any problem of body, mind, or spirit. Here you will learn how to use your pain as a stimulant for the cultivation of courage, strength, peace, compassion, understanding, and a host of other healing qualities. These qualities are the jewels of this life. They will help you broker and buffer the pain of this life.

LOCUS OF CONTROL

If you spend most of your time in steps 1-3, your locus of control is primarily outside. Most of us start here. When life presents overwhelming problems, it is often necessary to do some inner work. As you begin to practice methods 4-15, your locus of control gradually shifts to the inside. As qualities such as courage, peace, and strength slowly grow, you become less dependent on the outer world of people, activities, events, and things.

A balanced healing program includes work on both the horizontal and vertical axes. When you integrate the methods on both axes, you will become a more skillful pain manager. You will feel better and become a stronger and better person.

WHAT YOU WILL LEARN

If you choose to do this work, you will learn:

1. How to increase healing power for body, mind, and soul
2. How to skillfully manage any pain or problem: physical, mental, emotional, social, or spiritual
3. How to become a better person through the cultivation of healing qualities such as Love, compassion, forgiveness, courage, strength, peace, wisdom, and joy

4. How your pain can be the route to healing through the cultivation of spiritual qualities

5. How to find peace and strength within, despite the painful conditions of life

6. How to recover lost territories in the realm of people, activities, belief systems, and self-knowledge

7. How to exercise and strengthen the mind

8. How to transform painful emotion into self-knowledge

9. How to transmute bad habits into peace, strength, and contentment

10. How to reduce hyperactivity and build stillness into your program

11. How to use stillness as the doorway to higher states of consciousness

12. How to reduce the negative side of your ego and replace it with the highest healing qualities

13. How to lock Love, compassion, peace, and strength into brain grooves so that these healing qualities become your new mental habits

14. How to view your body as the carrier of higher states of consciousness as opposed to a source of fear and trouble

15. How to become increasingly able to help others on their journey toward healing and recovery

AN INSTRUCTION MANUAL

This is an instruction manual. Each chapter starts with a description of healing principles. It then gives step-by-step processes and examples that bring spiritual concepts from the lofty penthouse to the ground floor of the daily routines of life. While this manual is packed with powerful spiritual ideas begging for contemplation, it is no less rich in its practical, down-to-earth, how-to approach. The sacred wisdom of the ages requires ongoing study, contemplation, and practice, so for some readers, this book will be a lifelong resource. The meaning of a true pearl of wisdom is often well beyond the reach of most us and may take years or decades of contemplation to realize its full significance.

GROUP OR INDIVIDUAL USE

The model is for group or personal use. Healthcare professionals and physicians can teach the ten steps to their patients in hospitals and clinics. The model is also suited for self-help groups in the community or individual study and practice.

EDUCATIONAL FORMAT

I teach the steps in a group format using a style that is primarily educational. We read a short passage, then discuss and contemplate its significance. This teaching method is appropriate for discussion groups run in clinics or hospitals, as well as in self-help groups independent of healthcare institutions.

Our group does not focus on personal problems that require individual counseling. We do not try to fix other people's problems, nor do we ordinarily give advice or counsel. While all of us need advice or personal counsel from time to time, we always need the universal knowledge of how to expand our healing power, manage our pain more skillfully, and cultivate spiritual qualities. Groups should focus on spiritual practices that transform pain into spiritual power. However, we do not need a group or teacher. We can do this work alone at home.

THE SCIENTIFIC METHOD IN METAPHYSICS

In this work, you are encouraged to follow the scientific method in metaphysics. This method speaks to our ability to decipher spiritual fiction from fact even without blood tests and X-rays. In the laboratory of life, we can put profoundly important questions to the test of direct personal experience.

- Does compassionate service to humanity give peace of mind and strength?

- Does meditation work?
- Do higher states of consciousness actually exist?
- Does the body harbor the God of the Universe?
- Is Love more powerful than any pain or problem?

Listed below are the steps you can follow to prove or disprove such theories:

1. Test a theory by practicing a spiritual method.
2. Assume the agnostic position.
   a. Do not accept or reject the theory.
   b. Stay open and receptive.
3. The body is the test tube.
4. The experiment is on the life force itself: consciousness, energy, thought, feeling, desire, and behavior.
5. Prove or disprove the theory through direct personal experience.
6. If a method or concept works, keep it, and, if you are a health-care professional, teach it to your patients. If not, discard it.
7. Trust your ability to tell the difference.

POINTS TO REMEMBER

- There is a magnificently intelligent healing power that operates every cell in the body. We can help the healing power do its work when we have a balanced healing program including work on both the horizontal axis of people, activities, and belief systems, and the vertical axis of the twelve spiritually oriented cognitive-behavioral methods. All of us need:

1. People: a support network of loving, kind, courageous, strong, forgiving, and humorous people
2. Activities: a day filled with constructive and meaningful activities
3. Belief Systems: positive thoughts and wisdom

There is ample scientific evidence that each of these has a role in healing body, mind, and spirit. This scientific evidence is reinforced by my personal and professional experience. I have been impressed with the power that people, activities, and belief systems have in helping people manage the harsh realities of life.

• Individuals who fill their lives with positive people, activities, and belief systems have a much better chance of holding their ground when the world gets rough. There is pain relief and healing readily available to them. Although problems may not magically disappear, they become more manageable. On the other hand, when these three healing zones are dormant or abused, the problems of life tend to linger and grow.

• The elegant essence of religion is Love. Love is a composite of the one hundred healing qualities described in Step 7. Love is the greatest healer. It is part of the solution to all of our problems. We know how to make it grow. When we develop a spiritual practice, we cultivate Love, which helps us contain, reduce, or eliminate suffering. This work describes a variety of practices to make it grow. I encourage you to practice these methods so you can prove this to yourself through direct personal experience.

The next 3 chapters, Chapters 4-6, elaborate the ten steps.
Chapter 4 introduces the ten steps.
Chapter 5 describes steps 1-5: You will study the inevitability of suffering and how we make it worse.
Chapter 6 elaborates steps 6-10: You will discover the link between skillful pain management and the expansion of healing power.
Chapter 7 introduces The Universal Healing Wheel, the essential healing principle of the ten steps and any psychosocial or spiritual healing model.
Chapter 8 reviews the ten steps and how to skillfully manage the anxiety of change.

Chapter 9 introduces a universal healing method for any pain or problem.

Chapter 10 elaborates on the profound importance of the serenity prayer every step of the way on the recovery and healing path.

Chapter 11 defines key points for starting and maintaining a successful spiritual practice.

Chapters 12-23 describe in detail the twelve internal methods of the vertical axis.

Chapters 24-34 elaborate ten profound healing qualities.

Chapter 35 describes a balanced healing program.

Appendix A describes the guidelines for having a successful ten-step study group.

Appendix B defines some of the key terms used in this work. You might want to review these definitions before you begin your study of the ten-step model.

Appendix C gives an example of how the ten-step model can be used to stage disease and recovery.

The next section of the book describes the ten-step model. You will learn how to use the inevitable suffering of life to cultivate peace, Love, and joy. The result is a shift in the locus of control from the outer world of people, places, and things, to the inner world of peace, power, and strength: a world of our own definition.

CHAPTER FOUR

TEN STEPS TO PAIN MANAGEMENT AND SPIRITUAL EVOLUTION

Suffering Is the Route to Healing

- We seek unlimited peace, Love, and joy in an uncertain world where suffering is inevitable. Because we manage our pain poorly, we add to our troubles. The wisdom of the ages taught by the world's diverse spiritual traditions offers a solution to this dilemma by pointing out the connection between skillful pain management and the cultivation of spiritual qualities. When we develop a spiritual practice, we learn how to transform our suffering into spiritual power.

- *How we manage our pain determines whether we move forward, slip backward, or stay stuck in this life.* We can turn the tables on our pain and make it work for us. Then pain, rather than bringing us down, points the way toward expanded healing power and spiritual evolution.

- This chapter introduces a self-help method of ten principles that propel healing and spiritual evolution. The central premise is that life, through a series of painful lessons, teaches us that the peace, Love, and joy we seek in the outer world can and ultimately must be found within.

THE TEN STEPS

1. The Core Drive
2. Duality and Brutal Reality
3. The Compromise
4. Habits
5. Tools Become Barriers
6. The Seeker
7. Soul and Spirit
8. The School of Life
9. Spiritual Practice
10. Spiritual Experience

SUFFERING: STEPS 1–5

- Steps 1–5 describe the evolution of our suffering. Here you will find a description of two levels of pain:

  1. The inevitable suffering of life
  2. Reactivity: how we make it worse

- Step 1 describes the core drive: we want unlimited peace, Love, joy, and safety, more time, and no pain.

- Step 2 describes the inevitable suffering of life. Reality can be fierce and cruel. The very thought of this truth causes us to feel threatened, so we resist looking at the dark side. However, knowledge of what we are up against is our best defense. If we understand the root causes of our suffering, we can build a powerful healing program in response to it and be more likely to succeed. We must not shrink, even in the face of our most frightening problems. If we face our problems head on, we can build corresponding healing responses.

- Steps 3–5 describe how our attempt to achieve the core drive exclusively on the physical plane leads to a high degree of reactivity, thus adding unnecessary pain to the inevitable suffering of life. The search for Love and safety exclusively in the outer world actually causes more pain.

HEALING: STEPS 6–10

- Steps 6–10 focus on healing.

- Step 6 describes a period of insight and searching.

- Step 7 explores the nature of our true self and Higher Power.

- Step 8 describes pain management in the school of life. Pain is the teacher. Lessons have to do with the cultivation of healing qualities. Homework assignments and tests are designed to expose and eliminate the problems and flaws that restrict our ability to experience peace and joy. Pain is an intelligent guide, directing us to the work we need to do. When we learn how to extract the necessary lessons from our pain, we expand our healing power and move forward.

- Step 9 describes twelve healing methods derived from the world's great spiritual systems. These methods help us expand the healing power inherent in the body.

- Step 10 describes the experience that occurs when the reader practices the methods described in Step 9. Qualities such as Love, compassion, understanding, courage, perseverance, and humility grow. These qualities are the jewels of this life. They are healers. They help us eliminate or endure any painful condition of body, mind, or soul. They are more powerful than any barrier or challenge we may face. When we develop a spiritual practice, we slowly replace our limitations and flaws with healing qualities. We can then use these qualities to manage the turbulence of life.

POINTS TO REMEMBER

- Steps 1–5 describe the inevitable suffering of life and how we make it worse when we try to solve all of our problems externally.

- Steps 6–10 describe what you can do to heal your pain by working internally. Here you will learn:

  1. How to build a comprehensive healing program to help you manage any pain or problem
  2. How to expand healing power, become a more skillful pain manager, and become a better person
  3. How to turn the tables on your pain and make it work for you
  4. How to use the inevitable suffering of life to cultivate peace, power, and strength
  5. How to use pain as the route to healing by developing a spiritual practice
  6. How to find the Love and safety you crave at the very core of your inner being
  7. Through a series of painful lessons, we see how the peace, Love, and joy we seek from the outer world can and ultimately must be found within

While there is no easy way out of the dilemmas posed by life, there is much relief in the discovery that even in the throes of greatest turmoil, we exist somewhere on a ten-step map where suffering has a purpose: the development of spiritual power. We regain our bearings when we understand our pain is the stimulant for the growth of spiritual qualities.

By seeing the map, finding our place on it, and knowing there are always steps to take in the right direction, we get tremendous relief. We see that there is a sense of meaning, purpose, and direction to all that happens, and that we can take back control of our destiny. We make progress and feel better. We see that the results of our work are actually quite spectacular, even if we wish they weren't so slow to manifest. But we can put up with this challenge to our patience as long as we define the problem and take steps toward a tangible goal.

We encounter trouble no matter which route we take, but the way offered here is the path of least resistance, the way through our pain to peace, power, and strength. As we move forward through the ten steps, we find ourselves living the richest possible life, a journey where our spirit is in charge and we are ready for anything!

In the next chapter, you will study Steps 1–5. Here you will find a description of the inevitability of suffering and how we make it worse.

CHAPTER FIVE

SUFFERING
STEPS 1–5

The Inevitability of Suffering and How We Make It Worse

STEP 1: THE CORE DRIVE

- We want to live in a house filled with unlimited peace, Love, joy and safety: a home where no pain or death can enter. This is our core drive. We crave a perfect world consisting of three parts:

  1. The complete elimination of physical, mental, and spiritual anguish
  2. Unlimited peace, Love, joy, and safety
  3. Immortality (the feeling that there is more time)

- These elements drive all of our good and bad actions alike. Whether we rob a bank or serve the poor, the motivation is the same. We want:

  - No pain
  - Love and safety
  - More time, afraid as we are of the unknown and death

- Our quest to fulfill the core drive solely on the physical plane is doomed to fail, however, as material life is painful, the permanent solace we seek is transient, and death ultimately wins.

STEP 2: DUALITY AND BRUTAL REALITY

DUALITY

- We do experience peace, Love, and joy on the physical plane, but it is limited and change is inevitable. It is only a matter of time before reality shifts gears and brings forth new suffering, sometimes difficult or devastating, often brutal. This is the law of duality, which rules the story on the physical plane.

- Duality is the law of polar opposites, the ups and downs of life: pleasure and pain, good and evil, joy and sadness, Love and hate, desire and aversion, likes and dislikes, gain and loss, health and disease, prosperity and poverty, wisdom and ignorance, strength and weakness, cruelty and kindness, life and death, and so on. These opposites oscillate throughout our lives.

BRUTAL REALITY

- However we seek to avoid it, suffering is inevitable, time is limited, and the mysterious, infinite unknown, death, takes over in the end. It can be overwhelming. This is the harsh side of reality, here referred to as brutal reality. Brutal reality includes three elements:

  1. Death
  2. Pain and suffering
  3. The unknown

- In effect, brutal reality is the dark side of duality: pain, limitation, and impermanence. It has great power and ultimately cannot be controlled. It asserts itself unpredictably in anyone's life at anytime and in a seemingly endless variety of ways.

- We suffer brutal reality individually from disease, violence, racism, poverty, and injustice and collectively from cataclysmic events such as political upheaval, earthquakes, and war. Since life eventually leads to death, brutal reality ultimately reigns on the physical plane. While the ordinary changes of life are a source of adventure and excitement, death is terrifying, as it forces us to leave behind everything we know.

- In the card game of life, we must play the hand we are dealt. But death, that invisible, mysterious opponent, holds the ace. We do not like this power arrangement. In our attempts to get control and feel safe, we accumulate as many cards in the deck as possible, but brutal reality wins in the end.

- At death, when brutal reality finally plays its ace, we are thrust forward into the unknown at an accelerated pace. We are propelled into a personal form of future shock. There is a radical rapid shift into the heart of the mysterious infinite unknown.

STEP 3: THE COMPROMISE
THE SHOW

- We want to live painlessly and forever in perfect harmony. We try to achieve this core drive through the big show: the story of life on the physical plane. The action is attractive, fascinating, and seductive. It lures us into thinking we can achieve comfort and safety through our relationships, work, and recreation.

- We love the show. But the laws of duality and brutal reality rule the drama. Everything on the physical plane is temporary and limited, suffering is unavoidable, and death wins in the end. We try in vain to control our stories, but this is impossible. The external world will simply not deliver the absolute safety and perfect Love we crave. We can't get everything we want on the physical plane. In the collision between the core drive and duality, we discover the need to compromise.

THE ILLUSION OF SAFETY

• We compromise by creating the illusion of safety through relationships and activities. Family, friends, work, recreation, culture, and hobbies provide us with a measure of Love and security. There is healing here. Suffering is reduced. We do feel comfortable and safe. The illusion of safety is the balm of physical plane existence. It is the drug-elixir of life. We have to have it to function and thrive.

• However, it is only a matter of time before instability is upon us again. Suffering is unavoidable. Brutal reality makes its appearance at any time and in a great variety of forms throughout life and takes over in the end.

• We do not like this set-up. We resist the pain of reality. We do not accept the compromise. We do not accept the inevitable suffering of life. Instead, we make a desperate attempt to eliminate *all of our suffering* through faulty mechanisms such as the cultivation of bad habits that create pseudo-relief from our pain.

STEP 4: HABITS

1. Work
2. Relationships
3. Activity
4. Materialism
5. Computers/Internet
6. TV
7. Food
8. Shopping
9. Alcohol
10. Drugs
11. Sex
12. Power
13. Gambling
14. Money
15. Violence
16. Crime

• Most of the items listed above are good for us if only we could control the dose. But our relentless craving for perfect peace forces us all too often to act in desperate, destructive ways. We develop bad habits, power trips, materialism, hyperactivity, and codependency.

- In a mighty but misguided effort to ward off pain, we stuff ourselves with food, drugs, alcohol, and sex. In our restless search for permanent joy, we strive for wealth, possessions, and power over others. We become activity junkies, hooked on work, watching and playing sports, glued to television, the Internet, movies, music and so on ... all the while actually seeking eternal Love and safety in the external world where transience and limitation are the rule.

- Our troubles deepen as these bad habits have a negative influence on our work and relationships. Not only do we lose sight of the Love we seek, but also we infiltrate our relationships and activities with negativity. We dig ourselves into a deeper hole as we make the original, inevitable suffering on the physical plane worse through our misguided attempts to eliminate it.

Bad habits have a profound negative effect on our health and our response to health care interventions. You will learn how to eliminate bad habits in Chapter Twelve.

EXERCISES

1. What is your core drive?

2. What dualities are present in your life?

3. What is your brutal reality?

4. Describe how duality and brutal reality affect your life.

5. Describe the relationship between the core drive, duality, and brutal reality in your life.

6. What is "the compromise" described in Step 3?

7. How does this compromise play itself out in your life?

8. Do you have any bad habits?

STEP 5: TOOLS BECOME BARRIERS

REACTIVITY

- It doesn't matter what happens to us as much as how we react to it. Step 5 locates and defines the source of our reactivity, that part of our suffering that we add on to the inevitable suffering of life. This is important because we can contain, reduce, or eliminate reactivity if we are willing to do some work.

- Step 9 defines the nature of that work. In Step 9, spiritual practice, you will find a description of twelve techniques that help us reduce reactivity.

SIX TOOLS

- We use six tools to achieve the core drive of unlimited Love and safety, the place where no pain can enter.

  1. Mind
  2. Emotion
  3. Desire
  4. Body
  5. Activities
  6. Ego

- While these tools are useful in helping us find some measure of Love, safety, and pain relief, they become problems themselves. We add to our suffering with our restless minds, high emotional reactivity, excessive material desire, improperly cared for bodies, hyperactivity, and egotism.

Following is a discussion of how each of these tools helps us achieve our goals and how they too often spin out of control, add to our suffering, and become barriers to healing.

STEP 5.1: THE MIND

- A POWER TOOL. The mind is a very powerful and effective tool designed to help us in our pursuit of happiness. We use the mind to shape the meaning of our personal story, and it is a brilliant problem solver. When difficulties arise, the reasoning mind activates its "fixing mode." With its powers of understanding, reason, creativity, imagination, and positive thought, we analyze our problems and develop plans of action.

- GOOD MENTAL HEALTH. The mind does its best work when it is calm, positive, focused, strong, and resilient. This is good mental health. From this position, it can meet the challenge of any problem, test, or lesson that life presents. Unfortunately, the mind does not always work this well. It has a complex bag of tricks that keeps us from our core mission.

- A LIFE OF ITS OWN. The mind has a life all its own. It won't quit thinking often good, but sometimes useless, foolish, or destructive thoughts. It ruminates and obsesses long after it has completed its work of shaping meaning and solving problems. Even when we try to control it, the mind demonstrates its relentless independence, becoming at times a formidable opponent in our quest for happiness and the elimination of suffering.

- THE OVERHEATED MIND. When stressful problems arise, the mind often reacts like an electrical wire carrying too much charge. Overheated, it inadvertently attacks us with highly charged, negative, and often false thoughts. Negative thinking creates anger, depression, fear, and insecurity. We lose logic and flexibility. Distortion replaces truth. There is no problem solving. On the contrary, the mind in overdrive is a liability, contributing an additional layer of inner turmoil to our original painful problems.

- A RABBIT IN THE ATTIC. Ideally, when we have done all that we can to work on the reversible component of a problem, the mind would return to its natural state of peace and poise. Instead, even after it performs well in "fixing mode," the mind remains hyperactive and restless, in perpetual motion like a rabbit living in the attic. If we try to grab it, it hops out of our grasp. Fast and slippery, it darts from one topic to another, compromising our ability to focus, concentrate, and relax.

- RUMINATION. While at times the mind bolts like a bunny from one topic to another, it can also get stuck in a rut. When a car is stuck in the mud, it is natural to respond by pressing harder on the accelerator ... But this makes the problem worse. The motor overheats, the rut deepens, and mud spreads around. Similarly, the mind gets hung up on a problem and goes over the same thoughts again and again, even after a solution and plans have already been determined. We keep thinking about the problem, which only serves to deepen the mental groove that carries the overworked pattern of thought. This common occurrence is called rumination. We think too much. Perpetual replays of our personal story are a form of addiction. Hooked to the soap opera of our own lives, we lose contentment and satisfaction.

- LAYERS OF UNREALITY. An easily distracted, restless mind is a source of untold grief. It adds layer upon layer of unreality, distortion, and negativity over our true selves. It creates twists and turns that make life unnecessarily complex and stressful. It obsessively analyzes and fantasizes, creates unrealistic assumptions and expectations, and subjects itself to attractions and repulsions. It exaggerates the importance of events and infuses insecurity into our personal story.

- AN UNCONDITIONAL LOVE AFFAIR. Despite all of this, we seem to be in an unconditional love affair with the mind. We profoundly over-identify with it, no matter how much trouble it gives us. We consider our own thoughts, likes, and dislikes to be the final arbiter of truth. A bridge of arrogance spans events and the mind's interpretations of them. We let it dominate our consciousness even when it is wrong or hysterical.

- A CLEVER DICTATOR. The mind has a subtle, relentless grip on us. In the beginning we don't even realize the sly tyrant has taken over, as it uses tactics that are elusive and beyond our grasp. Unaware of its wily ways, the mind keeps us under its hypnotic control. This state of consciousness is so habitual we do not see the enemy within.

- REALIGN THE MIND. We need to understand how much trouble the shrewd and cunning mind causes. Then we can take steps to reduce its negative power and return it to an instrument of creativity, imagination, problem solving, and story shaping. In Step 9, spiritual practice, we learn how to do this. Here you will find a description of several techniques including contemplation, affirmation, mindfulness, and meditation. These techniques help us realign the mind to its natural state of peace, poise, resilience, openness, and flexibility.

An undisciplined mind is a weak mind. When you practice the methods described in Step 9, your mind becomes positive, calm, and strong. You will be ready for anything.

STEP 5.2: EMOTION

- SELF-KNOWLEDGE. Emotions are natural, healthy, and intelligent. They carry important information about our issues, problems, solutions, strategies, and lessons. When we learn how to extract this information from our feelings, we gain self-knowledge, knowledge of our personal story.

There are times when we have to go through emotional pain and learn from it in order to move forward. Translating emotion into self-knowledge is a valuable skill. When we know how to do this, we can transform our suffering into peace, joy, and strength.

- UNPROCESSED EMOTION. Too often, however, we suffer from highly reactive and volatile emotions that we do not understand. Most of us have had no training in emotional pain management. Because we don't know what to do with these feelings, we instinctively try to keep them from conscious awareness by denying their existence, avoiding them with bad habits, or pushing them into the subconscious and body where they are stored in latent form. The unprocessed emotion remains in the body and subconscious mind, however—waiting, if not begging, for recognition.

  While in storage, painful, unprocessed emotions have a negative impact on our physical, mental, and spiritual health. We develop negative attitudes and distorted thinking, and we behave in destructive ways. In the worst-case scenario, suppressed emotions overwhelm our defenses and we lose control, subsequently endangering self and others. Unprocessed emotions reap untold havoc on our lives and the lives of those around us.

- TRANSFORMATION OF EMOTION. There is a powerful narrative embedded in our feelings about our personal story. We need to learn how to process our emotions by letting our story unfold naturally. Then we need to learn to spiritualize our story. The spiritual practices described in Step 9 teach us how to do this. When we develop a spiritual practice, we learn how to transform painful emotions into self-knowledge.

STEP 5.3: DESIRE

- EXCESSIVE MATERIAL DESIRE. Step 5.3 revisits Step 4, Habits, from the perspective of excessive material desire, the root cause of attachments and bad habits.

- HEALTHY DESIRES. We love the show, the play of life on the physical plane. Its fascinating stories and alluring material objects capture our attention and desire. We want loving relationships, prosperity, and health. These desires are good. They help us achieve peace, safety and joy. Problems occur when we hold on to our possessions with fierce tenacity and when we ceaselessly desire more.

- ADDICTION. If not careful, our attachment to what we own and our thirst for more can slip into addiction. It is all too easy to become obsessed with power, sex, relationships, money, success, status, material objects, food, drugs, or alcohol. These addictions weaken and eventually paralyze our will, destroy our character, and bury our souls. Their root cause is excessive, uncontrolled desire.

- DESIRE BEGETS DESIRE. Even though some desires are positive, leading to success, health, and prosperity, they do not stop there. Desire begets desire. We want more things, even when we have enough. When desires are not met, we become angry, frustrated, and tense. When desires are satisfied, we are still not happy because another desire inevitably crops up and steals our peace. In our dissatisfaction and restlessness, we seek relief by quenching the next wave of desire. We cannot seem to get enough of what we think we want, because once we get it, we are stimulated to get more. If we keep pursuing happiness in this seemingly endless procession of want, we become caught up in a cycle of bad habits and addiction, greed and anxiety, attachment and exhaustion.

- A DOWNHILL COURSE. Excessive material desire is a root cause of dissatisfaction. Our attachments and bad habits separate us from others. We feel alone, insecure, and frightened. We act against our own will and the best interests of others. We are out of control, in a vicious cycle that is difficult to break. If we do not disrupt this cycle, we can experience panic, terror, depression, anger, and even rage. These painful emotions dominate our consciousness and impede our ability to find joy in this life. There can be no peace when our minds are restless and our emotions easily triggered. It is hard to love if we are on a power trip or greedy for more money.

- TRANSFORMATION OF DESIRE. The healing methods described in this work help us transform excessive material desire into inner peace and contentment. Then we can appreciate what we already have.

STEP 5.4: THE BODY

- OUR VEHICLE. The body is our vehicle for engaging life, the doer of all activities as we seek the many joys life has to offer.

- THE CHALLENGES. However, the body throws us many challenges. It annoys us when it pulls and tugs, gets tired and heavy, or is too hot or cold. It longs for relief from desire, hunger, and discomfort. It tosses us between pleasure and pain, illness and health, life and death. It subjects us to its demands, which sometimes lead us astray, into bad decisions and bad habits.

Some abuse the body by eating, drinking, and smoking too much. Many are in poor shape, not getting enough physical exercise. We all suffer from a variety of physical pains and progressive disability as the years pass, and ultimately, of course, the body ends in death.

- OUR GREATEST ATTACHMENT. We strongly identify with the body. It is our greatest attachment. We cling to the body in life and even at death. We hold on to it as though it were the only boat in the ocean. We think that letting go means drowning.

- FEAR OF DEATH. Fear of death causes many to become over-involved, even obsessed with their physical appearance, refusing to accept the body's progression into old age. Some of us choose cosmetic surgery, a stitch here, a tuck there, attempting to ward off what we fear the most: annihilation of the body and extinction of consciousness.

• A TEMPLE HARBORING HIGHER STATES OF CONSCIOUSNESS. Despite all of the trouble, the body is of magnificent design. It has inherent miraculous healing powers, spiritual qualities embedded in our genetic code, and it is the carrier of our potential spiritual enlightenment and liberation. The body is a temple, harboring higher states of consciousness. We can experience deep peace, Love, and joy of the soul when we develop a spiritual practice. Therefore, taking control of and being responsible for the maintenance of our bodies is imperative for healing and spiritual evolution.

STEP 5.5: ACTIVITY

• PERPETUAL MOTION. During the day, we walk, talk, work, shop, cook, clean, care for children and parents, exercise, study, read, play, go to church, mosque, or synagogue, play sports .... Most of us are in a state of perpetual motion from the time we get up in the morning until we go to bed at night. Being active is good, a natural part of life. Constructive meaningful activities expand our healing power and help us manage our pain. But popular culture would have us believe that work, recreation, and leisure will give us the deep peace of mind we seek. Experience dictates otherwise.

• OUTER LIFE. In the course of living, we find the joys and pleasures of the outer world are limited and ephemeral. The world of events, objects, and people is always changing. Everything has a beginning, middle, and end. Joy alternates with sadness, peace with anger, health with sickness, success with failure, and pleasure with pain. We cannot avoid the ups and downs of life. Worldly pleasures do not last and suffering is inevitable.

• INNER LIFE. Although we cannot be completely satisfied with our lives on the physical plane, the wisdom traditions point to our inner being as a source of lasting peace. Discovering the inner path to contentment is difficult, however, as the external world is powerful and attractive, continuously seducing us into the illusion that happiness is within our grasp and the price is right.

- STILLNESS. Activity becomes a barrier to spiritual growth when it is compulsive, addictive, or used as a substitute for searching within for the transcendent peace, Love, and joy bred of stillness. We can bring stillness into our lives when we learn such practices as contemplation, introspection, and meditation, as described in Step 9.

STEP 5.6: THE EGO

- CEO OF PHYSICAL PLANE CONSCIOUSNESS. The ego is the chief executive officer of our physical plane consciousness. Its job is to satisfy the core drive. It does this by establishing our place in the world of relationships, work, and recreation. This is good.

- SEPARATION. However, the ego has become a problem, as it has seceded from the union with our higher self, Higher Power, and creation. Like a rebel monarch, it declares itself the sole owner and operator of consciousness. It tricks us into thinking that material consciousness is the only reality. Forcing out all experiences of higher consciousness, it would have us believe that we are alone and limited.

- A DICTATORSHIP. The ego has surreptitiously taken over the control rooms of the mind, emotion, desire, body, and action. It uses these tools in its desperate search for immortality and permanent peace. The search is in vain, however, as the ego runs into the brick wall of limitation and inevitable suffering on the physical plane. Nevertheless, the ego does not give up its battle. It counters with an insatiable desire for recognition, success, and power. This results in excessive attention-seeking, inflated self-importance, accumulation, and empire building.

- SELFISHNESS. The ego behaves like a dictator, using a variety of tactics to gain power over others, including subtle manipulation and overt aggression. Concerned primarily with itself, the ego behaves as a greedy narcissist. "I! Me! Mine!" Territorial and self-important, it tries to manipulate others to its own ends and purposes. With a voracious appetite for control, it stifles dissent and ignores criticism.

- SELF-RIGHTEOUS AND INSECURE. Even if the ego's works give us success, power, and wealth, we are still in trouble. No matter how important we become, under the control of the ego we remain separate from the vast kingdom of peace within ourselves. Since it has no foundation, at its core the ego is insecure and fears extinction. Thus it is paranoid and defensive when it does not need to be and tries to be right all of the time, even when it is wrong.

- LACKS INTROSPECTION. Because the ego lacks introspection on its own problems, it remains self-righteous while it scapegoats others. The ego resists change and continues to hold on to outmoded ideas. It leads us into the dead end streets and dark alleys of our consciousness. With the ego in charge, we remain troubled, insecure, alone, and frightened.

- EGO REDUCTION AND SOUL EXPANSION. Clearly, we must address the problem of the ego on the spiritual path. In the section on spiritual practices, we learn how to reduce and ultimately replace the ego with the power and wisdom of the soul.

SUMMARY OF STEP 5:

- TOOLS IN ALIGNMENT. There are six tools that we use to achieve the core drive; they are mind, emotion, desire, body, activity, and ego. The tools in alignment are profound assets. They are our best friends.

Tools In Alignment

1. Mind: when positive, calm and focused, it is brilliant at solving problems and shaping meaning
2. Emotion: a source of self-knowledge
3. Desire: health, prosperity, and Love
4. Body: engage life, the doer of all of our activities, the source of our potential liberation and enlightenment
5. Activity: work, school, training, volunteer, recreation, culture, hobbies, sports
6. Ego: establish our place in the world of work and relationships

- TOOLS OUT OF ALIGNMENT. While these tools help us, they can also spin out of control and add to our suffering. This is referred to as reactivity.

Tools Out of Alignment = Reactivity

1. Mind: restless, relentless, a life of its own
2. Emotion: high emotional reactivity
3. Desire: excessive material desire resulting in attachments and bad habits
4. Body: heavy, tired, hurts, disability, death
5. Activity: hyperactivity
6. Ego: separation, selfishness, territorial, self-important

- A UNIVERSAL PROBLEM. The six tools out of alignment are a universal problem. It pins us to the mat of the status quo. It is the root cause of much of our suffering. These are the add-ons to the inevitable suffering of life.

- REACTIVITY IS REVERSIBLE. There is good news. Reactivity is reversible. We can get the six tools back in alignment when we develop a spiritual practice. In Step 9, you will learn a variety of spiritual methods that will help you do this work.

POINTS TO REMEMBER

The first five steps describe the evolution of suffering on the physical plane. In summary:

- Step 1: We want (1) complete elimination of suffering, (2) unlimited peace, Love and joy, and (3) immortality. This is the core drive.

- Step 2–3: We attempt to achieve the core drive through our relationships, work, and recreation but these prove inadequate since life on the physical plane is dual and brutal. There is limitation, impermanence, separation and suffering is inevitable.

- Step 4–5: We have six tools that help us achieve the core drive on the physical plane. While these tools help us achieve our goals, they spin out of control adding a great deal of suffering to the inevitable suffering of life.

- There are two levels of suffering:

  1. The inevitable suffering of life (Step 2)
  2. Reactivity: the six helpful tools spin out of control (Step 5)

- We cannot control duality and brutal reality—the inevitable suffering of life. However, we can control how we respond. We can intervene at Step 5. In Step 9, Spiritual Practice, you will learn a variety of methods that help reduce reactivity. This is very good news as we add a lot of suffering to the inevitable suffering of life.

EXERCISES

1. Step 5 describes how the mind, emotions, desires, body, activities, and ego are assets that become liabilities. Most of us remain totally unaware of this as it happens. As you begin and advance in your spiritual practice, try to become more mindful of when these tools are working for and against you. Review how each of these tools

presents both opportunities and challenges in your life. Ask yourself the following questions:

2. Does your mind both solve and create problems for you?

3. What kinds of problems does your mind create?

4. Would you like to be able to control your mind but don't know how?

5. Do you struggle with painful emotions that seem excessive and get you into trouble?

6. What are some examples in your life of how desire led to attachment and a bad habit or two?

7. Have your bad habits led to excessive emotional reactivity?

8. Are you mindful of your body as a carrier of higher states of consciousness?

9. Do you fill your waking life with continuous activity?

10. Do you have built-in periods of retreat and solitude for rest and regeneration?

11. Describe how your ego helps you and gets you into trouble.

12. Observe the functions of the ego. It takes a long time to learn all its tricks. Make a list.

• In this chapter, we studied Steps 1–5. These steps describe two levels of suffering:

    1. The inevitable suffering of life
    2. Reactivity, our reaction to the inevitable suffering of life

- Steps 6–10 address each of these levels. In the following chapters, we will learn how *pain management (Step 8) and spiritual practice (Step 9) lead to the recovery of the soul and Higher Power (Step 7) as the peace, Love, and joy we crave (Step 10).*

- Steps 1–5: Suffering

  1. Suffering
  2. Unskillful pain management
  3. Horizontal axis
  4. Locus of control primarily outside
  5. Descend

- Steps 6–10: Healing

  1. Healing
  2. Skillful pain management
  3. Vertical axis
  4. Shift the locus of control from outside to inside
  5. Ascend

CHAPTER SIX

HEALING
STEPS 6–10

Skillful Pain Management and the Expansion of Healing Power

STEP 6: THE SEEKER

- REVIEW OF STEPS 1–5.

  - STEP 1: THE CORE DRIVE. We want *permanent* peace, Love, joy, and safety, *no* suffering, and *unlimited* time.

  - STEP 2: DUALITY AND BRUTAL REALITY. We cannot satisfy this core drive on the physical plane where suffering is inevitable and limitations abound.

  - STEP 3: THE COMPROMISE. We compromise by creating an illusion of safety through our relationships, work, and recreation.

  - STEP 4: HABITS. However, since we do not accept the inevitable suffering of life, we often try to escape our pain by developing bad habits.

  - STEP 5: TOOLS BECOME BARRIERS. While mind, emotion, desire, body, activity, and ego help us achieve our goals, they spin out of control and add yet another layer to our suffering.

- THE SEEKER. Our pain deepens as the inevitable suffering of life is compounded by our own reactivity. We may develop symptoms and become less able to function productively. Moreover, there may be an impending or actual loss of control with danger to self or others. Our suffering leads us to a period of questioning. We recognize the need for help. We become seekers.

- THE EGO RESISTS CHANGE. This is a difficult stage to achieve, because of the ego. The ego, considering itself the king/queen of truth, denies any problems under its leadership. It sees no need for consultation. This sets up a fierce battle between our pain and our ego. Our pain demands that the ego get out of the way so new knowledge can flow in to save the day. Sensing a threat and a potential humiliating defeat, the ego clings to the status quo as it fights off new ways of understanding and perception.

- EGO REDUCTION AND HUMILITY. If insight is to prevail, however, we must seek help. We must reduce the ego to learn new and better ways of managing our pain. When our suffering becomes unbearable and the ego has finally had enough, it gives up a little territory and surrenders into the pain. At this point, humiliation becomes humility. The soft inner core of our being opens. Now we can learn. Now we can go deeper, ask the big questions, and seek new ways of understanding.

- THE SEARCH FOR WISDOM. Our search for meaning takes us to the dark side of duality: failure, defeat, loss, separation, abandonment, rejection, sickness, violence, poverty, war, death, and evil. What possible spiritual explanation can there be for slavery, the Holocaust, famine, or a terror attack perpetuated by criminal extremists? Why do murder, sex abuse, and rape exist? Why is reality so brutal?

While our minds crave an explanation, our souls yearn for relief.

But the spiritual mathematics in these shadows present a big challenge, and knowledge of the absolute is elusive. We persist.

Is there anything to hold on to? Is our search for permanent Love and safety futile on this earth where limitation and insecurity seem to have the upper hand? If the physical plane cannot satisfy our deepest yearning, is there another dimension to life, perhaps higher or subtler, that can help? Can the terror associated with the unknown be transformed into awe, curiosity for adventure, and creativity? Is there anything that doesn't change, which gives stillness and peace? Is there something in this life and after death in which we can trust? What can be done about our own character defects?

Our search takes us to the wisdom traditions. World religions and other healing models delve into the heart of the mystery and suffering of life and emerge with a prescription for our difficulties. We can heal ourselves if we learn how to manage our pain by practicing a variety of healing techniques described in Step 9. But first, we need a definition of the Higher Self and Higher Power.

POINTS TO REMEMBER: STEP 6

- Painful crises lead to a search for wisdom, meaning, and purpose.

- Ego reduction and humility open the door to learning more skillful ways of managing painful problems.

EXERCISES STEP 6

1. Has your suffering led you to search for meaning and purpose?

2. What is the meaning and purpose of your life?

3. What role does your belief system play in giving meaning and purpose to your life?

4. In your search for new and better ways of managing your suffering, you might find it useful to follow the scientific method in metaphysics. This method supports your ability to decipher spiritual fiction from fact. You can do this without lab tests or X-rays. This method is described in Chapter Three, How To Use This Book.

STEP 7: SOUL AND SPIRIT

HIGHER SELF

THE ESSENTIAL HEALING PRINCIPLE. Place all of the religions in a blender and swirl them into liquid religion. Take out your magical filter and command it to remove everything from the liquid that is not absolutely essential. Now pour the liquid through the filter into a small perfume bottle. The filter does its job of removing ritual, dogma, and other nonessentials. The perfume bottle now holds a product called the Elegant Essence of Religion. If you were to drink this one night before sleep and wake up in the morning transformed into a Christ, Krishna, Buddha, favorite master, saint, sage, or the highest person you can imagine, what would be in the bottle?

If you did the same exercise with every other healing model you can think of including the psychotherapies, 12-steps, DBT (Dialectic Behavioral Therapy), and other mindfulness-based cognitive therapies, what would be in the bottle?

On the next page, you will see a list of one hundred qualities that represent the essential healing principle of all psychological and spiritual belief systems. These qualities are the goal and product of any healing model directed at transformation of our inner being.

SPIRITUAL ALPHABET

HEALING QUALITIES

1.	Acceptance	35.	Honesty	69.	Pure awareness
2.	Appreciation	36.	Hope	70.	Pure consciousness
3.	Balance	37.	Humility	71.	Purity
4.	Beauty	38.	Humor	72.	Receptivity
5.	Belief	39.	Immortality	73.	Reverence
6.	Changelessness	40.	Infinity	74.	Rhythm
7.	Cheerfulness	41.	Integrity	75.	Safety
8.	Clarity	42.	Interconnectedness	76.	Security
9.	Community	43.	Introspection	77.	Self-control
10.	Compassion	44.	Intuition	78.	Service
11.	Confidence	45.	Joy	79.	Silence
12.	Contentment	46.	Justice	80.	Simplicity
13.	Courage	47.	Kindness	81.	Sincerity
14.	Creativity	48.	Knowledge	82.	Spaciousness
15.	Desirelessness	49.	Laughter	83.	Stillness
16.	Devotion	50.	Light	84.	Strength
17.	Endurance	51.	Listening	85.	Success
18.	Energy	52.	Loyalty	86.	Surrender
19.	Enthusiasm	53.	Mercy	87.	Sweetness
20.	Equality	54.	Mindfulness	88.	Tenderness
21.	Eternity	55.	Mystery	89.	Thoughtfulness
22.	Even-mindedness	56.	Non-attachment	90.	Tolerance
23.	Faith	57.	Non-injury	91.	Trust
24.	Fearlessness	58.	Oneness	92.	Truthfulness
25.	Forbearance	59.	Openness	93.	Unconditional Love
26.	Forgiveness	60.	Order	94.	Understanding
27.	Freedom	61.	Patience	95.	Unity
28.	Friendship	62.	Peace	96.	Usefulness
29.	Fun	63.	Perfection	97.	Warmth
30.	Generosity	64.	Perseverance	98.	Will
31.	Gentleness	65.	Play	99.	Wisdom
32.	Gratitude	66.	Positive thinking	100.	Witness
33.	Harmony	67.	Power	101.	Other
34.	Healing	68.	Practicality		

- THE GOAL. The Bible, Koran, Bhagavad Gita, and all sacred texts speak to these qualities. Christ, Buddha, Krishna, Rumi, the Baal Shem Tov, gurus, Zen masters, and yogis teach these qualities. They are at the core of every spiritual story. They represent the basics, the alphabet, the periodic table of spiritual elements. Likewise, all psychosocial healing models ultimately point to these qualities as the goal of inner being work.

- LOVE. In this work, the qualities listed in the Spiritual Alphabet are called Love. For our purposes, each time you read the word *Love,* you can consider that as one or a combination of these qualities. If you don't favor the word Love, you are encouraged to use one of the names below or any label that gives you inspiration.

- A VARIETY OF NAMES. You don't have to refer to the healing qualities as Love. You can call it Truth, Power, Wisdom, Self-Knowledge, Higher Self, True Self, Soul, the Buddha, Atman, the Image of God, Spiritual Qualities, Spiritual Alphabet, Healing Alphabet, Spiritual Properties, Healing Qualities, Life Savers, or the Attributes of Love. It doesn't matter what you call it. What does matter is the recognition that at the very core of our being exists a host of healing qualities that can help you manage any painful problem.

- THE TRUE SELF. Healing qualities describe who we really are. We are born with them. They are standard equipment, built into the human genetic code. As Dr. Herbert Benson argues in *Timeless Healing,* we are "wired for God." The higher self is pure and perfect, loving and calm, wise and compassionate. This is our genetic birthright.

- EXTERNAL IDENTIFICATIONS. The roles we play in life, our educational level, economic status, race, ethnicity, and age obscure our true nature. Our bodies, personalities, or roles do not ultimately describe us. Similarly, we are not our problems, flaws, or illnesses.

These superficial identifications veil our inner identity or true self, the soul where we find all of the spiritual qualities.

- A CALM CENTER. The soul is the deepest aspect of our being, a calm center that is always there, no matter how turbulent or chaotic our life. We can always turn to the soul for refuge, comfort, and rejuvenation. No matter what external problem we face, the soul offers safety, peace, harmony, and strength.

- INTERCONNECTED. The list of healing qualities is long and may appear formidable. It need not be. All of the qualities are connected, and Love is the root. If we improve our ability to love, the rest of the qualities simultaneously grow. Similarly, if we cultivate any one of the qualities, our Love grows. We can pick one or a few qualities to work on at any given time. It does not matter which ones we choose.

If you cultivate compassion, you will automatically become more patient and understanding. If you practice kindness, you will automatically become more forgiving and loving. When you practice courage and perseverance, you automatically become stronger and more peaceful. When you grow even one quality, the rest follow. It does not matter which ones we choose.

Nor does it matter what religion we practice. It does not matter if we practice a religion at all. What does matter is the level of our development of our souls' qualities, or Love. If the fruit of a religion or other healing model is Love, it is good; if not, there is a problem.

- MORE POWERFUL THAN ANY PAIN OR PROBLEM. Love and her consort qualities are the healers. They broker and buffer the pain of life. Such healing powers as compassion, understanding, forgiveness, and humility are more powerful than any painful problem. They will contain, reduce, or eliminate any barrier we encounter.

- ROOT CAUSE AND SOLUTION. The lack of healing qualities is a root cause of many of our life problems. Similarly, the cultivation of healing qualities is the inner solution to these problems. Knowing this kindles hope, which is necessary to start the healing process. Hope is the match that lights the fire necessary for deep growth and recovery.

- WE KNOW HOW TO MAKE THE QUALITIES GROW. We can cultivate Love and her companion qualities through meditation, prayer, contemplation, and other methods described in Step 9. These methods bring us to a quiet state needed to hear the still, small voice within. This voice, an inner guide, can show us the way to expanded compassion, kindness, and courage.

- THE HIGHER SELF. At the core of our being, we are all a composite of spiritual qualities: warm, loving, human beings filled with strength, wisdom, and joy. This is our spiritual identity, the higher self, our Buddha nature, the Image of God within. It is who we really are. Part of the spiritual journey is spent searching for and finding this inner reality, a search that also involves defining for ourselves the nature of our Higher Power.

HIGHER POWER

- HIGHER POWER. On the recovery and healing path, it is very helpful to define the nature of our Higher Power for ourselves. Once we have a working image of a Higher Power, we can tap into it as a source of the strength we seek. In this work, Higher Power refers to:

1. Higher meaning and purpose
2. The higher or true self

3. Higher states of consciousness
4. The God of your understanding

- A CAFETERIA OF OPTIONS. You can specifically define those aspects and images of a Higher Power that are comfortable, approachable, and accessible. Then you can use your concept as a source of continuous guidance in response to any problem or pain. Following are some of the ways that spiritual belief systems describe the nature of Higher Power:

  - OMNISCIENT, OMNIPOTENT, OMNIPRESENT. In Christianity, Judaism, Islam, Hinduism, and certain aspects of Buddhism, God is present everywhere as an all-knowing, all-powerful, conscious Universal Being to whom we may appeal and receive a response through grace.

  - GOD IS LOVE. There is a personal relationship with God as Father or Mother, Friend, Confidante, Beloved, Teacher, Protector, Guide, Creator, Healer, Counselor, or Physician.

  - CONSCIOUSNESS. Many people do not feel comfortable relating to their Higher Power in a personal way. They feel that any attempt to think of God in human terms is limiting, if not confusing. These individuals may pursue an elevation in consciousness but do not believe in a God to whom they can appeal. For example, some who practice Buddhism may focus on expanded awareness, energy, and consciousness.

  - THE MASTERS SUCH AS CHRIST, BUDDHA, KRISHNA, RUMI, THE BAAL SHEM TOV. God-realized masters embody the great spiritual qualities as a model for humanity to follow.

  - THE CHANGELESS ONE. This is the One Life that flows through, pervades, and unites everything, the eternal source of all that is, and the place to which we all return. It is the infinite and immortal formless form within which all form exists. There is no body, only pure consciousness and awareness; it cannot be cut, burned, or hurt in any way.

- A UNIFIED FIELD OF HEALING ENERGY. An omniscient loving power underlies and unites all. It is inside, outside, everywhere, extending forever in every direction, uniting all things and people. This is God as the Great Physician with infinite healing power. We can enter this unified field of healing energy via meditation and prayer.

- NATURE. Some commune with Nature, Energy, or Mother Earth.

- HIGHER MEANING AND PURPOSE. Others believe in a higher purpose and meaning. They seek healing qualities as part of their higher self. The tools for growth are reason, feeling, dreams, and the subconscious mind.

- GREAT SPIRIT, THE MASTER OF THE UNIVERSE, COSMIC CONSCIOUSNESS, COLLECTIVE UNCONSCIOUS, AND A HOST OF OTHER NAMES TOO NUMEROUS TO CATALOG.

- THE INFINITE MYSTERIOUS UNKNOWN. No words can describe this state. It is beyond the meager adjectives of human conception.

This is not a comprehensive list. There are many other concepts, images, and ideas.

You are encouraged to review these options, take what you need and leave the rest. In this work, I will employ all of the aspects described above in discussion, affirmations, and processes. If you have difficulty connecting to an image I am using, I encourage you to replace it with one that can work for you. For example, if I refer to God, you might choose consciousness. If I choose Father, you might prefer Mother. God may be seen as male, female, both, or neither. I alternate between male and female pronouns and other aspects such as Teacher, Physician, Ocean, Changeless One, or Counselor to emphasize the multi-faceted nature of the Higher Power.

POINTS TO REMEMBER: STEP 7

- A study of spiritual belief systems reveals the connection between healing qualities, the higher self, and our Higher Power. Healing qualities are the route to higher states of consciousness.

- The qualities listed in the healing alphabet tell a story about Love.

- Our true nature is Love.

- *Love* in this work is shorthand for the one hundred qualities comprising the spiritual alphabet. Love has a variety of meanings and can be controversial or confusing. Feel free to choose a different term such as Truth, Wisdom, Power, the Tao, or any other word that gives you inspiration.

- Are you a Christian, Jew, Buddhist, ethical humanist, Sufi mystic, atheist, or agnostic? That is the wrong question. Are you in peace, Love, and joy or something else? That is the question. It's about the qualities, not the vehicle. Your cells don't care about your religion. They do care about the qualities.

- The development of spiritual qualities is the central purpose of spiritual practice.

- When we activate Love, our healing power expands.

- Love is the essential healing principle found at the heart of all wisdom traditions.

- Love and her consort qualities are more powerful than any painful problem.

- Spiritual qualities impact healing operations in some yet-to be-determined way at the molecular, cellular, and electrical-magnetic levels of the brain and body.

- Full recovery and deep healing is not possible without Love.

- The cultivation of healing qualities is the key to any successful pain management program.

- If a healing model does not lead to the expansion of healing qualities, there is a problem. Why would we do the work if these were not growing?

- Developing a comfortable, approachable, and accessible concept of a Higher Power is useful for managing any pain or problem.

EXERCISES

1. What is your concept of true self or soul?

2. Review the list of spiritual qualities. What qualities would you like to grow?

3. Do you have a Higher Power?

4. What is your concept of a Higher Power?

5. Is your Higher Power loving and forgiving or judgmental and punitive?

6. To develop your concept of a Higher Power, think of some of the brutal realities that have or might occur. Is your connection to your Higher Power stronger than the worst experience that has

happened or that you can imagine? What would it take to get you through that?

SKILLFUL PAIN MANAGEMENT

STEPS 8–10
PAIN MANAGEMENT AND SPIRITUAL PRACTICE
GIVE US THE PEACE, LOVE, AND JOY WE CRAVE

- Step 7 defines the nature of the higher self and Higher Power as Love. Knowing this, however, does not give us the pain relief we seek. In steps 8–10, you will learn how to manage your pain more skillfully.

- Step 8 describes pain management in the school of life.

- Step 9 describes a variety of healing practices.

- Step 10 describes what happens when healing qualities expand.

STEP 8: THE SCHOOL OF LIFE

- DUALITY AND BRUTAL REALITY. The sacred traditions describe the experience of higher consciousness as a vast stillness, changeless peace, and infinite Love. Yet daily we experience turbulence from life on the physical plane. We have little or no control over the evolution and spin of the show. We love the positive side of the story, but the intrusion of brutal reality throws us into high mental and emotional reactivity. The harmony we seek disappears, and we no longer enjoy the show.

- LIFE IS SCHOOL. We cannot change duality, but we can change our response to it. We can learn new ways to manage pain by viewing life as school. The purpose of the school of life is to discover our true identity: unconditional Love and changeless peace. This involves accepting pain as a stimulant for the growth of spiritual qualities. We can turn the tables on the pain and make it work for us. We can do this by remembering three points when we are in pain:

1. Life is school.
2. Pain is the teacher if we open to its lessons.
3. The lessons have to do with the cultivation of healing qualities.

- THE TEACHER. Every experience, event, and person is a teacher in the school of life. Lessons have to do with expansion of Love and associated healing qualities. There are homework assignments and tests designed to bring out our painful physical, mental, and spiritual problems. The blocks to our spiritual growth must be exposed before they can be eliminated. Pain tells us where to work. It is intelligent. It bears messages. By enduring and working with our pain, we learn our lessons, expand our Love, and grow.

- HOMEWORK. Life expects us to do the homework every day. Daily assignments in the outer world often involve our jobs, school, relationships, chores, and service. Daily assignments in the inner world include practicing affirmations, meditation, mindfulness, and other spiritual methods.

- TESTS. When we attend classes and do the necessary homework, we learn lessons and pass the tests. To pass a test requires using our suffering as a stimulant for the cultivation of spiritual qualities. We are to respond to all of our painful problems with ever-increasing Love, compassion, understanding, strength, courage, and other qualities as listed in the spiritual alphabet.

- PLAYING HOOKY. When we pass our tests and achieve mastery, we move on to the next grade, where a new set of problems and higher standards emerge. However, when we play hooky from class and neglect our homework, assignments pile up and problems remain unresolved. We fail the test and repeat the class. When we avoid the inevitable suffering of life, it gets worse. If we keep playing hooky from the school of life, we end up in the school of hard knocks.

- SETUPS. Our daily routine often includes setups: events that cause us to overreact. For example, some of us have a lifelong problem with high emotional reactivity. When we begin our spiritual practice, we must make a conscious decision to remain calm and patient, no matter the provocation. With spiritual practices such as meditation and mindfulness, we slowly transform excessive emotion to even-minded patience. We know we have advanced when the circumstance that aroused excessive emotion in the past brings forth a peaceful response instead. When we master a certain level of grace, new, unexpected, and usually more difficult setups arise to test our ability to remain calm. In this way, the bar is raised so that we can continue to expand our peaceful response.

- BIG TESTS. Sometimes life assigns very painful problems that need much study and work. In these more difficult classes, there is great potential for learning and growth as long as we use our pain to cultivate strength, peace, and other healing qualities. On the other hand, if we resort to destructive, pain-killing devices such as substance abuse or other such bad habits, these difficult assignments will be lost as opportunities for growth, and their lessons will ultimately need to be repeated.

Many do well in the school of life when times are good, but poorly when tragedies or crises occur. A strong healing program must include all of life's events, including the most painful. When pain is accepted as the teacher, no barrier can stop us; even those that are apparently or obviously evil can be used to propel us forward to courage, strength, and wisdom.

- THE SCHOOL OF LIFE NEVER CLOSES. There are recesses, holidays, and vacations, but the school of life never closes. There is always room for improvement when developing spiritual qualities. It is wise to do the homework daily. There may be a surprise quiz at any time. And we cannot cram for the final exam the night before—the final exam being entry into the vast unknown mystery at the time of death. Don't you want to be prepared?

STEP 9: SPIRITUAL PRACTICE

- THE WORK. Following is a list of spiritual practices described in this book. This is where we do the work. You can practice these methods in response to any painful problem of body, mind, or soul:

- STEP 9.1: EXTERNAL SPIRITUAL PRACTICE. Many people go to synagogue, church, or mosque; perform rituals; sing and chant; listen to sermons; and study scripture. These good acts are a part of external worship. We get inspired, behave ethically, and may have some direct spiritual experiences.

- STEP 9.2: INTERNAL SPIRITUAL PRACTICE. The methods described in this work have to do with internal spiritual practice. These methods require an additional level of commitment, discipline, and time. The body is the temple. The pursuit is internal. The goal is translation of concept and belief into tangible experience and perception, going deeper into the realm of Spirit.

The internal spiritual practices described in this work are:

1. Affirmations
2. Habits
3. Progressive Muscle Relaxation
4. Breathwork
5. Contemplation
6. Meditation
7. Prayer

8. Mindfulness
9. Practicing the Presence of God
10. Service
11. Yoga
12. Transformation of Emotion

- THE REWARD. If you decide to do the work, the reward is great. You will cultivate spiritual qualities in response to the inevitable suffering of life. You will become a more skillful pain manager. Your healing power expands for body, mind, and soul. You will feel better and become a better person. You will conquer the inner world and become master of yourself.

STEP 10: SPIRITUAL EXPERIENCE
EXPANSION OF SPIRITUAL QUALITIES AND TRANSFORMATION OF CONSCIOUSNESS

- If you develop a spiritual practice as described in Step 9, you will experience an expansion of spiritual qualities and transform your consciousness. This occurs in four stages:

    a. STEP 10.1: NO CHANGE IS NOTICEABLE. Spiritual qualities are growing but the increase is subtle and imperceptible. Many people quit here as they are looking for immediate gratification and are not prepared for work, struggle, and discipline.

    b. STEP 10.2: YOU FEEL BETTER AND BECOME A BETTER PERSON. There is a tangible experience of ever-increasing peace, Love, strength, courage, compassion, and other qualities listed in the spiritual alphabet.

    c. STEP 10.3: TRANSFORMATION OF CONSCIOUSNESS. There is an unmistakable shift in consciousness sometimes described as superconsciousness, the peace that surpasses understanding, pure Love, ecstatic joy, unfathomable stillness, intuitive wisdom, a feeling of oneness with everything, and other wonderful expressions of Spirit. These experiences may last from a few minutes or hours to several days, but there is inevitably a return to ordinary consciousness.

d. STEP 10.4: MASTERY. There is a sustained state of superconsciousness. This is a very advanced stage and requires decades if not lifetimes of work and discipline. With continued practice, our spiritual qualities become strong enough that no external drama or condition of our bodies can shake them. We remain peaceful, positive, and poised no matter what life throws at us. We experience the soul and Higher Power as a durable Love born of ever-expanding compassion, understanding, wisdom, and joy. We know we are the immutable peace of the soul, connected to Spirit, eternally safe and protected. We know our Love is greater than any pain or problem. We can get through any barrier, no matter how insurmountable it appears. Nothing can stop us. Nothing can touch us. We are awake, aware, and ready for anything. Serene and compassionate service to humanity is the natural outcome of this state of consciousness.

- THE CORE DRIVE RESURRECTED: Step 10 is the core drive resurrected, but now we understand that getting the peace, Love, and joy we crave necessitates a shift in the locus of control from outside to inside.

A SUMMARY OF THE
KEY PRINCIPLES OF THE TEN STEPS

- Steps 1–3: we want permanent Love and safety in an uncertain world where suffering is inevitable.

- Steps 4–5: we manage our pain poorly and make it worse.

- Steps 6–7: we discover the essential healing principle of the great faith traditions as spiritual qualities or Love.

- Step 8: we learn how to use the inevitable suffering of life to cultivate spiritual qualities.

- Step 9: pain is the route to healing if we develop a spiritual practice.

- Steps 10: Healing qualities such as Love, compassion, courage, strength, and humility are the healers. They help us broker and buffer the pain of this life.

- Steps 1–10:

    a. Through a series of painful lessons, life teaches us that the peace, Love, and joy we seek in the outer world can and must ultimately be found within.

    b. Spiritual work results in a shift in the locus of control from the outer world of people, places, and things to the inner world of peace, power, and strength.

    c. Skillful pain management (Step 8) and spiritual practice (Step 9) lead to the discovery of the higher self and Higher Power (Step 7), as the peace, Love, and joy we crave (Step 10).

    d. Step 10 is the core drive resurrected, but now we understand that getting the peace, Love, and joy we crave necessitates a shift in the locus of control from outside to inside.

POINTS TO REMEMBER: STEPS 8–10

- Pain management and spiritual practice lead to the discovery that the soul and Spirit are indistinguishable from the unlimited Love we so crave. This is the core drive resurrected! But now, armed with the wisdom of the great world religions, we understand that the Love we have been seeking in the outside world can and must ultimately be found inside.

- We can prove that we have a soul made in the image of Love if we practice spiritual disciplines in response to life's problems.

- When we do the work, we experience ego reduction, pain relief, problem resolution, healing, guidance, and protection. Spiritual qualities such as courage, strength, gratitude, humility, and forgiveness slowly grow.

- As we advance, there may be an unmistakable change in consciousness. We experience the peace that surpasses understanding, unfathomable stillness, pure Love, ecstatic joy, cosmic sound and light, intuitive knowledge, visions, and pure disembodied consciousness.

- To grow spiritually, we have to effectively manage our pain and develop a spiritual practice.

- In the school of life, pain is the teacher and a stimulant for the growth of spiritual qualities. Through a series of painful lessons, we learn that what we were looking for on the outside, we can and must eventually find inside.

- Skillful pain management and spiritual practice lead to a variety of wonderful spiritual experiences!

- As we get better at managing pain and problems through the cultivation of spiritual qualities, our locus of control shifts from outside to inside ourselves. Eventually we come to understand that *everything we are looking for is inside.*

- If you decide to do this work, the reward is great:

a. You will cultivate spiritual qualities.
b. You will feel better.
c. You will become a better person.
d. Negative→Positive→Stillness→Higher Consciousness
e. You will conquer the inner world.
f. You will become master of yourself.

EXERCISES

1. Review the list of spiritual qualities. Which would you like to grow? (Step 7)

2. Using the metaphor of life as a school, how would you describe some of the classes that you are in at this time? (Step 8)

3. What lessons are you learning? (Step 8)

4. Discuss pain as a stimulant for the growth of your spiritual qualities. (Step 8)

5. Recall the purpose of spiritual practice: to reduce reactivity or the add-ons—the pain we add on to the inevitable suffering of life. We can locate this reactivity in the six tools that become barriers as described in Step 5.

Tools In Alignment
1. Mind: when positive, calm, and focused, it is brilliant at solving problems and shaping meaning
2. Emotion: a source of self-knowledge
3. Desire: our motivation to seek health, prosperity, and Love
4. Body: engages life, the doer of all of our activities, the source of our potential liberation and enlightenment
5. Activity: work, recreation, culture, hobbies
6. Ego: establishes our place in the world of work and relationships

Tools Out of Alignment = Reactivity

1. Mind: restless, relentless, a life of its own
2. Emotion: high emotional reactivity
3. Desire: excessive material desire resulting in attachments and bad habits
4. Body: heavy, tired, hurts, disability, death
5. Activity: hyperactivity
6. Ego: separation, selfishness, territorial, self-important

The six tools out of alignment are a universal problem, and this misalignment pins us to the mat of the status quo. It is the root cause of much of our suffering. These are the add-ons to the inevitable suffering of life.

We can get the six tools back in alignment by developing a spiritual practice. In Step 9, you will learn a variety of spiritual methods that will help you do this work.

Getting the tools back in alignment is like becoming your own spiritual chiropractor. The spiritual backbone in this metaphor is the six tools. When the six tools are in alignment, they are our best friends, powerful allies that help us achieve our goals. When out of alignment, they become our worst enemies, a source of unnecessary and often profound suffering. To get our spiritual backbone back in alignment, we give it a whack with any one or combination of the spiritual methods described in Step 9.

The relationship between Step 5 and Step 9 is where the leverage is. This is where we do the work. When we practice a spiritual method such as affirmations and breathwork (Step 9), we are getting our tools back in alignment (Step 5). This is the day-to-day, hand-to-hand combat, the grind-it-out spiritual work. This work requires discipline and life-long practice.

6. What is the next step in your spiritual development?

7. Are you willing to do some work?

8. Do you have a spiritual practice? (Step 9)

9. What spiritual methods do you use? (Step 9)

10. Do you need to expand your spiritual practice? (Step 9)

11. Have you experienced the growth of spiritual qualities? (Step 10)

12. Have you had a transformation of consciousness or a superconscious experience? What was it like? Do you have a word that describes this: God, Buddha, Nirvana, Christ Consciousness, or some other term? (Step 10.3)

You are now finished with your review of the ten steps. There is a lot of material there. It is complicated and may be overwhelming but there is good news. We can simplify and reduce the entire story into three variables: problem-method-quality. The next chapter describes the Universal Healing Wheel. All you need to become a more skillful pain manager is PMQ, or problem-method-quality. This is called the Universal Healing Wheel. It has a similar pattern to the teachings of the Buddha.

PART TWO
SPIRITUAL
PRACTICE

CHAPTER SEVEN

THE UNIVERSAL HEALING WHEEL

The Essential Healing Principle
Problem-Method-Quality

- THE UNIVERSAL HEALING WHEEL. To evolve, all you have to do is find a problem, practice a method, and cultivate a quality. When you do this, you will feel better, become a better person, and experience higher states of consciousness.

  This chapter introduces the Universal Healing Wheel, or problem-method-quality (PMQ). *PMQ is the essence of psychosocial-spiritual healing and the backbone of any and all of the processes described in this book.* The pattern of the Universal Healing Wheel is similar to that of the teachings of Buddhism.

- BUDDHISM. Twenty-six hundred years ago, the great metaphysician Siddhartha Gautama, the Buddha, began his campaign to relieve human suffering with a simple diagnosis and treatment plan, known famously as the Four Noble Truths. The first of these truths is: life is painful. The Buddha outlines the root cause of human suffering and prescribes a set of healing practices designed to cure the pains of life. Compassionate service is the medication; peace of mind is the result. The Buddha shows us how to heal our pain with practices such as mindfulness, meditation, and service. The result is serenity and joy. In essence, the Buddha is a masterful pain manager. He teaches us how to transform our suffering into spiritual power.

In his Four Noble Truths, the Buddha defines three simple variables that correspond with the elements of PMQ:

a. Problem: the inevitable suffering of life
b. Method: healing methods for the pain, including meditation, mindfulness, and service
c. Quality: the outcome of serenity, joy, and other spiritual qualities

In this work, problem-method-quality, or PMQ, correspond to steps 7–10:

- PROBLEM. Step 8, the School of Life, describes the inevitable suffering of life: any pain or problem of body, mind, or soul.

- METHOD. Step 9, Spiritual Practice, describes twelve internal methods that help us cultivate spiritual qualities.

- QUALITY. Step 7, Soul and Higher Power, and Step 10, Spiritual Experience, describe the expansion of healing qualities as the goal of all psychosocial-spiritual work. Skillful pain management (Step 8) and spiritual practice (Step 9) lead to the discovery of the higher self and Higher Power (Step 7), as the peace, Love, and joy we crave (Step 10).

Following is a list of the healing qualities described in Step 7. After that, you will review a few very important points about the qualities, followed by some examples of how the Universal Healing Wheel works in everyday living.

HEALING QUALITIES

1. Acceptance	35. Honesty	69. Pure awareness
2. Appreciation	36. Hope	70. Pure consciousness
3. Balance	37. Humility	71. Purity
4. Beauty	38. Humor	72. Receptivity
5. Belief	39. Immortality	73. Reverence
6. Changelessness	40. Infinity	74. Rhythm
7. Cheerfulness	41. Integrity	75. Safety
8. Clarity	42. Interconnectedness	76. Security
9. Community	43. Introspection	77. Self-control
10. Compassion	44. Intuition	78. Service
11. Confidence	45. Joy	79. Silence
12. Contentment	46. Justice	80. Simplicity
13. Courage	47. Kindness	81. Sincerity
14. Creativity	48. Knowledge	82. Spaciousness
15. Desirelessness	49. Laughter	83. Stillness
16. Devotion	50. Light	84. Strength
17. Endurance	51. Listening	85. Success
18. Energy	52. Loyalty	86. Surrender
19. Enthusiasm	53. Mercy	87. Sweetness
20. Equality	54. Mindfulness	88. Tenderness
21. Eternity	55. Mystery	89. Thoughtfulness
22. Even-mindedness	56. Non-attachment	90. Tolerance
23. Faith	57. Non-injury	91. Trust
24. Fearlessness	58. Oneness	92. Truthfulness
25. Forbearance	59. Openness	93. Unconditional Love
26. Forgiveness	60. Order	94. Understanding
27. Freedom	61. Patience	95. Unity
28. Friendship	62. Peace	96. Usefulness
29. Fun	63. Perfection	97. Warmth
30. Generosity	64. Perseverance	98. Will
31. Gentleness	65. Play	99. Wisdom
32. Gratitude	66. Positive thinking	100. Witness
33. Harmony	67. Power	101. Other
34. Healing	68. Practicality	

IMPORTANT POINTS ABOUT THE QUALITIES

An old Cherokee Indian was speaking to his grandson. "A fight is going on inside me," he said to the boy. "It is a terrible fight between two wolves. One is evil—he is anger, envy, sorrow, regret, greed, arrogance, self-pity, guilt, resentment, inferiority, lies, false pride, superiority, and ego. The other is good—he is joy, peace, love, hope, serenity, humility, kindness, benevolence, empathy, generosity, truth, compassion, and faith. This same fight is going on inside you, and inside every other person, too."

The grandson thought about it for a long minute, and then asked his grandfather, "Which wolf will win?"

The old Cherokee simply replied, "The one you feed."

- THE INHERITED WISDOM OF THE BODY. You already have every one of the qualities listed in the spiritual alphabet. You were born with them. They are part of the wisdom of the body, built into the genetic code as standard equipment. The jewels of this life lie at the very core of your being. You have within you right now the habits of a sage. You are not just good. You are very good.

- WE CAN MAKE THEM GROW. We know how to make the healing qualities grow. This book describes fifteen methods that will help you cultivate these qualities.

- ACTUAL HEALING POWERS. Spiritual qualities are not merely words but actual healing powers. We can deploy them in response to any pain or problem.

- MORE POWERFUL THAN ANY PAINFUL PROBLEM. The healing qualities are more powerful than our painful problems. They help us broker and buffer the pain of this life. Healing powers such as Love, compassion, understanding, forgiveness, and humility will contain, reduce, or eliminate any barrier we encounter. The cultivation of these wonderful healing qualities is an essential part of recovery. We need them for our deepest healing.

• HIGHER CONSCIOUSNESS. The healing qualities will help you in every aspect of your life. When you bring out these qualities in response to life's difficulties, your consciousness will rise to a higher state. Your life will be smoother, easier, and you will feel better. You will become a better person. The expansion of healing qualities ultimately leads to superconscious experiences.

• SHIFTING YOUR LOCUS OF CONTROL FROM OUTSIDE TO INSIDE. As you build your external world of people and activities, you can also build an inner world of peace, power, and strength. As the healing qualities slowly grow, you will be less reactive and more relaxed. The ultimate goal is to shift your locus of control from outside to inside in order to be less reactive, to remain at peace under all conditions.

SKILLFUL PAIN MANAGEMENT IN THE SCHOOL OF LIFE
ROLL THE UNIVERSAL HEALING WHEEL

• SCHOOL. Life is school. Pain is the teacher if you are open to its lessons. The lessons have to do with the cultivation of healing qualities. We are all presented with a variety of painful problems that we cannot escape. Rather than being dismayed or responding in a negative fashion, we can turn the tables on the pain and make it work for us by responding with healing qualities.

• THE UNIVERSE WILL NOT LEAVE US ALONE. Everybody suffers. The unavoidable suffering of life shows up as tests, trials, and temptations that inevitably interrupt our peace and stability. The universe simply will not leave us alone! It throws continuous challenges our way. Obviously, what happens to us in this life is important, but how we respond is even more important. In response to life's difficulties, we have the choice to react in a positive or negative fashion. However, no matter how hard we try to choose rightly, at times, we get lost in negativity. Sometimes our problems take over. We get stuck in old, negative thought patterns and habits that automatically choose our path for us. We cannot seem to get out.

- THE UNIVERSAL HEALING WHEEL. There is a way out. We can transform suffering into spiritual power by finding a problem, practicing a method, and cultivating a quality. This is the Universal Healing Wheel.

When locked in any painful struggle, roll the Universal Healing Wheel:

1. Problem: Identify the problem. This can be any problem of body, mind, or soul.

2. Method: Pick a method that will help you cultivate a quality. Following is a list of methods described in these lessons:

Horizontal Axis

1. People
2. Activities
3. Belief systems

Vertical Axis

4. Affirmations
5. Habit transformation
6. Progressive muscle relaxation
7. Breathwork
8. Contemplation
9. Meditation

10. Prayer
11. Mindfulness
12. The Presence of God
13. Service
14. Yoga
15. The transformation of emotion

3. Quality: Review the list of one hundred healing qualities. Pick one or a combination of qualities you need right now to help you with your problem.

• THE UNIVERSAL HEALING WHEEL:

1. Problem: any problem of body, mind, or soul
2. Method: any one or a combination of the fifteen methods
3. Quality: any one or a combination of one hundred qualities

• THE UNIVERSAL HEALING WHEEL IN SIMPLEST FORM:

1. Problem: I am anxious.
2. Method: I meditate.
3. Quality: I cultivate peace of mind.

• THE UNIVERSAL HEALING WHEEL IN A REAL LIFE SITUATION:

1. Problem: Today I had to deal with a rude bus driver and a cold-hearted nurse.
2. Method: I practice affirmations and breathwork.
3. Quality: I cultivate patience, kindness, compassion, and understanding.

Your day may be progressing pleasantly until one of the setups of life disrupts your harmony. Perhaps a rude bus driver does not accept your bus pass, or a nurse calls you from the doctor's office with the news that you need further testing because of a dark shadow in your chest X-ray. She does not give you any other information, and her attitude is cold and detached. On the recovery path, we try to respond to such difficulties with one or a combination of healing qualities. Though the bus driver was wrong and the nurse behaved unprofessionally, we try to remain calm, compassionate, and patient. Often, however, we lose control and contribute to the existing negativity with our own frustration and anger.

When life springs a challenge—such as the rude bus driver or the cold-hearted nurse—we can respond with frustration and anger, or we can do an inner workout. The inner workout utilizes our will with a practice method to cultivate a healing quality. For example, we could do some inner push-ups, such as deep breathing and affirmations of loving-kindness. With repetition and practice, we expand our ability to give a compassionate response to irritable, rude, provocative people. When we encourage these habits in ourselves, we cultivate inner strength and peace while others profit from our work because we do not add fuel to their fire.

To regain a positive response as soon as possible when you lose control, review the list of healing qualities. You might choose patience, kindness, compassion, and understanding as the qualities to inspire your response. Then consult the list of methods. You might try affirmations and breathwork to help you cultivate those qualities.

In these examples, the rude bus driver and the cold nurse are the problem. Breathwork, affirmations, mindfulness, and prayer are the methods used to cultivate the qualities of patience, kindness, compassion, and understanding. This is the Universal Healing Wheel. When you roll this wheel, you are healing.

The value of responding with patience, kindness, compassion, and understanding is clear. We feel better, and those around us—maybe even the bus driver and the nurse—feel better. Not only that, but our healing power goes up. Our cells love peace. When bathed in the vibrations of peace that come from practicing affirmations and deep abdominal breathing, the cells have a better chance to heal.

- INVOKE THE IMAGERY OF SCHOOL (STEP 8). When presented with a painful problem, it is natural to become frustrated, frightened, or angry. However, it is not a good idea to get stuck or to focus on these painful emotions. Instead, turn the tables on the pain and make it work for you by invoking the imagery of school. Say to yourself, "Okay, school is in session," and affirm:

  1. Life is school.
  2. Pain is the teacher if I open myself to its lessons.
  3. The lessons have to do with the cultivation of healing qualities.

- NEEDLE OF ATTENTION ON THE METHOD AND QUALITY. We need to recognize our problems, but we should not focus on them. Rather, we should focus on the method and the quality. Place your needle of attention on the methods and qualities—for example, deep abdominal breathing and peace—rather than on your anxiety. Then you will see the slow but sure development of peace or whatever quality you are cultivating.

- THE GROWTH OF HEALING QUALITIES IS SLOW BUT SURE. In the beginning, you may not feel anything. Don't be discouraged. The qualities are growing, but the growth is too subtle to feel. Persevere, and you will experience a tangible increase in qualities like peace, strength, patience, and courage in your life. You will feel better and become a better person. Keep rolling the Universal Healing Wheel and eventually you enter the room of stillness.

- THE ROOM OF STILLNESS. There is a calm center in the deepest part of our being. It is always there, no matter how turbulent or chaotic our lives. We can go there for refuge, comfort, and rejuvenation. No matter what problems of the world or body we face, the room of stillness offers us a continuous invitation. When we enter that room, we feel peace and safety. We will learn how to enter that room by practicing the methods described in this workbook.

- IN THE ROOM OF STILLNESS, HEALING QUALITIES EXPAND. The practice methods described in this work bring us to a quiet state needed to hear the still, small voice within. This voice, an inner guide, can show us the way to compassion, kindness, and courage. Healing qualities grow in the room of stillness. Peace of mind is the way and the goal.

- UNCONDITIONAL, SPONTANEOUS, AND AUTOMATIC (USA). Roll the Universal Healing Wheel every day and you will become a healing force in your own life and in the lives of others. Keep going and you will approach mastery. Once you master your healing practice, the qualities will manifest unconditionally, spontaneously, and automatically. You will give Love, respect, compassion, understanding, forgiveness, and other wonderful qualities to everyone you meet. Then you will be a sage, decorated with the jewels of this life.

THE METAPHYSICAL CAR

- The ten-step healing model described in this book works for any person: atheist, agnostic, religious, or spiritual. The only absolutely essential component is the Universal Healing Wheel. Everything else is optional. To illustrate how this works, think about building a metaphysical car.

- You can build a metaphysical car that will take you wherever you want to go on your recovery and healing journey. Even when you get stuck in a rut, it will get you out of trouble and help you move toward your destination. The car has three parts: a body, a wheel, and traction devices for the wheel.

1. BODY. The body of the car will be atheist, agnostic, religious, or spiritual. Which category best describes you?

2. WHEEL. Universal Healing Wheel: choose a problem, method, and quality.

   - Problem: choose any problem of body, mind, or soul.
   - Method: choose one or a combination of the fifteen methods.
   - Quality: choose one or a combination of the one hundred qualities.

The Universal Healing Wheel is the essential healing principle of any psychosocial or spiritual model. It is the lowest common denominator and cannot be reduced any further. We must have PMQ for deep healing and full recovery.

For many, PMQ is enough, but for others, it is not sufficient. Some need traction devices for the wheel.

3. TRACTION DEVICES. Traction devices for the wheel are the elements of the religions or other healing models that further enhance the healing process. Which ones will help you get traction so your car does not get stuck when the going gets rough? Here are a few examples: story; metaphor; parables; wisdom pearls; affirmations; prayers; Higher Power; Higher Consciousness; Mystery; the Unknown; God of Love; Omniscient, Omnipotent, Omnipresent Consciousness; Father; Mother; Friend; Beloved; Christ; Krishna; Buddha; the Image of God; Nature; the Collective Unconscious; Archetypes; the Subconscious; reason; traditional worship, ritual, sermons, music, art, committee work, and much more.

Remember this: one person's traction device is the next person's gag reflex. In this work, you will find a variety of descriptions of Higher Power. If you encounter terminology you don't like, you are encouraged to take what you need and leave the rest and to *nuke offensive language and substitute your own.*

- FOLLOW LOVE, NOT THE VEHICLE. It doesn't matter what kind of car you drive. What matters is the cultivation of healing qualities. You can be a Baptist, atheist, ethical humanist, or Sufi mystic. That is not as important as whether or not the qualities are growing. An ethical humanist may be more loving than a person practicing an orthodox religion. Follow Love, not the vehicle. The question we should ask of others and ourselves is not what kind of cars we drive, but rather, "Am I in the presence of Love, or something else?"

POINTS TO REMEMBER

- In this work, PMQ—or problem-method-quality—will be called the Universal Healing Wheel. The problem can be any problem of body, mind, or soul. To address these problems, the book describes fifteen methods. The result is the cultivation of one hundred spiritual qualities.

- The Universal Healing Wheel is the essential healing principle of any psychosocial or spiritual model. It is the lowest common denominator and cannot be reduced any further. We must have PMQ for deep healing and full recovery.

- PMQ is the essence of psychosocial-spiritual healing and the backbone of any and all of the processes described in this book. *PMQ is the physician for all people.*

- The essence of the ten steps, the Universal Healing Wheel, has a similar pattern to the teachings of Buddhism.

- PMQ corresponds to steps 7–10 in the ten-step model. Step 8 describes the problem, Step 9 describes the method, and Steps 7 and 10 describe the qualities. (PMQ = Steps 7–10 = Buddhism = the Universal Healing Wheel)

- As you build your external world of people and activities, you can also build an inner world of healing qualities: peace, power, strength, courage, and wisdom.

  1. You already have an army of one hundred spiritual qualities. You can call up any one or a combination of these qualities to help you win the battle of life.

  2. Healing qualities are part of the wisdom of the body. We need them for deepest healing. They are the jewels of this life. They are the healers. They buffer the pain of life.

- You can cultivate healing qualities in response to the inevitable suffering of life. This book teaches a variety of methods that will help you do this work. When you practice these methods, you will contain, reduce, or eliminate your problems and replace them with spiritual qualities. Spiritual qualities are more powerful than painful problems.

- Think about the events of your life and your responses to them. When you don't like the event or your response, try cultivating healing qualities. As the spiritual qualities grow toward unconditional, spontaneous, and automatic (USA), the locus of control shifts from outside to inside.

- Bring out the healing qualities in response to life's difficulties and you will see how much better you will feel. The qualities will help you in every aspect of your life. Your life will be smoother and easier.

- We are afraid of suffering, disease, disability, the unknown, and death. This fear or stress makes the inevitable suffering of life worse and slows down the healing process. The essence of mind-body medicine is reducing this reactivity and replacing it with healing qualities such as compassion, Love, understanding, strength, and peace. This is the work of steps 6–10 described in this model. It is equivalent to rolling the Universal Healing Wheel.

- If you *roll the Universal Healing Wheel* in response to the inevitable suffering of life, three things happen: (1) healing power expands, (2) you become a more skillful pain manager, and (3) you evolve spiritually.

- You may not be able to control outer events, but you own the space within you. It is your house; all of the rooms belong to you. You can choose the furniture and the decorations. Why not fill your house with the attributes of Love?

- Every affirmation, pearl of wisdom, quote, and technique in this work is an aspect of or doorway to the same larger space—a space filled with healing qualities and higher states of consciousness. Roll the Universal Healing Wheel, the essence of each technique, to enter this unified field of healing energy.

EXERCISES

1. Step 7 lists the one hundred healing qualities. The list is not dogmatic. Take what you need and leave the rest. Notice Quality 101: Other. You are encouraged to add any qualities you like. Review the list. Can you think of some qualities you would like to add or subtract?

2. When you have a spiritual experience, meet a spiritual person, read a sacred text, or discover a pearl of wisdom, try to describe the encounter in a single word. Collect these one-word affirmations as

your spiritual alphabet and compare it to the list of healing qualities cited in Step 7. What does your list look like?

3. Everyone brings something deeply good to the table right now. Which qualities are you good at? Which would you like to grow?

4. Look for the spiritual qualities in others. Focus on those qualities rather than any negative characteristics.

5. Practice one or a combination of the healing qualities throughout the day and, at night, evaluate how you did. Did you respond to the day's events with those qualities or in a negative fashion? Identify areas for improvement, and start anew the next day.

6. Roll the Universal Healing Wheel: see examples in Figure 1

   a. Find a problem you would like to work on. This can be any problem of body, mind, or soul.
   b. Go to the list of healing qualities. Pick one or a combination of qualities you need right now to help you with your problem.
   c. Pick one or more methods that will help you grow that quality.
   d. Practice cultivating your quality for a week.
   e. Read about that quality.
   f. Discuss it.
   g. Affirm it.
   h. Breathe it.
   i. Visualize it.
   j. Concentrate on it.
   k. Permeate your being with it.
   l. Create from it.
   m. Make it your faithful guide and companion.
   n. Write your experience.
   o. Share in a group or with a friend.

THE UNIVERSAL HEALING WHEEL

FIGURE 1

Problem	Method	Quality
Any problem of body, mind, or spirit	15 methods	100 qualities
Lonely	People: meet a friend	Joy
Bored	Activity: volunteer	Generosity
Loss	Belief system: go to church or AA meeting	Community
Physical illness	Affirmation	Acceptance
Addiction	Habit trans-formation	Contentment
Fatigue	Progressive muscle relaxation	Energy
Anxious	Breathwork	Peace
Confusion	Contemplation	Wisdom
Restless	Meditation	Even-mindedness
Fear	Prayer	Courage
Irritable	Mindfulness	Patience
Judgmental	Practicing the Presence of God	Unconditional Love
Guilt	Service	Forgiveness
Worry	Yoga	Harmony
Anger	Transformation of emotion	Understanding

7. Build your own metaphysical car. You can build a car that will take you wherever you want to go on your healing journey.

    a. The body of the car will be atheist, agnostic, religious, or spiritual. Which category best describes you?

    b. Universal Healing Wheel: choose a problem, method, and quality
   - Problem: choose any problem of body, mind, or soul.
   - Method: choose one or a combination of the fifteen methods.
   - Quality: choose one or a combination of the one hundred qualities.

    c. Traction devices: Traction devices for the wheel are the elements of the religions or other healing models. Which ones will help you get traction so your car does not get stuck when the going gets rough? Here are a few examples: Higher Power; Higher Consciousness; Mystery; the Unknown; God of Love; Omniscient, Omnipotent, Omnipresent; Father; Mother; Friend; Beloved; Creator, Christ; Krishna; Buddha; the Image of God; Nature; the Collective Unconscious; Archetypes; the Subconscious; Nature; reason; story; metaphor; the stuff of the religions or any other healing model.

8. The Dalai Lama says, "This is my simple religion. There is no need for temples, no need for complicated philosophy. Our own brain, our own heart is our temple; the philosophy is kindness." Do you see? It all has to do with the cultivation of spiritual qualities. When you have a painful problem, consult the list of one hundred spiritual qualities. Determine which qualities you need to help you manage your problem. Now, focus on your chosen quality. Give it all of your attention. You can use the qualities you choose as one-word affirmations throughout the day.

9. Review the Cherokee Indian parable on p. 100. Which wolf have you been feeding?

10. Notice how the growth of any one of the qualities in the spiritual alphabet leads to expansion of the others in the list. For example, if you become more patient, you will also have more compassion, understanding, and forgiveness. Patience, kindness, sweetness, and gentleness move together. Gratitude leads to reverence. Each quality is connected to the others, and they all lead to Love.

11. To see if you are growing, check your qualities. Ask, "Am I becoming more patient, kind, understanding, and peaceful? Am I growing in compassion, forgiveness, and gentleness? Is there more balance, rhythm, and harmony in my life? The answers to these questions make up your spiritual report card.

In the next chapter, you will find a review of the ten steps and a discussion of how to skillfully manage the anxiety of change.

CHAPTER EIGHT

SHIFTING THE LOCUS OF CONTROL

How To Skillfully Manage the Anxiety of Change

"THE LAST PLACE THEY WILL LOOK"

In a Native American parable, the Creator
gathers all the animals and says:
"I want to hide something from humans until they are ready
for it—the realization that they create their own reality."
"Give it to me. I'll fly it to the Moon," says the Eagle.
"No, one day soon they will go there and find it."
"How about the bottom of the ocean?" asks the Salmon.
"No, they will find it there, too."
"I will bury it in the great plains," says the Buffalo.
"They will soon dig and find it there."
"Put it inside them," says the wise Grandmother Mole.
"Done," says the Creator. "It is the last place they will look."

This chapter reviews the ten steps and why it is so difficult to change. Steps 1–5 describe the horizontal axis, where there is an external locus of control; that is, we work from the outside in, trying to achieve happiness in the outer world of people, activities, places, and things. In Steps 6–10, we shift from the horizontal to the vertical axis to work from the inside out; we move from the outer world of people, places, and things to the inner world of peace, power, and strength.

Many people remain on the horizontal track and do well. Others get into trouble and need the vertical axis for additional help and healing. The transition from horizontal to vertical healing is not easy.

This chapter will elaborate on why people resist change even when they should seek it out or embrace it.

THE TEN STEPS

1. The Core Drive
2. Duality and Brutal Reality
3. The Compromise
4. Habits
5. Tools Become Barriers
6. The Seeker
7. Soul and Spirit
8. The School of Life
9. Spiritual Practice
10. Spiritual Experience

STEPS 1–5: EXTERNAL LOCUS OF CONTROL (HORIZONTAL AXIS), WORKING FROM THE OUTSIDE IN

We want unlimited peace, Love, joy, and safety, more time, and no pain. This is the core drive, the Buddha, the image of God, or higher self. The core drive is the motivating force behind all of our actions at all times. It does not shut off. It can't. It is built into the genetic code. We have to have it. We want unlimited spiritual qualities and higher states of consciousness. The core drive is operating at all times, every step of the way, consciously, subconsciously, or both. We must have *unlimited* peace, joy, Love, safety, more time, and no pain.

In the beginning, we try to achieve the core drive exclusively on the physical plane, but these attempts are doomed to fail. We do get some peace, Love, joy, and safety from people, activities, places, events, and things. But on the physical plane, there is no such thing as permanent safety: suffering is inevitable, time is limited, and death wins in the end.

When we persist in our efforts to achieve the core drive on the physical plane, we create more pain. We develop bad habits, and the six tools spin out of control. This loss of control is akin to trying to accelerate your car out of a ditch: the harder you press on the gas pedal, the deeper in you get.

Recall a time when you were driving your car and doing well. Thought, feeling, desire, body, activity, and ego—the six tools that you use to achieve the core drive—are in good alignment and serving you well. You are headed for the goals of your core drive. You feel safe. There is no pain. The people, activities, and things in your life afford you a modicum of peace, Love, and joy. But, eventually, you run into the brick wall of loss, limitation, and suffering. Your car gets stuck in the mud.

Instinctively, you press down harder on the pedal to get your needs met. You redouble your efforts to find solace through your relationships, activities, places, and things. Instead, you get addicted and attached. You go deeper into the ditch and spray mud all over your car and everything else around you. The six tools spin out of control and become barriers—your greatest assets become your greatest liability. This phenomenon is called reactivity. Reactivity is what happens when the ego is in charge of the other five tools. A restless mind, unbridled emotions, excessive material desire, the body, hyperactivity, and egotism present an imposing array of problems for us to manage. When the six tools become barriers, a great deal of pain is added to the inevitable suffering of life.

We cannot control the inevitable suffering of life, but we can control how we respond to it. We can reduce and even eliminate our reactivity. Step 5, Tools Become Barriers, is monumentally important, for it is here that we do the work to eliminate the pain that we add to the inevitable suffering of life.

Although some people find what they need on the horizontal axis, others get stuck there. Driving their car on the horizontal track leads to reactivity, attachment, addiction, and heartbreak. This breakdown is an opportunity to advance to more skillful pain management, higher states of consciousness, and higher Love.

To get out of the mud, we need to replace our ordinary tires with the Universal Healing Wheel and traction devices described in Steps 7–10. With this tire change, an ordinary car is transformed into a metaphysical car, a car that will not get stuck. But this car is not so easy to get. Why?

STEP 6: THE SEEKER

Why is it so hard to get to Step 6, or to any kind of growth? Why are we so afraid of change? Let's go back to the power and importance of belief systems.

Belief systems are highly complex clusters of spiritual, religious, political, national, cultural, racial, familial, psychological, and personal thoughts, values, rituals, and behaviors. Their essential function is to create a story. The story may be literal, allegorical, or both. The story gives meaning and purpose, guidance and direction, inspiration and strength, pain management and healing, identity and control, self-esteem and well-being. It is a narrative that tries to make life coherent by explaining everything that happens to us and around us. It is no wonder that we hold onto our personal story with such fierce tenacity. In fact, belief system functions are crucial for the mental and emotional stability—if not the survival—of individuals and groups. Therefore, belief systems sometimes perpetuate themselves at any or all costs.

The two mechanisms that work to perpetuate belief systems are thought-repetition and repression of conflicting data. All of us employ these mechanisms: we accept information and ideas that are consistent with our belief systems and deny or repress conflicting information. This tendency has profound implications in health care, where part of our job is to help people shift from negative thoughts, feelings, and behaviors to positive ones. But change breeds fear and resistance. To understand how this works, lets review:

1. The cheeseburger effect
2. The uninvited guest in the living room
3. Fixed and opened belief systems

THE CHEESEBURGER EFFECT

Recall the cheeseburger story in chapter one. The cheeseburger represents the first event in the unraveling of an entire belief system. After I ate the cheeseburger, one by one I dropped the rites and rituals of my Jewish belief system until I got to the epicenter of the system: the existence of God. Is there a God? I don't know. Enter existential anxiety, or terror at the abyss.

Think of the rites and rituals of the belief system as pieces on a chessboard. The cheeseburger is a pawn. In the chess game of life, the pieces go down one by one. The king loses his protection and he too goes down. God is dead, maybe, and I am at the abyss.

In this metaphor, the loss of even one piece on the board is symbolic of the potential unraveling of the entire system. This is why people cling to all of the elements of their belief systems even when doing so makes no sense. There is a feeling that if you give up even a single piece of the system, you could lose the whole thing and come face to face with possible psychological annihilation—or even physical death—at the abyss. There is too much pain and power there. We can't stand it. So we keep our system intact, not willing to give up even an inch of territory.

THE UNINVITED GUEST IN THE LIVING ROOM

Here is another way to describe this concept. I invite you to my home for dinner. I ask if you would like something to drink, and you request a Coke with lemon and a glass of wine for your partner. I go to the kitchen and make the drinks. I come back and see that while I was in the kitchen, you rearranged the furniture and the pictures in my living room.

Incredulous, I say, "What are you doing? This is my house!"

"I like it better this way," you say.

"Fine, good for you, but here is what is going to happen. Put the furniture back, or go home. Even if you are the greatest interior decorator of all time, the furniture and decorations are placed where I am most comfortable. And even if it is dysfunctional, you cannot move it. It is not yours to move!"

Ideas and habits may be negative and create dysfunction, but they are the furniture and decorations in our living room. Any movement, even for the better, creates anxiety, even terror.

FIXED AND OPENED BELIEF SYSTEMS

There are two kinds of belief systems: fixed and opened. Fixed systems are inherited and carried to the grave. A good example of a fixed belief system is the orthodox wing of any traditional religious system. It provides all of the functions of belief systems: meaning and purpose, protection and guidance, community, and so forth. But one's inherited religion of origin does not always work. Some people spin out of their family program and look to other belief systems for help. Some find a new fixed system. Others pick and choose from a variety of systems, putting together their own story: an eclectic, opened system.

Transitioning between belief systems can cause anxiety, even terror. Moving from a fixed system to another fixed system or an opened system can be very frightening. Even little gaps in the system cause an anxiety rush. The way to prevent anxiety is to avoid all change. This is why people hang on to what they know with fierce tenacity: rites, rituals, concepts, images, aspects, habits, ideas, values, emotions, and attachments—nothing can change. Keeping everything the same keeps the peace.

What has this to do with health care? Healthcare practitioners make recommendations for lifestyle changes: adopt a healthier diet; exercise regularly; lose weight; stop smoking, drinking, and using drugs; cultivate positive thought and emotion; learn how to deal with your inner being; and so forth. The healthcare practitioner is the uninvited guest moving furniture around in the living room.

The cheeseburger effect and the uninvited guest in the living room speak to profoundly important barriers to recovery and healing: denial, defense, and resistance. We are afraid of even little changes. "If I allow even one little change," we think subconsciously, "the whole thing can unravel to the abyss."

Fear of change is the number one barrier to recovery and healing. It is the rate-limiting factor. People avoid change to avoid anxiety. At first glance, it doesn't seem like a little anxiety would stop people from moving forward, but this tendency isn't just about ordinary anxiety; even little changes can create the feeling that an entire belief system could unravel and leave the believer at the abyss. The abyss sits just underneath the living room. Or, you might say, the abyss and the living room exist in the same space. We try to keep the abyss at bay by arranging the furniture in the living room just so. When an uninvited guest shows up and tries to move the furniture around, we resist the change in order to keep the peace and avoid the abyss. Healthcare workers are uninvited guests in their patients' living rooms.

Patients push against healthcare workers all the time because our work is to help people confront and work through their anxiety. Without anxiety, there can be no growth. Although it is uncomfortable, it is necessary in order to achieve more strength and peace. For full healing to occur, we need to shift the existing struggle between healthcare professional and patient to a struggle within the patient's own psyche.

We need to learn how to control anxiety, or any other kind of pain, so that it does not control us. Remember this: how you manage your pain will determine whether you move forward, slip backward, or stay stuck in this life. *To become a more skillful pain manager, all you need to do is exchange the ordinary tire on your car with the Universal Healing Wheel and traction devices. With this simple maneuver, your ordinary car is transformed into a metaphysical car, a car that can get you out of the mud.*

STEPS 7–10: INTERNAL LOCUS OF CONTROL (VERTICAL AXIS), WORKING FROM THE INSIDE OUT

Recall Steps 7–10 describe the essential healing principle, which corresponds with PMQ, or problem-method-quality. Cultivating healing qualities in response to the inevitable suffering of life is the essence of mind-body work. When you roll the Universal Healing Wheel or drive your new metaphysical car:

1. The six tools go back into alignment.
2. Healing qualities grow.
3. Pain management skills increase.
4. We feel better and become better people.
5. Negative → positive → stillness → higher states of consciousness

When you practice PMQ, negative → positive → stillness → higher states of consciousness; "negative" stands for painful problems, or the inevitable suffering of life and our reaction to it; "positive" means spiritual qualities and, ultimately, stillness; stillness is the doorway to higher states of consciousness.

We run on the horizontal track trying to achieve the core drive through people, activities, things, and events. There are temporary victories on this axis, but the illusion of safety fights a losing battle against brutal reality; suffering is inevitable and death takes over in the end. The sooner we see this truth, the better. At that point, all we have to do is go to the vertical axis and roll the Universal Healing Wheel. This choice leads to the cultivation of healing qualities and, ultimately, the room of stillness, where we wait with patience until the door opens to an ecstatic domain of permanent safety. In this space, the core drive is resurrected, but now we see that the unlimited peace, Love, and joy we seek in the outer world can and ultimately must be found within.

Ideally there is a good balance between horizontal and vertical axis activity. On the horizontal axis, we give and receive Love and engage in constructive meaningful activities. On the vertical axis, we practice meditation, breathwork, affirmations, mindfulness, and other techniques to help us cultivate healing qualities in response to the inevitable suffering of life. Slowly, spiritual qualities grow until we reach mastery, where they become USA (unconditional, spontaneous, and automatic). The locus of control gradually shifts from outside to inside, until we are firmly anchored within. Then, no matter what the world or our bodies throw at us, we can respond with Love, compassion, kindness, and understanding. We remain even-minded under all conditions. We perform quiet anonymous acts of gentle, humble service to all of humanity. We bring our Love to brutal reality and serve there. We enjoy the show. We are ready for anything.

And remember, *you have an army of one hundred spiritual qualities.* Cultivate these in response to the inevitable suffering of life. Keep going and you will experience intermittent superconsciousness and ultimately, at mastery, a sustained state of superconsciousness. Love is greater than any pain or problem. Try this. Prove it to yourself.

In the next chapter, you will find a description of a Universal Healing Method. The Universal Healing Method includes the Universal Healing Wheel of problem-method-quality and adds external action, Higher Power, Will, and Grace.

CHAPTER NINE

A UNIVERSAL HEALING METHOD

A Ten-Step Method for Working
With Any Pain or Problem

- This chapter introduces a ten-step universal healing method that can be used for any pain or problem. Embedded in this method are a variety of principles necessary for deep healing and recovery.

- The universal healing method serves as a template for the methods, processes, and affirmations described in subsequent chapters. In chapters to follow, you will find variations on the themes presented here.

- The Universal Healing Method includes the Universal Healing Wheel of problem-method-quality and adds external action, Higher Power, Will, and Grace.

- The Universal Healing Method promotes a balanced healing program between outer and inner work, referred to respectively as the horizontal axis and vertical axis.

- Life is a series of tests and trials, every step of the way. We all experience physical, mental, emotional, and spiritual problems throughout our lives. These problems range from minor irritations to major crises. Following is a list of some of our most common problems:

a. Physical pain
b. Disease
c. Disability
d. Trauma
e. Restless mind
f. Painful emotion
g. Excessive material desire and attachments
h. Bad habits or addictions
i. Hyperactivity: always have to be busy
j. Egotism, selfishness, and separation
k. Loneliness and fear of being alone
l. Too dependent on others
m. Any conflict
n. Denial of problems
o. Controlling and rigid
p. Perfectionism
q. Negative attitude
r. Loss of status, possessions, people, or self-esteem
s. Feeling unworthy, guilty, or ashamed; self-hatred
t. Feeling rejected, abandoned, or humiliated
u. Hatred
v. Prejudice: judging others by their role, body, personality, age, race, religion, nationality, sexual identity, economic class, or disability
w. Indifference or boredom
x. Fixed false religious beliefs
y. Fear of the unknown, the abyss, and death
z. Lack of meaning and purpose
aa. Any other painful problem or character flaw

- When a painful problem arrives, it disturbs our peace and indicates an area where we could use some work. The school of life is in session. We have homework.

- Following are ten steps we can use to work our way through any pain or problem, however mild, severe, or extreme:

    1. Introspection: discover your issues and problems.
    2. Higher Power: get help from your Higher Power.
    3. External action: take action in the external world.
    4. Spiritual qualities: choose one or a combination of spiritual qualities in response to your problem.
    5. Spiritual methods: practice one or a combination of spiritual methods to cultivate spiritual qualities.

6. Will: apply all of your power to the chosen spiritual method.
7. Grace: gain access to the vast intelligent healing power within and around you.
8. Expansion of spiritual qualities: expand your qualities in four stages.
9. Repeat Steps 1–9: develop a lifelong process.
10. Mastery: attain superconsciousness in both meditation and activity.

1. INTROSPECTION:

- Introspection is self-analysis. It brings us to recesses of the mind that ordinarily remain hidden. It allows us to see our strengths and virtues as well as our flaws and limitations.

- In practicing introspection, we are encouraged not to deny or suppress our problems but to find them. All of us have issues and flaws. The advantage of finding out what they are is that once discovered, we can develop a plan for improvement.

- An honest look at our problems can be threatening or even shattering to the ego, but the goal is not to tear the self to shreds. The purpose of introspection is to discover what needs to change without inflicting any unnecessary guilt, low self-esteem, or humiliation upon ourselves. Rather than feel bad about our problems, we can feel good that we have the courage to face them and the integrity to change for the better.

- Retreat to a quiet place.

- To help create a safe healing space within, take several slow deep breaths. If you know a meditation technique, use it now to bring in as much stillness as you can. To facilitate the healing power, assume an attitude of compassion, understanding, and gentleness toward yourself.

- Now do a deep, honest, and fearless search for any issues, problems, or flaws that may need some work. Consult the list of problems cited in the beginning of this chapter.

- Make a problem list and a list of your strengths and accomplishments.

2. HIGHER POWER:

- We can get help from a Higher Power. To get help, we need to develop a concept or image that is comfortable and reachable.

- There are a variety of ways to conceptualize a Higher Power. Some examples are:

    a. The Omniscient, Omnipotent, Omnipresent God to whom you may appeal and get a response through grace
    b. A personal relationship with the God of Love manifesting as Father, Mother, Friend, Confidante, Beloved, Teacher, Protector, Guide, Creator, Healer, Counselor, Giver, or Physician
    c. A personal relationship with a saint, sage, prophet or God-realized master as the embodiment of spiritual qualities: Christ, Buddha, Krishna, Rumi, Mohammed, the Baal Shem Tov, and others
    d. God as the Great Physician, a vast unified field of Omniscient Love filled with infinite spiritual qualities and healing powers
    e. The Teacher (every person, event, experience, and all of life is the Teacher)
    f. The Creator, the source of all
    g. The Changeless One
    h. Higher meaning and purpose (for example, compassionate service to humanity)
    i. The higher self as an embodiment of healing qualities
    j. Higher states of consciousness
    k. Communion with Nature or Mother Earth

    l.   Reason, morality, and the subconscious

    m. The Collective Unconscious

    n. The Infinite Mysterious Unknown

    o. Many other concepts, images, and aspects

- Define the aspects or images of a Higher Power that are comfortable, approachable, and accessible.

- Install that image in your consciousness, and use it as a source of continuous guidance and inspiration.

- Your concept can help you in your relationships with people, in conducting the business of life, with minor irritations, or in major crisis.

- Sometimes we experience overwhelming pain. Sometimes we feel that we might shatter and never put the pieces back together again. Sometimes we do shatter. In any case, whether our problems are minor or extreme, our Higher Power can be a source of strength, courage, and wisdom.

3. EXTERNAL ACTION (ACTION ON THE PHYSICAL PLANE OR HORIZONTAL AXIS):

- We do everything we can to solve our problems on the horizontal axis or external world of people, activities, and belief system.

- For example, when we have symptoms of an illness, we go to the doctor for medicine.

- If we are in conflict with someone, we work on interpersonal communication and problem solving.

- When we suffer, we turn to our loved ones, work, recreation, sports, cultural events, and hobbies.

- We go to church, synagogue, or temple for traditional worship, inspirational sermons, communal prayer, chanting, readings, and other rituals.

- However, when a problem remains after we have done externally what we can, we use the problem as a stimulant for the cultivation of internal spiritual qualities.

4. SPIRITUAL QUALITIES (INTERNAL ACTION OR VERTICAL AXIS):

- Life is school. Pain is the teacher if we open to its lessons. The lessons have to do with expansion of spiritual qualities. We can respond to any problem with Love and its associated qualities. For example, we can cultivate patience when angry, peace when anxious, even-mindedness for excessive emotional reactivity, and strength for long-term illness.

- Review the spiritual alphabet. Here you will find an army of one hundred spiritual qualities. These healing powers are always available at no cost, in unlimited quantities, right inside of our bodies.

- Cultivate any one or a combination of these powerful healers in response to your problem, test, or trial.

- Do not focus on your problems or flaws. This makes them stronger. Instead, focus all of your attention on the spiritual quality.

- You are not your problems. You are a composite of the spiritual qualities listed in the spiritual alphabet. You are compassionate, loving, kind, understanding, courageous, and strong. This is your true identity. This is who you are no matter what the world or your body is doing.

5. SPIRITUAL METHODS (INTERNAL ACTION OR VERTI-
    CAL AXIS):

*   We can choose any one or a combination of the following methods
    to cultivate the desired qualities in response to any pain or problem.
    With regular and consistent practice of these powerful techniques,
    we can transform our suffering into spiritual strength:

    a. Affirmations
    b. Habits
    c. Progressive muscle relaxation
    d. Breathwork
    e. Contemplation
    f. Meditation
    g. Prayer
    h. Mindfulness
    i. Practicing the Presence of God
    j. Service
    k. Yoga
    l. Transformation of emotion

*   For example, to help transform high emotional reactivity to even-
    mindedness, we can use any of the methods described in this work.
    We might choose meditation, mindfulness, and service. We might
    change the combination of methods another day to affirmations,
    prayer, or breathwork. The choice is yours.

6. WILL:

*   What we put into our practice determines what we get from our
    practice. If we put in a meager effort, we get a meager outcome. If
    we give our best, we move forward at maximum speed.

*   Bring all of your heart, mind, might, and soul to your chosen

method and desired qualities. This is single-minded concentration. It involves the totality of your being.

• Conviction, dedication, and will are at full power, but there is no strain. Practice your method with intensity but not so intensely that you create tension. The mind is at its best when it is calm and concentrated.

• Longstanding patterns of thought, feeling, desire, energy, and behavior do not change overnight. There will be setbacks. When thrown off the horse, get back on. We learn by taking two steps forward and one step back. Resilience and perseverance mark the way. With long-term spiritual practice, nothing can stop you. (There is a more in-depth discussion of will in Chapter Ten: The Serenity Prayer.)

7. GRACE:

• We have access to a vast intelligent healing power within and around us. We can tap into this power and get help with any type of suffering through work and grace.

• Our job in the healing process is to define the problem, pick a spiritual method, determine which spiritual quality we need to develop, and exert maximum effort for as long as it takes. This means putting our whole being into the work. When we do our part at maximum effort, ask for help, and endure the problem as long as it is there, grace follows.

• We can conceptualize grace coming from a conscious God of Love or from the healing laws of the universe, which work for us when we cooperate with them. We can use whatever concept gives us inspiration and traction. The healing and transformation process works no matter how we label it.

- Grace opens the gate to the unified field of Omnipotent healing energy. We have no control over the gate. The Keeper of the gate, a mysterious, intelligent force or law, opens the gate for us. The gate may or may not open for elimination of disease, disability, or other painful problems. However, if we do the work described in steps Steps 1–6 of this method, the gate will always open to allow the expansion of spiritual qualities such as peace, Love, strength, courage, wisdom, and joy.

8. EXPANSION OF SPIRITUAL QUALITIES:

- The expansion of spiritual qualities occurs in four stages.

    1. In the first stage, we experience nothing. There is an expansion of Love, courage, peace, and strength, but the increase is subtle and imperceptible.
    2. In stage two, we feel these qualities expanding. This experience is tangible, concrete, and unmistakable. We feel better.
    3. In stage three, there is a distinct but time-limited transformation of consciousness. We experience unfathomable stillness, the changeless peace of the soul, ecstatic Love, pure joy, intuitive wisdom, cosmic sound, divine light, oneness with everything, disembodied consciousness, and other wonderful expressions of Spirit. Then, we return to ordinary consciousness.
    4. The fourth stage of sustained superconsciousness is described below in the section on MASTERY of this method.

- Although our experience is tangible in stage two and dramatic in stage three and four, the growth of spiritual qualities is slow. Do not expect results right away. There will be times when we think we are not moving at all. Sometimes we slip backwards, but sometimes we have to go backwards in order to go forward, and all effort is progress.

- When we make the effort, we are advancing, even when we can't see it. If we keep going, we will eventually see progress. Each time we practice affirmations, meditation, prayer, mindfulness, service, or other spiritual methods, we are putting wisdom, strength, courage, and other currency in our spiritual bank account. When the time comes and credit is due, we can take them out.

9. REPEAT STEPS 1–9:

*   Spiritual work is lifelong and continuous. This is not something we do for a few weeks or months. Life is always school. The only question is whether we attend the classes, do the homework, and pass the tests.

*   If we do the work, one by one our problems are contained, reduced, pulverized, or dissolved, and replaced by positive qualities and habits. Eventually we achieve mastery, a state of sustained super-consciousness in both meditation and activity.

10. MASTERY:

*   Upon mastery, when our soul merges with Spirit, we enter and never leave the boundless Ocean of Love. We come to know the Changeless One as unlimited stillness, silence, spaciousness, and serenity. With this expanded consciousness, we can receive any condition without losing our equilibrium. Our reason expands to intuition, separation to oneness, and human love to unconditional Love. We are fearless, humble, strong, enthusiastic, and cheerful. Our faith is perfect. Our highly attuned intuition receives guidance and wisdom from Omniscience. We are awake, aware, and ready for anything! We give peace, Love, and joy in our words, actions, and vibrations to all we meet. Even-minded in all conditions, we serve humanity with Love, compassion, and kindness. We perform acts of courage and heroism, but most of our work is quiet and anonymous acts of gentle, humble service. Liberated from the

bondage of fear and insecurity, we watch the colossal cosmic drama with calm detachment.

- Mastery, a sustained state of superconsciousness in both meditation and activity, is a very high state, difficult to achieve. Some think mastery is impossible, unreal, or too good to be true. To others, it seems inaccessible or overwhelming. It is not meant to be so.

- Advanced sages, saints, and masters are people who have realized their potential. I have included their description of higher states of consciousness as part of the spiritual map to remind us of our potential. Their descriptions of infinity, eternity, immortality, imperturbable peace, fearlessness, pure Love, and ecstatic joy sound good and intuitively seem right.

- I have experienced and verified some of the elements of superconsciousness, but I make no claim to mastery. I am a struggling student with many flaws, learning how to love. Nevertheless, I trust the teachings of the great ones. Throughout this work, I will describe the spiritual climb from beginning to end.

- I suggest you find your place on the path and work from there. Begin your practice now, today, or if you have already started, march on. Persist and persevere through all obstacles. I plan to travel the distance. I invite you to join me. I am not a master, but I can move in that direction, and so can you.

THE UNIVERSAL METHOD AND THE MYSTERY OF SUFFERING AND EVIL

- For many people, the biggest barrier to beginning a spiritual practice is this question: if God is Love, why is there so much suffering and evil in this world? Here are four possible explanations:

  1. THE MYSTERY. There is a God of Love, but we cannot answer

the question of why there is so much evil and suffering because His ways are mysterious. There are tests and trials, but their purpose is beyond our understanding. God works in strange and mysterious ways.

2. KARMA AND REINCARNATION. Karma is the law of cause and effect, and reincarnation is the transmigration of the soul. There is free will and choice. Good choices lead to good consequences, and bad choices lead to bad consequences. As you sow, so shall you reap. The soul reincarnates until we work out our negative karma, the related consequences of sin, through meditation, Love, and service.

3. AGNOSTICISM. An agnostic claims the existence of God is unknown.

4. ATHEISM. An atheist believes that there is no God and that events occur at random.

- In any case, each of us has to struggle with the challenges life brings without fully understanding why. To grow spiritually, we don't need answers to all of our questions. Nor do we need theological constructs or dogma. We do need the Universal Healing Wheel to discern our problems, develop a spiritual practice, and cultivate spiritual qualities. We can do this whether or not we believe in God, karma, or Grace.

- The centerpiece of this model is the Universal Healing Wheel: choosing a problem, method, and quality. Then we can add our concept of God, karma, and Grace or float all questions in the mystery.

- Pain is the teacher and stimulant for the cultivation of spiritual qualities. We can cultivate Love, compassion, kindness, and courage in response to tests and challenges without knowing answers to all of the questions. Whether or not we believe in God, we can always find problems, develop a spiritual practice, and cultivate spiritual qualities.

POINTS TO REMEMBER

• The ten-step method can help us accomplish the goal of spiritual work: the cultivation of spiritual qualities to help manage any issue, pain, or problem. This method is universal, applicable to anyone and to every problem.

• We can respond to painful problems with any one or a combination of one hundred spiritual qualities. Spiritual qualities are healers and purifying agents. They are standard equipment, built into the body, embedded in the genetic code as our birthright. We can tap into these healing powers at any time in response to any problem by practicing the spiritual disciplines described in this work.

• Events and our mental-emotional reactions to those events cause us to lose sight of the Omnipresent peace and wisdom of the soul. The spiritual methods described here help us reduce our reactivity and move towards, and finally into, the imperturbable peace of the soul.

• We may not be able to control everything in our environment, but we always have control over our will and thoughts. This is where the battle is fought and won. By choosing to practice a spiritual method, we can spiritualize any event. This means responding to life with a spiritual quality no matter what life brings.

• The formula for success in working with any pain or problem is:

1. Ask for help from your Higher Power.
2. Take action in the external world.

3. Apply maximum effort to a spiritual method for the cultivation of spiritual qualities.
4. Accept and endure as long as the problem persists.
5. Grace comes on its own schedule. The result is the expansion of peace, Love, strength, courage, wisdom, and joy.

- You may not be able to get rid of all your pain but you can change your relationship to it. Here is how. There are two layers of pain: the inevitable suffering of life, and our reaction to it. We cannot control the former, but we can control the latter. When you practice the techniques described in this book, you reduce reactivity, the add-ons to the inevitable suffering of life. You cultivate strength and peace no matter what your body or the world throws at you. You become a more skillful pain manager and your quality of life improves accordingly.

AFFIRMATIONS

- My spiritual practice is continuous and lifelong.
- I am always practicing a spiritual method.
- I am committed to spiritual practice for the rest of my life.
- I practice each spiritual method in the present, in the moments of my life.
- When I overcome difficulty, I expect new and more advanced challenges and tests.
- I practice with patience and perseverance. I never give up.
- I conduct all spiritual work with calm concentration.
- I give all of my heart, mind, might, and soul to the work.

EXERCISES

1. Define your Higher Power. To get help from a Higher Power, we need an image that is accessible and comfortable.

- Will you pick a master such as Jesus, Buddha, the Baal Shem

Tov, Rumi, or Krishna as an embodiment of spiritual qualities? Are there any other prophets, saints, or sages that give you
inspiration and guidance?

- Will you go to the Ocean of Love and find your guidance
  there?
- Will you observe nature and see in her the rhythm, harmony,
  beauty, and power that can carry you through anything?
- Will it be the Mystery, the Unknown, the absolute beyond
  conception?
- Will it be reason, morality, and the Higher Self?
- Is God like a Teacher, present in each event, person, and experience?
- Will you choose Love and service to humanity and surrender
  to the Mystery, accepting God as unknowable?

Whatever concept you choose, you will need your connection to it
to be stronger than the worst pain, evil, or problem that arises. Then
you can withstand the power of duality's brutal realities. What image
works for you?

2. Choose a problem, method, and quality; roll the Universal Healing
   Wheel.

The centerpiece of this work is the practice of a spiritual method to
cultivate spiritual qualities in response to painful problems.

   a. Review the list of problems described in the beginning of this
      chapter. Are you currently struggling with these or any other
      problems? Choose one or two on which you would like to
      focus.

   b. Choose one or a combination of spiritual qualities that will
      help you manage these problems.

   c. Choose one or a combination of spiritual methods that will help you cultivate your desired qualities. If you are not familiar with any spiritual practices, read the chapters on spiritual methods. Then return to this step.

Our differing, complex needs, capacities, and levels of receptivity require an individualized approach. There are as many pathways up the spiritual mountain as there are people. While all have some elements in common, no two paths are alike.

To best suit our needs, we can arrange and rearrange qualities and methods in any combination we wish. We can be flexible and individualize our program. If a method or quality seems too difficult, choose another. For example, if meditation is intimidating, try mindfulness and service. Later, the practice of meditation might prove less daunting.

The next chapter describes the Serenity Prayer, a prayer that helps us maintain peace of mind during all phases of recovery and healing.

CHAPTER TEN

THE SERENITY PRAYER

Will and Acceptance

- This work describes fifteen methods designed to help you become a more skillful pain manager. These methods will help you change, heal, grow, cultivate healing qualities, eliminate bad habits, get through barriers, accomplish your goals, and never give up.

- Before we begin our study of these methods, we will review the Serenity Prayer. This is a good place to start because it is intimately involved in the practice of each of these methods.

"THE SERENITY PRAYER"

God grant me the serenity to accept the things I cannot change,
courage to change the things I can,
and the wisdom to know the difference.

- The Serenity Prayer is in the Hall of Fame for all-time great prayers. It is a part of every twelve-step meeting. There is a reason for its popularity. The Serenity Prayer helps us sustain peace of mind during all phases of recovery work—including those times when we feel we are not making any progress—by addressing two great powers: will and acceptance.

- WILL AND ACCEPTANCE. Will and surrender are monumentally important every step of the way on the recovery and healing path. We need both to reach our full potential. In the pursuit of any goal, we need:

1. WILL. We need will to change what is changeable.
2. ACCEPTANCE. We need to accept what we cannot change. (Some people prefer the word acceptance. Others enjoy the word surrender. In this chapter, I will use these words interchangeably.)
3. WILL AND SURRENDER. Many problems require both will and surrender. We can work on a problem with will, and accept it as long as it remains.
4. WISDOM. With wisdom we can figure out which problems require will, acceptance, or both. This lesson describes how will and acceptance work separately and together for maximum recovery and healing.

WILL
HOW TO DEVELOP WILL POWER

- WILL HAS TWO ELEMENTS:

  1. Free will
  2. Will power

- FREE WILL. Free will is our ability to choose. It determines our direction.

- WILL POWER. Will power is the degree of intensity and passion given to our choices.

- WILL IS ENORMOUSLY IMPORTANT ON EVERY STEP OF THE RECOVERY PATH:

  a. Will is involved in determining if we choose the path of healing and how much time and energy we invest on that path.

b. Will shapes every moment of our lives, as we are always making choices in our thoughts, values, attitudes, desires, emotions, and actions.

c. Each of the practice methods described in this work requires the use of our will power.

d. We will review the importance of will in developing one-pointed, calm concentration in the performance of every practice method.

e. Will is intimately involved in our choice of thoughts, which in turn have a profound effect on how we see, feel, and act in the world. We will study this in the lessons on positive thought and the science of healing affirmations.

f. Will determines how much healing work we do. The more work we do, the better our results. Following is a discussion on how to expand will power.

CULTIVATING WILL POWER
FROM SPARK TO BONFIRE
"TWO FROGS IN TROUBLE"

From the writings of the renowned yogi, Paramahansa Yogananda:

Once a big fat frog and a lively little frog were hopping along together when they had the misfortune to jump straight into a pail of fresh milk. They swam for hours and hours, hoping to get out somehow; but the sides of the pail were steep and slippery, and death seemed certain.

When the big frog was exhausted, he lost courage. There seemed no hope of rescue. "Why keep struggling against the inevitable? I can't swim any longer," he moaned.

"Keep on! Keep on!" urged the little frog, who was still circling the pail. So they went on for a while. But the big frog decided it was no use. "Little friend, we may as well give up," he gasped. "I'm going to quit struggling."

Now only the little frog was left. He thought to himself, "Well, to give up is to be dead, so I will keep on swimming." Two more hours passed and the tiny legs of the determined little frog were almost paralyzed with exhaustion. It seemed as if he could not keep moving for another minute. But then he thought of his dead friend and repeated, "To give up is to be meat for someone's table, so I'll keep paddling until I die—if death is to come—but I will not cease trying. While there is life, there's hope!"

Intoxicated with determination, the little frog kept on, around and around and around the pail, chopping the milk into white waves. After awhile, just as he felt completely numb and thought he was about to drown, he suddenly felt something solid under him. To his astonishment, he saw that he was resting on a lump of butter, which he had churned by his incessant paddling! And so the successful little frog leaped out of the milk pail to freedom.

- TESTS. The unavoidable suffering of life shows up as tests, trials, and temptations that inevitably interrupt our peace and stability. Obviously what happens to us in this life is important but it is even more important how we respond. In response to life's difficulties, we have the choice to react in a positive or negative fashion. However, no matter how hard we try to choose rightly, at times we get lost in negativity. Sometimes our problems take over. We get stuck in old, negative thought patterns and habits that automatically choose our path for us. We cannot seem to get out.

- FIFTEEN PAIN MANAGEMENT OPTIONS. To get out of a negative rut, you can do some work on the horizontal axis by getting help from your support network, constructive meaningful activities, and traditional worship. And you can do some inner work by rolling the Universal Healing Wheel: identify your problem, pick a method, and cultivate a healing quality in response to your problem.

- WILL POWER. The next step is to apply all of your will power to the chosen method. But a spark of will power will not do. We need a bonfire! If our will is weak and we run into a large barrier, we will not have the power to get through. However, when our will is strong, we can burst through the barrier that stands in our way. The stronger our will, the easier barriers are to breach. With continued practice, we can get through anything. But what if your will power is weak? How can you make it stronger?

- PUSH-UPS. To understand the expansion of will power, imagine increasing physical strength. Let's say you're able to do twelve push-ups. You set a goal of twenty-five. To achieve twenty-five push-ups, you need to reach the current boundary of twelve and push past it with several repetitions of thirteen and then fourteen. With the sustained effort of pushing past your current limit, you will get to your goal of twenty-five push-ups. As you push through and expand your boundaries, your will power gets stronger.

- THE INVISIBLE MUSCLE. Will is the invisible muscle of our life, the power that gets us through an obstacle to our desired goal. As with physical muscles, our will power expands or atrophies depending on how much exercise it gets. We can use this principle to understand how will power grows.

- THE INNER WORKOUT. When life springs a challenge, we can add to the problem with frustration, anger, or negative actions, or we can do an inner workout. The inner workout utilizes our will with a practice method to cultivate a healing quality. For example, when you are trying to change a bad habit such as substance use, you will experience craving. If instead of using your drug, you do some inner push-ups such as deep breathing and affirmations of loving-kindness for yourself, you dissolve the craving and replace it with strength and peace, which you can then give to others who come your way. With repetition and practice, you expand your ability to find comfort and solace inside instead of from your drug.

- MAXIMUM EFFORT. For maximum spiritual growth, we should identify realistic, attainable goals and pursue them no matter what obstacles arise. We set our desire and effort at 100 percent. We do not let up.

- CALM AND CONTINUOUS. We do the work in a calm and continuous manner, chipping away at each barrier with all of our determination until it dissolves.

- EFFORT IS PROGRESS. Mistakes are part of the process. However, if we maintain our effort despite setbacks, eventually we progress.

- EVER-EXPANDING WILL POWER. As we work our way through obstacles and resistance, we exercise our will and thereby increase its power. The more we exercise our will, the more will power we build. This cycle repeats itself with new barriers, forcing our will to higher levels. This is how we can increase our will power from a spark to a bonfire, a necessity on the healing path. We will need ever-increasing will power to help us through the trials and tests of life.

<u>GOAL SETTING</u>

Following is an exercise in goal setting. This exercise will demonstrate how to use will, thought, and action to accomplish any goal:

1. Goal
2. Thought
3. Will
4. Action
5. Tests
6. Persistence
7. Success
8. Confidence
9. Goal

1. GOAL. Pick a realistic, attainable goal. Choose a goal that is good for you, others, and the world.

2. THOUGHT. Thoughts are very powerful, whether negative or positive. Keep your thoughts positive in the direction of your goal. Negative thoughts will only delay your progress. Remove all traces of negative thinking. You might try some of the affirmations related to will at the end of this chapter.

3. WILL. Use the full force of your will to accomplish your goal. Gather all of your strength, might, and determination until your intent is unbending. Set your mind to absolute victory. However, if your will is too intense, you create tension and reduce your effectiveness. Remain calm even as your will is at full power. Calm continuous use of the will is best. Your effort should remain smooth and steady. The formula for success is calm, single-minded concentration.

4. ACTION. With a positive mind aimed at your target and your will at full throttle, perform all of your actions in the direction of your goal.

5. TESTS. Expect many tests. Tests come in the form of difficulties, barriers, and obstacles. Exercise your will power and thought power against this resistance.

6. PERSISTENCE. Do not allow any negative influence to weaken the developing power of your will. Refuse to lose. Never give up. The only way to stop your growth is when you give up: then you lose. On the other hand, if you choose wisely and keep battling, you will move forward and ultimately succeed.

7. SUCCESS. When you follow the steps outlined above, your thought power and will power increase and you accomplish your goals.

8. CONFIDENCE. Confidence grows when you succeed.

9. GOAL. Set a new goal. Over time, you can pursue goals that are more complex and difficult to achieve. However, with too many goals, you can scatter your energy. Do not leave something half done to start a new goal. To avoid this problem, devote all your will power to mastering one goal at a time.

AN EXAMPLE OF GOAL SETTING

1. GOAL. Joe wants to quit smoking.

2. THOUGHT. Joe makes up his mind and begins using the following affirmations:

- I can change.
- With will and thought, I cultivate strength and peace.
- With great determination, I create new good habits and healing qualities.
- I make up my mind strongly now.
- I am busy doing my part because God helps those who help themselves.

3. WILL. Joe knows his cigarette habit is very powerful so he will need the full force of his will. He starts working with these affirmations:

- I have the will to change.
- I will change.
- I use the full power of my will to transform negative to positive thoughts.
- Nothing can stop me.
- I am strong.
- I give 100 percent of my effort.

4. ACTION. With his mind set at success, Joe conducts all of his activities in accord with his goal.

- My mind is set at success.
- My intent is unbending.
- I refuse to smoke.

5. TESTS. There are many tests. Cigarettes are everywhere. When Joe sees other people smoking, he wants to retreat to his bad habit but resists the craving by using the following affirmations:

   - I use any obstacle to stimulate my effort towards greater achievement.
   - The craving for cigarettes tries to throw me off balance, but my inner strength keeps me steady.
   - With great determination, I create new good habits.
   - The more work I do, the more results I get.
   - When I resist the craving, it disappears like a wave in the ocean, only to be replaced by strength and peace.

6. PERSISTENCE. Joe knows his battle against cigarettes is long-term. A friend offered him a cigarette at a party. He relapsed and gave in, but quickly picked himself up, using the following affirmations:

   - No matter how many times I fall down, I pick myself up and struggle again towards my goal.
   - When a host of difficulties and obstacles arise, I refuse to give up.
   - I possess the power of will and the power of thought. I make the effort now to draw these powers out through practice in the daily routines and challenges of my life.

7. SUCCESS. Joe experienced difficulties and setbacks on his way to success, but because of his persistence, he gave up smoking and no longer craves it. By exercising his will and affirmations, he replaced his smoking habit with peace of mind and strength. He affirms:

- I am victorious.
- I am successful.
- I am calm and strong.

8. CONFIDENCE. Because of his success, Joe is more confident in himself. He is especially buoyant, as he has discovered the scientific method of healing through affirmations and will. He is amazed at how the wonderful gift of will power works. By simply learning how to think correctly, he knows how to expand his healing power, positive energy, and will. He beat the habit because he was thinking scientifically. He affirms:

- I meet everybody and every circumstance with courage.

9. GOAL. Joe sets new goals as he realizes that he can use his new-found positive energy to benefit himself, others, and the world. He affirms:

- I am a strong willed person who can accomplish much good in this world.
- I exercise will and thought to help others and myself.
- I try to make this Earth a better place to live by using my tools of will and thought.
- No matter what challenge comes my way, I remain positive and live constructively.

- Clearly, will is important on the recovery and healing path as it helps us change, heal, grow, eliminate bad habits, move through barriers, accomplish goals, cultivate healing qualities, and serve the world.
- However, some conditions do not respond to will power. When we have applied all of our will, thought, and action to a painful problem and the problem remains, we can invoke will's partner, acceptance.

ACCEPTANCE OR SURRENDER
LEARNING TO LIVE WITH WHAT WE CANNOT CHANGE

- We need to learn how to accept the painful conditions of our current reality that cannot be changed.

- Acceptance is the opposite of resisting, running, or hiding. It means going through whatever comes our way in order to find our personal brand of knowledge, power, courage, humility, endurance, and wisdom.

- We must face our pain thoroughly and completely, for our most triumphant assets reside in the depths of our suffering. Pain is the teacher. It carries our personal story, meaning, and lessons.

- Athletes train their bodies for the exertion of their sport. People in recovery must also train. They work out their inner body of thoughts, feelings, desires, and energy. The inner workout includes introspection and transformation. Introspection is looking within to uncover issues, problems, bad habits, and flaws. Transformation is making the necessary changes.

- For introspection and transformation to occur, we must accept pain as our teacher. Suffering is packed with personal meaning. When we inspect our pain, it reveals the lessons we need to learn. The lessons always have to do with the expansion of healing qualities.

- The power of acceptance is great. When fully developed, it can get us through anything. Through acceptance, we gain the peace and strength on the other side of every painful problem.

- When we understand the healing principle of acceptance, we become inspired to drop our defenses and resistance, which do nothing but add tension and delay learning. Instead, we will enter the pain, eliminate negativity, and cultivate courage, strength, peace, Love, and joy.

• Moving into the center of our pain requires much courage, as we may have some dark days when nothing seems to make sense. However, if we trust pain as our teacher, we will see the evolution of our personal story taking the high road of wisdom.

• Pain is intelligent. It takes us where we need to go. It reveals its hidden meaning as it leads us through the maze of our troubles into the light and wisdom of recovery.

• When we apply our will to a problem and it remains, we can accept the problem as a guest-teacher who has come to reveal a hidden secret. Life is school. Pain is the teacher if we open to its lessons. The lessons always have to do with the expansion of healing qualities. Following is a technique for unpacking the secret knowledge carried in our pain.

A TECHNIQUE FOR ACCEPTANCE/SURRENDER

1. Higher Power
2. Introspection
3. Healing Qualities

1. HIGHER POWER:

• Ask for help from your Higher Power.

2. INTROSPECTION:

• Take several slow deep breaths.
• If you know a meditation technique, use it now to invite as much stillness as you can.
• Assume an attitude of gentle, compassionate understanding toward yourself.

- Surrender to the pain. Feel it fully. Listen to it. Learn from it.
- Ask the pain:

  a. Why are you here?
  b. What do you want?
  c. What do you have to teach me?
  d. What lessons do I need to learn?
  e. What problems remain hidden from my view?
  f. What healing qualities must I develop in response to you?

- The pain will point you in the direction of your inner work, which always has to do with expanding the healing qualities.

3. HEALING QUALITIES:

   - When we align ourselves with the healing qualities, we purify, heal, and transform.
   - Choose a method and begin the work of cultivating any one or a combination of healing qualities in response to your pain.
   - These qualities are not merely words but actual healing powers.
   - They help us manage our pain and suffering.
   - Such healing powers as Love, compassion, understanding, forgiveness, and humility will contain, reduce, or eliminate any barrier we encounter.
   - Focus on these qualities as your true identity.

- With acceptance, we drop our resistance and enter the pain that will not otherwise go away. Through introspection, we find our problems. Through transformation, we respond to our problems with peace, compassion, understanding, or any combination of healing qualities.

- Surrender, introspection, and transformation activate the healing power that resides and operates within every cell of the body. We can deploy this process of purification with any type of problem.

- The transformation of pain and problems into healing qualities through surrender is one of the inherent miracles of the body. Do not miss the opportunity to demonstrate this marvelous power when presented with a problem or condition that does not respond to your will. With practice, you will see how this miraculous, intelligent healing power works. It is incomparably brilliant!

- The purpose of suffering that does not respond to will is to help us decorate the rooms in our inner home with the great healing qualities. In this sense, all pain is a blessing.

- It is for you to decide if your suffering is God's will, but no matter what your beliefs, you can always be in school, learning the lessons and cultivating the qualities. To set yourself up for healing, surrender to the pain and let your story unfold in the direction of Love. This is the secret of pain management through acceptance. Make contact with and befriend the great power of acceptance. It will get you through anything.

MANAGING PROBLEMS WITH WILL, ACCEPTANCE, OR A COMBINATION OF BOTH

THE PRAYER OF RELINQUISHMENT

I am faced with this problem at the moment.
I won't run away from it.
I'll do my best to overcome it.
But the outcome is in the hands of my loving Father.
Whatever He wills, I accept.

- BALANCED USE OF WILL AND SURRENDER. The Prayer of Relinquishment describes the balanced use of will and surrender. The prayer reminds us to do our part of the work and accept life just as it is. While we use all of our initiative to work on a problem, we simultaneously surrender the results to our Higher Power. This is difficult. All of us miss the balance point between will and surrender countless number of times. Mistakes are inevitable. We are either too active or too passive. When too passive, we feel poorly about ourselves and do not live up to our potential. When too active, we create new problems.

- LISTEN IN STILLNESS. What is the right combination? How do we know whether a condition requires more or less will or surrender? Often, we do not; but we can improve. Stillness is the key. When we are alert, aware, and calm, we can hear the still, small voice within, guiding us to a balanced combination of will and surrender.

- WHEN WE DON'T DO THE WORK. Pain may come subtly at first, trying to gently coax and persuade us to discover and work on our problems. If we are mentally restless, however, we may not recognize its purpose. When we do not sense and listen to it, we cannot extract the necessary lessons. The underlying problem remains, and our pain grows. We feel tension and pressure.

  If we do not do the work at this stage, our pain may expand into symptoms, ultimately impairing our functioning and resulting in potential crisis and danger. At this point, there is neither a balance of will and surrender, nor wisdom to know the difference.

- WHEN WE DO THE WORK. With sustained practice, our foundation of inner peace broadens and deepens. We can maintain inner harmony and balance even when challenged by painful difficulties. The mind remains calm, and we hear the messages from that voice within. When we learn how to listen in stillness, we can find our problems through introspection, and transform ourselves through the cultivation of spiritual qualities.

- THE GREAT TEACHER. When we take responsibility for our problems by using pain as our guide, we make fewer mistakes in our attempts to balance will and surrender. As long as we remain calm and unruffled, pain, the Great Teacher in life, helps us know when to act and when to remain silent.

For deep recovery and healing, we must learn when to surrender and when to act with will. We need one-pointed, calm, continuous use of our will to change what we can, and to surrender and expand our healing qualities in response to what we cannot change. With time and practice, we can use will, surrender, or combinations of both in increasingly sophisticated ways, thus expanding our Love and our usefulness.

POINTS TO REMEMBER

- A sleeping giant lies within. You can wake up that giant when you learn how to exercise and expand your will power. You can take back lost territory by realizing your power and potential.

- You can exercise will consciously and continuously by simply re-membering to use it throughout the day.

- Will power is the invisible muscle of life. When you exercise your will, it gets stronger.

- With continuous will, thought, and activity, you can accomplish any realistic goal.

- While you practice your method with intensity, your effort should remain smooth and steady. Anxiety and tension reduce effectiveness. The formula for success is calm, single-minded concentration.

- Anxiety reduces will power, as it uses up the energy that we could otherwise use to accomplish our goals. Overcome obstacles by practicing deep breathing with affirmations of peace, courage, and faith.

- When we cannot change an outer condition, we retain the freedom to choose our inner response. We use our will to choose positive thoughts, values, attitude, feelings, desires, and actions no matter what other people do.

- We are control artists. Pride keeps us from letting go. We fear humiliation. We worry about appearing weak. We think acceptance implies passivity. We think if we give up control, we are going to get hurt. While it is true that when we surrender, we stop trying to solve external problems by changing others and controlling events, paradoxically, we gain control: surrender breeds an imperturbable state of inner strength and peace.

- Surrender is a powerful tool because it allows us to be at peace even though conditions and circumstances may be rough.

- We control very little. Let the game come to you. Stop dribbling so much. Stop trying to control other people. Be in it to Love, serve, and grow spiritual qualities in a relaxed way. Ultimately all we have is our qualities.

- We can invoke the Serenity Prayer for any circumstance at any time. It works for all of the moments of our lives. All we have to do is remember to use it.

- As we improve our ability to use will and surrender with wisdom, there is a corresponding expansion of peace, balance, and harmony in every domain of life.

- Practice the Serenity Prayer. Exercise will, surrender, and the wisdom to know the difference for years, and you will slowly enter the unified field of Love. At mastery, no condition of the world or body can throw you out.

AFFIRMATIONS OF WILL

- I can change
- I will change.
- I am successful.
- I make up my mind strongly now.
- My mind is set.
- My will is strong.
- I am ready to take on the challenge.
- I meet every circumstance with courage.
- No matter the challenge, I stay positive.
- I am filled with purpose, heart, and determination.
- God helps those who help themselves. I am busy doing my part.
- I possess the power of will and the power of thought.
- I use my will and thoughts to accomplish my goals, every step of the way.
- With will and thought, I work through any barrier.
- I act until my goal is accomplished.
- My will is calm, continuous, and concentrated.
- With great determination, I cultivate Love, peace, and strength.
- The more work I do, the more results I get.
- No matter how many times I fall down, I pick myself up and struggle again towards my goal.
- I use my will and thoughts to Love and serve.
- With will and thought, I make the Earth a better place to live.
- When difficulties arise, I refuse to give up.
- Love is my reason for being. I use my will to carry it out.

AFFIRMATIONS OF ACCEPTANCE

- I accept the things I cannot change.
- I don't try to change anything.

- I accept everything just as it is.
- I just let everything be.
- Everything is included in the path to enlightenment.
- Every problem, disease, and disability is an opportunity to advance on the spiritual path.
- I remain unruffled no matter what comes.
- I have done all that I can. Now I surrender to the will of the Universe, Life, God.
- The outside is just right, and the perfect Teacher is within.
- I have done all I can. Now I expand my healing qualities.
- Love is the greatest healer.
- Love transforms my suffering into peace, compassion, and understanding.
- No matter what circumstances arise, I trust in a higher, invisible order.
- I used to try to control everything. Now I have trust and remain calm in any circumstance.
- I know when to resist my problems and when to resign myself to them.
- In response to any painful condition, I cultivate strength, courage, and endurance.
- I remain loving, compassionate, and gentle with myself while I try to change for the better.
- Love burns up my problems until Love is all there is.

EXERCISES

1. What is the Serenity Prayer?

2. What are the two components of will?

3. What is acceptance/surrender?

4. What is the way to increase will power?

5. Describe the nine-step method for setting goals. Choose a goal, and apply this method.

6. Describe the technique for acceptance. Practice this method for any painful problem.

7. Can you think of a time when you were willful when you should have practiced acceptance?

8. Can you think of a problem you accepted when you should have been more willful?

9. Can you think of a time when you have used will and acceptance on the same problem?

10. Think of the saints, sages, or masters, and how they embody the qualities in the Serenity Prayer. They have a great capacity to immerse themselves in brutal reality, the courage and will to change what they can, the acceptance of that which they cannot change, and the wisdom to know the difference. They have extraordinarily powerful will, surrender, courage, wisdom, compassion, Love, and a host of other wonderful spiritual qualities. Their use of these qualities to skillfully manage their pain results in a high degree of spiritual evolution.

The next chapter outlines a variety of suggestions for starting a successful spiritual practice.

CHAPTER ELEVEN

GETTING STARTED

Suggestions for Starting a Successful Spiritual Practice

- THE PROMISE. In spiritual books and sacred texts, we read stories about the heroism, courage, power, and selfless service of the saints and masters. There are anecdotes about miraculous healings, descriptions of eternal life, and discourse on the nature of truth. Prayers, poems, affirmations, and pearls of wisdom allude to unlimited peace, unconditional Love, ecstatic joy, and wisdom. The world's religions claim that the body is the temple which secretly harbors the actual God of the universe, or, similarly, that the body carries higher states of consciousness.

- THE PROOF. We can test the truth of these and other wonderful spiritual ideas through direct experience, but only if we develop a spiritual practice. While there may be no absolute scientific proof, we can use our intellect, feeling, intuition, and personal experience as tools for interpretation. The experiment is life itself. The test tube is the body. The material worked with is consciousness, energy, thought, feeling, desire, and behavior. This is the scientific method in metaphysics.

- THE METHODS. Spiritual practice leads to concrete, tangible results reproduced across cultures and historical periods. The internal methods described in this work have withstood the test of history. Millions have found their value as tools for the cultivation of spiritual qualities and experiences. These methods are:

1. Affirmations
2. Habits
3. Progressive muscle relaxation
4. Breath work
5. Contemplation
6. Meditation
7. Prayer
8. Mindfulness
9. Practicing the Presence of God
10. Service
11. Yoga
12. Transformation of emotion

- THE QUALITIES. The purpose of practicing these spiritual disciplines is to cultivate spiritual qualities in response to the inevitable suffering of life. We can transform our suffering into peace, Love, joy, and wisdom when we practice yoga, meditation, mindfulness, and the other methods listed above.

Before we begin the detailed study of these spiritual techniques, we will review seventeen suggestions for starting a successful spiritual practice:

1. The goal: cultivate healing qualities.
2. Support: get a support network of like-minded people.
3. Solitude: learn how to be alone.
4. Self-reform: change the world by changing yourself.
5. Ego reduction: reduce your ego to expand your soul qualities.
6. Spiritual healing: recognize the difference between physical and spiritual healing.
7. Self-acceptance: accept where you are while striving to improve.
8. Discipline: suffering is a stimulant for the cultivation of spiritual power.
9. Expectations: spiritual rewards occur on their own timetable.

10. Calm concentration: the best practice position.
11. Stay in the present: minutes and moments.
12. Start slow: one step at a time.
13. Continuous practice: there is always work to do.
14. Pace yourself: it's a long climb.
15. Do your best: leave the rest.
16. A balanced healing program: fifteen pain management options.
17. The scientific method in metaphysics: direct personal experience.

THE GOAL

CULTIVATION OF HEALING QUALITIES

- We can have a variety of goals related to the outer world of people, activities, work, training, recreation, volunteer, sports, culture, and so forth. While we work on these outer goals, the inner goal is always cultivation of healing qualities.

- Once that inner goal is established, we must continuously visualize and constantly affirm the qualities we are seeking to cultivate. Repetition is the key to success. Throughout this work, you will discover a variety of practices that will help you grow healing qualities and keep this illumined goal before your eyes. This will keep you from getting confused and lost when the world gets rough.

SUPPORT

GET A SUPPORT NETWORK OF LIKE-MINDED PEOPLE

- We need support from others to achieve any material or spiritual goal. In the spiritual life, it is important to find people who have similar ideas, aspirations, and practices. The spiritual path is difficult. There are barriers, tests, trials, and temptations that lead us off the path.

- For support and encouragement, we need a network of people who love, care, understand, and forgive. When we see spiritual qualities such as strength, courage, and humor manifested in others, we gain the necessary guidance and inspiration to keep going, no matter what form resistance may take. When we tell our story to others who understand and validate our experience, we get comfort, solace, and relief.

- While a supportive network of like-minded people is essential for spiritual growth, it is no less important that we build in ample time for solitude.

SOLITUDE

LEARN HOW TO BE ALONE

- Popular culture would have us believe that success, money, power, and status bring security and happiness. Experience suggests otherwise. In the course of living, we find the joys and pleasures of the outer world are limited and ephemeral.

- The wisdom traditions point to our inner being as the source of lasting happiness, peace, and safety. Discovering the path of wisdom is difficult, however, as the external world is powerful and attractive, continuously seducing us into the illusion that we can find in it the joy and security we crave.

- The secret to discovering what is sacred and making it a part of our life is to develop a habit of solitude for study, contemplation, and meditation. But our addiction to the outer life makes it difficult to retreat for purposes of quiet reflection and stillness. Cultivating the new ground of solitude is akin to withdrawing from a substance of abuse like alcohol, drugs, or tobacco. When we retreat, we may feel anxious and crave our habitual pattern of activity. If we answer the call of this craving too quickly and fail to go through the rigors of the withdrawal, we do not bring the critical ingredient of solitude into our program.

- When we suffer, we turn to other people, work, recreation, and entertainment for support and relief. While it is obviously helpful to have the support of loving people and constructive meaningful activities, an important part of spiritual growth is shifting the locus of control from outside to inside. At times of crisis, the ultimate defense is inner strength and courage. Spiritual qualities are best cultivated in solitude, slowly, and over time through such practices as meditation and the contemplation of sacred texts. Without stillness and solitude, the growth of spiritual qualities is stunted.

SELF-REFORM
CHANGE THE WORLD BY CHANGING YOURSELF

- If we want to change the world, we need to start by changing ourselves. We will soon see how difficult a job that is! Gandhi once said he had three major opponents: the British people, the Indian people, and himself, and that by far, the most formidable was himself. Changing ourselves is more than a full-time job. When we focus on self-reform, we won't have the time or energy to dwell on the problems or flaws of others.

- Most of us have made the mistake of thinking that we can change other people. This is generally not possible. When we try to remodel the character of others, we can expect stiff resistance. The way to influence others is to develop a spiritual practice that enriches the spiritual qualities in the soil of our own consciousness. When we are more compassionate, understanding, forgiving, peaceful, and wise, those around us who can will profit from our development. They will be inspired to bring out these qualities in themselves. We gain more ground in this way than by pushing them.

EGO REDUCTION

REDUCE YOUR EGO TO EXPAND YOUR SOUL QUALITIES

- The goal of spiritual practice is the cultivation of the soul qualities of the spiritual alphabet. But these qualities cannot grow unless the ego is reduced and ultimately replaced as it occupies the space rightfully owned and operated by the soul. However, the ego does not give up its space so easily. It sets up camp in spiritual territory and will not budge, believing that any surrender of turf may lead to its own demise. On the spiritual path, then, a battle ensues between the fiercely territorial ego and the soul qualities, yearning to blossom with full expression.

- Our daily routines abound with opportunities to reduce the ego. By practicing the spiritual methods described in this book, we can replace the ego with spiritual qualities in a process of purification—sometimes purification by fire. Introspection is necessary, and pain is often involved. Those who are not willing or able to go through such rigors get stuck.

- The ego fights a bitter, resourceful war to the end. It resists every attempt of the soul to take over, and it does this in subtle and devious ways. Often we don't even know that it is present and in control. When we discover and work to dissolve a layer of ego, another layer quietly takes over, silently waiting for an opportunity to cause trouble. Ego reduction is slow and difficult. However, victory is inevitable to those who persist.

- When we submit our ego for reduction in a spiritual process, the rewards are great; as the ego is dissolved, humiliation is replaced by humility, insecurity by peace, resentment by compassion, anger by Love, ignorance by wisdom, and sadness by joy. The ego cannot survive the expansion of soul qualities that result from spiritual practice. The soul is more powerful than the trickster ego.

SPIRITUAL HEALING

RECOGNIZE THE DIFFERENCE BETWEEN PHYSICAL AND SPIRITUAL HEALING

- Spiritual practice results in the healing of the body, mind, and/ or soul. However, healing of the body may not always be possible since some conditions are chronic, progressive, and irreversible. In such cases, spiritual healing can still be relied upon.

- Spiritual healing is independent of the healing of the body. Spiritual healing is a process of purification, which involves reducing and ultimately replacing the ego with spiritual qualities. Our physical illness may improve, stay the same, or worsen, but we can always work on ego reduction and expansion of spiritual qualities. No matter the outcome of our physical pain and problems, with the practice of spiritual methods, we reduce the ego and grow spiritual qualities. We may get a chronic, progressive, or fatal illness, but our spiritual healing process continues as we cultivate unconditional Love, patience, courage, endurance, surrender, and self-control.

- Some people give up their work if they don't see their physical problems going away. This is a mistake; the point of spiritual work is the purification of consciousness, whether or not the body heals. In this sense, effort is progress, since spiritual work will always bring the expansion of spiritual qualities even while physical pain persists.

SELF-ACCEPTANCE

ACCEPT WHERE YOU ARE WHILE STRIVING TO IMPROVE

- The list of qualities in the spiritual alphabet is long and may seem daunting. Just thinking about unconditional Love is enough to stop some people from trying. If we think Love or any spiritual quality is unobtainable, we may not be able to look within, discover our current limitations, and begin the necessary work to improve.

- We can avoid this dilemma if we accept our current state while at the same time make an effort to improve. We can remain relaxed, compassionate, and gentle with ourselves even as we see the distance between where we are and the top of the high spiritual mountain we are climbing.

- Most of the time, there should be little or no guilt. When we are wrong, guilt may occur, but only to show us where to work; its purpose is not to create lingering feelings of low self-esteem. We should look at our past mistakes with compassion and forgiveness. We can use the past as a reference point and not dwell there. We should extract what lessons we can from the past and then let the experience go.

- Everyone makes mistakes. It is a part of the learning process. The key is to get the lesson and move on. Do not make the mistake the center of your life. Once you get the lesson and make the necessary correction, forget about it.

- To avoid neurotic perfectionism we give our best each day, knowing this is all that is expected. We can accept mistakes, failure, and awkwardness as part of the natural process of growth. We can see setbacks as opportunities to discover what we need for future successes. While engaged in the struggle to improve, we can cultivate humor, fun, laughter, and joy. This helps us not take ourselves too seriously.

DISCIPLINE

SUFFERING IS A STIMULANT FOR THE CULTIVATION OF SPIRITUAL POWER

- You may not have found a spiritual path that suits you. You may have only recently found your way and are just beginning. Or perhaps you are well along on a path with a teacher, teachings, and techniques that fit your needs. In any case, a good understanding of the nature of the struggle is important.

- The spiritual path is slippery. It is easy to slide off and fall. We might be tempted to throw in the towel early on, not foreseeing how difficult it would be, nor how uncomfortable. It is a mistake to underestimate the work, effort, and discipline required. The transformation of ordinary to spiritual consciousness is no easy task. Life is painful. Change is difficult and slow.

- Hard times are especially risky if we do not understand the connection between suffering and the development of spiritual power. If suffering appears meaningless, we may become frightened and turn to unhealthy pain-killing habits such as substance or sex abuse, excessive dependency on others, addiction to the Internet, television, and so on. On the other hand, if we understand that pain is a teacher and stimulant for the cultivation of spiritual qualities, we are much less likely to become frightened and abandon the path.

- A comprehensive spiritual program helps us expect, rise to, and work through any challenge. When difficulties arise, we respond with spiritual practices that help us cultivate Love, strength, courage, and endurance. The expansion of these and other spiritual qualities will help us transcend any challenge.

- When we have finished a set of problems or have passed some of life's tests, we experience the reward of happiness and tranquility. We love that part of the show when we celebrate life as pure entertainment and joy. It is only a question of time, however, before a new set of difficulties arises. As we move forward on our path, the bar is raised. More advanced problems and challenges arrive. How else would we develop our spiritual muscles? It is a marathon, not a sprint!

- Finding and following a spiritual path requires self-control, stamina, and balance. We need to follow the path with devotion and loyalty. This involves making choices that build strength, courage, and endurance. The struggle is daily, in the moments of our lives, and continues until our last breath is taken.

- We need discipline to maintain our direction when in crisis. We need patience and perseverance for the long course of life. We must face the pain of reality in order to achieve higher states of consciousness. Running away from troubles and difficulties does not work. There can be no denial or avoidance on the path. We may rest, take time out, pace ourselves, and even backtrack when necessary, but ultimately we must do all of the work.

- Reality can be harsh and brutal. However, with spiritual practice, we can face whatever comes our way, understand it, learn from it, and move on to higher spiritual realms where the rewards are great: the expansion of spiritual qualities and higher states of consciousness.

EXPECTATIONS

SPIRITUAL REWARDS OCCUR ON THEIR OWN TIMETABLE

- In any endeavor, it is good to have realistic expectations. Spiritual belief systems make many grandiose, idealistic promises, such as eternal peace, unconditional Love, and abundant joy. In the beginning, it is the hope for such experiences that gets many people involved in the rigorous discipline of the spiritual path. And after doing the work, it is a natural human tendency to expect the rewards promised. However, there will be times when there seems to be nothing but work, struggle, effort, and pain without compensation. Progress towards higher states of consciousness can be very slow or seem non-existent.

- It is best to have no expectations; if our demands are not met, we might stop doing the work. If we are patient and try not to imagine how fast our growth should be, we can persevere and stay on our chosen path. Though results are often slower than we would like them to be, spiritual growth always occurs if we make the effort. If we give our best effort without the expectation of reward on a particular schedule, we will eventually enjoy the fruits of our spiritual work. Peace, Love, joy, power, and wisdom lie on the other side of every painful problem, but they arrive on their own timetable.

CALM CONCENTRATION
THE BEST PRACTICE POSITION

- All of the methods described in this work require a calm, concentrated mind; but the mind loves to wander. It remains independent despite our best efforts to control it. In frustration, we fight back, but fighting mind with mind creates tension, taking us even further away from calm concentration. The way to prevent this frustration is to remain relaxed and non-judgmental when the mind wanders.

- Begin your practice. Choose any method. Notice when your mind drifts. Do not identify with a particular stream of thought. Gently bring your mind back to its state of calm concentration.

- This back and forth movement will go on for years. It is part of the natural process of spiritual work. The key is to accept the mind exactly where it is at the moment, because it could not be anywhere else. This will help you remain relaxed while you return the mind to its practice position.

- Bring all of your heart, mind, might, and soul to your practice. Leave nothing behind. Eliminate all distractions. Apply one-pointed, calm concentration to your chosen method and quality for best results. There should be intensity without tension.

- Mind, will power, emotions, energy, everything is channeled in a constructive way towards the cultivation of spiritual qualities. Channel all of your energy and inner faculties in a supreme conscious effort towards expansion of the healing qualities. Bring some zeal, hunger, intensity, and thirst to your practice. This inner workout is like doing mental push-ups. You might call it mental yoga.

- Practicing concentration can be fun or frustrating, depending upon our frame of reference. If we remain gentle, compassionate, and accepting of ourselves, we can play the game of concentration as a sport.

STAY IN THE PRESENT
MINUTES AND MOMENTS

- The next step in our spiritual development is here and now. Spiritual methods help us keep our attention and concentration focused on the present so we do not miss the opportunity to take the next step.

- We spend too much time dwelling on the past and future. We can learn from the past and plan for the future, however, the bulk of spiritual practice is in the seconds and minutes of our lives. When your mind drifts into the past or future during your practice, gently bring it back to the present. Concentrate on each moment by being here and now. When your mind wanders, bring it back to the here and now.

- Spiritual work is in the moments of our lives. Moments and minutes are more important than hours or years. Be aware of your attention and attitude in each moment. Attention breeds habits whether negative or positive. What you focus on is what you are becoming. Focus on the cultivation of healing qualities in the moments of your life.

- You may experience nothing but work or pain as you cultivate spiritual qualities. Do not be discouraged. Effort is progress. The expansion of spiritual qualities is the result of every little effort in each moment. Results are subtle, but they accumulate. Eventually you will experience the wonderful expansion of peace, Love, joy, power, and wisdom. Spiritual qualities are the route to higher states of consciousness. Keep going and you will experience the peace that surpasses understanding.

START SLOW
ONE STEP AT A TIME

- We climb a mountain one step at a time. Similarly, we build our practice each day by applying a spiritual method one step at a time. Spiritual qualities grow slowly. Patience is necessary. By taking small steps and building our program gradually, we will have a strong spiritual foundation upon which to build higher floors.

- You can start a practice such as meditation or mindfulness five to ten minutes twice a day and gradually build up your time. If this seems intimidating, try starting at thirty to sixty seconds twice a day. Give your best effort. Your concentration will expand. Eventually you will learn to stay with a method at will throughout the day.

- Practice any method for just a few moments and minutes and build your practice from there. Perseverance is the key. It gets easier, but you must persevere even on difficult days.

- You progress by taking one step at a time. Little by little, you get there. No matter what comes, press on. Eventually you will perfect the techniques.

- Start where you are right now and begin your patient daily practice.

CONTINUOUS PRACTICE
THERE IS ALWAYS WORK TO DO

- There is always spiritual work to do, whether life is smooth and stable or rocky and chaotic. If we practice the techniques when life is smooth, we can use them more effectively when it gets rough.

- Advanced students try to practice one of the spiritual methods at all times. This is possible since some methods, such as meditation and contemplation, require solitude while service, practicing the Presence of God, and mindfulness occur during activity. Slowly expand your practice until it is one continuous sacred ritual.

PACE YOURSELF
IT'S A LONG CLIMB

- Some individuals try to move forward on the spiritual path faster than is possible, but real spiritual growth occurs one day at a time. We need to relax and enjoy the day without adding undue pressure or stress by attempting to accomplish too much. We cannot do it all now. We can't live up in the penthouse when we haven't built the foundation or the floors in between. There are no shortcuts. We cannot skip any of the assigned classes. We need to do the homework daily. Then we can pass the tests and advance to the next grade.

- It is a long climb up the mountain. When we try to climb too fast, we slip, fall, hurt ourselves, or get exhausted unnecessarily. When we climb too slowly or not at all, we become bored or indifferent.

- To find the right speed, focus on one or two problems at a time. Bring all of your heart, mind, might, and soul to your work of cultivating spiritual qualities but remain calm without strain or tension. When you find the right speed, you will experience harmony, balance, rhythm, and flow.

DO YOUR BEST
LEAVE THE REST

- Your ability to focus on your spiritual method and quality will vary from day to day. On days when you are tired and need rest, you might just watch TV and eat popcorn. At other times, when you feel ready, you can do the deep inner work of transformation of emotion and meditation, the two most difficult techniques on the vertical axis. Pick a method or combination of methods that suits your needs at the moment, and do not worry about perfection. Just do your best and leave the rest.

A BALANCED HEALING PROGRAM
FIFTEEN PAIN MANAGEMENT OPTIONS

• This work describes fifteen psychosocial-spiritual methods that help us manage the inevitable suffering of life and our reaction to it. These are the methods we can turn to when doctors and other healthcare professionals cannot solve the problem.

Horizontal Axis

1. People
2. Activities
3. Belief systems

Vertical Axis

4. Affirmations
5. Habit transformation
6. Progressive muscle relaxation
7. Breathwork
8. Contemplation
9. Meditation
10. Prayer
11. Mindfulness
12. Practicing the Presence of God
13. Service
14. Yoga
15. Transformation of emotion

- EXTERNAL WORK: HORIZONTAL AXIS. Methods 1–3 describe our work in the external world of people, activities, and belief systems. When you are in pain, you can spend time with family and friends for solace and comfort. You can engage in constructive meaningful activities: work, school, training, volunteering, recreation, sports, culture, hobbies, and so forth. You can go to church, synagogue, or temple for traditional worship or to a group like Alcoholics Anonymous for support and wisdom. All of this helps and may be enough for some people. Others need to do some additional work in the vertical axis.

- INTERNAL WORK: VERTICAL AXIS. Methods 4–15: If you have done everything you can in the world of people, activities, and belief systems and you are still in pain, there are twelve additional methods you can use to help you with your problem. These are the methods of the vertical axis, the same methods referred to in PMQ, or problem-method-quality, of the Universal Healing Wheel. You can roll the Universal Healing Wheel no matter what conditions the world or your body throws at you.

- LOCUS OF CONTROL. If you spend most of your time in Methods 1–3, your locus of control is primarily outside. Most of us start here. When life presents overwhelming problems, it is often necessary to do some inner work. As you begin to practice Methods 4–15, your locus of control gradually shifts to your inner self. When you roll the Universal Healing Wheel, spiritual qualities such as courage, peace, and strength slowly grow. You become less dependent on the outer world of people, activities, events, and material things when you find inner peace, security, and contentment. At mastery, when your locus of control is deeply rooted inside, you will be even-minded under all conditions. For most of us, even-mindedness under all conditions is an affirmation, not a reality. On the way there, we can have fun with the challenge.

THE SCIENTIFIC METHOD IN METAPHYSICS
DIRECT PERSONAL EXPERIENCE

- In your search for new and better ways of managing your suffering, you might find it useful to follow the scientific method in metaphysics. This method supports your ability to decipher spiritual fiction from fact. You can put profoundly important questions to the test of direct personal experience in the laboratory of life.

- The method:
  a. The body is the test tube.
  b. The experiment is on the life force itself, consciousness, energy, thought, will, feeling, desire, choice, and behavior.
  c. Test a theory.
     1. Can I actually make the spiritual qualities grow?
     2. Is Love more powerful than any painful problem?
     3. Does compassionate service to humanity give peace of mind and strength?
     4. Does meditation work?
     5. Do higher states of consciousness actually exist?
     6. Does the body-temple harbor the God of the Universe?
  d. Assume the agnostic position.
  e. Practice a spiritual method.
  f. Prove or disprove the theory through direct personal experience.
  g. If a method or concept works, keep it. If not, discard it.

POINTS TO REMEMBER

- This book describes fifteen pain management options, three on the horizontal axis and twelve on the vertical axis. A balanced healing program includes work on both axes. Over time, there is a shift from dependence on the external world of people, activities, places, and things to the internal world of peace, security, and contentment no matter the condition of the outer world.

- The techniques described in this book will show you how to place your needle of attention on spiritual qualities referred to as Love or a substitute word of your choice. You will learn how to think, feel, visualize, and ultimately become these qualities. The qualities will then help you broker and buffer any painful problem.

- Spiritual qualities adding up to Love are more powerful than any painful problem. Clearly establish the cultivation of spiritual qualities as your goal, and keep this goal ever shining before you. You may get overwhelmed, but you won't get lost.

- Spiritual healing is the reduction of the ego and the expansion of soul qualities, independent of whether or not the body heals.

- We can test the reality of any spiritual idea through direct personal experience when we develop a spiritual practice. This is the scientific method in metaphysics.

- Spiritual work is difficult. It requires discipline, hard work, takes a long time, and often hurts. However, if you persist, it gets easier and the reward is great: expanded spiritual qualities and superconscious experience. If you persevere with courage and heart, you will learn, grow, and transform. Never, never, never give up.

AFFIRMATIONS

If you do not know how to do affirmations, please refer to Chapter Twelve.

- Love is the most powerful healing force.
- I balance support from my people and solitude for maximum spiritual growth.
- To change the world, I reform myself.
- I embrace ego reduction through expansion of soul qualities.

- My body may not heal, but I can always expand Love, peace, courage, and strength.
- I accept my present state as I make the spiritual climb.
- Peace, joy, Love, power, and wisdom are on the other side of every painful problem.
- Spiritual power comes on its own schedule. I wait patiently.
- I love myself exactly as I am at the moment but too much to leave me there.
- I accept myself exactly as I am right now but too much to leave me there.
- Mind makes me sick. Mind makes me well.
- I put every ounce of my energy into my spiritual practice.
- There is no such thing as a quick fix.
- I can learn. I can grow. I persevere with heart and courage.
- Where I place my attention is where I am going. I focus on healing qualities.
- I expect difficult days. I am awake, alert, and ready.
- I practice in the minutes of my life.
- All I have is the moments of my life. I practice there.
- Love is the way and the goal. I start my climb from where I am right now.

EXERCISES

1. How does the scientific method apply in metaphysics?

2. Why is it important to have a spiritual support network?

3. What is the purpose of solitude on the spiritual path?

4. How does a reduced ego assist in spiritual growth?

5. What is the relationship between ego reduction and spiritual healing?

6. What is the difference between the horizontal and vertical axis?

*   Armed with the Universal Healing Wheel, the Universal Healing Method, the Serenity Prayer, and the seventeen suggestions for starting a spiritual practice, you are ready for a detailed review of a variety of proven spiritual methods.

*   In the next section of the book, you will learn how to practice twelve spiritual methods. Regular, consistent practice of these disciplines will change your life. If you do the work, the virtues of the great saints and sages will slowly add on to you: peace and strength, compassion and courage, service and wisdom.

*   First, you will study two techniques: the science of affirmations, and habit transformation. Here you will learn how to change your destiny by changing your thoughts and habits.

*   Then you will learn five techniques that comprise a morning and evening program: progressive muscle relaxation, breathwork, contemplation, meditation, and prayer.

*   The final section describes five techniques you can practice while you perform your daily activities: mindfulness, practicing the Presence of God, service, yoga, and the transformation of emotion.

*   Practicing these disciplines will heal and transform your consciousness. You will experience an ever-expanding feeling of peace, compassion, and joy expressed in acts of gentle, humble service to all of humanity.

PART THREE
CHANGE YOUR DESTINY

CHAPTER TWELVE: AFFIRMATIONS

CHAPTER THIRTEEN: HABITS

CHAPTER TWELVE

AFFIRMATIONS

The Power of Thought

- MIND-POWER. What goes on in the mind is monumentally important. It has great power to do harm or good. It can be our greatest friend or our greatest enemy. It contributes to our health, and it can make diseases worse. It creates mental storms or gives us the peace we so desperately crave. Yet most of us remain unaware of how it works. We don't think about thinking.

- THE UNDISCIPLINED MIND. We allow our thoughts to wander freely like a pack of wild horses in the wilderness, with no goal or direction. Junk thoughts, false beliefs, distortions, and delusions play in the attic of our body-house without restriction. We get stuck in negativity. Fear, insecurity, worry, and doubt rule the day. The restless mind has a life of its own. It won't quit. There's a manic in the attic. We ask him to leave, but he won't go.

- THE WISDOM OF THE AGES. There is a way out. We can change the way we think. We can replace restless, destructive thoughts with the wisdom of the ages. Powerful, beautiful, deep, peaceful thoughts can be our invited guests and can ultimately take up permanent residence in our body-home.

- THE SCIENCE OF HEALING AFFIRMATIONS. This chapter introduces the science of healing affirmations. Here you will learn how to exercise the inherited but dormant powers of your mind. This work will help you in every dimension of your life. You will learn how to shift mental gears from negative to positive. Your relationships will improve. You will be more productive. Your healing power will grow. You will become a more skillful pain manager. You will evolve spiritually. You will feel better, become a better person, and experience higher states of consciousness.

- THE ATTRACTING POWER OF THOUGHT. Thoughts, both negative and positive, have great power; they are magnetic, but unlike ordinary magnets, they attract their equals—not their opposites—according to their vibrations. Negative thoughts attract negativity; positive thoughts attract positivity. Remembering this simple principle can change the course of your life. You can change your destiny by changing your thoughts.

- THOUGHTS ARE CHEMICAL, ELECTRICAL, AND MAGNETIC POWERS. The science of healing affirmations teaches us how to send powerful positive thoughts as chemical, electrical, and magnetic waves to our conscious and subconscious minds and to the cells in our bodies.

- FREE WILL AND CHOICE EXERCISED IN THE MIND. Through a simple maneuver involving free will and choice, you can learn how to deploy your own thoughts to break through limitations, transform bad habits, turn failure into success, and activate your healing powers.

- THOUGHT IMPACTS DISEASE AND HEALING. Thoughts have leverage in the inner workings of our cells having to do with transforming disease into health. By using affirmations to cultivate spiritual qualities, you can stimulate healing power. When you align your thinking with such qualities as peace, compassion, and loving-kindness, you set up harmonious conditions for the healing power to do its work. The right condition for healing is a mere thought away.

- THE PROBLEM AND THE SOLUTION IS IN THE MIND. The discovery that we are both the problem and the solution in the intimate proximity of our own minds is of enormous importance.

- RESPONSIBILITY AND WORK. A new level of responsibility and work is assumed when you learn how to apply the power of thought to affect any need or condition.

- A POWERFUL, POSITIVE HEALING FORCE. Life is a battle between negative and positive forces. In the mind, this battle takes place between positive and negative thoughts. Negative thoughts contribute to the disease process. Positive thoughts promote healing. Following is a description of how practicing affirmations can help you transform your mind into a powerful, positive healing force for yourself and others.

AFFIRMATIONS AND THE SUBCONSCIOUS MIND

- THE SUBCONSCIOUS STOREHOUSE. The subconscious mind is a vast storehouse of memories, thoughts, and experiences.

- NEGATIVE BRAIN GROOVES. Most of us have experienced rejection, humiliation, abandonment, and the loss of loved ones. Many have had terrible trauma, abuse, accidents, or illness. These harsh experiences can lead to negative thought patterns or habits that cause unnecessary, ongoing pain. These patterns are stored in our subconscious mind and brain cells in negative thought circuits that lock us into destructive ways of responding to the world. Some examples of this type of negative thinking are:

  - I am ugly, bad, guilty, and worthless.
  - I do not deserve to be healed.
  - I am a helpless, weak, inadequate loser.
  - I cannot change.
  - I am doomed to suffer.

- I deserve punishment.
- I will never be able to get out of this problem.
- I can't beat this habit.
- No matter what progress I make, something will come along to take it away.

- AUTOMATIC NEGATIVE THINKING. In response to life events, such negative attitudes emerge from the subconscious rapidly, automatically, and habitually. They often manifest in relentless repetitions referred to as ruminations or obsessions. The mind can get stuck in ruminations for minutes, hours, days, weeks, and longer. Some deeply embedded patterns can extend their influence over a lifetime. We have a tendency to underestimate the mind's negative power, much of which is submerged beneath our awareness.

- FROM NEGATIVE TO POSITIVE BRAIN GROOVES. The science of healing affirmations teaches us how to access the conscious and subconscious mind so that these negative patterns can be brought to awareness, rooted out, and replaced by positive new brain circuits and thought patterns.

- MENTAL HEALTH. The result is a positive, calm, focused, strong, and resilient mind, sharpened and ready for problem solving, managing life's harsh realities, and creating health, success, harmony, and joy. This is a good definition of mental health.

- THOUGHT-MEDICINE IN THE BRAIN-PHARMACY. Positive thoughts act like medicine released from the brain's own pharmacy. This thought-medicine cannot do its work, however, if negative ideas, beliefs, or attitudes neutralize its healing power. When a positive affirmation is stated, there is often an attack of negative thoughts or beliefs, which emerge from their storage place in the subconscious.

- THOUGHT SABOTAGE. For example, you may be fighting low self-esteem because of prior abandonment. To change your self-image, you affirm, "I am good, beautiful, worthy, and strong." However, your subconscious mind sabotages your efforts to create a new positive identity by releasing the negative counter-thought, "You are an insecure, awkward, homely loser." This negative thought has had control of your self-image for years. It is a well established thought circuit that does not give up its power so easily.

  The effect of the countering negative thought is the same as if you wrote something with chalk on a board and erased what you wrote. The negative thought maintains its power unless neutralized by a stronger, positive thought force.

- CREATE AN ARMY OF POSITIVE THOUGHTS. The science of healing affirmations teaches us to use our concentration, will, feeling, and faith to infuse the positive thought with the necessary power to take hold in the subconscious mind.

  With practice, the positive thought slowly grows in strength and associates with other positive thoughts such as, "I am a good person. There have been many victories. People actually do like me. I have a lot to offer."

  At some point, we can deploy an army of positive thoughts to rapidly and effectively neutralize the negative ones. Then, when the same provocative situation arises to test us, our mind stays positive, poised, and peaceful.

CREATING POWERFUL AND EFFECTIVE AFFIRMATIONS

Affirmations work, but they may not work for you if they lack the necessary potency to take hold and grow. Following are some suggestions for creating effective healing affirmations.

1. DEFINE YOUR PROBLEM.

- This can be any problem or condition of the body, mind, or soul.

2. DEFINE YOUR GOAL.

- Focus on the solution rather than the problem. Think more about where you want to be than where you have been. For example, if you are working with disease, focus on health. For fear, invoke courage or bravery. For anger, try peace, patience, forgiveness, or gentleness. For weakness, try strength. For failure, try success. You become and attract what you intend. Your goal will become your new habit.

- Keep your goal in the forefront of your consciousness, ever shining before you, making the way clear when you might otherwise be overwhelmed or confused.

3. PRESENT TENSE.

- State the affirmation in the present tense, as though the goal is already accomplished. You would not want to affirm, "I am going to be calm." You would affirm, "I am calm."

4. POSITIVE TERMS.

- State the affirmation in positive terms such as "I am calm," not the negative "I am no longer anxious."

5. INDIVIDUALIZE.

- Keep reworking the affirmation until it feels just right. For example, you may prefer "I remain even-minded under all conditions" or "Even-minded no matter the condition" or simply the one-word affirmation, "Even-minded." When it feels right, it will fit the rhythm of your being perfectly.

6. VISUALIZATION.

- You can reinforce the power of your affirmation by associating it with a mental picture or visualization. In this way you can think, see, and feel the reality of the affirmation.

- For example, we can all imagine circumstances that make us nervous, angry, or agitated. We can rehearse these scenes in our minds by creating thoughts and pictures of ourselves remaining calm despite provocation. The more we rehearse, the more likely the subconscious and conscious minds will help us stay relaxed when the actual stressful condition arrives.

7. PRACTICE.

- Practice and repetition are most important. Without repetition, there can be no progress. Deeply embedded negative thoughts, beliefs, and attitudes have been around for a long time in the subconscious mind. When the brain cells are loaded up with thought habits that have to do with disease and limitation, it takes time to form thought circuits that have to do with health and possibility.

- The first round is just the beginning. It takes time to realize the deeper pearls of wisdom, and it takes time to root out the subconscious brain grooves that carry negative thought patterns. This is a life-long project that goes to the deepest and most hidden corners of our being.

- We need to repeat affirmations continuously for chronic, deeply embedded conditions, and we need to ignore an unchanged or contrary condition as we repeat the affirmation. Many people give up early, not understanding the effort required or unwilling to do the work. Some habits, patterns, or conditions may change with ease, while others may take a long time to heal or replace. We need patience; it may take months, even years, to transform deeply ingrained habit patterns of thought, feeling, desire, or behavior.

• Perseverance is the magic of healing work. The more we use positive affirmation, the quicker change occurs for the better. With continued practice, the affirmation takes on a life of its own. It repeats itself by itself. The thought gains momentum and strength, eventually becoming powerful enough to become reality. Repetitious positive thoughts gradually replace and finally dominate the negative patterns of the conscious and subconscious minds.

8. INTENSITY.

• To be effective, you will need to bring all of your attention and energy to your practice. Each method described in this book requires all of your heart, mind, might, and soul for maximum benefit. There must be sufficient intensity and concentration of feeling, thought, will, and faith to give the exercise—in this case, the affirmation—sufficient energy and power to make the necessary changes.

• If the affirmation is spoken without passion or planted in a restless, unfocused mind, it will have less power. Muscles atrophy from lack of exercise. Similarly, those who have not been doing an inner workout weaken their powers of concentration and will, the tools necessary to break through the barriers of limitation into conscious possibility.

• With practice and repetition, your will power and concentration slowly grow. As you strengthen your affirmation, be sure not to create tension by going too far. Calm concentration without tension increases the force of the thought. The goal is to repeat the affirmation as many times as you wish with calm concentration, deep feeling, and will.

- When you realize your attention has wandered, bring it back to the affirmation with as much focus as possible. Repeating the affirmation with increasingly intense concentration and feeling mobilizes healing power.

- At first, our healing affirmations may be like sparks blowing in the wind with no apparent effect. With patient, persistent practice, these thoughts get stronger. They light healing power ablaze. Although it kindles slowly, if we keep adding affirmative fuel to the healing power, there will be a bonfire. Then the affirmation permeates our conscious and subconscious minds, every cell, fiber, molecule, and atom of our being, as well as surrounding space, eventually bringing into existence the very thing being affirmed.

9. FAITH.

- The life energy operating the bodily cells, tissues, organs, and systems has within it the power of healing. This brilliant power heals our cuts, bruises, colds, and other ailments without our action. We can trust it, and there is evidence that the more we trust it, the better it works.

- Affirmations are more effective when practiced with faith and belief. Doubt and insecurity undermine the authority of the new positive thought and work against the life energy and healing power. For maximum benefit, perform your affirmation with faith, trust, and belief in its power to heal.

WHEN TO DO AFFIRMATIONS

- We can do affirmations any time: at rest, in meditation, or during activity.

- Affirmations are more effective when the mind is relaxed, opened, and less defensive, such as just before going to sleep or just after awaking. Its maximum benefit occurs when the mind is still during or after meditation.

- We can practice affirmations before, during, or after a particular problem surfaces. For example, if we are struggling with anxiety, we can practice affirmations of peace while we are anxious. But we can also practice when we are feeling serene, which is a good time to fortify the subconscious for the tests of life that are sure to come.

THE TECHNIQUE FOR AFFIRMATIONS DURING PERIODS OF REST OR MEDITATION

- You are always affirming something in your conscious and subconscious mind. You can find out what is in there and get rid of what you don't like by practicing the following technique. You can perform this technique during periods of rest and before, during, and after meditation:

  1. Sit
  2. Breathe
  3. Relax
  4. Open
  5. Affirm
  6. Feel
  7. Visualize
  8. Repeat

1. SIT:

- Sit with the spine straight.

2. BREATHE:

- Take several slow deep breaths.

3. RELAX:

- Relax the body and calm the mind.
- Throw out all problems, restless thoughts, fears, insecurities, and doubts.
- Gather as much concentration and stillness as you can.

4. OPEN:

- Open yourself to the idea that affirmations work and that all conditions of the body, emotions, mind, and spirit are changeable.

5. AFFIRM:

- Choose an affirmation, and repeat it with increasing intensity.
- With your will and concentration, eliminate all other thoughts.
- Hold the affirmation in the center of your being for several minutes.
- At some point, notice the affirmation repeating itself even when you do not try to remember it.

6. FEEL:

- Feel the affirmation.
- Allow it to permeate your conscious and subconscious minds, every cell, fiber, molecule, and atom of your entire being and surrounding space.

7. VISUALIZE:

- Visualize yourself as you imagine yourself to be when the affirmation has become completely real.

8. REPEAT:

- When the mind wanders, bring it back to the affirmation.

THE TECHNIQUE FOR
AFFIRMATIONS DURING ACTIVITY

- We can perform this technique when we are engaged in activities that do not require our full attention such as walking, raking leaves, washing dishes, cooking, shopping, cleaning, or driving in rush-hour traffic.

- We can also do this technique when our mind wanders into negativity, when we are upset, or when we want to change the direction of our thoughts for any reason.

1. STOP:

- When you notice your mind is in a negative space, give it a command to stop.

2. FOLLOW STEPS 2–8 ABOVE:

- You can repeat your affirmation, mantra, or chant throughout the day.

- Every thought sets up a corresponding vibration. When you repeat a word, thought, or chant reflecting a healing quality such as peace, Love, or compassion, you will eventually experience peace, Love, and compassion.

- Avoid mechanical or dry repetition. Feel the affirmation in your heart. When your repetition becomes mechanical, bring it back into your heart and infuse it with feeling.

- Repeat the silent chant when you are working, cooking, shopping, cleaning, driving, walking, exercising, playing sports, or helping others.

- Repeat the affirmation with interest, attention, and feeling.

WRITING AND RECORDING AFFIRMATIONS

- You can write affirmations on note cards and keep them in your pocket at all times. You can pull the card out during the day whenever possible.

- Pick a relevant affirmation, and repeat it until the idea deeply ingrains itself in both the conscious and subconscious minds.

- We can also record affirmations.

HOW MANY PROBLEMS SHOULD BE ADDRESSED AT ONE TIME

- We can work on one or many problems at the same time, but it is wise not to put too many affirmations into our program at first. It is better to concentrate on one or a few affirmations with intense concentration than to dilute our power by spreading ourselves too thin.

THE DIFFERENCE BETWEEN PRAYER AND AFFIRMATION

- Affirmations and prayer are similar. In prayer, we seek help from our Higher Power. An affirmation is a statement of the prayer as though the result is already accomplished. For example, one might pray, "Lord, grant me even-mindedness under all conditions." The corresponding affirmation would be, "I am even-minded under all conditions."

- Those who understand themselves to be co-creators and co-operators with their Higher Power can combine the use of prayer and affirmation. For example, it has often been said that God helps those who help themselves. When we work with affirmations, we are helping ourselves. Prayer is the request for God's grace as a means of getting help with the problem.

ONE-WORD AFFIRMATIONS

• When we need to do some work in a particular area, we can affirm any healing quality with one word. For example, when we feel restless, we can talk to our body. It will take instructions. We can give the body a one-word command such as "relax," "harmony," "balance," or "rhythm." We can talk to our mind. Eventually it will listen. We can think, "patience," "peace," or "poise." When someone is giving us a hard time, we can affirm, "understanding," "compassion," or "forgiveness."

ACCEPTING THE THINGS WE CANNOT CHANGE

• We can apply affirmations to get rid of any unwanted condition or to attain a desired goal. However, there is no promise of a cure or even improvement in simply doing affirmations. Some conditions will not change, no matter how long or perfectly we practice.

• When healing occurs—if it is going to occur—is not up to the individual. Do not set a time limit. Desire for change is good but should not be confused with an expectation of results on our own schedule. Such expectations may create unnecessary tension, an attitude of entitlement, and disappointment.

• Stay realistic, and avoid magical thinking. Perform affirmations, prayer, and other techniques with the realization that the outcome is not up to us. If we improve, we are grateful. If we continue to struggle with our current problems, we can cultivate acceptance, strength, and courage.

• It is natural to want a physical cure or to accomplish our goals in the external world, but this is not always possible. We can, however, always continue working with our inner being, seeking emotional stability, peace of mind, and spiritual wholeness. For most of us, there is more than a lifetime of work to do in these areas.

- For those conditions that improve slowly or not at all, affirmations of surrender or acceptance may be of use:

  o I surrender to the will of God.
  o I accept the things I cannot change.
  o Pain is the teacher. I work with it. I learn from it. I am not afraid.
  o Or you might try one-word affirmations such as, "accept," "surrender," "yield," "open," "soft," "patience," or "silence."

EXAMPLE

Joe has a very difficult time accepting criticism without feeling rejected. When others are critical, he reacts with anger and fear. He loses control of his emotions, yells, and becomes verbally aggressive. Later, embarrassed by his immature behavior, he feels guilt, shame, and remorse.

Joe wants to change. He starts the practice of affirmations. He affirms, "I am at peace under all conditions. I remain calm when challenged. I am a warm, compassionate, loving human being. I am as good as any other person. I remain calm even if the other person is mean and wrong." With his imagination, he visualizes himself at peace no matter how angry others get. These pictures go into his subconscious mind.

Joe performs his affirmations and visualizations with calm concentration, will, feeling, and faith. His subconscious mind forms a new habit pattern of staying calm, just as Joe pictures himself to be when others get angry.

Later, an angry person confronted Joe in the street. Instead of reacting with anger and fear, he remained calm. He was even able to stay supportive of the other person and give him a kind word. He withdrew from the scene without adding oil to the other person's fire. Joe marveled at the power of affirmations to heal his long-standing problem.

Joe was also wise to the fact that his healing was not complete. From his study of the science of healing affirmations, he knew that his progress might not be in a straight line, that his record might not be perfect. He knew that he might not handle other situations as well and that negative thoughts of discouragement and insecurity would arise.

Despite the inevitable setbacks, Joe continued his practice of affirmation with diligence, patience, and perseverance. Although he knew it would take time, he was confident that he would ultimately master his long-standing problem by calmly concentrating on his affirmations with all of his heart, mind, might, and soul. Eventually, Joe achieved mastery.

POINTS TO REMEMBER

- Nothing is closer to us than our own thoughts. It is in this realm that we can change our reality and our destiny.

- We look at the world through our thoughts as though they are glasses. Negative thoughts fashion a dark vision of the world. Change your glasses. Think positive thoughts rooted in Love.

- Healing power is a part of the wisdom of the body. We can help it do its work when we think positive thoughts.

- Spiritual qualities are the healers. When we align our thinking with such qualities as peace, compassion, understanding, and forgiveness, we maximize the chemical and electromagnetic forces that control healing.

- We can work on any problem by affirming any one or a combination of one hundred healing qualities. Choosing thoughts in alignment with these qualities lights the fire of healing power. In so doing, we make an immediate contribution towards the transformation and healing of the world by reforming ourselves.

- In each moment of our lives, we have a choice concerning our thoughts and attitude. A negative thought unchallenged becomes the truth. As soon as we perceive a single negative thought, we can eliminate it with an army of positive thoughts. When feeling restless, affirm peace. When judging others, counter with an affirmation of loving-kindness.

• We compound our problems with our excesses. In response to the difficulties of the world, we respond with mental restlessness, high emotion, bad habits, and greed. Our selfishness gives us the illusion of protection while creating more fear and insecurity. Instead, we can respond with compassion, peace, and understanding—powerful healers that neutralize all types of negativity.

• In a state of deep meditation, we can plant our affirmation and visualization in the subconscious mind. With continued practice, this thought-picture grows in strength and power until it has enough force to become a new habit.

• Healing qualities are the gateway to higher consciousness. We can create the qualities we lack through concentration, will, thought, and faith. Pick a healing quality, breath it, affirm it, and practice it in your actions. Each time we align our thinking with healing qualities, we move one step closer to higher states of consciousness.

• When we see something we dislike, we can affirm our vision of goodness and beauty. We can apply the scientific principles of healing affirmations to eliminate all traces of negativity.

• Even when our thoughts are distorted and wrong, we endorse them as the gospel. Remember this: negative thoughts are just thoughts, not facts. We don't need to believe them. We can take away their invasive destructive power and replace them with the wisdom of the ages, healing thoughts centered in Love, compassion, kindness, and understanding. The body, mind, and soul love this.

- Fill your mind with wisdom when you first get up in the morning, and give yourself a tune up any time of day or night.

- You are the prime beneficiary of loving-kindness affirmations, as the affirmation must pass through your cells on the way to others. So too with anger and other harsh emotions.

- You have the power to magnify or reduce your pain. Here is how it works: Pain is both physical and psychological. All pain is experienced in the mind and can therefore be influenced by the mind. Fearful thoughts magnify the inevitable suffering of life—this is called stress, or reactivity. When you strengthen your mind by practicing affirmations and the other methods described in Step 9, it can remain calm even when the body presents challenges such as disease and disability. Some people refer to this as a positive mental attitude, the power of positive thinking, mind-power, or mental yoga.

- We can do much more to heal ourselves through positive thought. Negative thinking leads to negative emotions and vibrations, which impede the healing process. Positive thoughts, feelings, and vibrations stimulate healing power. Of course, we need to eat right, exercise, and eliminate our addictions to tobacco, alcohol, and drugs, but it is equally important to replace thoughts of fear, insecurity, worry, and doubt with affirmations of peace, strength, and courage. We may not be able to eliminate disease and disability, but we can always soothe ourselves with positive thoughts.

- Applying the power of positive thought to healing your life is simple, relaxing, and enjoyable. The results are of great benefit over time. Practice affirmations. You will be amazed when you see how the wonderful power of thought can change your life! Never underestimate the healing power of positive thinking.

- "So watch your thought and its ways with care, and let it spring from Love born out of concern for all beings" (the Buddha). With affirmative thought, we can give ourselves inspiration and guidance, comfort and solace, transformation and purification.

AFFIRMATIONS
FOR SUCCESS IN WORK

- I am successful in all aspects of my work.
- I focus on completing one task at a time.
- I am calm, efficient, and productive.
- I enjoy making a contribution to the welfare of others.

FOR SUCCESS IN RELATIONSHIPS

- I am in harmony with all people.
- I contribute to the health and welfare of everyone I meet.
- I am understanding and compassionate, even when others are wrong and provocative.

FOR CULTIVATION OF SPIRITUAL QUALITIES

- I am at peace no matter what the world does.
- Compassion and kindness permeate my thoughts, feelings, and actions.
- Love is the great healer. I give Love and kindness to all I meet.

HEALING

- The infinitely intelligent healing power permeates every cell of my body.
- The infinitely intelligent healing power cleans my cells.
- The infinitely intelligent healing power eliminates debris.
- The infinitely intelligent healing power creates antibodies against disease-causing microbes.
- The infinitely intelligent healing power generates new cells where needed.

- The infinitely intelligent healing power energizes my body.
- The infinitely intelligent healing power relaxes my body.
- The infinitely intelligent healing power melts disease.
- The infinitely intelligent healing power coordinates all the activities of my body.

EXERCISES

1. Review and study the nine guidelines for creating powerful, effective healing affirmations.

2. Describe and practice the technique for affirmations during meditation or rest.

3. Describe and practice the technique for affirmations during activity.

4. Watch the trend of your thoughts. When you become aware that your mind is negative, bring in a positive affirmation. For example, when your thinking is stuck in fear, insecurity, worry, and doubt, substitute such thoughts as, "I am strong. I am courageous. I can do this work. I can win this victory."

5. Notice how you feel when your mind is negative and when it is positive. What is the difference?

6. Notice the difference in the direction your life takes as you shift from negative to positive thoughts.

7. What is the difference between a prayer and an affirmation?

8. Describe how subconscious negative thoughts sabotage affirmations.

9. As you repeat your affirmations, try writing down the negative thoughts that surface from your subconscious. This will demon-

strate the nature of the negative images and attitudes that could be controlling you at this time. By doing this, you can find out what beliefs prevent realization of your intended positive thought.

10. Reflect on the brilliance of the healing power. Meditate on it. This will increase your trust in its magnificent intelligence. As you increase your faith, trust, and belief in your own healing power, your affirmations will be more effective.

11. Write out some affirmations on note cards and keep them in your pocket at all times. Pull out the card and practice these affirmations during the day. Select an "affirmation of the day."

12. Review the one hundred healing qualities in the spiritual alphabet. You can use these as one-word affirmations. Try using one-word affirmations as your word of the day. For example, you can chant "peace, peace, peace" throughout the day. This will help you get through any physical, mental, emotional, or spiritual problem. If negative thoughts emerge from the subconscious mind such as "I can't do this. Peace is impossible for the likes of me," take notice and let them go. With consistent long-term practice, these negative thoughts will be replaced by thoughts aligned with healing qualities such as peace, strength, courage, and kindness.

13. Life is school. Pain is the teacher if we open to its lessons. The lessons have to do with the cultivation of healing qualities. There are lots of tests in the school of life. Tests are any painful problem of body, mind, or soul. There are tests of the world and tests of the body. We don't like tests. But every test is an opportunity. We can react with a negative attitude or a healing quality. Can you find the blessing in disguise? Can you accept the painful problem and respond with a healing quality?

14. Many people suffer from thoughts of sin, guilt, fear, and punishment. Such thoughts are harmful to the immune system and may

lead to disease. Try shifting gears toward thoughts that stimulate healing power. Bring in some affirmations of kindness, understanding, and forgiveness for yourself.

15. The mind is like a living room. The thoughts you let in become your furniture, decorations, and guests. Who and what is in your living room? Do you need some new furniture? New decorations? How often do you clean the room?

16. To illustrate the power of thought, Dr. Blaslotto at the University of Chicago conducted a study of three groups and tested each group on how many free throws they could make. Then he had the first group practice free throws every day for an hour. The second group visualized themselves making free throws. The third group did nothing. After thirty days, he tested them again. The first group improved by 24 percent; the second group improved by 23 percent without touching a basketball, except mentally; the third group did not improve, which was expected. Such is the power of the mind.

17. Affirmations are mental push-ups. When you practice affirmations, you are tapping into your inherited mental power. This is called mind-power or mental yoga. Pick a goal, and line up all of your thoughts toward accomplishing that goal. Don't let a single negative thought come in. If you dwell on the negative thought or experience, that becomes the goal. Train your mind to eliminate all traces of negative thought.

18. You can practice affirmations to help achieve your horizontal axis goals: success, prosperity, relationships, and health. You can simultaneously practice affirmations of acceptance when the world, or your body, does not conform to your wish. And you can always cultivate spiritual qualities internally, no matter what your body or the world is doing.

19. Throw loving-kindness-light affirmations to all of your cells, all people, and all creation.

In the next chapter, you will study how habits form and change. You will learn how to transform bad habits into constructive meaningful activities, the habits of a seeker, and the habits of a sage.

CHAPTER THIRTEEN

HABITS

How to Eliminate Bad Habits

We are creatures of habits—thousands of habits. Habits are actions performed on automatic pilot. We don't have to think about the action to perform it. Habits reside in neurocircuits. These neurocircuits control our thoughts, feelings, attitudes, values, and actions. Some of these habits are positive and some are negative. For recovery and healing, we need to transform negative habits into positive ones. We already know how to do this. Lets start with the Buddha. He says,

> *The thought manifests as word;*
> *the word manifests as deed;*
> *the deed develops into habit;*
> *and habit hardens into character.*
> *So watch the thought and its ways with care,*
> *and let it spring from Love*
> *born out of concern for all beings.*

The Buddha suggests we root our thoughts in Love and compassion. In this chapter, we will study how to lock healing qualities such as Love and compassion into our brain grooves, thus making them our new mental habits.

- HABITS RULE DESTINY. A cocaine addict, a working person raising a family, a seeker practicing meditation and service, and a highly conscious sage all have the same motivation. We all want avoidance of suffering and permanent Love, peace, and safety.

What separates us are our habits. Our life is a sequence of habits that determine our course and evolution. Habits rule destiny.

- HOW HABITS FORM AND CHANGE. We all have a mix of good and bad habits. Bad habits cause untold suffering. Good habits help us manage the inevitable suffering of life and expand healing power. For full recovery and deep healing, we must release the energy captured by bad habits and transfer this power to new good habits.

To understand how we got where we are and how to change direction, we need to understand how habits form and change. To understand habit formation and transformation, we need to look at:

1. Brain grooves
2. Attention
3. Repetition

- BRAIN GROOVES. Any pattern of thought or action repeated many times results in a habit with a corresponding neurosignature, or brain groove. The brain is composed of approximately one hundred billion cells, called neurons. A brain groove is a series of interconnected neurons that carry the thought patterns of a particular habit.

- ATTENTION. Attention feeds the habit. When we give our attention to a habit, we activate the brain groove, releasing the thoughts, desires, and actions related to that habit. The brain is like a jukebox. It records everything we have ever done and stores these records in the subconscious. Where we place our needle of attention determines what record plays. We can play records of addiction or, as suggested by the Buddha, records that "spring from Love born out of concern for all beings." As the old Cherokee wise man said, the wolf you feed is the wolf that wins. (See Chapter Seven, Universal Healing Wheel, homework exercise number nine, p. 113.)

- REPETITION. The brain is malleable. We can change our thoughts and behavior by recruiting new cells to form new brain grooves. Every thought and action is recorded within the interconnected nerve cells, and each repetition adds new depth to the brain groove. If we repeat a thought and action enough times, a habit is formed. Continued repetition strengthens the power of the habit. Inattention and lack of repetition weakens the power of the habit. These principles apply to the formation of both bad and good habits. Negative thoughts and actions create harmful habits. Positive thoughts and actions create good habits.

- HABIT TRANSFORMATION. We can use these principles to eliminate and replace bad habits with good ones. We can gradually starve bad habits to death by not giving them our attention. As we pay more attention to forming a good habit, the new brain groove slowly gains power. Eventually, the new positive brain groove dominates the negative groove, and good habits drive out the bad. Without this transformation, recovery and healing are impossible.

- SKILLFUL PAIN MANAGEMENT IN THE SCHOOL OF LIFE. When we are assigned painful problems in the school of life, we need to do the homework. All too often, however, we play hooky by escaping into the pleasures of a bad habit. If we repeat this behavior, at some point we get addicted. We end up with the original problem and a host of additional difficulties associated with addiction: wild emotions, mental storms, paranoia, rage, humiliation, chaotic relationships, job loss, disease, and death. We can avoid this by doing our homework, by learning how to be good pain managers. Learning how to manage our suffering is critical for deep healing and full recovery. However, most of us slide down the path of bad habits early in our lives in our attempt to avoid pain.

- ADDICTION. Bad habits include smoking, use of drugs or alcohol, excessive eating, compulsive gambling, compulsive shopping, addiction to the Internet, computer, or television, addiction to sex, money, fame, work, activity, or power, or dependency on others at the expense of independence and individuality (a condition known as codependency or relationship addiction).

Although bad habits are pleasurable in the beginning, their eventual evolution into emptiness and torment is inevitable as they force us to act in ways contrary to our true nature. We want to express Love, compassion, kindness, patience, and courage.

• TWO ROOMS. Life is painful no matter what route we take. How we manage the pain determines whether we move forward, slip backward, or stay stuck in this life. We can think of the choices we have in managing our pain as two separate rooms in our house. There is pain no matter which room we choose, but room number one is the room of healing, and room number two is the room of addiction.

The room of addiction is attractive and seductive. It lures us into thinking there is an easy way out by giving us pain relief in the beginning, but over time, it creates more pain. The room of healing may not look so attractive in the beginning, and it may even appear intimidating or frightening. It may involve more pain in the beginning, but that pain takes us to strength, peace of mind, and courage.

The pain of bad habits is worse than the pain of healing. Cultivating good habits is hard, but it is more difficult to maintain bad habits. The pain of addiction takes us down. The pain of healing takes us up.

• POSITIVE HABITS. There are hundreds of good physical, mental, emotional, and spiritual habits. These fall into three categories:

1. Constructive meaningful activities: activities related to health,

work, training, volunteering, school, relationships, culture, sports, recreation, or hobbies.

2. Healing methods (the habits of a seeker): the methods described in this and other healing models
3. Healing qualities: (the habits of a sage): qualities such as Love, compassion, forgiveness, courage, strength, and others listed in the healing alphabet.

- REFRAIN TONIGHT. The time to create positive habits is now. Every time we repeat a thought or action of a bad habit, it maintains or gains power. Procrastination weakens our will to the point that we think we cannot change. Before we know it, the habit has locked us in a prison of our own making. We may not even know if a habit already has enough power to imprison us for decades; we only discover its power when one day we try to stop it and find out we cannot.

> *Assume a virtue if you have it not.*
> *Refrain tonight,*
> *and that shall lend a kind of easiness*
> *to the next abstinence, the next more easy;*
> *for use almost can change the stamp of nature,*
> *and either lodge the devil or throw him out*
> *with wondrous potency.*
> — Shakespeare, *Hamlet*

TECHNIQUE

- Neurocircuits or brain grooves carry both good and bad habits. Attention and repetition determine which brain groove is active and gaining power. Place your needle of attention on the neurocircuit of a bad habit, and it gains power. Place your needle of attention on a good habit, and it will gain power. What you pay attention to and repeat will determine the course of your life. Following is a technique for transformation of habits from negative to positive:

1. Introspection
2. Avoidance of everything associated with the bad habit
3. Affirmations and will
4. Constructive, meaningful activities
5. Healing methods (the habits of a seeker)
6. Healing qualities: (the habits of a sage)
7. Support
8. Solitude
9. Perseverance
10. Victory

1. INTROSPECTION:

• Make a list of the habits you would like to change. Examples of bad habits include smoking, substance abuse, gambling, compulsive eating, addictions to sex, computers, money, power, or work, and codependency or addiction to people.

2. AVOIDANCE OF EVERYTHING ASSOCIATED WITH THE BAD HABIT:

• People, environment, routines, and our own thoughts are the breath that gives life to the brain groove of a bad habit. With continued stimulation, a bad habit grows, our will weakens, and we slide off the recovery and healing path.

• However, the neurocircuit for the bad habit remains dormant in the subconscious if we give it no thought or attention. We can gain power over a bad habit by avoiding exposure to everything associated with it. Stay away from the negative environment, people, and actions that supported the habit until the new brain groove is strong.

• Avoid thinking about the bad habit as much as possible. We are subject to craving in an instant if not careful. Even a passing thought or image of the negative habit can awaken desire. The more we let the idea play in our minds, the more at risk we are of recurrent addiction. Starve the bad habit to death by inattention.

3. AFFIRMATIONS AND WILL:

•   Review the lessons on affirmations and will to see how thought-power and will power can erase even the deepest grooves of long-standing habits.

•   The mind has the key that can unlock the door of a bad habit, as a single thought or visual image can stimulate craving. We need to choose our thoughts carefully. Thoughts associated with our bad habits do pass through our consciousness against our will, however. To prevent these thoughts from becoming action, we must work against them. As soon as we become aware of the unwanted thought, we can knock it out with will and affirmations.

•   We can invoke our will at full power, deploy our favorite affirmations, and turn to good actions. These include constructive meaningful activities, the habits of a seeker, and the habits of a sage.

4. CONSTRUCTIVE, MEANINGFUL ACTIVITIES:

•   Make a list of activities related to your work, chores, relationships, leisure, recreation, hobbies, and self-nurturance. These activities are a part of your repertoire of positive habits. You can use these activities to ward off the thoughts and impulses related to your bad habits. Such a list might include playing and watching sports, listening to or playing music, watching television, surfing the Internet, watching movies, reading, writing, studying, exercising, doing arts and crafts, playing board games, completing crossword or jigsaw puzzles, gardening, paying bills, shopping, cooking, cleaning, taking a nap, getting a massage, and so on.

5. HEALING METHODS (THE HABITS OF A SEEKER):

*   The habits of a seeker include any technique that leads to the growth of healing qualities. For our purposes, these are affirmations, progressive muscle relaxation, breathwork, contemplation, meditation, prayer, mindfulness, practicing the Presence of God, service, yoga, and the transformation of emotion.

6. HEALING QUALITIES (THE HABITS OF A SAGE):

*   The habits of a sage are the qualities listed in the spiritual alphabet: Love, compassion, understanding, forgiveness, courage, strength, endurance, peace, and joy. When a bad habit takes over, the habits of a sage are reduced or non-existent. As healing and recovery advance, these spiritual qualities grow and the power of addiction is less. In full recovery, craving ceases as these qualities completely replace the bad habit.

*   If constructive meaningful activities, the habits of a seeker, and the habits of a sage keep the door of the bad habit locked, craving is kept at bay. We are safe. On the other hand, if despite our best efforts, the door of bad habits opens, the seductive music of craving may bring us to the brink of relapse. On the way to full recovery, there will be times when craving is dangerously strong and impossible to resist. If this occurs, we must surround ourselves with people who will protect us from negative actions.

7. SUPPORT:

*   We need to surround ourselves with people who support our goals. Friends and family associated with our bad habits often try to pull us back. When we move forward, they take it personally. Moreover, we are afraid of finding new people. We must get through this fear to create a support network of people with like-minded goals who

act as our bodyguards, protecting us from ourselves in moments of vulnerability.

8. SOLITUDE:

- To heal completely, we need to practice discipline when we are alone. This is a tall order. Many of us are afraid of the unknown and afraid to be alone. With continued practice, however, we will gain the necessary courage and self-control to resist craving even when we are alone. Then we do not need bodyguards. Eventually, craving ceases.

9. PERSEVERANCE:

- Change is difficult. Some strong bad habits may take years to break. Tests, trials, and temptations come. Setbacks occur. Back and forth movement between old and new patterns is a natural part of the process. Do not give up.

- When you slip and fall, be sure to create the mental habit of gentleness with yourself while using the remorse, regret, or disgust you may feel as an incentive to push you on to greater efforts. Get the lesson from your mistake, and move on. Don't let guilt, shame, and embarrassment dominate your consciousness. Replace feelings of self-contempt with Love, compassion, kindness, understanding and forgiveness for yourself.

10. VICTORY:

- Focus on your goal, and avoid thinking about the problem. Thinking about the problem only serves to rev up the negative brain groove that carries it. Keep feeding the positive habit to make it stronger and starving the negative habit to make it weaker. Give the best of your effort, concentration, and attention to the new habit until it takes over and becomes a natural, effortless, and automatic part of your repertoire.

- Stay with your support network and constructive meaningful activities. Go to 12-step meetings, other healing circles, and church, synagogue, or mosque if that is part of your program. Practice your healing methods and cultivate healing qualities. Keep battling, and you will win. Craving ceases. Peace and strength expand. Life becomes easier and more natural.

- As we practice the methods of a seeker, we reinforce the neurocircuits containing spiritual qualities such as Love, compassion, understanding, strength, and courage until these become unconditional habits. In the end, we realize our true spiritual identity by reconditioning our brain with soul qualities. We do not have to think about our practice. We express the habits of a sage, the Love qualities, automatically, naturally, and easily.

POINTS TO REMEMBER

- The ego, in its drive for immediate gratification, gets us into trouble with addiction and attachment. Not only do we lose preexisting strength, but also spiritual qualities cannot grow. Our souls yearn for Love and are willing to pay the price of work and patience.

- In the beginning of our self-healing work, it may be difficult to get traction. We can gain momentum by setting reasonable goals, taking small steps, achieving modest successes, and building from there.

- Neurocircuits or brain grooves carry both good and bad habits. Attention and repetition determine which brain groove is active and gaining power. Place your needle of attention on the neurocircuit of a bad habit, and it gains power. Place your needle of attention on a good habit, and it will gain power. What you pay attention to and repeat will determine the course of your life.

- The next step in our development is in the immediate moments of our lives. However, when we do not like what is going on, we leap out of the moment into an unhealthy habit. We hypnotize and narcotize ourselves in order to avoid unpleasant feelings. Instead, choose constructive meaningful activities and the healing methods of a seeker to develop the healing qualities of a sage.

- Reactivity is located in Step 5, Tools Become Barriers. The restless mind, high emotional reactivity, excessive material desire, physical problems, hyperactivity, and the ego get locked into neurocircuit-driven habits that are difficult to change. We can change, however, if we form new neurocircuits carrying the habits of a seeker and the habits of a sage. The habits of a seeker are the methods described in Step 9, and the habits of a sage are the healing qualities described in Step 7. Break bad habits of thought, attitude, emotion, desire, energy, and action so you can emerge from the past and find yourself renewed: fresh, spontaneous, and in the moment.

AFFIRMATIONS

- I can eliminate any bad habit.
- I expand my will power through practice.
- With my expanded will power, I escape from bad habits.
- One by one, I eliminate all bad habits.
- Nothing can stand in my way.
- Nothing can touch my will.
- Nothing can shake my resolve.
- My will power grows stronger each day.
- My mind is set.
- Nothing can stop me.
- I will succeed.
- Old friends who would have me indulge my bad habits are out.

- With will and thought, I conquer every bad habit, one at a time.
- I am not my bad habit. My true self is warm, compassionate, loving, and kind.
- I am stronger than any negative desire or temptation.
- No matter how many times I fail, I will rise and conquer.
- As I strengthen my body through physical exercise, I strengthen my will with mental exercise.
- With will and thought, I cast out this bad habit from the neurocircuits in my brain.
- With will and thought, I cultivate the habits of a sage: Love, peace of mind, compassion, and strength.

EXERCISES

1. Make a list of your good and bad physical and mental habits. Which habits would you like to change now?

2. What barriers keep you from changing your bad habits?

3. Make a list of constructive, meaningful activities that you will use to avoid bad habits.

4. What self-healing methods would you like to practice?

5. What healing qualities would you like to develop?

6. What will you do when craving for a destructive habit returns?

7. Practice the ten steps for replacing bad habits with positive habits.

8. It is a good idea to have a spiritual practice even when you are doing well. Practice now, so that when the going gets rough, the brain grooves that carry the habits of seekers and sages will have more power. Then, when painful problems emerge, you will be able to focus on your method and quality. You will be able to maintain strength and peace, even in the face of duress.

9. There are three stages to think about when dealing with a bad habit:

   a. The Safety Zone: Here, there is no craving. You are safe and protected from the bad habit.

   b. The Ambivalent Zone: there is craving, and you are at risk of returning to your bad habit.

   c. The Roller Coaster: You cannot control the impulse and indulge your bad habit. This is akin to going for a ride on a roller coaster. You give the man your tickets, sit down, pull the bar over your lap, and go for the ride. Once the ride starts, you can't get off until you get to the finish line. Then you have the option of getting off or going for another ride. When you finally get off the roller coaster, you are weak and dizzy. Sound familiar? When craving starts and you enter the ambivalent zone, what will you do to avoid getting on the roller coaster?

10. Keep a log. Each day you can inspect the status of your habits. Give yourself credit for your successes. Recognize your slips, but do not dwell on the bad habit; this only reinforces the associated brain groove. Instead, cultivate the mental habit of being gentle with yourself while you focus on the good habits you are creating. Always be compassionate, loving, kind, and forgiving towards yourself.

In the next section, we will study five techniques that comprise a morning and evening program: progressive muscle relaxation, breathwork, contemplation, meditation, and prayer. In the next chapter on progressive muscle relaxation, you will learn how to energize and relax your body.

PART FOUR
MORNING AND EVENING PROGRAM

CHAPTER FOURTEEN

PROGRESSIVE MUSCLE RELAXATION

Energizing and Relaxing the Body

Progressive muscle relaxation calms our mind and body through tensing and relaxing our muscles. An anxious mind results in a tense body. Progressive muscle relaxation calms the body, which in turn calms the mind.

This technique is effective for reducing anxiety, fear, panic, depression, insomnia, and fatigue. In addition, when the body and mind are relaxed, it is easier to practice other methods such as contemplation, mindfulness, and service. Many people use this technique to relax the body in preparation for deeper states of meditation.

GUIDELINES

1. Practice the entire routine described below in your morning and evening program for ten to fifteen minutes. You can also tense and relax specific muscles when stressed or fatigued.

2. Make this part of a regular routine including spiritual study, breathwork, meditation, and prayer.

3. Concentrate exclusively on tensing, relaxing, and energizing each muscle. Use your will and concentration to eliminate all other thoughts. This is not a time to worry, plan, fantasize, or solve problems. It is a time to relax and gain energy. When the mind wanders, bring it back to focus on tensing, relaxing, and energizing your muscles.

4. To reinforce your intention of energizing and relaxing your muscles, you can use an affirmation such as "energize" when you tense the muscle and "relax" when you relax the muscle.

5. Tense each muscle at maximum strength but without strain for three seconds. Then relax for three seconds. The movements are smooth and continuous, not abrupt or jerky.

6. Repeat each exercise three to five times.

7. When tensing a particular muscle, keep the rest of your muscles relaxed.

TECHNIQUE

1. Position: practice sitting, lying, or standing.

2. Eyes: close your eyes and focus at the point just above and between your eyebrows.

3. Breath: You may breathe in as you tense and exhale as you relax each muscle, or simply maintain calm, natural, smooth, relaxed breathing in the background. When you inhale, imagine that you are inhaling energy. When you exhale, imagine exhaling tension.

4. Foot: Make several circles with your left foot in each direction. Then tense the left foot muscle by curling the toes downward. Repeat this exercise with the right foot.

5. Calf: Tense and relax the left calf muscle three to five times. Repeat this exercise with the right calf.

6. Thigh: Tense and relax the left thigh muscle three to five times. Repeat this exercise with the right thigh.

7. Buttock: Tense and relax the left buttock three to five times. Repeat this exercise with the right buttock.

8. Lower abdomen: tense and relax the lower abdomen three to five times.

9. Upper abdomen: tense and relax the upper abdomen three to five times.

10. Full abdomen: Pull your abdominal muscles all the way in and hold for two seconds, then relax your abdomen. Repeat this exercise five to twenty times.

11. Fist: Tense and relax the left fist three to five times. Repeat this exercise with the right fist.

12. Forearm: Tense and relax the left forearm three to five times. Repeat this exercise with the right forearm.

13. Upper arm: Tense and relax the left upper arm three to five times. Repeat this exercise with the right upper arm.

14. Chest: Tense and relax the left chest three to five times. Repeat this exercise with the right chest.

15. Lower back: tense and relax the muscles in your lower back three to five times.

16. Middle back: Tense and relax the muscles in your middle back three to five times. You might imagine squeezing an orange between your shoulder blades.

17. Upper back: tense and relax the upper back muscles three to five times.

18. Neck: Tense and relax the left neck muscle, then the right neck

muscle, then the front neck muscle, and then the back neck muscle. Repeat this exercise three to five times.

19. Head: gently tense the muscles in your neck while you roll your head three to five times slowly in each direction.

20. Facial muscles: Notice any tension that you have here. Tighten your facial muscles by smiling wide, closing your eyes tightly, and wrinkling your forehead. Tense and relax each area three to five times.

21. Inhale and tense your whole body. Hold for a count of five. Exhale and relax, releasing the tension from your entire body.

22. Now take inventory of your body. Notice any lingering tension. Tense and relax three to five times where necessary.

23. Take several smooth, slow, deep breaths. On inhalation, imagine taking in life energy. On exhalation, imagine releasing any remaining tension in your body. Eliminate all negative thoughts. Concentrate on the peace and energy you have gained from these exercises.

24. Spend a few minutes feeling peace and energy spread to all parts of your body.

25. Open your eyes and feel awake, alert, and refreshed!

POINTS TO REMEMBER

- Practice progressive muscle relaxation slowly, with deep concentration. Eliminate all thought of problems, difficulty, and worry.

- Your muscle movement in these exercises should be smooth and continuous, not abrupt or jerky. It is important to tense each muscle to maximum strength without strain. Tense your muscle for three seconds, and relax for three seconds.

- Each time you tense and relax a muscle, you are energizing and relaxing that muscle. When you tense and relax all of your muscles at the same time, you fill your entire body with calm energy.

- Tense and relax your whole body three to five times whenever you feel anxious or fatigued.

AFFIRMATIONS

- I permeate every cell in my body with energy and peace.
- I fill my body with energy and peace.

EXERCISES

1. Notice the contrast when you tense and relax any muscle. Muscle tension, followed by a conscious effort to relax the muscle, allows you to recognize the difference between tension and relaxation. Once you notice this difference, it is easier to induce relaxation.

2. Include progressive muscle relaxation in your morning and evening spiritual routine. It is easier to meditate when your body is relaxed.

3. Practice progressive muscle relaxation any time you feel anxiety or fatigue.

4. You can memorize the instructions for progressive muscle relaxation or make a recording, so you can listen to the instructions as you perform the exercises.

In the next chapter, you will study the second method of the morning and evening program, breathwork. You will learn how to use your breath to relax and heal your body, mind, and soul.

CHAPTER FIFTEEN

BREATHWORK

Using Breath to Heal Mind, Body, and Spirit

- This chapter introduces breathwork, the second method of the morning and evening program.

- There is a right way to breathe. By learning how to breathe correctly, we can enhance our physical, mental, emotional, and spiritual wellbeing.

- In this chapter, you will learn how to take slow, deep, abdominal breaths. The benefits are profound.

- For the body: abdominal breathing gives an immediate relaxation response. Everything slows down including heart rate, respiratory rate, and blood pressure. Muscles relax. There is more energy, better sleep and digestion, and improved pain management.

- For the emotions: breath control reduces anxiety, depression, anger, guilt, and other painful feelings.

- For the mind: conscious breathing helps cultivate a positive, calm, strong, focused and resilient mind.

- For the soul: When we learn how to breathe, we can find our calm center, a necessity for all cognitive-behavioral and spiritual practices.

- With cognitive-behavioral methods including breathwork, many will be able to reduce and ultimately get off addicting anti-anxiety and pain medications.

- Following are some simple, enjoyable breathing exercises. These exercises can be practiced anywhere, anytime, and in any position including sitting, standing, walking, or lying down.

- As with other methods, the benefits of breathwork develop gradually and cumulatively with daily practice.

ABDOMINAL BREATHING

- To breathe correctly, we need to understand the difference between chest and abdominal breathing.

- Notice your breath. If you expand your chest or rib cage more, you are a chest breather. If you expand your abdomen or stomach more, you are an abdominal breather.

- Stress causes rapid, shallow, noisy, and irregular chest breathing which in turn results in more stress, locking us into a negative cycle. For example, anger and fear are inevitably associated with rapid, uneven, shallow breathing.

- Abdominal breathing, on the other hand, induces relaxation and has an immediate anti-anxiety effect. The heart rate slows, blood pressure decreases, and the mind and muscles relax. We regain our calm center and reduce the likelihood of getting stuck in a negative mental or emotional state.

- In addition to relaxation, abdominal breathing gives the body more oxygen, resulting in more energy.

- We should breathe abdominally when we feel well or when we have stress, restless thoughts, painful emotions, or fatigue.

- You can practice abdominal breathing as part of your morning and evening program or at any time. The goal is to make a habit of abdominal breathing.

Following are several wonderful breathing techniques.

FOCUSED ABDOMINAL BREATHING
WITH AFFIRMATIONS

1. Focus on your breath. Make a conscious effort to breathe slowly, regularly, quietly, smoothly, and deeply. Chest breathing is common when anxious or in pain. If this occurs, go back to slow, deep abdominal breathing.

2. Inhalation: Inhale slowly. Expand in this order:

   a. Abdomen
   b. Lower chest
   c. Upper chest

3. Exhalation: When you breathe out, exhale slowly, fully and completely. Squeeze all the air out of your lungs in reverse order:

   a. Upper chest
   b. Lower chest
   c. Abdomen

4. Affirm: Try any affirmation that makes you comfortable or simply focus on the breath. You might affirm:

   - Breathing gently, calming down.
   - Breathing gently, problem melts.

5. If the mind wanders, gently bring it back to the breath.

6. Breathe slow and deep five to ten minutes in your morning and

evening program, or any time of day. You might try ten to fifteen quiet, deep breaths whenever you need to refocus and energize.

7. If you feel light headed, stop for twenty to thirty seconds and then start again.

With practice, abdominal breathing replaces chest breathing. The result is a relaxed body, peace of mind, and vitality.

THE CALMING BREATH

This breathing exercise produces a feeling of peace. Practice the calming breath when you are anxious, restless, or at any time.

1. Make a conscious effort to make your breath slow, regular, quiet, smooth, and deep.

2. Inhalation: inhale fully to a count of eight.

3. Hold: hold the deep breath to a count of eight.

4. Exhalation: exhale fully to a count of eight.

5. You can count to two, four, six, twelve, or even up to twenty. Choose whatever number you wish. Use that same number for the inhalation, holding it, and the exhalation. It does not matter how fast you count.

6. Repeat this six to eight times in your morning and evening program, or any time of day.

THE BREATH OF FIRE

The breath of fire stimulates, energizes, and relaxes the body. Try it when you get up in the morning or any time you are sleepy, fatigued, or anxious.

1. With mouth closed, breathe through your nose at a rate of two to three breaths a second. One breath includes inhalation and exhalation.

2. The inhalations and exhalations are continuous, smooth, and of equal length.

3. Practice this exercise for fifteen to thirty seconds. Increase in small increments up to several minutes at a time.

THE BREATH AND EMOTIONAL PAIN MANAGEMENT

Abdominal breathing helps us work through emotional pain. This allows us to experience the truth of our feelings. When we process anger, anxiety, depression, and other difficult emotions, we gain self-knowledge and peace of mind.

1. Notice what you are feeling.

2. Remind yourself that repressed feelings remain, while processed feelings dissipate.

3. Breathe right into the center of the feeling. Sometimes just breathing into the feeling clears it.

4. If the feeling persists, stay with it and let it speak to you. When the feeling reveals its truths it moves on, and you gain self-knowledge. Refer to Chapter Twenty-Three, Transformation of Emotion, for additional details on emotional processing.

POINTS TO REMEMBER

• Abdominal breathing is one of the keys to physical, mental, emotional, and spiritual health.

- The way we breathe has a profound effect on how we feel.

- We do not have to practice breathing for months or years to get results. The relaxation response can occur immediately.

- Breath is always available. We can use it at any time to get centered, calm, comfortable, and still.

- Abdominal breathing increases our awareness of our body, feelings, and the environment.

- Breathwork helps dissolve painful emotions.

- Breathwork helps replace mental restlessness with peace of mind.

- Breathwork helps curb addiction and craving. Breathe right into the heart of the craving to make it disappear.

- Breathwork helps manage physical pain. Breathing into the pain helps to control fear and cultivate strength.

AFFIRMATIONS

Practice the following affirmations as you breathe slowly and deeply:

- Breathing gently, calming down.
- Breathing gently, problem melts.
- Aware of breath: relax-peace.
- Follow breath: relax-peace.
- Breathe in and out: relax-peace.
- Breathe deeply. Feel peace.
- Breathe deep. Feel better.
- Breathe deep. Nothing to fear.
- Breathe deep. Ready for anything.
- I use my breath to stay present.

- I relax my body. I calm my mind. Relax. Peace.
- I slow down my breathing to slow down my thoughts.
- I use my breath to heal myself.
- I fill my mind with thoughts of peace.
- Whatever comes, I can do.
- Fears examined melt away.
- Drop of water wears down stone.

EXERCISES

1. Describe the benefits of conscious breathing for the body, mind, emotions, and spirit.

2. What is the difference between chest and abdominal breathing?

3. Describe and practice focused abdominal breathing with affirmations.

4. Describe and practice the "calming breath."

5. Describe and practice the "breath of fire."

6. Practice deep abdominal breathing the next time you are upset or angry. Notice the effect.

7. Practice deep abdominal breathing the next time you are craving food, alcohol, drugs, or anything else you are trying to avoid. Notice the effect.

8. Practice deep abdominal breathing the next time you are suffering from physical pain. Notice the effect.

In the next chapter, you will study the third method of the morning and evening program: contemplation.

CHAPTER SIXTEEN

CONTEMPLATION

A Technique for Realizing Wisdom

"Contemplation for an hour is better than
formal worship for sixty years."
— Mohammed

• This chapter introduces contemplation, the third method of the morning and evening program.

• The contemplation of wisdom is a special method of study that allows us to realize the powerful knowledge hidden in the great wisdom texts. The Bible, Bhagavad Gita, Koran, and the poetry of Rumi, Hafiz, and Whitman are just a few examples. These texts are packed with pearls of wisdom that we can integrate into our being.

• You do not need a Higher Power or a religion to practice the contemplation of wisdom. All you need is some quiet time and your favorite wisdom, which can come from any source, secular or spiritual.

• The aim of ordinary reading, such as a newspaper or novel, is the accumulation of knowledge and/or entertainment. For these purposes, we generally read straight through without pause.

• Contemplation requires a different type of reading. Here the goal is cultivation of spiritual qualities for healing, pain management, and spiritual evolution.

- Following is a method of contemplative study. With this technique, we slow down our reading so we can go deep into our consciousness, in order to convert the words into personal realization.

TECHNIQUE

The pearls of wisdom found in sacred texts reflect the healing qualities that already exist within us. To realize any healing quality, set aside some time and follow these steps:

1. Choose a topic
2. Study
3. Affirm
4. Act
5. Introspect
6. Mastery

1. CHOOSE A TOPIC:

- Pick an area where you would like to do some work, such as becoming more compassionate.

2. STUDY:

- Find a quiet place to study. Eliminate all distractions: turn off the TV, radio, and telephone.

- Find a passage in your wisdom book having to do with compassion. Read this passage to get the overall picture.

- Go back and read the material again, this time jotting down the important points. When written, the material is impressed much deeper in the mind and consciousness.

3. AFFIRM:

- Affirm one complete thought. This may be a sentence, a few lines, or a paragraph.

- An example of a thought on compassion from the Dalai Lama is "The feeling of kindness, Love, and compassion is the essence of brotherhood and sisterhood. This compassionate feeling is the basis of inner peace."

- With your will and concentration, eliminate all other thoughts.

- Place the affirmation in the center of your being, and keep it there for several minutes. When your mind wanders, bring it back to your affirmation.

- Let the vibratory power of your affirmation spread throughout your body and surrounding space.

- Visualize yourself spreading Love, compassion, and kindness with each action throughout your day.

- If you know a technique of meditation, you can include your affirmation and visualization before and after your practice. Affirmations are most effective when the mind is relaxed and opened, as during meditation.

4. ACT:

- Place note cards with affirmations related to compassion in your shirt pocket or other convenient places. Pull these cards out when you have a spare moment.

- Review these affirmations as a reminder of your theme for the day.

- You might give your mind a one-word affirmation such as "compassion."

- Remember to let compassion be the governor of every thought, attitude, feeling, and action.

- Notice how an oft-repeated affirmation will come into your conscious mind automatically. This is a sign that compassion is becoming a mental habit.

- Through repetition and practice, compassion slowly expands.

5. INTROSPECT:

- In the evening, you can review your performance that day with respect to your chosen theme. When you fall short—and you will—take note of it and keep trying. For most of us, such a great quality as compassion requires a lifetime of practice. There will be many setbacks. This is natural.

- Do not allow your ego to slow your progress by denying mistakes and blaming others. Instead, humbly accept your limitations as part of the human condition. This will help you be more compassionate with yourself as well as others.

6. MASTERY:

- After many years of daily study and practice, compassion slowly takes hold, eventually becoming a habit. It guides all of your thoughts, feelings, and actions.

- As compassion slowly expands, it surrounds, feeds, permeates, and saturates every aspect of your being. In the end, you become compassion itself.

POINTS TO REMEMBER

- Without contemplation, the inherent healing power of wisdom pearls remains locked up, waiting, if not begging, for liberation. We have seen many preach about the enlightened life but come up short because they do not know how to transfer the life of the sacred written word into their daily lives. We can avoid this perilous trap by practicing contemplation.

- With contemplation, we can crack open the shell of a pearl of wisdom to reveal its hidden secrets and release its soothing healing powers.

- Through contemplative practice, we convert the great ideas and healing qualities embedded in wisdom texts from shallow words in our heads to real vibrations that permeate consciousness and action.

- Affirmations of Love, compassion, understanding, and kindness are healing vibrations that go to our cells and to the cells of other people.

- The contemplation of wisdom is in the hall of fame of cognitive-behavioral and spiritual practices. It converts such great qualities as compassion or any other healing quality or idea from the surface superficiality of mere words to feeling, experience, and action.

- It is good to have a positive thought in your mind. It is even better to let it drop down to the center of your being, permeate your entire consciousness, and become a part of who you are. Wisdom thoughts are faithful guides and protectors when they become one's constant companions.

- The healing qualities described in the great wisdom traditions are within us. We can understand them better in contemplation and embody them through repetitive action. With practice, patience, and perseverance, we expand and express these virtues in our thoughts, feelings, and actions. We become peace, joy, kindness, compassion, courage, and strength. This is realization of wisdom. It is a part of deep healing and full recovery.

- Include this powerful technique in your healing program. Start your morning and evening program with a period of contemplative study. You will see that it not only works but also is supremely enjoyable.

EXERCISES

1. What is the difference between ordinary reading and contemplative study?

2. You do not need a Higher Power or a religion to practice the contemplation of wisdom. All you need is some quiet time and your favorite positive thoughts, which can come from any source. Some people get their wisdom from spiritual writings or church. Others find it in secular work and the community. Others get it from their family, relationships, their conscience, or the Image of God or Buddha within. Some have street smarts. Where do you get your wisdom?

3. Describe the six steps for contemplating wisdom.

4. What healing quality would you like to develop? Choose a reading that reflects that quality. Follow the six steps for contemplating wisdom.

5. When you are alone and suffering, remember this: healing qualities—which are already inside of you—are more powerful than painful problems. We can make them grow by practicing contemplation. Find one of your favorite wisdom books, read a meaningful passage, and sit with it for a few minutes. Then focus on one thought and the healing quality it reflects. Place that

thought and healing quality at the center of your consciousness, and let it spread to every atom and fiber of your being as well as the space surrounding you. Notice how your pain is slowly contained, reduced, or eliminated as Love, peace, compassion, courage, and strength grow.

6. Describe how the ego interferes with the growth of healing qualities.

7. What is realization of wisdom?

8. Why is introspection necessary for realizing wisdom?

9. Fill your brain with wisdom in the morning. It will set the tone for the rest of the day.

10. It takes time to cultivate the true compassion of a master, or to develop any of the wonderful healing qualities in the spiritual alphabet. Be patient and humble—your growth will slow down if you make the mistake of thinking you have already mastered the qualities. Acknowledge your limitations. With consistent daily practice, the qualities slowly grow until they become the unconditional, spontaneous, and automatic habits of a sage.

In the next chapter, you will study meditation, the fourth method of the morning and evening program. You will learn how to bring stillness into your program.

CHAPTER SEVENTEEN

MEDITATION

A Technique for All Seasons

- This chapter introduces the principles of meditation, describes its risks and benefits, and outlines a practice technique. Here you will learn how to replace negative thought with positive thought and positive thought with stillness. When you add stillness to your program, problems are contained, reduced, and eliminated. You become a more skillful pain manager. Your healing qualities grow. You feel better, become a better person, and experience higher states of consciousness.

- In our culture, we are encouraged to surround ourselves continuously with stimulating activities. Between work, relationships, recreation, sports, the arts, radio, television, the Internet, magazines, and newspapers, we have plenty to keep us busy. Most of us have become activity junkies, staying in motion the entire day.

- In response to the barrage of continuous happenings in the outside world, the mind becomes restless and hyperactive, getting no rest except in sleep. We crave peace of mind, but we have distracted ourselves from the tranquility that is only found in the stillness and silence at the core of our beings. Meditation—an ancient technique currently undergoing a revival in popularity—brings such inner peace. During meditation, the body and mind slow progressively, eventually reaching absolute stillness.

- Right now, there is a place inside of us that is absolutely still and quiet, but our mental restlessness bars us from entering. The hyper-

245

active mind keeps us from even knowing it is there. Meditation is the solution to this problem.

• When you learn how to meditate, you will be able to slow the mind down, replace negative thought with positive thought, and, eventually, get into the room of stillness. The experience of peace in the room of stillness surpasses understanding; there you will find beauty, joy, compassion, light, energy, power, elation, and ecstasy.

• Before introducing the meditation technique, it will be helpful to review how the mind works when it is in alignment and doing its job correctly and what happens when it becomes misaligned and turns into a liability.

MENTAL HEALTH

THE MIND IN ALIGNMENT

• The mind does its best work when it is *positive, calm, focused, strong,* and *resilient*. In this position, it is our best friend. It helps us create, shape meaning, solve problems, accomplish goals, manage pain, and heal. It remains peaceful and poised no matter what the world and body throw at it. It is ready for anything. This is the definition of good mental health.

• Unfortunately, the mind doesn't always work this well. When presented with stressful problems, the mind goes out of control. Instead of helping us manage our problems, it adds untold suffering. Instead of acting as our best friend, it becomes our worst enemy. What happens?

MENTAL DISTRESS

THE MIND OUT OF ALIGNMENT

• All kinds of events impinge on the screen of the mind—events from our inner being, from our bodies, and from the outer world. Some of these events are painful and frightening, harsh, or even brutal; they can be difficult to manage. In response to this barrage of events, the mind becomes restless and hyperactive and, aside from sleep, gets no rest.

- The mind is highly sensitive and reactive. When stressed, it takes off into a great variety of negative states spontaneously and automatically, against our will. Sometimes these negative patterns are quiet, subtle, and difficult to detect. At other times, they create their own bad weather: tornadoes, hurricanes, cyclones, and a variety of noisy storms—all for nothing.

- The mind creates untold and unnecessary fear, insecurity, worry, and doubt. It knots us up like a pretzel, makes us feel terrible, and keeps us from effective action. Like a robber, it steals our peace and replaces it with profound and unnecessary torment and suffering.

- Meditation offers a solution to the dilemma of mental restlessness. It brings us to the room of stillness, where healing qualities such as Love, peace, compassion, courage, and strength slowly grow. The mind returns to its position of peace and poise.

DEEP HEALING IN THE ROOM OF STILLNESS

- There is a place inside that is absolutely still, silent, spacious, and serene. Here we feel safe and protected. This is called the room of stillness. In this room, the most profound healing takes place.

- In the room of stillness, we reach the deep healing power of the spiritual qualities, which slowly and subtly overpower our ego and our problems. In the stillness of deep meditation, Love burns up hate, kindness dissolves cruelty, courage defeats fear, and hope replaces despair. When we come out of meditation, the priceless gems of Love, kindness, courage, and hope permeate our thoughts, feelings, and actions. With renewed strength and courage, we are in a better position to manage the harsh realities of life and can help others do the same. Stillness provides the opportunity for deepest healing.

FIVE STAGES OF MEDITATION

- There are five stages of meditation, each with a greater degree of stillness. The progression from one stage to the next is dependent on meditating longer and deeper. Although these stages are progressive, they are not mutually exclusive. There is overlap. They are separated here for descriptive purposes only. The stages are:

- STAGE 1: MEDITATION FOR THE BODY. The relaxation response.

- STAGE 2: MEDITATION FOR THE MIND. A positive, calm, focused, strong, and resilient mind.

- STAGE 3: MEDITATION FOR THE SOUL. No mind; a shift in identity to the soul; an expansion of healing qualities; stillness.

- STAGE 4: MEDITATION ON THE HIGHER POWER. Communion, guidance, protection, intuition, prayer, and further expansion of healing qualities.

- STAGE 5: INFINITY. A dramatic transformation of consciousness sometimes referred to as liberation or enlightenment; the full blossom of healing qualities.

- *As you move through these stages, there is a natural progression from negative thought to positive thought to stillness to higher states of consciousness.*

STAGE 1: MEDITATION FOR THE BODY
THE RELAXATION RESPONSE

- The non-meditating mind is restless and hyperactive. This is the active state from which we all start. The first step up from this level is meditation for the body.

- When we focus on a single point such as a word, phrase, or the breath, our thought process slows down. The heart, lungs, muscles, brain, and every other organ, tissue, and cell in the body relax. The heart rate, respiratory rate, and blood pressure decrease, as does the rate at which the body burns energy. This profound effect is called the relaxation response, the easiest level of meditation. It can occur in a few minutes.

- The relaxation response is good for health and healing: the trillions of cells in the body get a chance to regenerate, repair, and resist disease. Meditation helps us manage chronic pain, insomnia, high blood pressure, and any condition caused or worsened by stress.

- For some, these health benefits are reason enough to meditate. For others, there are additional motivations such as strengthening the mind with positive thoughts and deeper peace.

STAGE 2: MEDITATION FOR THE MIND
A POSITIVE, CALM, FOCUSED, STRONG AND RESILIENT MIND

- In the first stage of meditation, there is no attempt to restructure thinking. There is simply a slowing down of the mind. In stage two, the goal is to slow the mind down further and replace negative with positive thoughts by using the technique of affirmation.

- Affirmations are particularly effective during and right after meditation; the mind is more receptive at this time. Meditation helps clear the soil of our consciousness of hyperactivity so that we can plant new ideas and suggestions. When we restructure negative or distorted patterns of thought with affirmations, we reframe problems in a realistic, positive way.

- You might review the lesson on affirmations and practice this technique during meditation. The combination of meditation and affirmations results in a strong, positive, calm mind. When the mind is peaceful and positive, it is better able to create success in relationships and activities, deal with painful problems in the school of life, and foster our enjoyment of life.

- For some, the achievement of a positive, strong, calm mind is sufficient motivation to meditate. Others may be interested in the next phase of meditation, discovery of the soul. With longer and deeper meditation, it is possible to bring the mind to a position of complete stillness. This leads to the discovery of the soul and expansion of spiritual qualities.

STAGE 3: MEDITATION FOR THE SOUL
NO MIND; STILLNESS

- The goal in stage one is to slow the mind down and relax the body. The goal in stage two is to further slow the mind and replace negative thoughts with positive. The goal in Stage 3 is to proceed with slowing the mind down to complete stillness. We transition from negative to positive thought and from positive thought to stillness.

- Stopping the internal dialogue is referred to in Buddhism as "no mind" or "empty mind." To bring the mind to complete stillness requires longer and deeper practice.

- The path of progressively greater degrees of stillness in meditation leads ultimately to the soul. The soul is always completely still, no matter what tempest is happening outside. The soul, also known as the witness, is our true identity and the home of all of the spiritual qualities. We can find the soul, the place of perfect peace, inside, through meditation, whether we are in a personal or impersonal relationship with our Higher Power.

- To find the soul in the stillness of meditation is a valuable skill. It not only brings deep peace no matter the external condition, but also reveals our true identity. It is in this stillness that we see our consciousness not completely identified with our body, mind, ego, and the external drama of life. We can see that we are the soul, that we are warm, compassionate, loving, courageous, and strong. It is difficult to get to this state of higher consciousness. It takes years of daily practice.

- On the way to progressively greater degrees of stillness, the mind continues to churn with all kinds of useless thoughts related to our concerns and insecurities. These thoughts come like waves, one after another. We are unable to stop them. However, we can counter them with our mantra, breath, prayer, affirmations, and visualizations. We can replace negative thoughts with positive thoughts. In addition, we can watch thoughts come and go from the witness, the place of stillness inside.

- To reach the soul, we need to stop identifying with our thoughts as though they were the ultimate judges of reality. We must reduce the power of our thoughts so that we can give control of our consciousness back to the soul. We can do this in meditation by watching our train of thoughts without getting aboard the train. The mind will go on and on indefinitely, even after we start meditating. However, rather than being swept along with the movement on the train of thought, we can simply watch it go by, noting that thoughts are merely thoughts. They are not the whole of reality. They are not who we are. They are not in control of our lives. In this way, we can reduce their importance, their charge, and their ruling power.

- As meditation proceeds and the mind quiets, we have a chance to step back from the drama of life and view the story as if it were a movie or a play. We are still actors, but now rather than identify with the characters we play, we become the observer or witness. This detachment gives us a chance to relax in the face of our troubles. We gain perspective and objectivity as we begin to see that we are not our thoughts, ego, problems, or role in the drama. As we step out of the movie-mind and approach the soul, we realize that our ego and problems must be dealt with, but they are not who we are. We are the soul, a composite of the most wonderful qualities.

- If we practice with diligence and discipline, if we persist and refuse to quit, if we give it our best over days, weeks, months, and years, slowly but surely the mind calms and is replaced by stillness. There are progressively greater degrees of quiet resulting in a state of absolute stillness.

- When we enter and delve into this domain of stillness, we arrive at a state where we want to be all the time. Here we find the peace that surpasses understanding, a Love that is pure, perfect, and unconditional, and a joy so intense that we call it ecstasy. This is a place of no pain and no problems, where nothing can harm us and nothing can touch us. This is the soul.

No weapon can pierce the soul; no fire can burn it; no water can moisten it; nor can any wind wither it. The soul is uncleavable; it cannot be burnt or wetted or dried. The soul is immutable, all-permeating, ever-calm, and immovable—eternally the same.
The Bhagavad Gita: Chapter II: verse 23-24. P. 221-223
Paramahansa Yogananda

- When we stop the waves of activity from the world, body, senses, and mind and sit in the stillness and spaciousness of deep meditation, we absorb strength, courage, compassion, and wisdom. We become who we really are: compassionate, loving, serviceful human beings, capable of managing any problem or pain in the school of life. We enjoy the show in the theatre of life. We are ready for anything, including meditation at the next level, communion with our Higher Power.

STAGE 4:
MEDITATION WITH OUR HIGHER POWER
RECEPTIVITY AND ATTUNEMENT

- There is an Omniscient, Omnipotent, Omnipresent Power that is in us, surrounds us, and extends outward and endlessly in every direction. By making contact with this power in meditation, we can get help for others, the world, and ourselves. We can get guidance, healing, advancement in the development of any spiritual quality, and help with pain and problems.

- Meditation is an ideal time for communion with our Higher Power; stillness promotes receptivity and attunement. For those who have a personal relationship with their God, this is a good time to pray, talk, share, listen, and feel. When the mind and body are still, we can send and receive with more clarity than when the mind is restless.

STAGE 5: INFINITY
DEEP, VAST, STILL, AND CHANGELESS

- This stage is reserved for highly evolved souls: saints, sages, gurus, and masters. After many years of deep and long meditation, prayer, and service to humanity, there can be a dramatic transformation in consciousness, sometimes referred to as liberation or enlightenment. This experience is like entering an infinite ocean of Spirit.

- Think of life as an ocean. On the surface of the ocean are waves. At times, the surface is calm. Other times, the waves are variously choppy, turbulent, stormy, or dangerous. Beneath the surface, the ocean is deep, vast, still, ubiquitous, and immutable. Consider the deep part of the ocean as a vast repository of healing qualities and higher states of consciousness.

- Now think of the waves as change in life and the underlying ocean as that part of life that is changeless. In ordinary consciousness, we bob about on the surface of the ocean, riding the waves of change. Our awareness remains tethered to the changing waves at the surface by our restless mind, volatile emotions, excessive material desires, the body, hyperactivity, and egotism (Step 5, Tools Become Barriers).

- When we reach absolute stillness and relinquish our mind, our consciousness can slip beneath the changing surface waves of the ocean and merge into the depths of the vast Changeless One below. This results in a magnificent shift in consciousness: unity, infinity, and eternity replace limitation, division, and impermanence. In advanced yoga meditation, this is called *samadhi*. Here there is absolute safety and protection from the problems of the body and the problems of the world.

- Entry tickets to this realm of superconsciousness are reserved for those who have achieved an egoless state of highly developed spiritual qualities. In this stage, the advanced meditator bathes in an infinite ocean of peace, joy, Love, power, wisdom, and other soul qualities. Some get to travel. The vehicle for travel in this neighborhood is fearlessness. The fuel is Love. The destination is other worlds.

- Those who enter the greater world of Spirit return to the surface world of duality to share with us what they have found, not with words so much as through acts of gentle, humble service. They are able to manifest and express their soul qualities under all conditions. With calm and strong minds, powerful Love, durable faith, and courage, they are ready for anything.

- The Love of such an advanced soul is palpable and tangible. If we are receptive, we can receive and feel their loving power through attunement. Many students try to spend too much time with such masters in order to receive their power, but the true spiritual adept will direct the student to practices that will allow them to gain these spiritual qualities for themselves. Meditation is one such method, a power tool of the ages and of great importance to our work in cultivating peace, Love, joy, power, and wisdom.

RISKS

- Now that you have reviewed the benefits of meditation and before you begin your practice, please review the following statement about risks.

- Meditation is not without risks. Some people become frightened rather than relaxed. Old wounds can be stirred up. You might experience a flood of emotional or mental anguish.

- Some find meditation useful in working through such periods of agitation or crisis. Others cannot meditate when in crisis but can meditate later when they feel better. Some should not meditate under any conditions.

- If your meditation causes a frightening increase in inner turmoil or symptoms, stop temporarily and consult with an expert in mental health and meditation.

- Presented below is one of many approaches to meditation. You can explore this or other methods until you find what works best for you. It may be of great value to have a teacher of meditation.

THE TECHNIQUE

1. Sacred space
2. Posture

3. Release all concerns
4. The breath
5. Prayer or affirmation
6. Mantra
7. Concentration
8. Stillness
9. Prayer
10. Closure and re-entry

1. SACRED SPACE:

• Go to a quiet place in your home. Try to return to the same place each time. This is your sacred space. You might want to build an altar. Turn off the phone and all other distractions so you can remain undisturbed for the duration of your meditation.

2. POSTURE:

• Sit on a chair with your back straight and make yourself comfortable. You may prefer to sit on a cushion on the floor with legs crossed or in the lotus position. Close your eyes and lift your gaze to the point just above and between your eyebrows. Try to keep your attention fixed on this point throughout meditation. This is known as the third or spiritual eye. If you notice your attention has shifted to a lower level, gently bring it back up. There should be no strain of the eyes when you do this. Relax your body and all muscles. During the meditation, keep your body as still and relaxed as possible for as long as you can.

3. RELEASE ALL CONCERNS:

• Relax your mind, releasing all thoughts, concerns, and problems. Forget everything and everybody. Let go of the drama of life for the period of this meditation. Use your will to toss out the world and all its problems, cares, and concerns. Relax and surrender to the stillness and peace that is always present within you.

4. THE BREATH:

- Breathe slowly and naturally as you adopt a quiet, open, receptive state.

5. PRAYER OR AFFIRMATION:

- Start your meditation with a prayer, affirmation, or visualization that relates to peace and compassion for yourself and all people. In this way, the heart progressively opens.

6. MANTRA:

- Pick a word or brief phrase that comes from your belief system. Repeat it silently. Words such as "one," "ocean," "Love," "peace," "harmony," "our Father who art in heaven," "shalom," or "om" can be used. You might try focusing on your breath without the repetition of a mantra. If you try this method, make your breathing slow, quiet, and regular. Your mantra or point of focus will protect you from the turmoil of the world and the restlessness of your own mind.

7. CONCENTRATION:

- Try to maintain your concentration on the mantra. You will notice your mind wander off into its typical pattern of mental chatter. As soon as you notice that your mind has drifted off, bring it gently back to the mantra. This pattern of going back and forth between the mantra and the routine chatter of the mind is a natural process of meditation. Do not worry about how well you are doing. When thoughts return, gently return to the point of focus. Do not strain.

The correct position is calm concentration without tension. Gradually, thinking slows and finally stops.

8. STILLNESS:

The ever-increasing stillness bred of meditation brings the body and mind to a state of deep peace, rest, and relaxation. When you stop the superficial waves of thought and are immersed in stillness, relax and feel the peace. Don't think. *In this state of open, quiet receptivity and stillness,*

    a. *Healing qualities grow.*
    b. *The ego shrinks.*
    c. *Problems burn up.*

9. PRAYER:

- Toward the end of your meditation, you can commune with your Higher Power, seeking guidance, protection, or healing for yourself and others. You can close your meditation with a prayer for all who need help as well as *for harmony and peace between all individuals, nations, races, and religions.*

10. CLOSURE AND RE-ENTRY:

- Do not stand immediately when you are finished. Continue to sit quietly, enjoying the peace that occurs from slowing down your mind. Then open your eyes and sit for another moment before rising. You are now prepared to give the benefits that you have gained from meditation to all who need your help. Your peace, joy, Love, and other healing qualities grow in meditation. You will be able to offer these to your loved ones and to all whom you meet.

- Meditate for ten to twenty minutes in the morning and evening.

If this is too long, meditate for even one minute at a time. You can gradually extend this as motivation and time allow.

- Some will meditate on a regular basis. Others will meditate whenever it feels right or fits into their schedule. Best results occur with regular, long, deep meditation. Advanced practice can be one to two hours, twice a day. Longer meditations of three to ten hours are reserved for special occasions or retreats. You can increase your time in meditation slowly according to your desires and needs. The amount of time spent in meditation can vary depending on your level of responsibilities to family and work and on your desire to go inward.

WHAT TO EXPECT

There are three common experiences in meditation:

1. WORK. It felt like a lot of work, and nothing special happened.

2. PAIN. It was difficult and maybe even painful. The most common difficulties are restlessness, boredom, and frustration with the rebellious mind that will not quit thinking about everything. There may be physical or psychological discomfort. Many are afraid to look inward for fear of what they might discover.

3. HIGHER CONSCIOUSNESS. We experience stillness, peace, beauty, joy, Love, compassion, light, energy, power, elation, or ecstasy. Often, however, these results are subtle. If we look for a big experience, we may miss the more refined changes in our vibration or consciousness. We want elation all of the time, but this is not possible. In order to get to the higher states, it is best to have no expectations, anticipating some of the meditations to be work, slightly difficult or painful, or nothing special.

RESULTS ARE SLOW,
CUMULATIVE, AND LIFELONG

- Think of the results of a meditative practice as a lifelong process of ever-increasing relaxation of the body, peace of mind, and opening of the heart. Do not worry about your progress, expertise, or whether or not you had a good meditation. Just practice.

- In the beginning, you may not feel anything special. Although some may feel results immediately, for most, it is likely to be difficult at first. Do not be discouraged. This is usual. Since the benefits emerge slowly, patience is helpful.

- As with all spiritual practices, effort is progress. If you are meditating, you are making progress. You will succeed if you let the process unfold on its own schedule, have no expectations, and make no demands. If you persist, it gets easier. In the beginning, you may not want to sit. Later, you will not want to get up.

REGULARITY

- The key to success in meditation is regularity. Mastery is achieved through practice, as with any discipline or art. Think of playing the piano or any instrument. Without practice, there can be no progress. For best results, meditate in the morning and evening.

BRIEF MEDITATION

- You can meditate for a few minutes any time of day. Once meditation is part of your daily routine, try meditating briefly wherever you may be. Tense the whole body for a few seconds and relax your muscles. This releases physical tension. Breathe slowly and deeply, then focus on your mantra for a few minutes.

BURNING UP PROBLEMS IN THE STILLNESS OF MEDITATION

- Many have a habit of thinking about their problems during meditation. This is very seductive; we think we are doing good work by facing our issues and working on them. To a degree, this is true. It is a good idea to set aside some time to reflect and learn from our experiences. The description of how to do this is in the lesson on Transformation of Emotion described in Chapter Twenty-Three. This is self-knowledge born of introspection, not meditation. The purpose of meditation is stillness through concentration.

- Thinking about problems is one of the tricks the mind will play on you, as it resists stillness by staying active. Your problems are important and require work and thought, but not in meditation. *What is important during meditation is getting beneath the thought waves on the surface and into the stillness below, for absorption of healing qualities.* In order to do this, you have to free your mind of all thoughts, including those related to problem solving. Whenever you become aware that you are thinking, return to your mantra. It is through concentrating on your mantra that you can attain stillness.

- When you try to focus on your mantra and find your mind keeps going to a problem, ask yourself, "Is this problem solving or rumination?" If it is problem solving, review Chapter Twenty-Three, Transformation of Emotion. When you decide it is rumination, keep going back to your mantra to get out of the negative habitual mental rut that has no function at this point.

- Now, review Step 8 of the technique of meditation: STILLNESS. When you stop the superficial waves of thought and are immersed in stillness, relax and feel the peace. Don't think. *In this state of open, quiet receptivity and stillness, spiritual qualities grow, the ego shrinks, and problems burn up.*

- In the room of stillness, we reach the deep healing power of the spiritual qualities. It is here, in stillness, that we slowly and subtly replace our problems with spiritual qualities. Spiritual qualities are healing powers. They have more power than our problems. In the stillness of meditation, Love burns up hate, kindness dissolves cruelty, courage defeats fear, and hope replaces despair. When we come out of meditation, the priceless gems of Love, kindness, courage, and hope radiate their light through our thoughts, speech, and actions.

- Bring deeper and longer meditation into your daily practice to speed up the evolution of your healing and recovery. The mind, every cell in the body, and the soul crave the serenity bred of deep meditation.

POINTS TO REMEMBER

- Everything that happens to us passes through the mind. The mind is like a receiving station that gets messages from the outside world, our bodies, and our inner being. The mind cannot avoid the pictures coming at it from the outside world. It is as though there is a movie going on that won't quit. The mind is also subject to the messages of the body and the inner being, messages that convey cold, heat, hunger, fatigue, pain, fear, anger, and sadness, to name just a few examples. Most of what is coming at us from both the outside and inside is beyond our control, but we can control how we respond mentally. We can reframe the pictures coming at us from the outside world in the direction of our choice. We can shape the meaning of the story of our experience toward recovery and healing. Those who persist in their practice of meditation experience ever-increasing peace of mind. There is a progressive ability to stay calm no matter what the world or body throws at us. The mind is peaceful and poised, ready for anything.

- Every painful problem has a mental component because it must pass through the mind. The mind can make the problem worse by following one of its negative habit patterns, or it can help contain, reduce, and, sometimes, completely eliminate the problem. In meditation, we can restructure the mind's habitual negative responses into positive healing qualities.

- The mind has great negative and positive power. It can lock us up in our own body-prison or liberate us into higher states of consciousness. You can remain a prisoner of your own mental restlessness, or you can use your mind to heal, manage your pain, and cultivate ever-increasing peace, joy, Love, power, and wisdom.

- We gain access to a reservoir of untapped healing power by focusing the mind where we want it to be rather than letting it have its way with us.

- Stillness is key. Stillness expands healing qualities such as compassion, Love, understanding, courage, strength, and patience. Then we can use these qualities to more skillfully manage our painful problems in the school of life.

- In meditation, healing qualities such as patience, kindness, and compassion grow. We feel better and become better people.

- We can more gracefully give Love, compassion, and understanding when the mind is calm than when it is restless and hyperactive.

- In meditation, there is a natural progression from negative thought to positive thought to stillness to higher states of consciousness. You might want to reserve defining the nature of your Higher Power until you experience higher states of consciousness. Premature discussion or formulation might be an intellectual exercise without the benefit of experiential data.

- Positive thought is good, but the peace experienced in the room of stillness is even better; there is no thought—only stillness, silence, spaciousness, and serenity.

- We can use people and activities to satisfy a part of the core drive on the horizontal axis, but the ultimate fulfillment is Love and safety in the room of stillness. The room of stillness offers protection from all conditions of the world and of the body. The room is not just an idea—it is a place, an experience. This advanced stage is difficult to achieve. It takes years of long and deep meditation. With practice, you can get into the room of stillness. At mastery, you can stay there.

- When we get comfortable with the contemplative practices of the great traditions such as meditation, we learn to treasure our connection to the silence and stillness within. As we advance in healing, we balance our active outer life with an inner life of tranquility. The benefits of adding the dimension of stillness to our healing program are profound.

AFFIRMATIONS

- In meditation, I still my wandering mind and eliminate all thoughts.
- In the stillness of meditation, I discover the deep, permanent peace that has been with me all along.
- In meditation, soul qualities replace my ego. I become strong, calm, understanding, and patient.
- In the room of stillness, I feel absolute safety and protection.
- The deepest healing is in the room of stillness.
- In the room of stillness, I commune with my Higher Power. I speak to my God with devotion. The still, small voice within shows me the way.
- Stillness, silence, spaciousness, serenity.

EXERCISES

1. Describe the five stages of meditation.

2. Practice progressive muscle relaxation before meditation. This relaxes the body, making meditation easier.

3. Review and practice the meditation technique described in this chapter.

4. The key to success in meditation is regular practice, just as with playing a musical instrument. Without regularity, you will still be a beginner in twenty years. Occasional practice does not work. We need to practice in the morning and the evening. Develop the habit of meditation for ten to twenty minutes at the beginning and end of your day. If this is too long, start with one to two minutes. Expand from there in small increments. The results are cumulative, slow but sure. The more you practice, the more you feel the effects. There may be phenomenal experiences at first, but meditation is not just joy. It is work.

5. One of the keys to success in meditation is balancing concentration with relaxation. Bring your power of concentration to your mantra and relax your body and mind at the same time. Intense concentration does not require strain. The correct position is calm concentration without tension. Never strain during your practice. When you strain, you lose the goal of meditation, which is peace. When you learn how to do this, you will become progressively more awake, alert, aware, and calm.

6. What is the difference between self-knowledge born of introspection and meditation?

7. Describe how meditation reduces problems, shrinks the ego, and expands healing qualities.

8. When stressed, your mind can be your best friend or your worst enemy. When you are having problems, notice if your mind stays positive and poised or if it goes into one of its negative habit patterns and adds to your trouble. Try meditation for a few months and see if this makes a difference.

9. There are two outcomes you can follow from your meditation practice: First, how far in or deep did you go in meditation? Second, when you come out of meditation, how well are you able to manifest the quality you are cultivating—for example, even-mindedness under all conditions or compassion for all of humanity?

10. Meditation reduces stress and anxiety. This fact alone is reason enough to meditate. What's more, our overall physical and mental health improves with meditation. Those who commit long-term to their meditation practices will discover *stillness is the springboard to higher states of consciousness.* You don't need a God or even a theory about the cosmos to explore this terrain. Just go there and see what happens. When you get into the room of stillness, stop, wait, and be patient. Stay there as long as you can. Does the invisible door of stillness open? Did you experience expansion, ecstasy, light, or some other aspect? Later, you can develop your theory or concept based on what happens to you in stillness. For many, it is the higher states of consciousness described throughout this book. What would it be for you?

11. Consider finding a meditation teacher and group. Group meditation reinforces individual effort and experience.

   In the next chapter, you will study prayer, the fifth and final method of the morning and evening program.

CHAPTER EIGHTEEN

PRAYER

Communion with Your Higher Power

- This chapter introduces prayer, the fifth and final technique of the morning and evening program.

- There is a time for joy and a time for struggle. The brutal reality of death, suffering, and the unknown mysteriously loops its way through the show of our lives, making its appearance in a variety of costumes without apparent cause or reason. We do what we can to understand the mystery while we position ourselves in the drama. We work with will, thought, and action to achieve our goals. We use our inner and outer resources to work with and through our problems. Nevertheless, when we have finished our work, we remain vulnerable. Some problems linger. We suffer. We feel isolated, disconnected, and separate.

- To get help, we pray. Prayer is a telephone call to our Higher Power as Friend, Counselor, Guide, Protector, Father, Mother, Beloved, Teacher, Healer, Higher Self, or higher states of consciousness. We seek counsel, support, knowledge, protection, solace, power, understanding, healing, forgiveness, and communion. We try to influence circumstances, conditions, and events in our immediate environment as well as in environments thousands of miles away.

- Although controversy remains, there is scientific evidence that prayer works.

Following is a description of some elements that may contribute to the effectiveness of prayer:

1. ONENESS. There is a unified field of intelligent consciousness, an Omnipotent Power that underlies and unites all. When we invoke this vast healing power, it helps those we are praying for and ourselves. We do not enter this field. We are already in it. It is already in us. There is no separation. All is one. In prayer, we remind ourselves that this power is inside, outside, everywhere, extending forever in every direction, uniting all things and people.

2. HUMILITY. In ego consciousness, we feel separate from the vast healing power in and around us. In fact, were the ego to have its way, we would not even believe in the possibility of getting help from a Higher Power. Furthermore, the ego does not like to admit we have problems. To get help from a Higher Power, we need to identify our problems and know our limitations. This requires ego reduction. When we reduce our ego and accept our powerlessness, we create a channel for the flow of God's healing power. While we do all we can to achieve our goals and solve our problems, we ask for help from Omnipresent Intelligence.

3. INDIVIDUALITY. Prayer consistent with our individuality and belief system gives meaning and comfort. We can create our own ritual and pray with our own heartfelt words.

4. STILLNESS. Prayer is most effective when the mind is still. Some methods that promote stillness are meditation, progressive muscle relaxation, affirmations, breathing, mindfulness, practicing the Presence of God, yoga, and will training. Stillness is essential during prayer, allowing us to make contact with higher, subtle, vibratory realms where we can follow the command, "Be still and know that I am God." By listening to the still, small voice within, we can be aware of new thoughts and feelings that come in response

to prayer. When still, we are more receptive to help, blessings, and guidance from God.

5. CONCENTRATION. In prayer, we open a channel of communication between the Omnipresent healing power and ourselves. The channel is most open when we focus exclusively on the perfect healing power of Spirit and the object of our prayer. All other thoughts should be eliminated. When we reach a high degree of concentration, we become one with the object of our prayer. The more we concentrate, the more powerful our prayer.

6. VISUALIZATION. In visualization, we imagine the desired goal of the prayer. The image should be as clear and specific as possible. For example, we can visualize a white healing light dissolving away disease, flaws, or imperfection.

7. DEVOTION. We can connect to the Omniscient, Omnipresent healing power through Love and compassion. Prayer is most effective when it comes from the heart, from our passion, and from our pain.

8. WILL POWER. Will power is an essential element in prayer. Do not give up after one or two tries. Be patient and keep praying with intensity. Help does not come on our schedule.

9. FAITH. Doubt and disbelief undermine the power of prayer. Faith connects us with the infinite healing power of God and the possibility of getting help.

10. AWARENESS. Remain open and aware. Help comes in many ways, often subtle and different from our expectations. There may be a response through our thoughts, feelings, desires, or actions. We might hear the still, small voice within. We may see changes in other people, events, circumstances, or conditions. There may be

guidance or protection, arrival of resources, lessons to learn, or an
expansion of healing qualities.

11. ACCEPTANCE. After we pray, we do all we can to solve our problem. Then we accept the outcome and surrender in peace to life as
it is. We acknowledge pain and tragedy as part of the natural way
of things. We resist the desire of the ego to be ruler of the universe.
Rather than trying to control events, we gain an appreciation for
the unfolding of the story, no matter which direction it takes. We
must be willing to bask in the mystery, tolerate ambiguity, and
face the unknown. We accept on faith that what occurs, including
continued struggle, is best.

We align ourselves with what is, acknowledging that God knows
what we need more than we do. We surrender to God's will through
attunement and receptivity, believing there is meaning and order in
the face of mystery and suffering. We trust that the healing power
knows what to do. "God is the Doer, not I." "Thy will be done, not
mine."

12. PEACE. While the reasons for the outcome improving, deteriorat-
ing, or staying the same may be beyond our understanding, acceptance brings tranquility of the soul. While there is a time for
struggle and a time for joy, the ultimate lesson is to transfer the locus of control from outside to inside, where serenity is ever-present.
When we completely accept the outcome, we contact our inner
stillness and silence. In that quiet place, we accept all outcomes
as part of the drama. When we make peace with life, the serenity
that is always there begins to emerge. As this peace grows, the soul
heals. Surrender takes us deep, to the domain of the soul, where we
cannot be touched, hurt, cut, or burned.

TECHNIQUE

1. Invoke

2. Request
3. Act
4. Grace
5. Accept
6. Peace

1. INVOKE. With humility and reverence, invoke the Presence of God. Bring in as much concentration, devotion, and stillness as you can. This sets up a channel of operations for the infinitely intelligent, healing power of God.

2. REQUEST. We can ask for:

- Essential needs such as safety, food, clothing, or shelter
- Help with work or relationships
- Healing or purification of body, mind, and soul
- Healing relationships between individuals, groups, races, religions, and nations
- World peace
- Peace of mind
- To become a better person by growth of any one or a combination of spiritual qualities
- Forgiveness
- Receptivity to the help, guidance, and blessing that is always there
- The Presence of God as peace, joy, Love, or wisdom
- Insight about the nature of our problems and ways to work with them
- Help and guidance for our problems
- Answers to our questions
- Alignment with God's will. In stillness and silence, we pray for the experience of God's presence without asking for anything but His will.
- Success, wealth, or fame

3. ACT. We use our will, thought, and actions to do what we can to change or remove a condition or circumstance. For illness, we may try medicines, surgery, special diets, or other healing practices. During activity, we can practice mindfulness or the Presence of God to stay connected, attuned, and receptive to His guidance.

4. GRACE. There is a partnership between God and us. We do our part by exercising thought, will, and action. We maintain awareness of His healing presence and guidance, and we ask for help. God does His part. He determines the outcome, and we do our part by accepting it.

5. ACCEPT. Surrender to whatever the results may be. When we do not get what we ask for, we can trust that this is best and look for lessons in our not receiving.

6. PEACE. We gain serenity of the soul by accepting the outcome, whatever it may be.

POINTS TO REMEMBER

• Prayer is an expression of our unity with God and all people. In prayer, we connect to an Omniscient, Omnipresent power through the cultivation of Love and compassion. With this Love, we ask for help for others and ourselves.

• We can pray for something and get it. We can pray for something and not get it. We can also pray and not ask for anything. We just commune with our Higher Power. With an attitude of complete faith, devotion, and surrender, we do not attempt to change the course of life's drama. With reverence, gratitude, and humility, we extract the lessons from life and enjoy life as it is. In prayers of gratitude and devotion, we express thankfulness for our many blessings, and give our Love to God.

- We can have a joyful conversation with God or speak to God with a single word. We can also pray without words. God is in our hearts. He already knows what we need. There is great beauty in communing with God in silence.

- In our prayers for world peace, we can ask God to impact the hearts and minds of our leaders.

- We can change the world by changing ourselves. Pray to become a better person. Pray for Love, understanding, and wisdom. This is the practical way to change the world.

EXERCISES

1. Describe the elements that contribute to the effectiveness of prayer.

2. Describe the six steps in the technique for praying.

3. You are now equipped with five techniques that comprise a morning and evening program. In the beginning, set aside forty-five to sixty minutes and practice these techniques:

   a. Progressive muscle relaxation: ten minutes
   b. Breathwork: five minutes
   c. Contemplation: fifteen to twenty minutes
   d. Meditation: ten to twenty minutes
   e. Prayer: five minutes

You have finished your review of the five morning and evening techniques. In the next section, we will study five techniques that comprise the daily activity program: mindfulness, practicing the Presence of God, service, yoga, and the transformation of emotion.

PART FIVE
DAILY ACTIVITY PROGRAM

CHAPTER NINETEEN

MINDFULNESS

"I Am Awake"

- When the people asked the Buddha if he was a God, an angel, or a saint, he said, "No." "Then who are you?" Buddha replied, "I am awake." What is the Buddha trying to tell us? What is it that we are to awaken from? Why is it important to be more conscious?

- The field of awareness in ordinary states of consciousness is contaminated with a variety of negative thought patterns. We remain largely unaware of these negative patterns and how they prevent us from reaching higher states of consciousness. In mindless states of unawareness, we are hypnotized, functioning like robots on automatic pilot, sleepwalking our way through life.

- This chapter will describe the importance of awakening from ordinary to higher consciousness and how mindfulness, a two-thousand-and-five-hundred-year-old practice taught by the Buddha, can help us with this transformation. Mindfulness is the first technique of the daily activity program.

ORDINARY CONSCIOUSNESS

MINDLESSNESS

- LET THE STORY UNFOLD. The story of life is unfolding in the now, the place where we learn, enjoy, help others, heal, find our courage, work with our problems, manage our pain, and experience inner peace. To accomplish this, we need the mind to work with and accept the story as it unfolds.

- ONE MOMENT AT A TIME. The mind is at its best when it accepts and works with one moment at a time, no matter what life throws at it. This requires discipline. Without discipline, the mind will try to escape, and when it does, it creates more problems. The undisciplined mind is the biggest culprit. It is a source of untold suffering. It wreaks havoc on our peace.

- THE UNDISCIPLINED MIND. The undisciplined mind disrupts our lives by taking us out of the present moment, where our life is at its fullest. Repeatedly, the mind takes us out of our current moments when it does not like what is going on. Here are some examples:

1. It fights when angry.
2. It runs when afraid.
3. It competes when jealous.
4. It creates imagined calamities
5. It projects fantasies from its desires.
6. It is strongly attracted to the past and the future. While it is good to learn from the past and have hopeful plans for the future, the mind goes overboard in its replays and projections. We relive past hurts, resentments, and regrets, which only serve to recycle anger, depression, and guilt. Our projections of the future breed unnecessary fear and insecurity.
7. It builds a rigid structure of selfish, dogmatic, overvalued thoughts, opinions, likes, and dislikes.
8. It tries to get our needs met by controlling and pushing events and people. However, the world does not conform to our egotistical desires; when things do not fit, we create new desires. Instead of working with what we have that is good, it escapes into fantasy, to what we think we want next.

The mind is set up to deal with one moment at a time. Instead, when it doesn't like what is happening, it tries to avoid the moment and escape. This results in negative thought patterns, which only serve to compound our problems. We end up with the original problem and an increase in mental restlessness and rumination, signs that the mind is overheated.

MINDFULNESS

- EVEN-MINDED TRANQUILITY. Mindfulness, an ancient technique of Buddhism, helps us manage our inner reactions to a turbulent and unpredictable world. We want to respond with poise and peace, but all too often our thoughts and feelings will not cooperate. While there can be no respite from troubles and pain, mindfulness helps us receive the tests and trials of life in calm repose. By avoiding the destructive excesses of the mind, we can receive what life brings with even-minded tranquility.

- AWAKE, AWARE, AND READY. To transform ordinary consciousness to higher consciousness, we bring the mind under control by placing it where we want it to be: in the current moment, awake, attentive, and ready. It is in this alignment that we are most able to heal, learn, solve problems, manage suffering, relax, serve, and enjoy.

- YOUR NEXT STEP IS IN THE CURRENT MOMENT. Aligning the mind and attention with the present is a crucial element in the healing process. The next step, the step we need to take, is in these moments; they hold the continuity of our story, a story pregnant with lessons, entertainment, and opportunities to produce, create, love, and serve. In the lower state of ordinary consciousness, we miss these opportunities because we are preoccupied with other fields of awareness.

- NO NEED TO MAKE ANY CHANGES EXCEPT PLACEMENT OF THE MIND. To practice mindfulness, there is no need to make any changes other than the placement of the mind as we go about our usual activities. With practice, the mind remains calm and poised no matter what occurs in the material world. We remain in balance. We get the rhythm of the story. There is no force in it. We are ready for anything.

A MINDFULNESS TECHNIQUE

1. Stop
2. Breathe
3. Present moment
4. Frame:
   a. Witness
   b. School
   c. Entertainment
   d. Service
   e. Warrior
   f. Ritual
   g. Other

1. STOP:

- When the mind lapses into one of its negative habit patterns, it draws you away from the opportunities of the moment. You go for a ride on the negative thought train. Because you identify with the negativity, you think this is who you are.

- When you become aware that your mind is wandering, give yourself a one-word command: stop. This will help you stop thinking and then you can focus on your breath.

2. BREATHE:

- Take a breath and gently bring the mind back to the reality of the moment.

- By simply becoming aware of your breath, you can stop the rambling mind, relax, and return to the present moments of your life.

- This simple maneuver of using your breath to control your mind will help you develop your powers of concentration.

- You can develop single-minded concentration by continually bringing your attention back to your breath, every time the mind wanders.

- With practice, you will be able to stay increasingly in the present, bringing your mind out of its aimless spin, back into alignment with the present moment.

3. PRESENT MOMENT:

- Give your full attention to each moment.
- Focus on what is going on inside.
- Focus on what is going on outside.
- Focus on your body.
- Focus on what you are doing.

4. FRAME:

- When you use the breath to calm your mind and place it in the present moment, you have an opportunity to choose from a variety of frames of reference for life, as it occurs.

- We cannot control most of what is going on outside, but we can control how we respond.

- We can choose frames that inspire, heal, soothe, purify, entertain, and transform.

- We can create any frame we wish.

- In this lesson, we will review six frames:

    a. Witness
    b. School
    c. Entertainment
    d. Service
    e. Warrior
    f. Ritual
    g. Other

THE WITNESS

EVEN-MINDED UNDER ALL CONDITIONS

When you become aware that you have gone for a ride on the negative train of thought and you want to get off the train, practice cultivating the witness as follows:

1. Stop
2. Breathe
3. Present moment
4. Witness

- There is a place inside that is always calm. We want to remain in that place, peaceful and poised no matter what the world and body throw at us. We can achieve this state by cultivating the witness.

- To invoke the witness, take a slow deep abdominal breath and affirm: "Stillness, silence, spaciousness, and serenity."

- The witness replaces the restlessness and ruminations of the undisciplined mind with stillness, silence, spaciousness, and serenity. The witness does this by observing the changes of life without reacting. It remains silent and serene. It watches events unfold from a position of stillness and peace.

- The witness does not try to change anything. It does not add, subtract, delete, or edit. It accepts reality as it is while we change our frame from reactivity to stillness. We focus on the stillness and silence within and the outer present moment.

- As the witness grows through the practice of mindfulness, you can slowly bring the dimensions of spaciousness and serenity to the events of your life.

- With the breath as a means of centering yourself, you can begin the process of disengaging from your identification with the negative patterns of the uncontrolled mind.

- With a single breath, you can invoke the witness. Here, there is a peaceful and compassionate space, large enough to hold all.

- Breathe and refocus on the calm witness early and often to reach for the peace and enjoyment that resides there, inhibited only by your undisciplined mind.

SCHOOL

CULTIVATING SPIRITUAL QUALITIES

When you become aware that you have gone for a ride on the negative train of thought and you want to get off the train, practice the following method:

1. Stop
2. Breathe
3. Present moment
4. School

- When life gets difficult inside or outside, we try to get away. We run and resist by going into unawareness or fantasy. But the school of life is merely presenting a lesson that we need to learn.

- Allowing the mind to wander is the equivalent of playing hooky from school. In mindfulness, we do not fight with the teacher or run. We pay attention, listen, and cooperate in order to graduate to the next level.

- Peace is not found by running away from problems; rather, we find peace by facing the problem or difficulty and going through it.

- Through the breath, we can enter rather than run from unpleasantness. By entering deeply into the present, we can extract the lessons and move on.

- When you are in pain, affirm:

  1. Life is school.
  2. Pain is the teacher if I open to its lessons.
  3. The lessons have to do with the cultivation of spiritual qualities.

- Consult the list of healing qualities listed in the spiritual alphabet. Which qualities do you need to develop to help you manage your current problem?

- Remember, the healing qualities in the spiritual alphabet are more powerful than any painful problem. By invoking and affirming these healing qualities, you create an inner atmosphere conducive to healing. As the healing qualities slowly burn up trouble-making negativity, you will experience a corresponding shift to peace and strength.

- Love, kindness, acceptance, and forgiveness are more powerful than any pain or problem. Be patient, understanding, compassionate, and gentle with yourself. This will help you face your problems, get the necessary lessons, and move forward.

- The teacher and the lessons are found in the moments of our lives. You cannot move up the chain of awareness without learning from these moments, and you cannot learn if you are not in school; that is, awake, aware, and focused on the present.

- The goal is to stay calm and suffer at the same time. We can do this if we create a healing space large enough to hold any problem or pain. Then we can allow our painful problems to exist in consciousness without the destructive aspects of denial, repression, or expression.

  a. Denial and repression drive our painful problems into the subconscious and into the body, where they are stored as negative energy. The problem remains hidden and unresolved.

  b. Destructive expressions of our pain manifest in a variety of ways, including exertion of power over others, irritability, anger, and aggression. In effect, we spread our pain and problems to others.

- Alternatively, we can cultivate an internal healing space for the pain. We can do this by invoking an enlarged space filled with healing qualities. When we let our pain and problems play in an enlarged, peaceful, compassionate space, negative energy is released that has been repressed over the years within our subconscious and the body. By accepting pain and problems with compassion, we end the fear of releasing negativity. By stopping the fight within, the tension of repression dissolves.

- There is a profound feeling of peace when we turn the table on our suffering by offering no resistance. By fully accepting the inevitable suffering of life without repression and resistance, we gain internal power.

- To shift gears from ordinary to higher consciousness, we need to think less, be aware of our breath, remain in the present, and accept pain as the teacher. Stay calm, be kind and gentle with yourself, and do the work. The result is strength, serenity, spaciousness, and stillness.

- When we gently and courageously enter our pain, we gain the knowledge and strength that will help us take on the next set of problems or lessons. This is pain control through acceptance or surrender. Additional details on how to process emotional pain into self-knowledge are described in Chapter Twenty-Three, Transformation of Emotion.

ENTERTAINMENT
A SPECTACULAR SHOW

When you become aware that you have gone for a ride on the negative train of thought and you want to get off the train, practice the following method:

1. Stop
2. Breath
3. Present moment
4. Entertainment

- The unfolding drama of life is not always about school and learning. Life is entertainment. Our stories are filled with beauty, joy, laughter, and fun. It is difficult if not impossible to see life as entertainment, however, if we are immersed in the drama, consumed by our problems and suffering.

- By taking a step back from the role we are playing, we can take ourselves less seriously. We can do this by framing life as a movie or a sport. We are actors in a role, players in a game.

- By not identifying completely with our role, we gain distance and perspective. When we reduce our tendency to exaggerate the importance of events, we eliminate some mental restlessness and high emotional reactivity. When we calm the mind and create more operating space within, we can enjoy the show.

- To remember life as a spectacular show, give yourself a one-word affirmation such as "entertainment," "show," "drama," "play," "movie," "game," or "sport." This frame helps us to not take everything and ourselves so seriously.

<u>SERVICE</u>
HELPING OTHERS

When you become aware that you have gone for a ride on the negative train of thought and you want to get off the train, practice the following method:

1. Stop
2. Breathe
3. Present moment
4. Service

- Mindfulness practice helps us escape the influence of negative thoughts and turbulent emotions. When we are more peaceful inside, we can give kindness, Love, and service to others.

- Gracious, warm, loving service to all of humanity and creation is a natural consequence of the sustained practice of mindfulness.

- To invoke the servant, affirm, "compassionate service to everyone I meet."

WARRIOR

READY FOR ANYTHING

When you become aware that you have gone for a ride on the negative train of thought and you want to get off the train, practice the following method:

1. Stop
2. Breathe
3. Present moment
4. Warrior

- The practice of mindfulness slowly replaces unbridled thoughts, feelings, and desires with serenity and stillness. Mental reactivity and turmoil subside. With a more powerful and resilient mind, the difficulties of life are less likely to throw us off course.

- We can deal with whatever comes and hold our ground. We do not have to run or hide. We can stay in the moment, take a stand, and hold our position. We are awake, aware, and ready for anything, including work, pain, change, the unknown, even death. This is the stance of a warrior.

- To invoke the warrior, give your self the following command: "awake, aware, ready for anything."

RITUAL

MAGICAL MIRACLES EVERYWHERE

When you become aware that you have gone for a ride on the negative train of thought and you want to get off the train, practice the following method:

1. Stop
2. Breathe

3. Present moment
4. Ritual

- We spend a lot of time in routine daily activities: eating, strolling in the park, chatting on the phone, standing in line, cutting the grass, running to the store, baking, washing dishes, brushing teeth, tying shoes …. There is meaning in any of these routines of life, but we miss it. Because we assume the mundane is boring, the mind wanders. We lose touch with the magic and miracles secreted in every moment, everywhere, outside and inside.

- The practice of mindfulness brings awe back to the routines of life by focusing on our activities and creating a context of special meaning and importance. For example, we can appreciate the moments that might otherwise be lost in boredom by recognizing the Omniscient Wisdom that is always with us.

- Omniscience is the infinite intelligence that permeates our body and the entire universe.

- As we perform any routine activity, we can think of how the body follows our command when we tell it what to do.

- We can think of the unfathomable intelligence that creates and operates our vision and hearing as we go about our chores and tasks.

- When reading, we can think of the brilliance that allows us to understand the words right now.

- While eating, we can think of how the stomach and intestines digest food by breaking it into molecules that are sent to the right places in the body for energy, repair, immunity, and a host of other functions.

- When washing our hair, we can think about how the body responds to our commands.

- The intelligence that creates and operates the body is phenomenal. We are magicians, performing astounding feats throughout the day, but ordinary consciousness makes the miraculous mundane.

- Maintaining awareness of the Omniscient Power that permeates the universe is part of capturing the wonder, magic, and mystery of being alive, in what might otherwise appear to be the humdrum of everyday routines.

- We can start such a practice with any routine, anywhere, any time. By consciously looking for the positives inside and outside, we can find them. A blessing in disguise lurks everywhere; we must only work to uncover it.

- If we bring the full powers of a calm, concentrated, and positive mind to our routine activities, we can capture the blessings and make them our own.

- With breath, focused attention, and creative framing, we can extract the gifts of life—peace, joy, beauty, and the magic of being—from the most mundane activities.

- Give yourself a one-word command: "Omniscience." This will attune your consciousness to the magnificence of creation, from particle and wave to galaxy.

CHOOSE YOUR OWN FRAME

When you become aware that you have gone for a ride on the negative train of thought and you want to get off the train, practice the following method:

1. Stop

2. Breathe
3. Present moment
4. Choose your own frame. There are unlimited numbers of frames you can use to help you stay in the moment. Be creative.

REPETITION

- It takes years to bring the mind under control. Expect it to wander from the present moment into its old negative habit patterns. Do not frame this as success and failure, as this will cause frustration and tension.

- When you go for a ride on the train of thought and find yourself back in a lower state of consciousness, remain kind, compassionate, and gentle with yourself. Stop, breathe, and reenter the moment with the frame of your choice.

ONE CONTINUOUS SACRED RITUAL

- With practice, we can become increasingly aware, awake, and attentive in each of the moments of our lives. As our will power and concentration increase, we can begin to string the moments together. By maintaining our focus on what we are doing at all times, we learn to stay in the present more and more, even when life gets rough. We see that we can remain in reality whether it turns good, bad, or ugly.

- When our concentration is highly developed, we can stay in the present and maintain harmony and balance no matter what life does. All of our moments become part of one continuous ritual in response to the truth of life just as it is—with all of its sorrow, beauty, and joy. When we recognize that all we have are these moments, that there is nowhere else to go, we gain strength and peace.

- When we bring the unruly mind under control through mindfulness, we gain access to the calm witness, the student in school, the actor in the movie, the servant of humanity, the warrior who is ready for anything, and the magical ritual.

  o The witness remains even-minded under all conditions.
  o When difficult or painful, life is school. We enter our pain to extract the necessary lessons.
  o When life is entertaining, it is like a movie or a sport. When we frame life as a movie, we are observing the show or acting in a role. This gives us some perspective and protection from over-involvement. Playing with life as though it is a sport or game lightens our burden. We don't take it so seriously.
  o We are in service when we help others. We feel peace and joy.
  o The warrior is ready for anything.
  o The ritual transforms the ordinary and mundane to magic and miraculous.

When we rotate these frames, life becomes one continuous sacred ritual, offering up its knowledge and lessons, entertainment and joy, and opportunities to Love and serve.

BENEFITS FROM THE PRACTICE OF MINDFULNESS

- An all-purpose increase in awareness of everything
- Improved powers of concentration
- Enhances ability to stay on task
- More present and calm
- Better at listening
- Removes debris and rubbish from our consciousness
- Purification and healing
- Helps us accept what we cannot change
- Helps us get some distance from our train of thought
- Stops the pursuit of negative thoughts

- More compassion, Love, and kindness to the self and others
- Reduces mental restlessness and emotional reactivity
- Better problem solving
- More skillful pain management

POINTS TO REMEMBER

- The field of awareness in ordinary states of consciousness is contaminated with a variety of negative thought patterns. We remain largely unaware of these negative patterns and how they prevent us from reaching higher states of consciousness. In mindless states of unawareness, we are hypnotized, functioning like robots on automatic pilot, sleepwalking our way through life. Mindfulness, an ancient practice taught by the Buddha, helps us awaken from ordinary to higher consciousness.

- Mindful introspection allows us to see the forces that control and distract us. Through continuous observation of the flow of our thoughts, feelings, desires, aversions, impulses, and fantasies, we come to understand ourselves better. We can see how our desires, fears, and insecurities cause tension and how, with the technique of mindfulness, we can release ourselves into the stillness, silence, spaciousness, and serenity of the witness.

- It takes years to bring the mind under control. Expect it to wander from the present moment into its old negative habit patterns. Do not frame this as success and failure, as this will cause frustration and tension. When you go for a ride on the train of thought and find yourself back in a lower state of consciousness, remain kind, compassionate, and gentle with yourself. Stop, breathe, and reenter the moment with the frame of your choice.

- We can practice mindfulness anywhere, anytime. All we have to do is stop, breathe, get into the present moment, and reframe. It is like the simple flick of a switch.

- To be fully aware of all of the elements of our lives, we need to pay attention. Mindfulness is a walking meditation or meditation in action. We can turn every action into a mindful, meditative exercise by giving whatever we are doing our full attention.

- The present moment is both the teacher and the entertainer. There are lessons to be learned and experiences to be enjoyed. Sometimes the lessons are painful. Other experiences are enjoyable and entertaining. Stay alert to get the most out of life, whatever the experience.

- The mind is geared to deal with the present. The past and future are too much to bear. There is more than enough reality here and now. Why add to the burden by leaning forward into the future or bending backward into the past?

- Mindfulness is an exercise designed to increase our concentration and attention so we can be awake and ready for anything, including work, pain, change, the unknown, or death.

- Highly developed intense concentration in the present moment results in a sense of flow, rhythm, harmony, and balance.

- Mindfulness is a part of the performance of all of the methods described in this work. Attention, concentration, and awareness are needed for all cognitive-behavioral or spiritual practice.

- The peace, joy, Love, power, and wisdom we are looking for is right here in the moments of our lives. However, we must be awake, aware, and focused; otherwise, restless thoughts, reactive emotions, and excessive desires will take us away.

- In ordinary consciousness, we identify with the stream of negative and disruptive thoughts, feelings, desires, impulses, and fantasies that pass through our awareness. With the practice of mindfulness, we create a space large enough to hold the negativity. In this space, we do not identify with negativity, and therefore do not need to repress or express it, both of which are destructive. Instead, we go to the compassionate witness of the true self and create a healing space within. This is a furnace of sorts: here we can burn up the junk thoughts, feelings, desires, and fantasies that keep our consciousness from rising.

- Rather than being negative, panicky, or agitated when life gets rough, ride the ups and downs like a rodeo cowboy on a bucking horse. With continued practice of mindfulness, the restless mind, hyperactive emotions, and excessive material desires will not bump us off the horse. We stay calm and focused even when the ride is rough.

- With deep, sustained, long-term practice of mindful service and meditation, our inner space expands so that we can receive the harsh realities of life with peace and poise.

- Stay awake and aware in the present moment, since it is in the here and now that life offers up its knowledge and lessons, entertainment and joy, and opportunities to Love and serve.

- Be compassionate, yet unencumbered. Give peaceful, joyful, loving service to all of humanity, and enjoy the show.

AFFIRMATIONS

- With the breath, I anchor myself in the present moment.
- I calmly embrace the present moment.
- I calm myself and get back to the present moment.
- I invoke the witness, watching and observing.
- I invoke the witness, still and silent.
- I invoke the witness, patient and breathing.
- I invoke the witness, serene and spacious.

- Compassion is the fire that burns up my problems in the healing furnace inside me.
- By steady absorption in the moment, I get the rhythm of the story.
- I respond to the show with peace and poise.
- I am kind and gentle with myself under all conditions.
- I add Love and compassion to every moment of my inner life.
- I receive all events with gentle compassion for myself.
- I receive all events with gentle compassion for you.
- I live fully in the present.
- I practice the presence of peace.
- I live fully in the present where change and healing occur.
- I am grateful for the blessings of entertainment and joy.
- I accept suffering as an opportunity to cultivate healing qualities.
- I see magical miracles everywhere.

EXERCISES

1. What is the difference between ordinary and higher consciousness?

2. Describe the four steps of the mindfulness technique.

3. Describe and discuss the six frames of reference listed in Step 4 of mindfulness practice.

4. Can you think of any additional frames that might help you?

5. Life is school. How might the practice of mindfulness help you learn the lessons meant for you?

6. Life is entertaining. How might the practice of mindfulness help you enjoy life more than you do now?

7. There are thoughts without awareness and thoughts with awareness. Your witness is conscious, calm, and non-judgmental. Watch your

thoughts from the witness. This is impartial self-analysis. Stand back and observe without prejudice. Try this now.

8. When completely immersed in the turbulence of ruminative thoughts, feelings, sensations, fantasies, and impulses, remember the witness, that place inside where there is stillness, silence, space, and serenity. When you are in turmoil, try these one-word affirmations:

   • Stillness
   • Silence
   • Spaciousness
   • Serenity

   This may help you get through difficult times.

9. Be aware of your inner being, your body, and the sights, sounds, and feel of the environment. Look for the positives within yourself and in your present environment. Try this technique:

   a. Stop
   b. Breathe
   c. Present moment
   d. Find something positive in your inner being.
   e. Find something positive in your body.
   f. Find something positive in the environment.

10. You are either in Love or something else. When you notice negativity:

    a. Stop
    b. Breathe
    c. Present moment
    d. Affirm Love or another healing quality

11. Notice when you are managing your pain skillfully or unskillfully. When you observe unskillful pain management:

    a. Stop
    b. Breathe
    c. Present moment
    d. Affirm: "Life is school. Pain is the teacher if I open to the lessons. The lessons have to do with the cultivation of healing qualities."

12. Ask yourself, "Am I in the drama over-reacting or watching the drama from the serenity and stillness of the witness?"

13. Always practice mindfulness with an attitude of compassion and understanding for yourself. Try this now.

14. To create a healing atmosphere for yourself, affirm Love and kindness. Try this now.

15. Meditation and mindfulness work in tandem. Both techniques reduce the excesses of the mind so it can be in alignment with the higher purposes of the heart and soul. Both techniques require one-pointed concentration. If you practice meditation and mindfulness, you will build a powerful control center at the very core of your being. Events, the doings of other people, and your own reactivity will not ruffle you because you have more space and strength inside. This takes time to develop. Begin your practice now.

16. The Sacred is with you all the time. Relax, open, listen, attune, and receive. Can you feel it?

17. Every action, no matter how mundane, is a part of one uninterrupted sacred ritual. Offer every action in service to humanity and to your God or Buddha. Then you will have strength and peace.

You have completed your review of mindfulness, the first of five techniques recommended for your daily activity program. In the next chapter, you will study a similar technique: practicing the Presence of God.

CHAPTER TWENTY

PRACTICING THE PRESENCE OF GOD

A Personal Relationship

- WE CAN TALK TO GOD AND GET A RESPONSE. This chapter introduces the second technique of the daily activity program, practicing the Presence of God. We can talk to God and get a response. We can have a personal relationship with an Omniscient Power whose nature is gentle, compassionate, loving, and wise, a living presence beyond philosophy or belief. Contact is not only possible, but this magnificent benevolent power knows what we need and wants to give it to us.

- ONE OF HIS GREATEST TRICKS. In order to give us the help we need, God performs one of His greatest tricks. He reduces Himself from Infinite Power to a number of aspects we can relate to: Father, Mother, Friend, Healer, Lover, Teacher, Guide, Protector, and Counselor. Then, through these aspects, He offers guidance, protection, friendship, healing, purification, and the expansion of soul qualities. As our healing qualities grow, we feel better, treat others better, and make the world a better place.

- WHY DON'T WE KNOW HIM? It seems too good to be true that such a wonderful relationship is available in the world of limitation and suffering, as we know it in ordinary consciousness. If it is true that an all-knowing, infinite power can mysteriously manifest at our level and enter our lives bearing priceless gifts, why don't we know Him? How can we find Him? And how can we keep Him in our lives?

- TRAPPED IN MATERIAL CONSCIOUSNESS. This great invisible power bearing the gifts of friendship, peace, healing, and wisdom knocks on the door of our consciousness, but we do not hear it. We have lost our connection to the subtle vibrations offered by the gracious Omnipresent Power, stuck as we are in the grosser vibrations of material consciousness.

- DEAF TO THE FRIEND TRYING TO HELP. We focus on the fascinating story and alluring objects of the material world. Tests and trials come. We get trapped in our thoughts, feelings, desires, habits, attachments, and egos. Separated, mired, and hooked by these limitations of material consciousness, we remain deaf to the Friend trying to help.

- WE DON'T KNOW HOW TO MAKE CONTACT. Material consciousness creates an invisible shield, a seemingly impenetrable defense against our experience of the subtle vibrations of compassion, kindness, gentleness, and warmth offered by the Grand Healer. We don't experience the next layer of reality just behind the veil of ordinary consciousness because we are not mindful of the possibility and we don't know how to make contact. We need a technique to help us work through the limitations of material consciousness so we can contact God, prove His existence to ourselves, explore His nature, and partake of His wondrous gifts.

TECHNIQUE

Following is a technique for practicing the Presence of God:

1. Stop
2. Breathe
3. Present moment

4. Frame: practicing the Presence of God

   a. Any method described in this book: affirmations, habit transformation, progressive muscle relaxation, breathwork, contemplation, meditation, prayer, mindfulness, service, yoga, and transformation of emotion
   b. The sacred meaning of story
   c. Conversation with God

5. God responds

   a. Omniscient, Omnipotent, Omnipresence
   b. Healing
   c. Meditation
   d. Phenomenon

6. Hide and seek, find and keep

- SIMILAR TO MINDFULNESS. Notice the similarity between the technique for practicing mindfulness, and that of the Presence of God. Both focus on our experience of higher states of consciousness. The difference is in the concept of a Higher Power. Mindfulness practice does not require a personal relationship with God. Practicing the Presence of God presupposes the existence of God as a conscious power with whom we can have a relationship.

- CONCENTRATION IN THE PRESENT MOMENT. As in the practice of mindfulness, we need to employ our powers of concentration and awareness in the present moment, as we can know God best in the present.

- MANY WAYS TO PRACTICE. Follow the same steps as with mindfulness, but now, at Step 4, the frame is practicing the Presence of God through any of the spiritual methods described in this book, the sacred meaning of story, and conversing with God. Each of these spiritual practices results in a direct experience of God.

- FORGET AND REMEMBER. When the mind wanders into one of the many variations of ordinary consciousness, stop, breathe, focus on the present moment, and bring God to your awareness by choosing one of the frames listed in Step 4. When you relapse and realize you are back in ordinary consciousness, refocus on the Presence of God. As in meditation and mindfulness, you will forget and remember many times for years to come; this is the nature of spiritual practice.

STEP 4A: ANY METHOD DESCRIBED IN THIS BOOK

- The practice of any method described in this work results in the cultivation of spiritual qualities adding up to Love. When our Love is strong enough, it breaks into another realm, an unmistakable transformation of consciousness to Divine Love. This is practicing the presence of God as Love.

STEP 4B: THE SACRED MEANING OF STORY

- GOD IS THE TEACHER. God's presence can be distilled from the sacred meaning of stories. We can experience the Presence of God if we watch our personal and collective stories unfold from the point of view of God as our Teacher, training us to cultivate Love through a process of purification, the goal of which is perfection.

- THE LESSONS ARE ABOUT LOVE. The Teacher is eager to train us in the art of Love, gratitude, reverence, humility, surrender, intuition, and faith. She sets up the entire universe of human experience as a training ground for the expansion of Love and Her associated qualities, until they become unconditional. She designs events and circumstances so that we can discover, remove, and replace our faults with the healing qualities of Love. Everything in our life experience is raw material to train us to be more loving in our thoughts, feelings, desires, and actions. To observe the story of life unfolding from this point of view is to practice the Presence of God as the Teacher of Love.

- GOD IS PERFECT LOVE AND SO ARE WE. God is untainted and unlimited peace, joy, Love, power, and wisdom. We are made of these same Love qualities in combination with our problems, flaws, and imperfections, which act as barriers between God and ourselves. When we slowly reduce and replace our imperfections by expanding Love qualities, we approach the gateway to Her presence: She is Love; it is her domain.

- PICK A LOVE QUALITY AND MAKE IT GROW. The Teacher of Love does not care about our role, power, money, status, age, class, or religion. She only cares about what is in our hearts. Actions saturated with Love, kindness, humility, and understanding are pleasant in Her sight. Pick a quality such as Love or one of her associates: peace, gentleness, sweetness, gratitude, appreciation, or surrender. Cultivate your chosen quality by focusing on it in your meditation and through affirmations and visualizations. Bring it to every thought, feeling, action, and event. Hold on to it and make it grow. This is practicing the Presence of God.

- DON'T CHANGE ANYTHING. JUST BE IN LOVE. We don't have to change anything in our life, except to respond to events and problems with God's qualities. When we respond to cruelty with kindness, to ignorance with understanding, to suffering with compassionate service, and to fear with courage, we practice the Presence of God.

- FULFILLING THE SACRED INTENT OF STORY. In the end, when we have burned off our imperfections and become pure, we enter Her kingdom of unlimited peace, joy, Love, power, and wisdom, fulfilling the sacred intent and meaning of our life story.

STEP 4C: CONVERSING WITH GOD

- AN INFORMAL CONVERSATION. Prayer is formal, structured communication with God. We can also have an ongoing, spontaneous conversation with God. Some of us may find conversing with an invisible power strange at first. Because of our feeling of separation, we think no one is there. A few suggestions might help.

- A WORKABLE, ACCESSIBLE CONCEPT. To make contact with God, we need a workable, accessible concept of who God is and who we are. We can speak to God's Omnipresent Formless Form or to a more concrete aspect such as Teacher, Father, Mother, Friend, Healer, Counselor, Confidante, Beloved, Creator, King, Guide, or Protector. We can approach God as a babe, child, student, servant, witness, disciple, devotee, warrior, or simply a human being.

- DIFFERENT ASPECTS FOR DIFFERING NEEDS. We can pick a concept based on our need at the time. If we need advice, we can call the Counselor. If we are lonely or need to share, we can call the Friend. If we need healing or purification, we can call the Physician. If we need forgiveness, we can call the Mother. If we need to extract the meaning and lessons from the events of our lives, we can call the Teacher. If we need wisdom, strength, or courage, we can call the Father. If we need Love, we can call the Beloved.

- START THE CONVERSATION. As in any relationship, we begin by starting a conversation. The conversation can occur at any point during the day, from the time we get up in the morning to just before sleep. We can be as natural and relaxed as we would be with a friend or formal and reverent. The communication should be honest, direct, and heartfelt.

- WEAVE GOD INTO THE FABRIC OF YOUR LIFE. We can weave God into the fabric of our daily lives by sharing our needs, goals, problems, joys, and successes. We can share what has happened in our day, what is happening in our lives, our feelings, idle thoughts, anything, and everything. We can be angry and argue. We can ask for guidance, protection, or support. We can ask questions. We can ask for help with our own problems and bad habits and for aid in all that we do for others. We can express our desire to be closer to Him, to be more like Him. We can confess our embarrassing secrets and ask for understanding and forgiveness. It is liberating and healing to tell the truth to the One who already knows what we have done and what is in our hearts.

STEP 5: GOD'S RESPONSE

- WE START THE CONVERSATION. We can initiate our communication with God through the sacred meaning of story, conversing with God, or through any spiritual method described in this work. How does God respond?

- IT IS NOT EASY TO GET A RESPONSE. We cannot make contact with Him without intense, continuous, and long-term communication. We need to practice with all our hearts, minds, might, and souls until we get a response, however long it may take.

Most of us will not get a response in the beginning. As a result, many stop practicing. Some drop their practice because of indifference or boredom. Others give up when life becomes difficult. Some quit their practice when life becomes easy.

- KNOCK WITH INTENSITY, AND YOU WILL RECEIVE. If we take advantage of all our moments by practicing the Presence of

God and never giving up, we break down the invisible shield that we have built up between God and ourselves, experience God's response, and get the help we need.

- GOD RESPONDS IN A VARIETY OF WAYS. God's response varies according to our individual predilections and our level of spiritual development. Following is a discussion of four ways that God may come into our lives:

    a. Omnipresence, Omniscience, and Omnipotence
    b. Healing
    c. Meditation
    d. Phenomenon

STEP 5A: OMNIPRESENCE, OMNISCIENCE, AND OMNIPOTENCE

- ABUNDANT EVIDENCE. Clues and evidence speaking to God's Omniscience, Omnipotence, and Omnipresence abound. God is a conscious intelligent power whose presence is ubiquitous. Her manifestation is ever-present in all of nature and in our bodies and consciousness. She occupies every millimeter of space, from the infinitesimal to infinity. She operates every level of reality, from microcosmic particles and waves to macrocosmic solar systems. Her unfathomable power keeps the whirling atoms, planets, and galaxies moving in harmonious balance with each other.

- BILLIONS OF FORMS. Her infinitely intelligent power creates, sustains, operates, and dissolves a seemingly endless parade of billions of forms, including us. The marvels and beauty of nature—birds, ocean, sky, sunsets, and flowers—are Her costume. The entire universe, all forms and every human body, are Her temple.

- CONTINUOUS SIGNS. The entry point to Her realm is acknowledgement of the continuous signs of Her power, beauty, and intelligence. We need to remind ourselves that Her unseen, invisible intelligence is always sustaining and guiding atoms, galaxies, and us.

- TAP INTO HER BOUNDLESS RESOURCES. God wants us to use Her boundless resources in our daily lives. We can get Her help if we remember to connect our thoughts, will, feelings, desires, actions, and all events with Her.

- GET HELP WITH ANY PROBLEM. God's power and energy permeate every scene, in every moment, at every level of detail. By remembering Her Omnipresence, we can get help with any problem or crisis.

- EVERYTHING COUNTS. No moment or detail is too small. It is easy to get tricked or fooled into apathy or boredom by quiet moments such as traffic jams or waiting in line. However, we can use these seemingly mundane events to see God in everything, and everything in God. If we persist in our practice, we will come to the realization that God is an unlimited source of power, Love, and wisdom that we can tap into at any time.

STEP 5B: HEALING

- GOD IS THE HEALER. God responds to our spiritual work by healing our mind, body, and soul.

- HEALING THE MIND. The mind becomes positive, calm, focused, resilient, and strong. Destructive emotions are skillfully transformed into self-knowledge. Excessive material desires are transmuted into contentment and satisfaction.

- HEALING THE BODY. Healing power for the body expands. We can get help with any disease or disability. While our physical problems may not magically disappear, we can always expand the healing qualities of the soul.

- HEALING THE SOUL. Soul qualities such as peace, gentleness, and understanding replace restlessness, aggression, and ignorance.

- HEALING OTHERS. As our healing qualities expand and our problems burn up, we get more space to receive the suffering of the world. Then we can respond with compassionate action, thus contributing to the healing of others and the environment.

STEP 5C: MEDITATION

- SUPERCONSCIOUSNESS. In meditation, God manifests as unfathomable stillness, the peace that surpasses understanding, ecstatic joy, pure Love, and intuitive wisdom. Some experience a breathtaking and thrilling, yet soft and gentle surge of power, a soothing embrace, or a feeling of absolute safety. Advanced meditators experience samadhi, the ecstasy of complete union with God.

STEP 5D: PHENOMENON

- A VARIETY OF SPIRITUAL EXPERIENCES. Some people experience phenomenon such as aura, light, visions, prophetic dreams, intuitive knowing, guidance, protection, answered prayers, synchronicity, healing powers, or entrance into the "zone," the experience of supreme flow, rhythm, and harmony.

STEP 6: HIDE AND SEEK, FIND AND KEEP

- GOD APPEARS. When we align ourselves with His will, God makes an appearance through:

  1. His Omniscient, Omnipotent, Omnipresence
  2. Healing body, mind, and soul
  3. In the Love and stillness of meditation
  4. Phenomenon

- GOD DISAPPEARS. With continued practice, we gradually

become more attuned and receptive to His will, guidance, and counsel. As we see His great healing principle at work in our lives, our trust in Him grows. However, as we go through tests and trials, God disappears behind the veil of ordinary consciousness. We feel separate again, dry and seemingly alone as we struggle with our problems.

• HIDE AND SEEK. God's appearance and disappearance, His play of hide and seek, has a purpose: character development through the culture of unconditional Love. God is unconditional Love and associated qualities. His wish is that we become like Him through a process of purification, through expansion of our soul qualities. During difficult times when God is hiding, our job is to seek Him through the pursuit of Love qualities until they become unconditional.

• USA: UNCONDITIONAL, SPONTANEOUS, AUTOMATIC LOVE QUALITIES. We can respond to events with manifestations of God's Love such as kindness, compassion, peace, and understanding, or with cruelty, hate, violence, and ignorance. When our response is one of the many forms of negativity, we need to work through it until we get back to Love and its companion soul qualities. God appears and disappears until such qualities become unconditional, spontaneous, and automatic.

• LEARNING TO TRUST THE PURIFICATION PROCESS. His play of hide and seek goes on indefinitely as we work through our pain and problems. He often hides as we do the work but eventually the Gentle Lover returns. We learn to trust His purification process, as He inevitably reappears with infinitely creative versions of His sweet Love. The experience of even a trace of His sweetness is addicting. In our yearning for more, we avail ourselves to His healing process of purification—sometimes purification by fire. We learn to trust the process of His appearing and disappearing as we realize His intention for us: to become the tender gentle Love that He is.

- A MULTIFACETED POWER. Eventually it becomes impossible not to love Her intimately and deeply. She has given us the greatest possible gift: immersion in Her presence, where we can contact the unconditional sweet Love of the Father-Mother, the perfect, ubiquitous guidance from the Counselor, the healing and purification from the Physician, the training from the Teacher, and friendship from the Friend. As Her colossal, stupendous, multifaceted power plays hide and seek with us, we play find and keep with Her.

- PERMANENTLY IMMERSED IN HIS OCEAN. In the end, we find ourselves permanently immersed in His Ocean. We see that everything is in Him, as fish swimming in water. Then we experience His Love no matter what difficulties life brings. Surrounded, fed, permeated, and saturated with His Love, we give only that to all we meet. Secure in the knowledge that we are always in Him and He in us, we bow in reverence and awe.

- INFINITY, ETERNITY, AND IMMORTALITY. Think cosmic thoughts as you fold laundry and put the kids to bed. Instead of zoning out, realize that the Great One is always here, right now. Every moment is a manifestation of infinity, eternity, and immortality!

POINTS TO REMEMBER

- On the spiritual path, there is only one desire: the Presence of God.

- To enter His realm, God expects us to learn how to behave. To behave properly, we need to become like Him, a composite of pure Love qualities. Then the all-powerful, all-knowing God of the universe gradually, gently enters an intimate relationship with us by revealing His compassion and wisdom.

- To find God in an event, follow the Love. If you cannot find Love, bring it out from within yourself. Wherever there is Love, there is your temple and there is your God.

- God hides behind the veil of ordinary consciousness. We seek Him through the cultivation of unconditional Love in the present moment. When we fill our moments with Love, we experience the Presence of God. God is Love. Love is our home.

- The Teacher wants us to respond to all events and people with Love qualities. The challenges are many. It is difficult to respond with compassion when we are insulted, provoked, or abused. However, the ultimate practice of the Presence of God is responding with Love no matter what happens in our environment.

- Pain is a directive signal, telling us where we need to do some work. It is a stimulant for the development of spiritual qualities. We accept pain as necessary for transformation and purification of consciousness towards forbearance, endurance, courage, strength, humility, patience, or any combination of qualities. Pain is an opportunity to work in the direction of God.

- Practicing the Presence of God is the same as practicing the presence of any spiritual quality. As we breathe, affirm, and grow a spiritual quality, we increase our experience of the Presence of God. When we realize that we have lost our peace and our mind is restless, we can stop, breathe, focus on the present, and affirm any one or a combination of the Love qualities needed at that moment.

- All of the spiritual qualities are connected and grow together. For example, if we choose to expand peace of mind, we will also grow patience, compassion, and forgiveness. Thus, through the practice of peace, we connect our lives to God; it is His will that we permeate our thoughts with His peace.

- There are times when we have absolutely no control over the environment, but we always have power over our thoughts and will. This is where the battle is fought. This is where we can bring God into every thought, feeling, and action. This is where we can make the relationship personal.

- Practicing the Presence of God is a secret, sacred, silent act. No one knows.

- Selfless service to humanity brings us to the Presence of God: this is His will.

- Selfless service to the environment brings us to the Presence of God, which is also His will.

- As our spiritual qualities grow and our experience of the Presence of God correspondingly deepens, our ability to serve God and humanity is refined and expanded. We become increasingly useful.

- A conversation with God might go something like this: "I read about You in sacred texts. You are described in the most glowing terms. The saints say You are a gentle, loving, compassionate being. You come as peace, stillness, and joy in meditation. Some are given glorious visions, healings, or miracles. Where are You for me? I experience nothing but separation. When and how will You reveal Yourself to me?" After you pour your heart out, you wait for a response. She says, "I want you to be with Me, but first you must learn to behave. Look for the sacred meaning in the events of your life. Purify yourself by fostering Love qualities. Then you will know Me as your Teacher. Seek my guidance and counsel. Then you will know Me as Wisdom. Practice service, and you will know Me as the Giver. Practice meditation, and you will feel Me enter the temple of your body as the sweetness that you crave. Then you will know Me as your Father, Mother, Beloved, Friend, Healer, Confidante, Protector, and Guide."

AFFIRMATIONS

- I come from and return to Spirit.
- I move, live, and have my being in Spirit.
- I am a fish swimming in the ocean of God.
- I love and serve in the omnipresent temple of God.
- I worship the Lord equally in every body-temple.
- I serve the God housed in my body.
- I serve the God housed in your body.
- I stay in the present, where I can know and feel God.
- Every person, form, and story serves as a reminder of His presence.
- I bow to the manifestation of the Divine Mother before me right now.
- I love the manifestation of the Divine Mother before me right now.
- I serve the manifestation of the Divine Mother before me right now.
- I am always in the mind of God.
- I am always in the heart of God.
- I am always on the throne of God.
- I am always at the feet of God.
- I am one with God.

EXERCISE

1. Why do we feel separate from God?

2. We can speak to God's Omnipresent Formlessness or to a more concrete aspect such as Teacher, Father, Mother, Friend, Healer, Counselor, Confidante, Beloved, Creator, King, Guide, or Protector. We can approach God as a babe, child, student, servant, witness, disciple, devotee, warrior, or simply a human being. Can you think of any additional aspects? Which do you prefer?

3. Describe the six steps for practicing the Presence of God.

4. What is the sacred meaning of story?

5. Describe the elements of having a conversation with God.

6. What are four ways that God can respond to the seeker?

7. Always check to see where you are. Where are your mind and feelings? Are you here and now or on automatic pilot? Of what are you practicing the presence? Is it God, a Love quality, or something else?

8. In ordinary consciousness, we find it difficult to believe that God is here with us right now. However, to practice the Presence of God, we need to begin thinking, feeling, and acting as though we are in the temple of God at all times, because in reality we are, even though material consciousness hypnotizes us into thinking that God's presence is an illusion. How should we behave in the presence of the Creator of the Universe? What would it be like to have thoughts, feelings, and actions consistent with being at the feet of God?

9. What would change if you had an appointment with God in 3 hours?

10. How would you behave in Her Presence?

11. How would you treat the person you are with if s(he) is God in disguise?

12. What would be different if everything is God and God is everything?

13. We do not need to change anything to practice the Presence of God. Simply perform every action to please God no matter what

the circumstances are. You might want to start practicing this right now. Practicing the Presence of God is keeping our attention on God at all times. We can do this since God is always present in one or more of His aspects. We can see the hand of God in events by watching for these aspects. Pick a concept, practice, and experience the results. Try the following technique. When you have gone for a ride on the train of thought and you want to get off the train:

a. Stop
b. Breathe
c. Present moment
d. Concentrate on any aspect of your Higher Power: Father, Mother, Friend, Beloved, Confidante, Creator, Teacher, Healer, Changelessness, Love or any healing quality, and so forth.

14. A gentleman passes you by on the street and your ego-mind thinks," He is not very attractive or stylish and he should lose some weight." You observe this judgmental thought and counter with a thought from the soul, "God sends unconditional Love to all of His children. I send Love and kindness to this man as well." Do you see? It's a simple flick of a switch to practice Her presence. "Those who think Me near, I am near." (Paramahansa Yogananda)

You have now studied two techniques for your daily activity program: mindfulness and the Presence of God. In the next chapter, you will review service.

CHAPTER TWENTY-ONE

SERVICE

Adding Our Light to the Sum of Light

I slept and dreamt that life was joy.
I awoke and saw that life was service.
I acted and behold! Service was joy.
— Tagore

In this chapter, we will explore the third method of the daily activity program: service.

- ADD YOUR LIGHT TO THE SUM OF LIGHT. The colossal suffering of the world takes many forms: ignorance, violence, poverty, homelessness, disease, tyranny, corruption, racism, unemployment, and injustice. We want to help. We want to heal the world. This natural compassionate drive is an expression of the soul, our true identity. Although we cannot influence the vast problems of the world as much as we would like, we can do our part, however small. We can add our light to the sum of the light. The world's religions would have us do just that.

- SPIRITUAL GIANTS. True religions emphasize serving others in need. Spiritual giants like Jesus, Buddha, Krishna, Mother Teresa, and Gandhi name selfless service as the path to enlightenment. Masters in the art of service, they gave of themselves for the evolution of others and experienced the joy that comes as a result.

- THE BODHISATTVA. An example of the highest service is the

319

bodhisattva. The Buddhists define a bodhisattva as one who vows to return to Earth in as many incarnations as are necessary in order to relieve all human suffering.

"THE BODHISATTVA'S VOW"

So long as space remains,
so long as sentient beings remain,
I will remain
in order to help,
in order to serve,
in order to make
my own contribution.
— Interpreted by the Dalai Lama

- LESSONS FROM THE GREAT ONES. Masters, saints, and bodhisattvas model grand service to humanity. Although we may not have such a major role in the big picture, we can take some valuable lessons from their lead in order to be helpful in our immediate sphere of influence.

- SMALL ACTS OF GENTLE, HUMBLE SERVICE. Small acts of gentle, humble service have impact. Wherever we are, we do what we can. Mother Teresa said, "I can't help thousands. I can help only the one who stands before me." John Newton added, "If two angels were sent down from heaven, one to conduct an empire and the other to sweep the street, they would feel no inclination to change employments."

- COMPASSION IN ACTION. It does not matter what role we play. What does matter is how we play it. We do not need to change anything. What we do need is to bring Love, kindness, and compassion to our actions. It is our attitude that counts, whether we are postal workers, waiting on tables, health care professionals, bus drivers, or staying at home with children. We can perform any task in a state of ordinary consciousness or in the consciousness of service. The difference is Love. Love converts an ordinary act to service. Service is Love in action.

- GIVE WITHOUT ATTACHMENT TO OUTCOME. The greatest service is giving inner and outer resources without attachment or expectation. Ordinary action generally focuses on external rewards and recognition. When we perform an act of service, giving our time, energy, and resources as an expression of our Love, the reward is inner peace, satisfaction, and joy. In this sense, service itself is selfish, since we do it because it makes us feel good.

- SERVICE HEALS INDIVIDUALS. Service is a universal healer, a potent medicine for individuals and the community. For individuals, it works as an antidote to the poison of guilt and as a powerful antidepressant. It takes us out of our tiresome self-ruminations, bolsters our self-esteem, and replaces feelings of insecurity with confidence. As service places us on the common ground with all of humanity, we grow in humility and equality. When we connect to others through service, our internal agitation is silenced.

- SERVICE HEALS COMMUNITIES. Service is also a powerful medicine for the community. It works against those forces that tear us apart. Political, religious, sexual, racial, and national identities create division and conflict. Loving service, by nature expansive and inclusive, is the glue that binds us back together. Service is anesthetic to our troubles. It stops the internal wars, heals the divisions between us, and shows us who we really are.

- SERVICE IS NOT ABOUT REFORMING OTHERS. Unfortunately, the very religions that promote service are often guilty of blocking its full expression. When a religion claims to be the one and only true way, it contributes to separation. All too often, when we think we are saved and safe, we become complacent and arrogant. Busy trying to convert others, we neglect the critical necessity of transforming ourselves. We hamper our ability to help others if we are not in an ongoing process of self-reform at the same time.

- THE HIGHEST SERVICE IS TIED TO SELF-REFORM. Self-reform is integral in effectively serving humanity. The work starts inside. We need to deal with our own issues before we can successfully understand and assist others with theirs. We can do the necessary inner work by practicing the methods described in this book. Such practices as introspection, affirmations, meditation, and transformation of emotion are digging tools that can reach the deepest recesses of our being to root out all traces of negativity. It is only through rigorous inner work that we can eliminate our flaws and replace them with spiritual qualities. Then such jewels as humility, reverence, gratitude, and equality decorate our service to humanity.

- SERVICE IDENTITY. Each of us has a unique way of expressing Love. With daily practice, we can find our distinctive service identity and personality. Next is a daily routine that may be of use in helping you discover your service voice. When we find our service voice and rhythm, our actions are naturally permeated with passion, focus, joy, warmth, and enthusiasm.

LOVE AND SERVICE: A DAILY ROUTINE

- MORNING PROGRAM AND EVENING PROGRAM:

  1. Progressive muscle relaxation
  2. Breathwork
  3. Contemplation
  4. Meditation
  5. Prayer

- DAYTIME PROGRAM:

  1. Mindfulness

2. Practicing the Presence of God
3. Service
4. Yoga
5. Transformation of Emotion

- MORNING PROGRAM. The morning program is designed for self-healing. We start with progressive muscle relaxation and breathwork, which calm the body and mind. Contemplation converts spiritual ideas into reality; we fill our brains with wisdom. Meditation, affirmations, and prayer generate healing power that permeates every cell in the body and surrounding space. When we finish the morning program, we are aligned with Love and Her consort qualities.

- DAY PROGRAM. We can maintain the momentum gained in the morning program by practicing mindfulness or the Presence of God. These disciplines convert ordinary acts to service by introducing compassion to our actions. Without changing anything, we can focus on the Presence of God or perform each action mindfully.

  If we pay attention to the details and the routine connections between us, we won't miss the myriad opportunities throughout the day to give and receive Love. We have all had experiences with waiters, doctors, teachers, or any worker performing their task with indifference or disdain. In the consciousness of service, we infuse the same tasks with kindness and joy. *Spiritual qualities are the currency of service.*

- EVENING PROGRAM. After the day's activities are completed, repeat the morning exercise program. During the period of contemplation, review the day's activities with attention to successes, challenges, and ways to improve your ability to love and serve.

- BALANCE. Many of us have a difficult time dealing with our own suffering, let alone the monumental pain of the world. We may try to avoid all suffering by denying problems and escaping into the distractions, entertainment, and pleasures of life. Some of us take on too much suffering of others, resulting in high emotional reactivity and burn out. How much is enough? Is there a way to find balance?

The daily routine described above offers a way to stay in balance while we help others and ourselves. The morning and evening programs are for self-healing. The day program is for helping others through mindful action or practicing the Presence of God.

Through the practices of the morning and evening programs, we can withdraw from the pain and problems of the world and ourselves. In meditation, we leave suffering behind and enter a place of freedom, joy, peace, and beauty. We come out of meditation refreshed, ready to take on the next wave of problems. This is the full cycle of healthy spirituality, a way to stay balanced through renewal and regeneration.

SUGGESTIONS

- It's not what you do but how you do it. Add Love to every action.
- Start by taking care of yourself. Be kind, gentle, and loving to yourself. Then widen your circle of service to friends, family, and community.
- Pick a cause.
- Transmit your gift of compassion for the victims of social injustice and inequality.
- Go on a campaign to lift the spirits of the sick and dying or the poor and homeless.
- Volunteer at a soup kitchen.
- Read to a lonely senior.
- Fight religious and racial persecution.
- Stand up for fairness.

- Protect the meek and vulnerable.
- Be a big brother or sister to a neglected child.
- Talk to those shunned by others.
- Shop for a senior.
- Take a disabled person for a walk.
- Hold the door open for everyone.
- Let cars go ahead of you.
- Let someone ahead of you in line.
- Ask a sales person how their day is going.
- Thank the bus driver.
- Affirm loving kindness for everyone who goes by.

- THE HEALING POWER OF LOVE. In service to humanity, we discover who we really are and what really helps. We come to know Love as the power that heals the self first and then others. As we change ourselves, we change the world. The healing power of Love is a magnet that draws to itself all good things.

> *I sought my soul, but my soul I could not see.*
> *I sought my God, but my God eluded me.*
> *I serve my brother and I found all three.*
> — Anonymous

POINTS TO REMEMBER

- The goal of all spiritual practice is Love and service. Compassionate action is part of the wisdom of the universe. When we apply the law of Love, we solve problems. When you help others, you help yourself.

- Service is a universal healer, a potent medicine for individuals and the community.

- In Hinduism, selfless service is called karma yoga or right action. All actions are performed in the consciousness of Love in service to God, to please God. While there is an attempt to excel and succeed, the results of action are left to God alone. We gain peace of mind when we leave the outcome to God. No matter what the world does, just keep helping.

- Work done in the consciousness of Love is itself a sacred ritual. You are in the Presence of God when you help others. This is the real church. This is mindfulness.

- Our ability to serve improves with practice. People are complex. As we practice, our understanding is increased, so we can serve in a more refined and sophisticated manner. We become more useful.

- Service = Love in action → joy

- Whom you are with at any given moment is the most important person in the world.

- Balance meditation and service for maximum spiritual growth.

- Seek guidance and direction in your routine meetings and relationships. You can do this by invoking stillness and silence at the start of an act. When calm and attuned, the still, small voice within reveals the best way to express Love in that situation.

- No matter what the world does, cultivate Love and practice service. Maintain a positive, calm mind and open, compassionate heart. Receive the good, the bad, and the ugly, and return only good. The ones who make a difference bring anonymous, humble service to others. They are healers. They will quietly change the world.

- We may not be able to solve or fix other people's problems, but we can support them with compassion. We can be there and listen so they know they are not alone. We may not tell them what to do, but we can tell them what gets us through. We can help them do what they can. We can support their power, which can get them through any physical, mental, emotional, or spiritual barriers.

- No matter what happens, we can love and serve. We can do the work of ego reduction and the expansion of Love.

- Follow Love, serve all of humanity, and keep your eyes open. You will find your place in the world. You will see healing and transformation. You will see expansion of Love and her sister qualities. You will experience ever-increasing joy.

AFFIRMATIONS

- I help everyone.
- I am here to love and serve.
- I serve others with Love.
- I meditate on Love and give only that.
- I focus on Love and forget everything else.
- I fill every moment with Love.
- I fill every breath with Love.
- I fill every action with Love.
- The person I am with now is the most important person in the world.
- The person I am with now is God in disguise.
- I serve on the altar of the God within you.
- I serve on the altar of the Buddha within you.
- I think of others. I am sensitive to their needs.
- I give my time to others.
- I give what I can.
- I am a peaceful servant of God.

EXERCISES

1. What is the difference between an ordinary act and an act of service?

2. Describe the morning, daytime, and evening routine of Love and service.

3. How does the daily routine for Love and service help maintain balance?

4. Make a list of ways you already serve.

5. Do you have a desire to expand your service?

6. Make a list of ways you might like to serve in the future.

7. What are some of the barriers keeping you from expanding your service?

8. Anytime you feel bad and do something, however small, for someone else, notice the effect. You will feel better. It may be subtle, but it is there.

9. Most of us are comfortable serving those closest to us. It is natural to help family, friends, and neighbors in need. To expand Love and service to those that we do not know can be more challenging:

    a. You can start by extending loving-kindness affirmations, common courtesies, and thoughtful gestures to all who cross your path.
    b. You can formally volunteer in an organization that helps those in need.
    c. You can begin to see all people as members of one family, as brothers and sisters, aunts and uncles, cousins, grandchildren and grandparents, as though they are your own.
    d. When you practice mindfulness or the Presence of God, you transform an ordinary action to service by adding compassion.

In the next chapter, we will explore yoga, the fourth method of our daily activity program.

CHAPTER TWENTY-TWO

YOGA

A Way to Brahman or God

- A COMPASSIONATE, ALL-KNOWING POWER. This chapter introduces yoga, the fourth method of our daily activity program. Yoga is a gift to the world from the Hindu tradition, a system of principles and methods designed to help us achieve a great reward: making contact and getting help from a compassionate, all-knowing power that exists just behind the veil of ordinary human experience. Yoga is a scientific body of knowledge with precise instructions to dissolve the layers of ordinary limited human awareness and discover that we are in reality one with the Grand Spirit known as Brahman or God.

- A SECRET BURIED TREASURE. A yogi is one who practices yoga. The yogi learns how to break through the confining boundaries of ordinary perception to make the spectacular discovery that we are carrying with us at all times the promise of the core drive. Eternal peace, pure Love, and ecstatic joy—what we have been looking for in the external world—is a secret, buried treasure in the center of our very own being. What we really want is right here, right now, inside.

- LIBERATION FROM SUFFERING. Yoga is God-realization through the union of soul with Spirit. We are created in the image of God. God implants His image in each human body as the soul, His representation of Himself in each person. The first stage of yoga is to make contact with the soul. Then the soul merges with Spirit. When we make contact with the soul, we experience expansion of peace, Love, and other spiritual qualities. In the end, when the soul unites with the Spirit, there is complete liberation from limitation and suffering, and entry into infinite, immortal, eternal peace.

- THE VEIL OF ORDINARY CONSCIOUSNESS. In ordinary material consciousness, we do not experience the unlimited power of the soul and Spirit. Why? What is in the veil that prevents us from entry into the vast eternal kingdom? How do we get through these barriers to make contact with the soul and Spirit?

- IDENTIFICATION. The central problem is one of identification. We accept ordinary material reality as normal. We believe impermanence and change have ultimate power. We experience limitation because we identify with our body, personality, and role in the drama of life. We think we are our desires, habits, attachments, flaws, and problems. We identify with our ego, which causes us to feel separate from others, creation, and the Creator. Because of these identifications, our perception and experience is limited to the vibrational frequencies detectable by the ordinary mind and five senses.

- PURIFICATION AND ATTUNEMENT. The soul and Spirit, on the other hand, are vibrating at a frequency too subtle to detect by the mind and five senses. Any attempt to experience the soul and Spirit with the mind and senses is doomed to fail. This is where yoga enters the picture. Yoga offers a variety of methods to refine and purify our consciousness so that we attune to the more subtle frequencies of soul and Spirit.

- THE GRAND PRIZE WITHIN. To uncover our true self as eternal peace, pure Love, and ecstatic joy is a tall order. We need a set of spiritual practices that address everything that pins us down to the status quo, the level that we have come to know and accept as our home or "normal" consciousness. Because we cling to our current understanding and perception of reality, no matter how painful, difficult, and chaotic it might be, we cannot solve the cosmic puzzle and find the grand prize within. *However, when we have finally had enough suffering, when we have a passionate, burning desire to change, when we are ready to do some work, yoga answers the call by helping us unplug from the material world as we know it, so we can finally enter the kingdom of Omnipresent Love.*

FOUR PATHWAYS TO GOD

- Love, service, meditation, and wisdom are basic to any spiritual path. Tapping our innate faculties of feeling, action, concentration, and reason, yoga offers four powerful techniques to help us plow our way through the multiple layers of ordinary reality to discover the God of the universe. The four techniques are:

  1. Love, or Bhakti Yoga: the way of transforming feeling to devotion
  2. Service, or Karma Yoga: the way of transforming action to service
  3. Meditation, or Raja Yoga: the way of stillness through concentration
  4. Wisdom, or Jnana Yoga: the way of transforming thought to wisdom

     God can be known through Love, service, meditation, and wisdom, but not until we reduce the restlessness and excesses of the body, mind, emotions, desires, and ego by practicing one or a combination of these four yogas.

- We can practice bhakti, karma, raja, and jnana yoga in a variety of combinations, depending on individual preferences and circumstances. Some practice all four methods daily in a balanced way. For others, one or two of the practices may dominate. These are not distinct categories. They overlap. It is a matter of emphasis. The common denominator of any combination practiced diligently over time is the gradual replacement of restlessness, hyperactivity, destructive emotions, and excessive material desires with stillness and peace, compassion and kindness, courage and strength.

BHAKTI YOGA

THE PATH TO GOD THROUGH LOVE AND DEVOTION

- **LOVE IS GREATER THAN MAYA.** God is eternal Love, and so are we. Everything else is maya. This is bhakti yoga; its purpose is cultivating an immutable union between the Love of the soul and the Love of God. *Maya* is a Hindu term that describes the impermanence, limitations, separation, and consequent suffering of the material plane. The bhakti yogi remains in the consciousness of Love no matter what troubles or difficulties arise in the world of maya. In bhakti yoga, we accomplish this by loving God with all of our hearts, minds, might, and souls, and by loving our neighbors as ourselves. "It doesn't matter what happens, Lord. All that matters is that I love You and You love me."

- **CHANNEL ALL TO LOVE.** In bhakti yoga, we capitalize on the feeling of Love that is naturally in our heart by directing it toward God. We also channel likes, dislikes, emotion, passion, dependencies, and attachment in the direction of Love. We leave no trace of our being behind. We channel all to God as Love.

- **ONLY LOVE.** The bhakta strives to be within God's Love at all times. This is a difficult task, as stressful events often provoke a response of tension, irritation, annoyance, impatience, and worse. The bhakta wants no part of this, for a negative response is a return to the hypnotic sleep of maya. To be awake is to be aware that we are always in the presence of God's Love.

- **CHOOSE AN ASPECT THAT AROUSES DEVOTION.** To remain in God's Love, the bhakta cultivates a real, intimate, personal relationship with the Divine. We can do this by choosing an aspect of God that arouses devotion. That aspect becomes a point of focus for the bhakti yogi's Love.

- A PERSONAL RELATIONSHIP WITH GOD. God is both personal and impersonal. For most people, it is difficult to apply Love to an impersonal aspect of God, such as an incomprehensible, abstract power. However, we can form a personal relationship with God as the Father, Mother, Friend, Beloved, Teacher, or as one of the Divine incarnations such as Christ, Krishna, or Buddha. These aspects naturally evoke a loving response.

- HIDE AND SEEK. Loving God does not come easily or early on the spiritual path. In the beginning, we do not know God; it is not natural to love what we do not know. We can start the process by thinking about God. Then we can talk, share, and listen, as in any human relationship. With consistent meditation, service, and conversation with God, at some point She responds by revealing Herself as peace, joy, Love, power, wisdom, ecstasy, or some other manifestation. Then She goes back behind the veil, playing hide and seek. We return to ordinary consciousness and resume our spiritual work. During dry spells, we develop and mature our unconditional Love, surrender, devotion, trust, strength, and courage. How else would we develop our spiritual muscles?

- FIND AND KEEP. Nevertheless, we yearn for God's return. Our heart's desire is to find and keep Her. We want more than just a taste of Her sweetness. If we persist in our spiritual work, God appears again, perhaps with the Mother's tender Love, warmth, and exquisite beauty. God may manifest as our unconditional Friend and Confidante, One who knows, understands, and accepts us no matter what we have done. If attuned and receptive, we may know God as our infinitely wise Father, Guide, and Protector. When we are in pain, we can know God as the Teacher, giving us the experiences that we need for spiritual growth. As we get to know our Father, Mother, Teacher, and Friend, it is easy and natural to love Him in an intimate, ever-evolving, ever-new romance.

- UNCONDITIONAL LOVE. God is an infinite ocean of pure, unconditional Love, an ocean we cannot enter until our Love is likewise pure and unconditional. In bhakti yoga, we accomplish this by applying all of our spiritual muscle to respond with Love to all people in every circumstance. All we have to do is love no matter what happens and not worry about the rest. This is following God's will through attunement with His aspect of all-powerful Love.

- ETERNAL ROMANCE. We can apply God's Love, the most powerful healing force in the universe, to any pain or problem. When difficulties come and we find ourselves reacting poorly, we can find our connection to God's Omnipresent Love by going to the deepest part of our hearts, where He resides. By repeatedly returning to God's Love, we break our identification with maya and reduce our suffering. In our eternal romance with the almighty, gentle Father-Mother God of the universe, we get the peace-joy that we crave.

KARMA YOGA
THE PATH TO GOD THROUGH ACTION

- SELFLESS ACTION. Karma yoga is union of the soul with Spirit through selfless action. Here we take advantage of our activity throughout the day. In karma yoga, we transform ordinary action to selfless action dedicated to God; service becomes the principle means of union of the soul with Spirit.

- LOVING SERVICE. Every thought, feeling, and action is an offering in loving service to God. There is no thought of personal gain or impressing others. We surrender the results, outcomes, expectations, and rewards to God. "I work to please God alone."

"Thou art the doer, not I." "Thy will, Lord, not mine." Every action is powered by His energy and will.

- NON-ATTACHMENT TO OUTCOMES. The ego is attached to outcomes. The ego derives its power in the battle for victory over defeat, gain over loss, and pleasure over pain. When the ego takes credit for success, it puffs up; when it fails, it grieves. In either case, it maintains its territory. To the yogi, however, the ups and downs of life are one and the same; the outcome is in God's hands. When motivated by the ego, we add to the separation between God and ourselves. The same act performed selflessly moves us closer to God. As servant to the King, the karma yogi claims nothing for the self, no matter what level of personal sacrifice.

- EGO REDUCTION AND SOUL EXPANSION. In the practice of karma yoga, the sole intent is to follow God's will with every action. The Creator is the Author of the act. The yogi is the worker. Once the act is completed, the yogi disconnects from the results of the action, letting the story of life unfold as determined by God. When we surrender the results of our actions to God, we deprive the ego of consequences. The ego shrinks, allowing the soul to come into awareness.

- EVEN-MINDED, ENTHUSIASTIC, GRATEFUL, HUMBLE. We play our service-role, fulfill our tasks and responsibilities, and do the best we can. We strive for success in all endeavors but remain even-minded in any outcome. We perform each act with calm concentration and efficiency. Understanding that all work is God's work, we perform every act, however mundane or routine, with enthusiasm, gratitude, and humility. We avoid indifference, an aspect of laziness and selfishness. Accepting difficulties as coming from God the Teacher, we learn and move on.

- ONE CONTINUOUS SACRED RITUAL OF LOVING SERVICE. Wherever we are and whoever we are, we can turn this moment into serviceable action by dedicating it to God, humanity, and the greater good. Then every movement and action powers our way to God. It does not matter what we do. Our task may be simple or complex, routine or important, painful or enjoyable. What matters is that we hold the consciousness of God at all times and seek His guidance as we perform and give our best. Then all tasks merge into one continuous, sacred ritual of loving service to God.

- STILLNESS IN ACTION. By non-attachment to the results of action, we can enter the arena of worldly activity, serve with compassion and understanding, and remain calm even in the face of turmoil. The stillness of the true self remains constant in the midst of activity. The *Bhagavad Gita* refers to this as inaction in action. As stated by Paramahansa Yogananda in *Autobiography of a Yogi*, "I, the soul, watch the cosmic movie with calm detachment while at the same time I play my assigned role perfectly with zeal, ambition, and the supreme desire to please God." Karma yoga, meditation in action, is a source of joy. Joy is in the action, in working for God and humanity, in service. The outcome belongs to God.

RAJA YOGA
THE PATH TO GOD THROUGH MEDITATION

- AN INVITATION TO MEDITATION. *"Be still and know that I am God"* is an invitation from the Bible (Psalm 46:10) to meditate. In meditation, we can achieve the motionless state, which profoundly facilitates our ability to commune with God. Raja yoga describes the way to a direct experience with God in the stillness of meditation.

- PATANJALI. Patanjali, an ancient master of yoga, outlined an eight-step model designed to achieve stillness and communion with God. By following the eight steps, we learn how to achieve stillness by stopping the world, body, senses, and mind. To understand the eight steps, one must first understand *prana, pranayama*, and the *chakras.*

- PRANA. Prana is the life energy present in the human body. We send prana outward towards the world for daily activities, and in and up the spine to the brain for God-realization.

- CHAKRAS. There are seven centers of concentrated prana in the spine and brain, called chakras. Yoga opens up the chakras, so that energy can travel upward into the higher centers in the spinal cord and brain resulting in God-communion.

- PRANAYAMA. Pranayama is control of prana by reversing the outward flow of life energy, directing it to the higher chakras in the spine and brain. The result is expansion of peace, joy, and Love.

- THE EIGHT STEPS OF PATANJALI:

  1. YAMA is moral conduct. All religions have rules for moral conduct, such as the Ten Commandments. Yama refers to abstention from harming others, falsehood, theft, and greed.
  2. NIYAMA is religious observance. Devotion, service, moderation, discipline, study of scripture, purity, and surrender, along with the moral conduct described in Step 1, provide a platform from which all else is built.
  3. ASANA is right posture. Hatha yoga is a set of body positions and exercises that prepare the body for meditation. In meditation, it is essential that the body is still and the spine straight.
  4. PRANAYAMA is control of prana or life energy. Energy directed outward in ordinary activity keeps us locked in the status quo of mundane consciousness. Pranayama reverses the flow of outward energy and directs it inward and upward, toward the spinal cord and brain. This stills the mind and senses.
  5. PRATYAHARA is interiorization. Pranayama (Step 4) results in interiorization of the mind, energy, and consciousness from

outer attachments and bodily organs to the higher centers in the spinal cord and brain.

6. DHARANA is concentration. The interiorized mind is completely still so it can concentrate on a single point, such as a mantra.

7. DHYANA is meditation. This is direct concentration on God.

8. SAMADHI is union of the soul with God. This is the most advanced stage of meditation. There is complete union or merging with God.

• STILLNESS OPENS THE DOOR TO HIGHER STATES OF CONSCIOUSNESS. When the mind slows and finally stops, consciousness and energy shift from the outer world, restless thoughts, and sensations of the body to the higher centers in the spine and brain. In stillness, God reveals Himself on His schedule, through His grace, as peace, joy, Love, energy, light, wisdom, and guidance. We realize His beauty and power. When meditation is over, we manifest His Love and wisdom through service to humanity.

JNANA YOGA
THE PATH TO GOD THROUGH WISDOM

• FROM ORDINARY THOUGHT TO WISDOM. The path of jnana yoga capitalizes on our God-given gift of reason by transforming ordinary thought into wisdom. Through the practice of jnana yoga, intellect evolves to intuition, or direct knowledge of the truth. For those inclined to practice jnana yoga, thought is an enjoyable, stimulating, vibrant source of inspiration and realization.

• YOU BECOME WISDOM. In jnana yoga, we do not just think or theorize. We embody wisdom and become one with the truth through a process of listening, perceiving, and assimilating. The process starts with the study of scriptural truth. Then we bring the idea to contemplation and meditation for realization. We maintain this wisdom during activity, through affirmation, concentration, and will.

- ONENESS. For example, in the beginning, we think the world as we know it in ordinary consciousness is the only reality. The jnana yoga thinker, however, is convinced of the oneness of it all underneath the complex surface of ordinary consciousness. Despite the appearance of complexity, the jnana yogi affirms God is One. (S)he maintains the affirmation of oneness in the face of the counter-pull of mundane thoughts and the senses that support the illusions of maya. The jnana yogi understands through discrimination that the nature of the world and its phenomena are illusory, and that only the oneness of God is real. This is union of the soul with God through discriminatory intellect and wisdom.

THE YOGI IN THE SCHOOL OF LIFE

- TWO KEY PROCESSES. In the practice of yoga, two key processes converge to accomplish the goal of union of soul with Spirit. These processes are:

1. The school of life
2. Pranayama

- THE SCHOOL OF LIFE. God sets up His school of life, where we have the opportunity to learn critical lessons for purposes of evolution of the soul towards Spirit. There are many classes, subjects, and tests. When we learn the lessons and pass the tests, we transform and heal. In a process of purification, the ego shrinks and spiritual qualities expand.

- PRANAYAMA. Bhakti, karma, raja, and jnana yoga similarly lead to evolution of the soul to Spirit. Practice of the four yogas slowly and progressively opens the higher chakras in the spine and brain. Consciousness and energy travel upwards through the chakras to higher centers in the brain and spine, eventually resulting in a tangible experience of God's wisdom and power.

- CONSCIOUSNESS IS REFINED AND THE SOUL EVOLVES. Each person learns their tailor-made lessons in the school of life. Ego, problems, and flaws burn up in the fire of devotion, service, meditation, and wisdom. The higher chakras in the spine and brain open. Consciousness is refined and the soul evolves. With sustained practice, we reach a critical mass, tipping the scales in favor of the soul over the ego.

- THE SECRET VEILS OF MAYA LIFT. In the end, when we conquer the ego, when the secret veils of maya lift and when the soul dissolves in the one true reality, we find that God has hidden Himself as joy and peace in the human body-temple itself. Then, in perfect attunement with God's will, we can follow the command of the sacred scriptures: to love God with all of our heart, mind, might, and soul and our neighbor as our self. Such a servant of the King can give patience, sweetness, kindness, and gentleness to all of humanity.

- THE HIGHEST STATE OF CONSCIOUSNESS. God's eternal peace, pure Love, and ecstatic joy are the highest states of consciousness, the beginning of all creation, the endpoint of evolution, and the ultimate grace. We are made of this pure and perfect, unending Love. We come from, move, live, have our being, and ultimately melt back into this sacred consciousness. This is yoga, evolution of the soul, and God-realization.

POINTS TO REMEMBER

- We are more than our egos, bodies, or personalities. We are not our problems, symptoms, flaws, or disabilities. We are made in the image of Spirit. We need to transfer our identity from our problems to soul qualities. Soul qualities will take us to higher states of consciousness.

- We can experience what is just underneath the world as we know it when everything we understand as reality is reduced to zero in the absolute stillness of yoga meditation. This includes the ego, personality, body, senses, mind, personal story, world story, and fund of knowledge. When we escape from everything we think we are and enter the domain of stillness, we can experience the ecstatic joy of the soul and God.

- The science of yoga teaches us how to still the waves of mental restlessness, excessive material desire, and emotional reactivity in both meditation and activity.

- Yoga is not easy. It takes a lot of work and a long time to reach such superconscious states as the changeless peace of the soul, pure light, or cosmic sound. It is a long, arduous journey to Omniscient Love. Maya has great power. The way is paved with strife. Nevertheless, yoga works. Progress is slow but definite. Many quit because they want a quick fix. Practice, patience, and perseverance are prerequisites for success.

- The way to God is paved with unconditional Love. This is devotion, bhakti yoga. We do everything with one intention: to love God and people.

- The way to God is paved with service to humanity. This is karma yoga. We add Love to every action.

- The way to God is through stillness. This is meditation or raja yoga. Stillness is the doorway to higher states of consciousness.

- The way to God is through discriminative intellect. This is jnana yoga. We convert ordinary thinking to wisdom.

- Bhakti, karma, raja, and jnana yoga work together. The practice of one feeds the other three.

- In the beginning, the goal of selfless service is not possible because of the ego. However, if our intent is selflessness and we continue to practice yoga to the best of our ability, the ego slowly dissolves.

- Service work is not about success or failure. The work is our responsibility. The outcome is not ours.

- The yogi cuts into the ignorance, suffering, and injustice of the world by adding compassion, humility, and understanding.

AFFIRMATIONS

- I conduct this act immersed in Your Love with the sole desire to please You.
- I am always at the feet of God.
- I am always on the altar of God.
- I serve every person as a manifestation of God.
- I love unconditionally.
- Love is the only reality.
- God is one.
- God is stillness.
- God is in the stillness.
- God is beyond the stillness.

EXERCISES

1. What is yoga?

2. Why is it impossible to experience the soul with the ordinary mind and the five senses?

3. What keeps us locked up in ordinary consciousness?

4. Describe in detail the four types of yoga.

5. What are the eight steps of Patanjali?

6. What does stillness have to do with knowing God?

7. Describe how the school of life and the four yogas work together to advance the soul in its movement toward Spirit.

In the next chapter, we will study the fifth and final technique of our daily activity program: the transformation of emotion.

CHAPTER TWENTY-THREE

TRANSFORMATION OF EMOTION

Converting Emotional Pain to Self-knowledge

"THE GUESTHOUSE"

This being human is a guesthouse.
Every morning is a new arrival.
A joy, a depression, a meanness,
some momentary awareness comes
as an unexpected visitor.

Welcome and entertain them all!
Even if they're a crowd of sorrows,
Who violently sweep your house
empty of its furniture,
Still, treat each guest honorably.
He may be clearing you out
for some new delight.

The dark thought, the shame, the malice,
meet them at the door laughing,
and invite them in.
Be grateful for whoever comes,
Because each has been sent
as a guide from beyond.
— Rumi

- In this chapter, we will review the fifth and final technique of our daily activity program: the transformation of emotion. Here you will learn how to transform painful emotion into self-knowledge.

INTROSPECTION

- Often, we can successfully work through painful emotions by practicing any one or a combination of the other techniques described in this work. Most of the time, we go to the horizontal axis to manage painful emotion. Here we tell our story to those we trust. We engage in constructive meaningful activities. We go to church, synagogue, or mosque for traditional worship.

- If these options do not suffice, we can turn to vertical axis techniques such as affirmations, habit transformation, progressive muscle relaxation, breathwork, contemplation, meditation, prayer, mindfulness, practicing the Presence of God, service, and yoga. Sometimes, however, even these methods do not liberate us from the grip of painful feelings. In such instances, it may be necessary to stop all of these practices, stay alone, be with the pain, and let it teach. This involves introspection or self-analysis.

- Introspection allows us to see our strengths and virtues, flaws and limitations, and the needs and desires that motivate our actions. Material for review includes attitude, thoughts, emotion, behavior, habits, conflicts, character flaws, relationships, and our ability to love, serve, give, and be useful.

- Introspection is necessary for deep healing. There are times when we have to examine our pain and extract the necessary lessons in order to go forward. If we choose any other option, the pain lingers.

- To succeed in introspection, we must learn to successfully navigate our way through painful emotions. Painful emotion is a teacher bearing the gift of self-knowledge. Self-knowledge is information gained when we explore our emotions. Most of us experience emotional pain in response to ordinary daily events. These feelings carry meaningful information about our story.

- Emotions are natural, normal, healthy, and intelligent. Within the painful emotion are problems and solutions begging for recognition, work, synthesis, and resolution. When we extract this important information from within our emotions, suffering is contained, reduced, or eliminated. It is only when emotional pain is not processed that it causes us additional difficulties.

- Anger, depression, fear, guilt, and other painful emotions are powerful energy forces that need to be managed wisely or they can overwhelm our defenses, cause us to lose control, and in the worst-case scenario, endanger others and ourselves. Yet most of us have had no training in emotional pain management.

REPRESSED EMOTIONS ARE STORED IN THE SUBCONSCIOUS AND BODY

- Because we don't know what to do with painful emotions, we instinctively try to keep them from conscious awareness by denying their existence, drowning them in substance abuse or pushing them into the subconscious and the body where they are stored in latent form. When we resist experiencing pain, the energy of the unprocessed feelings remains in the subconscious and the body. The subconscious and body become carriers of suppressed, unresolved emotions and the unprocessed lessons embedded within them.

- While in storage, these emotions can have a negative impact on our physical, mental, and spiritual health. We develop negative attitudes, distorted thinking, and behave in destructive ways. For example, unprocessed anger leads to judgment, criticism, blaming, and fighting with others. Instead of processing the anger into self-knowledge, we pass it along to others, making their lives more difficult.

SETUPS

- We attract events, circumstances, and people who elicit the painful feelings and problems hidden in the subconscious and body. These are setups. A setup is any circumstance that brings forth painful emotions. Setups come to reveal the issues requiring some work. The painful emotion, the carrier, tells us where to work.

- If we do not do the work, the problem remains. When we miss the opportunity to get the necessary lessons, we continue to attract people and circumstances that bring out these suppressed feelings. We continue to attract similar circumstances until we learn the necessary lessons.

- For example, if we are codependent, we continue to attract codependent partners until independence is learned. We may remain stuck in a codependent relationship or find new people and repeat the codependent pattern until we sufficiently process the underlying, unresolved pain related to dependency into new knowledge and strength.

SELF-KNOWLEDGE

- The alternative to these negative scenarios is to learn how to extract the messages embedded within the feelings. We can process the emotional pain into a story with knowledge and lessons. Our feelings carry problems, solutions, and strategies that contribute to understanding life. To get this knowledge, we need a fearless, objective, honest introspective process. The ego is the greatest opponent to such a process.

- The ego will try to tell the story solely from its point of view.

Self-justification is one of its greatest tricks. It does not admit to mistakes. Since it lacks introspection on its own problems, it remains self-righteous while it treats others as scapegoats. It projects problems rather than taking responsibility. The ego is selfish, insecure, defensive, controlling, and self-important. In the face of criticism, it becomes frightened and aggressive. While it may accurately discover others' faults, it is blind to its own.

- To combat the ego, we can turn to introspection guided by the higher self. The higher self is not afraid to look inward. It wants to find flaws and replace them with healing qualities. It is ready to look in every secret chamber of our consciousness in order to root out the barriers that prevent our full expression of Love. Our true self knows we will feel better when we do this work. It is willing to suffer any pain in order to rise.

- The soul reviews our story, looking for the root cause of our pain. "What am I to learn from this? Where am I at fault in this story? Where can I improve? How could I have behaved more skillfully? How can I use this pain to find and replace my flaws with spiritual qualities? Where did I fail to express Love in thought, feeling, and action? Am I giving the best of my Love, humility, understanding and gentleness to everyone throughout the day? Do I give understanding, compassion, and forgiveness to others but not enough to myself?"

- Upon introspection, the ego and soul fight for control. For example, when we are mistreated, we are quickly angered and name what the other person has done wrong and what the remedy should be. We take defensive actions, such as setting boundaries, deploying interpersonal communication for problem solving, and correcting injustice. This is good.

- Often, however, the wrongdoer is not cooperative, leaving us angry and resentful. It is easy to get stuck here; the ego tends to act like a self-righteous victim, defining the faults and weaknesses of others as the source of our discomfort. It may be right but this only serves to prolong our suffering since we end up bearing the pain given to us by the wrongdoer.

- The true self, on the other hand, assumes responsibility for any lingering pain as a stimulant for the development of spiritual qualities, even if the pain comes to us by way of injustice. The soul uses the transformative power of Love to counter any remaining anger and resentment. By responding to cruelty with strength, to ignorance with understanding, and to suffering with compassion, the soul spiritualizes our story, consequently giving us the peace of mind we seek.

- The implications of the introspective process are profound. We stop blaming others for our problems. We abandon the victim stance and take responsibility for our emotions. We become more concerned with our own behavior than we are with another's. Regardless of whether others are right or wrong, we use our suffering as an opportunity to cultivate strength, courage, endurance, and peace.

Following is a systematic technique designed to help us extract the knowledge embedded in our emotional pain, so it becomes our ally rather than our adversary. Before reviewing the technique, please read the next section regarding risk.

RISK

- Processing raw emotional pain into self-knowledge is not for everybody. Opening a dialogue with emotional pain can be frightening, requiring a dive into uncharted territory and facing the unknown. We must explore and even become friends with our fears. We stand alone and "ride the pain waves." There is likely to be considerable resistance. We should never underestimate how frightful this may be. We should never push anybody into such a process.

- Some cannot and should not engage in exploring their pain in such a manner without seeking professional help; it might flood their defenses, causing alarm or panic. In such circumstances, the individual can work with the other techniques described in this work. If you feel that processing emotional pain to gain self-knowledge is too intense, please avoid it at this point and consult with a professional counselor. For those ready to review the technique, the steps are outlined below.

PROCESSING PAINFUL EMOTION INTO SELF-KNOWLEDGE

This technique applies to any emotion:

1. Create a safe healing space
2. Ask for help from your Higher Power
3. Let the story unfold
4. Spiritualize the story

1. CREATE A SAFE HEALING SPACE:

- An honest look at character flaws can be threatening, even shattering to the ego. However, the goal is not to tear the self to shreds. The purpose of introspection is to discover those aspects that need to change without causing unnecessary guilt, low self-esteem, or humiliation.

- Sit quietly. Use your breathing and meditation techniques to bring in as much stillness as you can.

- Be gentle and compassionate with yourself. Remain calm and accepting. Rather than feel bad that you have problems, feel good that you have the courage to face them and the integrity to change for the better.

2. ASK FOR HELP FROM YOUR HIGHER POWER:

- We are connected inside to an infinitely intelligent healing power whose nature is Love and compassion. We can ask for and get help from the Great Physician, the Healer within.

- Open yourself to the wisdom of your Counselor and Friend, asking for help to understand the nature of your suffering. Ask for the necessary courage and strength.

3. LET THE STORY UNFOLD:

- There is a pressure inside of each emotion, pushing it to tell its story. Right or wrong, the feeling wants to be heard, accepted, and validated. We need to let our emotions tell their stories without judgment.

- Go to your serene and spacious witness. In a relaxed, receptive state, with your defenses down, observe your feelings.

- Feelings such as depression, anxiety, fear, anger, guilt, shame, jealousy, and abandonment may surface. Identify and label them.

- Feelings often overlap and merge. It is possible to feel angry and sad or other combinations all at once. With practice and patience, you will be able to identify overlapping feelings.

- Relax and breathe.

- Feel each emotion fully. Let the feeling come through without resistance. Do not fight. Take full responsibility for the emotion. It is there for a reason. It is intelligent, pointing you in the direction of work that needs completion. When you experience the feeling and take responsibility for it, it releases the intelligent information it carries. In a context of compassion, gentleness, and understanding, let the emotion tell its story.

- In the story, we can find our strengths and faults. We can define the spiritual qualities we already have; however, we should not stop there. We can build on our strengths only if we define and work on our remaining problems and issues.

- Introspection allows us to see the recesses of our mind that otherwise remain hidden. Without fear, go to the deepest, darkest places in your consciousness, to those recesses needing exposure and work. Take out your inner mirror. Turn on the light of introspection. Ask the pain:

  o Why are you here?
  o What am I to learn from you?
  o Show me why I repeat the same mistakes.
  o What flaws do I have that contribute to my current problems?
  o Show me anything and everything I need to learn to become a better person.
  o Direct me to the work I need to do in the external world and within myself.

- If we stay with our feelings long enough, we can determine the significance of our suffering. Our pain takes us to the root cause of our troubles. This is good news; once we discover our flaws and attachments, we are en route to deep healing. But first, we must learn to spiritualize our story.

4. SPIRITUALIZE THE STORY:

- You can see how important it is to find your problems; for if you do not find them, you cannot improve. However, it is equally important to avoid reliving your problems. In this step, we replace our flaws with healing qualities. Guided by spiritual qualities, the story unfolds in the direction of Love.

- Never identify with your weakness. Dwelling on flaws actually makes them stronger. Our flaws and problems are reinforced through the repetition of thought. The self becomes confused, identifying with negativity, thinking this is its nature. Always remember: *you are not your problems and flaws.* This is very important!

- In order to avoid obsessing on errors or flaws and thinking that is who you are, discover the problem and construct its opposite positive healing quality. Focus on that quality. When you discover a negative quality in your nature, do not concentrate on it. Instead, direct all your energy to the cultivation of the opposite good quality.

- For every negative quality, there is a polar opposite, positive quality. For anger, there is patience. For selfishness, there is Love. For anxiety, there is peace. For resentment, there is forgiveness.

- You can do this by creating affirmations related to the healing quality you wish to cultivate. With this method, one by one, problems are contained, reduced, and dissolved, replaced by positive qualities and habits. The true self emerges as peace, strength, courage, and compassion, overwhelming all traces of negativity.

- We learn many valuable lessons from our emotional pain as our life story unfolds. By completing an introspective process, our emotional pain exhausts itself and disappears, leaving in its wake new knowledge and strength.

- When we permeate our strategies for dealing with life's problems with Love and understanding, we spiritualize our story. In clearing and healing our emotions, we gain the peace of the soul.

TRANSFORMATION OF EMOTION INTO SELF-KNOWLEDGE

AN EXAMPLE

Joe's wife has been complaining that he has been irritable with her and their children. He decides to see if she is right. First, he reviews the lessons in this book on affirmations, will, habits, and introspection. Then he finds some quiet time. He asks for help from his Higher Power. He looks inside with an attitude of honest, fearless compassion.

Joe surrenders into his pain. He adopts an attitude of total acceptance to whatever story his emotions have to tell. As Joe lets the story unfold, he realizes he has indeed been impatient and angry with his family.

Further exploration of his feelings leads him to realize that he has been struggling at work. His boss treats him poorly. Colleagues are more competitive than cooperative. The work itself has become boring. Joe realizes that he needs to change his job, but until he can make that change, he does not want to abuse his family. He fights off his ego's tendency to blame others and seeks to spiritualize his story.

Joe knows that there are times when he has absolutely no control over the environment, but he always has choice about his will, thoughts, and actions. Joe decides to fight the battle against his anger. He consults the list of healing qualities. He finds a number of qualities that he can use to antidote his irritability. These include peace, patience, kindness, tenderness, gentleness, sweetness, understanding, compassion, forgiveness, tolerance, acceptance, openness, and surrender.

He writes affirmations on some note cards: "I am patient, kind, and understanding under all conditions. Sweetness of speech is the rule of the day. I accept the things I cannot change." Patience, kindness, understanding, and sweetness of speech are the watchwords he uses for every action. He practices these qualities in all of his actions throughout the day.

Joe finds it difficult to respond with spiritual qualities when the demands are great at work and at home. Nevertheless, with perseverance he sees slow but definite results. His family is happier. Joe gradually becomes more patient as he looks for a new job.

In allowing his emotions to tell their story, Joe discovered his issues and problems. Then he infused the story with healing qualities, realizing another degree of his true self.

POINTS TO REMEMBER

- How we manage painful emotion can make the difference between success and failure, health and disease, poverty or prosperity, Love and despair.

- Painful emotions are a part of the normal, natural, intelligent healing process. When we learn how to process emotion into self-knowledge, we gain strength and peace.

- We can process feelings daily or as they arise. If we wait too long, they add up and may become too hot to handle, forcing us to express them destructively.

- Emotions are a rich source of information. If we are able to experience sadness or anger without excessive use of alcohol, drugs, food, gambling, sex, or violence, we may discover why we are experiencing these feelings. Emotions tell a story with lessons having to do with the cultivation of spiritual qualities. When we finish the story, it will not keep coming up.

- During introspection, the ego tells the story from its point of view. This is good. We can learn many things about ourselves by listening to the ego and seeing how it works. However, the ego tends to be self-righteous. It blames others, making itself into a victim. The soul, on the other hand, looks to replace our imperfections with spiritual power. It spiritualizes the story by bringing out our soul qualities.

- Emotions come in waves. Learn how to surf the waves. If you ride them, they dissipate, leaving behind a story packed with meaning, lessons, peace, and power.

- Letting the story unfold and spiritualizing the story may take longer for some problems than for others. For deep long-term problems, these two steps may alternate and overlap for months, even years.

- True self-analysis is essential for deep healing and recovery. Be honest with yourself. To have a clear conscience is one of the greatest joys.

- The ego keeps us tiny by inflating the importance of its story. When we reduce and finally replace the ego with the soul, we realize the true self as a composite of the great healing qualities: Love, compassion, understanding, forgiveness, strength, courage, warmth, and more.

EXERCISES

1. What is introspection?

2. What is self-knowledge?

3. Overwhelming emotions reduce our intellect, imagination, and choices. We become destructive. Describe the technique for transforming emotion into self-knowledge. How can you use this technique?

4. Can you think of some occasions where your emotional discomfort carried the lessons you needed to learn? How did you extract that knowledge from the pain?

5. How can you spiritualize your story?

You have completed your study of twelve methods proven over the ages to be effective tools for cultivating healing qualities. In the next section, we will discuss how healing qualities help us manage pain and problems. From the one hundred qualities listed in the spiritual alphabet, ten are chosen for detailed discussion, study, and work.

PART SIX
SPIRITUAL QUALITIES

CHAPTER TWENTY-FOUR

INTRODUCTION TO SPIRITUAL QUALITIES

- THE GOAL. The goal of all spiritual work is cultivation of soul qualities. Soul qualities are healing powers built into the body as standard equipment. They help us broker and buffer the pain of life. Such healing powers as courage, compassion, understanding, and humility help us manage our problems skillfully.

- INTERCONNECTED. The qualities are related. They grow together. An increase in one leads to expansion of the others, and they all lead directly to Love and ultimately to joy. If we increase patience, we automatically become more compassionate. If we listen more carefully, we will be more understanding. Gratitude leads to reverence, peace to Love, and when Love is great enough, it transforms into joy.

- SCHOOL. Life is a school. Pain is the teacher if we let it be. The lessons have to do with expansion of spiritual qualities. We can expand any quality by practicing the methods described in this book. This work has no end. We can expand any quality indefinitely. Greatest expansion comes when we focus all our attention on the chosen method and quality rather than on our problem.

- WE ALWAYS NEED MORE. Our circumstances present us with the opportunity to cultivate any one or a combination of one hundred soul qualities. We always need more understanding, forgiveness, strength, and forbearance. We always need warmth, thoughtfulness, and sensitivity to the needs of others. There is always a need for justice and equality. We crave friendship, humor, fun, and laughter. We have an unbending need for peace, Love, joy and wisdom. These and other soul qualities help us skillfully manage anything life throws at us.

- THE GOLD STANDARD. Love qualities are the gold standard, the ideal, the best. They guide us. They set the boundaries and pathway. We are either in or out of bounds, on or off the path. When our thoughts, feelings, and actions are not in alignment with Love, we have work to do. The work is to practice any one or a combination of spiritual methods to expand Love until it is unconditional. Soul qualities are the goal, the product, and the true measure of our success.

- THE JEWELS OF THIS LIFE. No matter what barriers would stop us, we can respond with soul qualities. These are our tools, the habits of a sage, and the jewels of this life. In the next section, there is a discussion of how soul qualities help us manage any pain or problem. When your back is against the wall and you are still in pain, you can call up your army of one hundred healing qualities. We will now begin our review of ten qualities in detail. We will start with Love.

CHAPTER TWENTY-FIVE

LOVE

The Command to Love

- *JUDAISM.* *"You shall not take vengeance or bear a grudge against any of your people, but you shall love your neighbor as yourself" (Leviticus 19:17).*

- *CHRISTIANITY.* *"You shall love the Lord your God with all your heart, soul, mind, and strength, and your neighbor as yourself" (Mark 12:28–34).*

- *ISLAM.* *"Paradise will be occupied by those who love one another for God's sake, those who sit together for God's sake, and those who visit one another for God's sake" (the Hadith).*

- *BUDDHISM.* *"Whatever happiness is in the world has arisen from a wish for the welfare of others; whatever misery there is has arisen from indulging selfishness" (a Buddhist proverb).*

- *HINDUISM.* *"O Arjuna, the best type of yogi is he who feels for others, whether in grief or pleasure, even as he feels for himself" (the Bhagavad-Gita 6:32)*

- *TAOISM.* *"The supreme good is like water, which nourishes all things without trying to. It is content with the low places that people disdain. That is like the Tao" (Tao Te Ching 8)*

- *NATIVE AMERICAN SPIRITUALITY.* *"Whatever befalls the*

Earth befalls the sons and daughters of the Earth. We did not weave the web of life; we are merely a strand in it. Whatever we do to the web, we do to ourselves" (Chief Seattle).

This chapter describes the healing principle of Love from the mystic traditions of Hinduism, Christianity, Judaism, and Sufism. It describes God's Love as the Great Healer and our purpose on this earth to learn how to love when we do not.

Some readers will find it refreshing that a healing and pain management model speaks to God's Love, as this concept is already a part of their belief systems, if not their central premise. Others will find this discussion unacceptable, even toxic.

Recall this advice from Chapter Three: Take what you need and leave the rest. Nuke offensive language and substitute your own. If you don't believe in God, let alone God as Love, ignore this term and instead substitute spiritual qualities, healing qualities, qualities, the Tao, the Way, the Great Spirit, compassion, or any other term that gives you traction. The main point is to expand healing power inside. Some of the great books and teachers describe this power as Divine Love. Please read on and use whatever term is most acceptable to you.

THE COSMIC PURPOSE OF LIFE

• THE GRAND PLAN. The purpose of life is Love. The grand plan for each individual and the human race is evolution of consciousness toward higher realms of Love and service. The universe is set up as a school, our Teacher, the God of Love. The lesson plan is simple. *We are on this Earth-school to learn how to love when we do not.*

• A COSMIC GAME OF CHOICE. God sets up Her school of life where we learn critical lessons that propel our evolution toward Love. The most important discovery is that God has invented a cosmic game of choice. We can use our free will to choose Love or something else. Our troubles are the result of poor choices. We move in the right direction when we choose Love.

- THE COMPASSIONATE WAY. Lack of Love is a fundamental cause of our problems. The solution is Love. We are to follow the path of kindness and compassion, thereby becoming Love itself. When we learn how to love, we fulfill life's purpose. The entire setup of creation intends this to happen. All events point in this direction.

- AN INSATIABLE DRIVE. As described in Step 1, the Core Drive, we have an insatiable drive for unconditional Love. We must have it. In the beginning, we look to family, friends, and lovers to satisfy our craving for perfect Love. We all start here. However, human love can only satisfy a part of this need. Divine Love is the only experience that is completely fulfilling.

- A DESPERATE SEARCH. When we look to people for pure Love, we fail; human love is imperfect. We all have egos, flaws, attachments, and bad habits. These barriers impede our ability to manifest perfect Love. When our need for unconditional Love remains unmet, we get anxious. In frustration, we desperately seek Love in all the wrong places. We end up with codependency, multiple partners, addiction, and other such bad habits. The solution lies in the transformation of human love to Divine Love.

- PURIFICATION TOWARDS PERFECTION. We can achieve this change through a process of purification towards perfection. This requires discipline, effort, and ego reduction. It takes time and it hurts, so we are slow to enter the process; even when we start, we resist its completion. However, this is the purpose of life. We are here to learn how to love unconditionally. Until we begin transforming human to Divine Love, there will be restlessness, frustration, and dissatisfaction. To eliminate this unnecessary suffering, we must expand and perfect our Love until it is unqualified. Until then, we cannot realize the core drive.

- START WITH CURRENT RELATIONSHIPS. We can use our current relationships as a starting place. In our lives, we give and receive love in a variety of roles, including as a parent, child, sibling, coworker, friend, neighbor, or romantic partner. In the daily grind of these relationships, problems inevitably emerge. Rather than be dismayed, we can use these as opportunities to expand and purify our Love. We can do some interpersonal work to improve communication and problem solving. However, the transformation of human love to Divine Love is ultimately about self-reform and self-mastery. It is not about others' behavior. It is about our response.

- SELF-REFORM. Instead of looking to others, we bring Love from within ourselves. Instead of trying to control and change others, which usually causes resistance, we learn how to be content and comfortable inside. There is no expectation, demand, or need for others to behave in a certain way. We give Love, no matter what. This higher Love gives complete satisfaction while setting up the condition for others to change when they can.

- DIVINE LOVE IS ALWAYS INSIDE. God's Love is Omnipresent, always available as the universal balm for any problem or pain. We can tap into Divine Love at any time; it is already with us, implanted in the bodily temple as the soul, or Image of God. We already have the superconscious Love we are looking for. It is always inside, regardless of our outer condition.

- REMOVE ALL TRACES OF NEGATIVITY. Through mindful introspection, we can identify any flaw that impedes the free flow of Love. Then we can apply a spiritual method such as mindfulness or meditation to cultivate the Love that is already there. We leave no stone unturned, working to remove all traces of negativity, however long that might take.

- DIVINE LOVE IS AN EXPERIENCE. Most people have never experienced Divine Love. It is different than human love or any other experience. We cannot imagine it until we experience it. At first, it may seem unattainable. However, we can find it by purifying and expanding our human love. When our Love is strong enough, it eventually breaks into another realm described by saints, sages, and masters as ecstasy, the peace that surpasses understanding, bliss, nirvana. Here, words fail. The Love of God has to be experienced.

- ENTER THE HOUSE OF LOVE. When we cooperate with the command to love and do our work, there is a radical transformation of consciousness. God's cosmic broom sweeps away junk thoughts, harsh emotions, and restless discontent. A flowing river of healing energy gently overpowers the ego. The veil of ordinary human consciousness lifts and separation ends. We enter the House of Love. Here we experience light, intuitive knowledge, unfathomable stillness, and ecstatic joy. We feel safe, secure, and immortal. The feeling is exquisite! We want to stay forever, but we return to ordinary consciousness, since there is more work to do. We are never the same, however: the memory of ecstatic Love marks our return. One taste of Divine Love is addicting. Hooked for eternity, we yearn for more forever. We are willing to do whatever it takes to get more until we become pure Love. Then we can return to our true home and stay forever.

- THE GREAT HEALER. Unconditional Love is the greatest force in the universe. It breaks down the barriers and walls between us. In its presence, over time, all that is not Love dissolves. It is the glue that binds together the fragments of our inner and outer lives. It eliminates anxiety, distrust, depression, indifference, apathy, frustration, and anger. It harmonizes our relationships and all of the events of our lives.

- ENDLESS VARIETY. Every one has a uniquely individual Love

story. There is no end to Love's variety as it plays through each of our stories, leading us through trials to higher ground. As the story unfolds, we discover Love is the means and the end, the way and the goal.

- THE TEACHER OF LOVE CALLS. We see the Teacher of Love calling us to cultivate compassion in response to all of the events in our lives. Every scene and every moment is a lesson from God, beckoning us to join Her in Her temple of Love.

- LOVE IS A LAW. Every person and thing is a window through which we can see God. When we are in Love, the universe reveals its secret truths and hidden magic. Love is the Mother of the Universe, the Healer of healers, the Power of powers. It can transform any problem into knowledge and wisdom. It gives us the necessary traction to move through our barriers. It is the healing force that can change the world. When we are in Love, everything falls into place. Love is the only religion. Where there is Love, there is God. This is the law of Love. It works every time. You can prove it to yourself through direct personal experience in the test tube of life. Following are some techniques to help you do this.

TECHNIQUES

- OMNIPRESENT LOVE. We live in an infinite ocean of pure Love, an actual field of indivisible perfect energy. We are in it, and it is in us. It permeates every cell of our bodies, every atom, and all space. In ordinary states of consciousness, however, we do not feel it. Our ego, pain, and problems cause us to feel separate from Omnipresent Love.

- THE UNIVERSAL BALM FOR ANY PAIN OR PROBLEM. Although we feel separate, we can access Love and use it as the universal balm for any problem. Following are some exercises that can help us connect to that Love. By practicing these and other exercises, we can prove to ourselves that Love is the most powerful force in our lives.

BURNING KARMA IN THE FIRE OF LOVE

- The fire of Love is strong enough to move us through any barrier if we love God with all of our heart, mind, might, and soul and if we love our neighbors as ourselves. To make Love an active force in your life, follow these steps:

1. Introspect
2. Invoke
3. Affirm
4. Visualize
5. Serve
6. Repeat
7. Transform

1. INTROSPECT:

- Following is a partial list of barriers that interfere with our ability to give and receive Love. See if you can recognize which of these have a negative effect in your life. At any point during your day, mindfully identify any obstacle that interferes with your ability to love.

  a. Restless mind
  b. Highly reactive emotions
  c. Excessive material desire and attachments
  d. Bad habits
  e. Hyperactivity
  f. Fear of being alone
  g. Too dependent on others
  h. Physical pain
  i. The ego and narcissism
  j. Unskillful pain management

k. Denial of problems
l. Character flaws
m. Negative attitude
n. Feeling unworthy, guilty, ashamed, self-hatred
o. Feeling rejected, abandoned, and humiliated
p. Hatred
q. Prejudice: judging others by their role, body, personality, age, race, religion, sexual identity, nationality, economic class, or disability
r. Indifference or boredom
s. Fixed false religious beliefs
t. Fear of the unknown and death
u. Other painful problems

2. INVOKE:

*   Invoke the presence of God's Love. It is always available inside, outside, and everywhere as the universal balm for any pain or problem.

3. AFFIRM:

*   Love is the most powerful force in life.
*   I am in the Ocean of Love.
*   I am all of the qualities in the spiritual alphabet.
*   The God of Love is one. The polarizing forces of hatred, conflict, and frustration cannot touch Her.

4. VISUALIZE:

*   Visualize Love in your heart as a flame of light. Visualize the Love-light spreading to every cell in your body, to all people, nations, creatures, and ultimately to all creation. Picture the light melting every barrier. Feel the Love burn up all that is not Love inside, outside, everywhere.

5. SERVE:

- When you practice this exercise, your expanded and purified Love saturates your thoughts, feelings, and actions. Small acts of gentle, humble service are the natural result. You can give your Love in every action to all whom you meet.

6. REPEAT:

- We are either in Love or something else: a large category filled with all kinds of problems that do not go away so easily. When anything shows up that is not Love, repeat Steps 1–5 until you become Love itself.

- This is a lifelong project. Do not give up. Persevere and practice. The reward is great.

7. TRANSFORM:

- The reward is ever-increasing soul qualities such as contentment, harmony, and strength. When our Love is strong enough, it eventually breaks into the peace that surpasses understanding, pure light, and ecstatic joy.

EXPANDING LOVE IN MEDITATION

- We do not love everybody all of the time. God does. We can improve our ability to love by communing with God in the stillness of meditation. Review the technique for meditation described in Chapter Seventeen.

- Now you can practice the following exercise:

  1. Meditation
  2. Stillness
  3. Prayer

4. Purification and expansion
5. Action
6. Repetition

1. MEDITATION:

• Practice your technique of meditation. Bring in as much stillness as you can.

2. STILLNESS:

• The ever-increasing stillness bred of meditation brings the body and mind to a state of deep peace and relaxation. When you stop superficial thought and immerse in stillness, relax and feel the peace. Do not think. In this state of opened, quiet receptivity, Love qualities grow, the ego reduces, and problems burn up.

• In the stillness of deep meditation, think of the people in your life who are difficult to love. Include family, friends, neighbors, colleagues, strangers, and enemies. Place them and yourself in a bouquet. Offer the bouquet to God.

3. PRAYER:

• Now commune with your Higher Power, seeking healing for yourself and others. Speaking to God in the language of your heart, you might say something like this: "Lord, purify and expand my Love. I cannot do it. You can. You know I don't love these people. I know that You do. I need Your help, grace, and blessing. Create a space large enough in me to hold all. Eliminate all barriers that impede the flow of Your infinitely compassionate, all-understanding Love."

4. PURIFICATION AND EXPANSION:

• Relax, stay open, wait, and be patient. In stillness, you will experience your connection to the source of Love. Feel Love surround, permeate, and purify every cell and fiber of your being. Visualize Love expanding to include your troubled relationships, your family, friends, all people, and all of creation. Bathe in the sacred healing pool of Love as long as you can. Here, soul qualities replace all traces of negativity.

5. ACTION:

- When you come out of meditation, bring your expanded and purified Love to all you meet. Send affirmations of Love and kindness to your friends, family, strangers, and enemies. Let your generosity flow in every interaction. Help everyone.

6. REPEAT:

- In meditation, ego and problems burn up and soul qualities expand. This is a life-long process. Repeat this purification and expansion process until only Love is there.

LOVE EVERYONE EQUALLY

- We place people in categories according to their roles in life, body type, age, race, religion, nationality, sexual identity, educational level, and economic class. We are attracted to some, repelled by others, and indifferent to the rest.

- In the spiritual world, everyone is equal. No one is above or below another. We can work against attraction, repulsion, and indifference by giving Love freely and equally to all. We cannot get to God otherwise; this is where She lives.

1. OBSERVE:

  - Observe what qualities attract and repel you. Notice how personality, body type, age, clothes, weight, size, race, religion, sexual identity, or nationality determine whether you are attracted, repelled, or indifferent.

2. AFFIRM:

- I treat each person as God in disguise.

- I respond to every person with even-minded Love.

- I bow to the Image of God within you.

- I worship the Lord equally in every body-temple.

- I bow to the manifestation of Divine Mother before me right now.

- I serve the manifestation of the Divine Mother before me right now.

- I see the face of God in every face.

- I see the Cosmic Mother in every face.

- I see the Cosmic Mother everywhere.

3. REPEAT:

- Repeat this technique until you can give your Love equally to all people.

THIRTY WAYS TO PRACTICE LOVE

1. INTROSPECTION. Avoid criticism and judgment of others. Instead, work at being a better person by reforming yourself. When you become critical of others, tell your mind to be quiet. Instead of judging them, work to reform yourself by cultivating Love.

2. THE GOLDEN RULE. Do unto others as you would have them do unto you.

3. UNDERSTANDING. Slow down and go deep. Think about others. Try to understand why people do what they do.

4. AWARENESS. Be aware and sensitive to the needs of others.

5. COMPASSION. Have compassion for others when they make mistakes, just as you would have in return.

6. SELF-CONTROL. Learn to cool off your own emotions so you do not spread pain to other people in acts of unkindness or aggression.

7. PEACE. Cultivate peace, the platform upon which Love is built.

8. JOY. Cultivate Love, the platform upon which joy is built.

9. RELATIONSHIP. Be an unconditional friend. Friendship is a way to cement Love in our relationships.

10. WISDOM. Concentrate on the thoughts of saints and sages. Bring their wisdom into your life.

11. SPIRITUAL PRACTICE. Jesus said that the Kingdom of Heaven is within. To find Love inside, practice mindfulness, meditation, and the Presence of God.

12. SOLITUDE. Learn how to be alone.

13. BALANCE. Balance stillness and meditation with activity and service.

14. PRAYER. Send affirmations of Love and kindness to others during prayer.

15. LISTEN. Open your receptor sites. Reflect on what others are going through.

16. SURRENDER. Accept that which you cannot change with deep serenity.

17. EQUALITY. Understand your true position: equality with all people.

18. ACCOUNTABILITY. Identify and transform bad habits, destructive emotions, excessive material desires, and the sly tricks of the ego, all of which disrupt your ability to love.

19. SPACIOUSNESS. Create enough room inside to hold others in all of their folly. Understanding creates more space. This does not mean we accept negative behavior. We need to set limits when others violate our boundaries. We can set outer limits and create inner space at the same time.

20. BOUNDARIES. Love includes protection. The bottom line is safety for the self and others. We defend the boundary of Love by setting limits.

21. SERVICE. Work against selfishness by thinking about how to improve your Love and service a little bit more each day. Connecting to others through service promotes healing.

22. CONCENTRATION. When we do not listen carefully, we are not in Love. A calm, focused mind repaired and healed by meditation and mindfulness helps us understand.

23. INTIMACY. Love is holding on. Distance and detachment can be an excuse to avoid the suffering of intimacy. True learning occurs in the trenches. How else can we correct our flaws if not in the daily grind of relationships?

24. DETACHMENT. Love is letting go. Clinging and enmeshment stunt our growth.

25. ONENESS. God is one. Love is one. Live as though there is only one person here.

26. SOUL QUALITIES. Love is all of the spiritual qualities. If we cultivate any spiritual quality, Love grows.

27. PAIN MANAGEMENT. We need to work with and through our pain to expand and purify our Love. The inner connection to Love and safety can only come if we face all of our troubles. Our suffering leads to inner strength and wisdom if we endure with courage.

28. OPEN. You love best when you are relaxed, open, listening, and empathetic.

29. COMMUNICATION. With good communication, we solve our problems. Everything falls into place.

30. LEARN. Learning to love is a lifelong process.

THE WAY TO SUPERCONSCIOUS LOVE
AN AFFIRMATION

I am here to bring out my Love and the Love of other people.
I do not do this by working on others,
I do this by working on myself.
Love is about self-reform and self-mastery.
It is not about other people's behavior.
It is about how I respond to them.
I do not worry about others.
I do not expect or need others to behave in a certain way.

I do not try to get Love from others.

This is what makes me vulnerable.
I find Love within myself and give it to others.
This is what makes me strong.

In the end, I am Love.
I can give only that,
Free and content no matter the outer condition.
This is the way to superconscious Love.

<u>POINTS TO REMEMBER</u>

- Confusing spirituality boils down to a very simple principle: Love. Follow Love and everything will fall into place.

- The command to love is at the center of every great tradition. We are to love, serve, and give. We are here to learn how to take the high ground of understanding, compassion, and forgiveness, even when treated poorly. In your heart of hearts, you are Love itself.

- The command to love is crystal clear. We are to love God with all of our heart, mind, might, and soul, and our neighbor as ourselves. Nothing is excluded. When something other than Love surfaces, it has to go. There are no exceptions or exclusions. This makes it both easy and hard. It is easy because the mission is absolutely clear, and hard because there is much within that we must eliminate.

- In response to any problem, we can cultivate Love. This gives us the necessary traction to move through any barrier. This is the law of Love. It works every time. We can prove it through practice.

- We need the ego to establish ourselves in the world. At some point, however, we need to reduce the ego, think more about others and less about ourselves.

- When we look for Love on the outside, we are vulnerable: we may or may not get it. We already have what we need. When we learn how to love within ourselves, we are in a position of strength.

- We can use Love continuously as a powerful healing force in our lives.

- God is the Love that was there in the beginning and will be there in the end. It embraces all people, creatures, and creation. It is the cohesive force that holds everything together.

- The Love of God is here, unconditionally embracing, understanding, and forgiving no matter what we have done. We come from, live in, and ultimately return to Her Love. We can get that Love in meditation and give it to all who cross our path.

- Our bodies, personality, race, education, religion, sexual identity, status, role, flaws, problems, mistakes, and illness are but costumes disguising our true identity. Underneath all of these layers and identifications is our true self, the Image of God, the image of Love. We are Love.

- Selflessness is selfish, since it gives the best feeling.

- Serenity, sweetness of speech, and compassionate acts of kindness are healing powers.

- For inspiration, we can go to church, synagogue, or mosque, listen to sermons, participate in rituals, sing, chant, meditate, and practice mindfulness. Then we need to translate our inspiration into acts of loving kindness and service.

- Every action is worship if done in Love.

- When we make an effort to bring more Love and kindness into the world no matter how the world treats us, we are making progress.

- We can spiritualize our moments by adding Love or any other healing quality.

- To love God is to love Love.

- Love is built on truth. There can be no deception to self or others.

- God reduces Her almighty power to a sweet, tender, gentle Love. She gives me that. I give that in turn.

- We cannot get to God's Love with words. He is in the stillness. When we go there and come back, we find words inadequate to describe it.

- Divine Love is a place and an experience. Words can only point the way. You have to go there.

- "Love's the only engine of survival" (Leonard Cohen).

- "Dance me to the end of Love" (Leonard Cohen).

- To get to higher Love, we must surrender the ego and what we know and go through hoops of fire. There may be times when it feels like nothing and nobody is there to help. Some have to experience terror at the abyss to get to Omniscient Love.

- It's all about Love. Start your climb.

AFFIRMATIONS

- I express God's sweet, gentle Love to all I meet.
- I am not seeking Love from you. I am in Love.
- No matter how the world treats me, I respond with Love and kindness.
- I live, move, and have my being in Love.
- Love permeates every atom, cell, and molecule of my being.

- Love is the guiding force of my evolving story.
- Love is the most powerful force in the universe.
- Love is greater than any pain.
- Love burns karma: mine, yours, and ours.
- Love, Love, only Love.
- I love God, others, and myself completely and unconditionally.
- I am a part of everything because I love.
- A boundless Love watches over me through all of life's experiences.
- I respond to cruelty with kindness.
- I respond to harsh words with sweetness of speech.
- I send Love and kindness to those who hurt me.
- I act in kindness to those passed up by others.
- Warmth is the word of the day.
- God loves me as I am but too much to leave me there.
- I love myself as I am but too much to leave me there.
- I channel every word and act through warmth and gentleness.
- Show me the problem. I show you the Love.
- Love + Intelligence = God = Wisdom
- I receive the Love of God. I give the Love of God.
- Love does not keep score.

EXERCISES

1. What is the command to love?

2. What is the difference between human love and God's Love?

3. Name the barriers that inhibit your ability to give and receive Love.

4. Describe and practice the following techniques:

   a. Burning karma in the fire of Love
   b. Expanding Love in meditation
   c. Love everyone equally

5. The creative intelligence of Love is unlimited. There is no end to the variety of ways people can give and receive Love. Review and practice the thirty ways to Love. What would you add to this list?

6. Love is both intimate and detached as described in number twenty-three and number twenty-four in the list of thirty ways to love. There is a time for both. For example, a mother protects her child fiercely but must also let the child go. Can you think of other examples?

7. Love is the ultimate beacon through the fog of ego and suffering. We need the beacon. What images of Love give you inspiration or traction?

8. What methods and qualities do you use to stay in Love when reality is harsh?

9. Notice the endless variety of ways people give and receive Love throughout the day.

CHAPTER TWENTY-SIX

PEACE

The Changeless Peace of the Soul

- THE INEVITABLE SUFFERING OF LIFE. We want unlimited peace. We seek it on the horizontal axis: the world of people, activities, places, and things. However, our search for a lasting peace in the ever-changing external world is in vain. Everything on the physical plane is temporary and limited, suffering is unavoidable, and death wins in the end. No matter how hard we try, the external world will simply not deliver the permanent peace we crave.

- REACTIVITY. As described in Step 5, there are six tools that help us achieve a degree of peace in the world. However, when we try to realize the core drive exclusively on the horizontal axis, these assets spin out of control and become liabilities. The restless mind, reactive moods, uncontrolled desires, physical problems, hyperactivity, and egotism steal from our peace and deepen our troubles.

- THE SEEKER. Suffering causes us to seek and question. Our search takes us to the wisdom of the ages in sacred texts. Here we learn that the permanent peace we seek is inside.

- CHANGELESS PEACE. Changeless peace is everywhere, all around us and inside us. It is the ground of all being. We already have the deep, permanent peace we seek. It is always with us, inside. We can dwell there every moment of our lives. No condition of the world or body can touch it. To find this unlimited peace, we must look within. If we do not find it there, we will not find it.

- THE WORK. The permanent peace of the soul is our natural state, our True Self, and our birthright. We can have soul-peace no matter what condition befalls us; however, we must do some work. We must introspect, face reality, and solve our problems. We must conquer our bad habits, restless mind, reactive moods, excessive desires, and egotism. We must go beneath the superficial waves of the world, slow down, and go inside. We must love and serve. In short, to get the lasting peace of the soul, we need to skillfully manage our suffering and develop a spiritual practice. If we do the work, peace slowly expands until it becomes permanent. Following is a suggested pathway to the immutable peace of the soul.

TEN STEPS TO SOUL PEACE

1. Solitude
2. Introspection
3. Contemplation
4. Affirmations
5. Meditation
6. Mindfulness
7. Practicing the Presence of God
8. Love and service
9. Grace
10. Peace of the soul

1. SOLITUDE:

- When we suffer, we turn to the world for support and relief. While it is obviously good to have the support of wise, compassionate people and meaningful activities, an important part of spiritual growth is shifting the locus of control from outside to inside.

- At times of crisis, the ultimate defense is the deep peace of the soul. To attain this, we need quiet time alone for introspection, contemplation of spiritual wisdom, affirmations, and meditation.

- Our addiction to the outer life makes it difficult to retreat. Cultivating the new ground of solitude is akin to withdrawing from a substance of abuse like alcohol or drugs. When we retreat, we may feel anxious and crave our habitual pattern of activities. If we answer the call of this craving too quickly and fail to go through the rigors of withdrawal, we will not bring the critical element of solitude into our program. It may be difficult or impossible to find the perpetual peace of the soul unless we have periods of retreat for introspection, spiritual study, and meditation.

2. INTROSPECTION:

- Instead of running to our favorite escape such as television, the Internet, radio, food, sex, shopping, or golf, we can sit in quiet solitude and look inside. If we stay with the feelings that come up, we discover what we have been avoiding: painful emotions, bad memories, flaws, mistakes, fear of loss, fear of the abyss, fear of death, and fear of fear. These painful problems arrive in the school of life to get our attention and show us where to work. We can work on these problems with any of the spiritual practices described in this book. When we do the work, peace expands. Peace is on the other side of every painful problem.

- In order to build durable peace, we must face all of our problems. We must go through whatever comes our way. We have to work through every layer of pain. If we avoid a problem, it continues to show up in different forms, directing us to necessary work. If we do the work, peace slowly grows. Eventually, we can remain at peace under all conditions, including the transition to the great unknown: death.

- Staying in the pain is not just a good idea; it is the bridge between attachment, dependency, addiction and spiritual power. When the going gets rough, we panic, drop the experience, and escape to one of our worldly habits. On the other hand, if we ride every wave of pain until it dissipates, peace increases until it becomes permanent.

- Attaining immutable peace is a tall order. We need some additional tools. Following is a brief review of contemplation, affirmations, meditation, mindfulness, practicing the Presence of God, Love, and service. With these practices and grace, our painful problems eventually melt into the unlimited peace of the soul and Spirit.

3. CONTEMPLATION:

- Contemplation of wisdom helps us manage the problems and fears we discover through introspection. Review Chapter Sixteen on contemplation. Study a passage from your favorite sacred book related to peace of mind under all conditions. Then practice even-minded peace throughout the day.

4. AFFIRMATIONS:

- In retreat and in activity, we can repeat affirmations of peace. The repetition or chanting of the affirmation helps us maintain peace of mind no matter what happens. Choose one or a combination of the following affirmations, or make up your own:

  - Peace is on the other side of every painful problem.
  - I am calm.
  - I am poised.
  - I am peaceful.
  - I am patient.
  - Peace is everywhere.
  - I swim in the ocean of peace.
  - Peace expands, filling my body and all space around me.
  - Peace flows through every thought, feeling, and action.
  - Peace flows through every cell in my body.
  - I am a peace warrior.

- I stand serene in the center of life's storms.
- I never lose my peace.
- I am in the peace of the soul no matter what comes to me.
- Peace is in every movement of my body.
- All worries dissolve in the light of powerful, peace thoughts.
- I choose peace in all situations.
- Peace is the order of this day.
- Peace flows through me like a gentle wind.
- Peace eliminates worries.
- Peace eliminates mental restlessness.
- Peace vitalizes every cell of my body.
- Peace is inside and outside, left and right, above and below, in front and behind … everywhere.
- I do everything with peace.
- I stay deep in the ocean of peace, below the choppy surface waves that try to bait me.
- No one can steal my peace.
- Nothing can touch me.
- Nothing can ruffle me.
- It does not matter what the world or my body does. I am at peace.
- The rougher it gets, the softer I get.
- I inundate my mind with constant thoughts of peace.
- I affirm continuous peace.

5. MEDITATION:

- The ultimate retreat is in the stillness of meditation. Here we find the deepest peace, more than in any worldly activity.

- The Bible says, "Be still and know that I am God" (Psalm 46:10). The peace of the soul and Spirit is there, in the stillness.

- We can commune with God in meditation and get His peace. When we detach from the choppy surface waves of His ocean and enter the deep stillness below, we know His peace as the foundation of the universe.

6. MINDFULNESS:

*   We can practice the presence of peace in every waking moment of our lives. Practicing the presence of peace during activity is meditation in action, or mindfulness.

*   When we are restless and distracted, we lose contact with serenity. To counter this, we can use breathing and affirmations related to peace in response to all events. When the chaotic world enters our life and we respond with a chaotic mind, we can follow these four steps:

    a. Stop: the first step is to realize that our mind is in a chaotic or negative state.
    b. Breathe: take several slow, deep, abdominal breaths.
    c. Affirm: use one or several of the affirmations above to help return the mind to its natural state of peace and poise.
    d. Act: we can perform every action in the presence of peace.

7. PRACTICING THE PRESENCE OF GOD AS PEACE:

*   God's peace is omnipresent, eternal, infinite, and perfect. It is the underlying force behind all creation. We can get a glimpse of the harmonious operations of this cosmic power in the balanced movements of the planets and galaxies and in the beauty of nature: flowers, sunsets, oceans, mountains, and sky.

*   We can align ourselves with this great power by practicing the Presence of God as peace in every action.

*   When the mind is restless, follow these steps:

    a. Stop: realize the mind is restless or negative.

b. Breathe: take several slow, deep, abdominal breaths.

c. Affirm: affirm the Presence of God as the omnipotent peace that rules the universe and the beauty that infuses nature.

d. Act: Perform every action in the presence of that peace. Omnipresent peace permeates every millimeter of space. The more we focus on peace, the more we will feel it in our lives. Eventually we stay deep in the ocean of peace, no matter what happens on the surface.

8. LOVE AND SERVICE:

- Practicing selfless service reduces the ego and cultivates soul-peace. Personal difficulties dry up and blow away in the face of Love and service. Where there is loving service, there is peace.

9. GRACE:

- God manifests changeless peace amid the most turbulent conditions. By grace, we can be in this peace. First we must do our part. In solitude, we can introspect, contemplate, affirm, and meditate. In activity, we can be mindful, practice the Presence of God, Love, and serve. With these practices, we purify our consciousness and help other people. With determination and will, we do our best and never give up. Slowly, peace expands.

- To get to the perfect peace of the soul, however, we need help. As we do our part, we can submit our problems to our Higher Power, asking for inner calm. With practice, our peace slowly expands until it is strong enough to weather the trials of life. This peace, this stillness, is a gift from God.

10. PEACE OF THE SOUL:

- Buried underneath the rubble of our personal problems is the perfect peace of the soul. The soul is the witness. The witness is still, silent, spacious, and serene. Neither the world nor the body can touch us here. No pain, desire, impulse, or fear can enter. This is our haven. It is always at the center of our being. We can take shelter here no matter what happens. Nothing can be more important than finding changeless peace within. When we know this place, we need not fear any condition.

- We can slowly work our way to this peace by practicing retreat, introspection, contemplation, affirmations, meditation, mindfulness, the Presence of God, and loving service. With these practices and God's grace, we learn how to live in the world and simultaneously maintain peace and poise. Then we are a force of peace in the world.

- At mastery, we can stay deep in the ocean of peace, unaffected by the turbulence of the surface waves of change. We know God inside as perfect peace, and outside as the infinite peace that rules the universe. When we learn how to be quiet within, we can experience the Changeless One who underlies all creation.

PRAYER OF ST. FRANCIS OF ASSISSI

Lord, make me an instrument of Your peace:
where there is hatred let me sow Love;
where there is injury, pardon;
where there is doubt, faith;
where there is despair, hope;
where there is darkness, light;
where there is sadness, joy.

O Divine Master, grant that I may not so much seek
to be consoled as to console;
to be understood as to understand;
to be loved as to love;
for it is in giving that we receive;

it is in pardoning that we are pardoned,
and it is in dying that we are born to eternal life.

POINTS TO REMEMBER

• There are three layers: events, our ego's reaction to events, and the perfect peace of the soul. The middle layer, our reaction, is very powerful. We need to take away its power and give it to the soul. All of the spiritual methods described in this work reduce egotistical reactivity and expand the peace of the soul. We can cultivate soul-peace in response to problems by practicing solitude, introspection, contemplation, affirmations, meditation, mindfulness, the Presence of God, and loving service.

• Peace is the platform upon which all other spiritual qualities are built.

• We can dwell in the peace of the soul no matter what happens. It is our home in pain and pleasure, success and failure, health and disease, life and death. This elevated state of consciousness is accomplished through surrender or acceptance. We can use every event to bring us closer to our soul-peace. In this sense, everything is a blessing.

• God is peace. If we perform an action in peace, we are with God.

• We can train our minds to remain calm under all conditions.

• When we have inner peace, we are more skillful, successful, loving, understanding, and receptive. We worry less, enjoy more, have better health, and get along better with others. We are more perceptive, make better decisions, and solve more problems.

• The God of peace is trying to show you deeper levels of peace than you have ever known. However, He cannot speak when you are restless. Meditate. Stop the world, body, senses, and mind. Be still and know that He is the peace that surpasses understanding.

EXERCISES

1. Popular media promotes fast-paced reality based on consumer spending, material consciousness, hero worship, youth, sex, power, money, and violence. These images enter our consciousness, speed up our minds, and undermine our common humanity. Take a break from your usual routine. Do a media fast. For a few days or longer, reduce or eliminate television, the radio, magazines, newspapers, and use of the computer.

2. Reduce your addictions. Review the lesson on habits. Use these principles to reduce your addictive behaviors to drugs, alcohol, food, cigarettes, television, power, people, sex, money, and work. These habits and attachments may help you avoid your problems and give you a false sense of security. However, these same problems will return later to haunt you with more force and vigor.

3. Take some time for retreat and reflection. In solitude, ask yourself what you are running from.

4. Practice the ten steps to soul-peace or design a similar program for yourself. Practice daily. Keep going. Realize ever-deeper levels of peace. The goal is to find and keep the permanent peace of the soul-Spirit.

CHAPTER TWENTY-SEVEN

HUMILITY

The Mother of All Virtues

- THE EGO. We are tiny, infinitesimal specks in an infinite universe. The ego puffs up that speck to make it look like the grandest thing that has ever happened. Confusing its little story with the whole of reality, the ego leads us into the blind alley of self-importance and arrogance. We can counter this by learning humility, the greatest of all spiritual virtues.

- THE TRUE SELF. Humility takes us to our true identity, the soul connected to Spirit. The true self is compassionate, kind, and courageous. However, the false god of ego blocks our awareness of the soul, keeps us separate from Spirit, and prevents us from experiencing higher states of consciousness. To become who we really are, we must reduce the ego by cultivating humility. The antidote to the ego, humility, is the key that unlocks the door to the higher self and Higher Consciousness. Without it, there can be no entrance.

- SEVEN PATHWAYS TO HUMILITY. In this lesson, there is a description of seven routes to humility:

  1. Self-reform
  2. Omniscience
  3. Equality
  4. Service
  5. Love

6. Darkness
7. Knowing our place

THE WAY OF SELF-REFORM

- EGO REDUCTION. The only way to advance to higher Love is to find our flaws and fix them. The ego inhibits this work, trying to be right and look good all the time. It is afraid to look within and uncover imperfections. It is unable to give up its power without embarrassment and humiliation. Nevertheless, what we give up in egotistical power we gain in spiritual power. The spiritual way is ego reduction and the expansion of soul qualities.

- CULTIVATE SPIRITUAL QUALITIES. To reduce the ego, we stop blaming, criticizing, judging, and trying to change others. We understand that the best way to change others is to reform ourselves. We become students, always ready to learn. We listen to feedback from others and from our conscience. We identify our mistakes and flaws, but they do not define us. Our problems are simply signposts on the road to the soul and Spirit. The work is cultivation of spiritual qualities.

- HUMILIATION TO HUMILITY. Life teaches humility when we open to the lessons. It takes courage to look inside and make the necessary changes. When we do the work of introspection, the humiliation of the ego transforms into the humility of the soul.

THE WAY OF OMNISCIENCE

INTELLECTUAL HUMILITY

- TINY BUT SIGNIFICANT. Intellectual humility is knowledge of our true and rightful place in the universe. God is vast. We are tiny but not insignificant. We are made in the image of God. We are co-creators. We have power, free will, and a role to play. Our job is to manifest and express God's greatness by ridding our consciousness of its egotistical impurities and cultivating His qualities.

- OMNIPOTENCE. To gain perspective, drive your little bus of knowledge to the border of the infinite unknown and look out the window. There you will find countless illustrations of the intelligent power that runs the universe. For example, imagine the Earth rotating on its own axis every twenty-four hours at one thousand miles per hour, around the sun at sixty thousand miles per hour, while moving as part of our galaxy at six hundred thousand miles per hour. The Earth travels in mathematically precise harmony, rhythm, and balance with the other planets and stars. The ride is smooth. There are no bumps. We don't feel any movement. The ocean's water does not spill into space. No matter where we are on the planet, we think we are on "top," yet those on the "bottom" do not fall off.

- OMNISCIENCE. The creative power of the universe is omniscient. It is inside, outside, and everywhere. It operates on every level of creation. It permeates every centimeter of space. It runs the cells of our body while holding the universe together. We move, live, and have our being in this infinite ocean of intelligence. Although we cannot be outside of its presence, neither can we plumb its depth: our human intelligence can take us only so far. Even the IQ of a genius is puny in comparison.

- OUR KNOWLEDGE IS INFINITESIMAL. No matter how much knowledge we accumulate, what we do not know remains infinite. The sum total of everything we know individually and collectively remains infinitesimal compared to the infinite knowledge of God. God's knowledge will always be infinitely beyond our grasp. God knows everything. We know very little. Yet the ego persists in projecting its tiny speck of knowledge as the nature of reality.

- OMNISCIENT, OMNIPRESENT POWER. To combat the ego and maintain a humble stance, we can focus on God's infinite intelligence. Omniscience permeates atoms, galaxies, and us. All we have to do is remember. Even when we forget, we are only a thought away.

- KNOWLEDGE AND MYSTERY. The self-important ego gets us into trouble by overestimating its knowledge. However, we can view the world with one eye on our knowledge and the other on the unknown. In this way, we remain at the actual boundary of our current knowledge and the mysteries of life. With this receptive stance, we recognize when we do not know the answers. When we know our true place in this mysterious, infinitely intelligent universe, there can be but one response: humility.

THE WAY OF EQUALITY

- EQUALITY AND HUMILITY. In the world of roles, there are divisions with status determined by wealth, education, position, age, power, race, religion, or sexual identity. Our egos get caught up in competition. As we surf the waves of success and failure, we develop feelings of superiority and inferiority. The perception of superiority is associated with arrogance, pride, and domination. Feelings of inferiority breed insecurity, anxiety, and doubt. Some people suffer from both states. Equality and its partner, humility, are healing powers that cure these ills. We approach true humility when we see ourselves as equal to others, not better or worse.

- EQUALITY AND LOVE. In the spiritual world, all are equally included in the circle of Love. Role and status have little importance. We look neither up nor down but across, eye to eye, squarely, honestly. The realization of our equality in God's Love gives us humility, a source of deep peace and strength.

THE WAY OF SERVICE

- GENTLE, HUMBLE SERVICE. The ego strives for greatness in the world. The way of the soul is simple acts of gentle, humble service to humanity. In humility, we make no distinctions, equally serving the mighty and the meek. Small, anonymous acts of service mark the true path of Love. Humility grounded in unselfish Love is the mother of all powers. Without it, no virtue can grow. The way to God is paved with acts of selfless service.

THE WAY OF LOVE

- EXPANSION OF SOUL QUALITIES. As we advance on the path of self-healing through ego reduction and the cultivation of soul qualities, the mind and heart become increasingly quiet. Patience, kindness, and gentleness expand. We have more space inside. We are content, receptive, understanding, and forgiving.

- REDUCE REACTIVITY. Progressively anchored to the soul, we are able to accomplish something very difficult and profoundly needed: an ever-increasing ability to tolerate the problems and provocations of other people. We find ourselves reacting less to what other people do. We are more gracious in the face of their limitations. We yield to opposing views, insults, and condemnation, even malice. We have no need to defend ourselves, even when we are right, because we do not feel threatened.

- WHEN TO REACT AND WHEN TO ABSORB. Humility does not imply enabling others to be abusive. We continue to give feedback, set limits, and maintain boundaries. However, we are often unnecessarily reactive. The highly volatile ego defends its territory at the slightest provocation. The soul knows when to react and when to absorb.

- PATIENCE, KINDNESS, AND UNDERSTANDING. We can

make a small contribution to healing the world by accepting the pain of others without reacting. Steadfast and firm in the face of provocation, we can transmute our own and others' pain with our Love. When we refrain from adding fuel to their fire, others have a better chance of successfully dealing with their own problems. When we respond to other people's problems with patience, kindness, and understanding, we reduce the suffering of the world and fulfill the destiny of the soul.

THE WAY OF DARKNESS

- THE CAVE OF DARKNESS. On the way to spiritual knowledge, some of us pass through the cave of darkness, a place of severe pain where we face the unknown, death, and/or evil without immediate answers to our questions. War, ethnic cleansing, racism, domestic violence, rape, child sex abuse, and other horrific conditions can bring us to this cave of darkness. Here our spiritual belief systems come under their most rigorous challenge. This is a critical place: if our sacred knowledge holds here, it will hold anywhere.

- FIERCE TRAINING. There are many classrooms in the school of life but none like this. The training here is fierce. The cave is dark. All evidence of spiritual life is gone. The world seems to be against us. There is no solace from our usual sources of family, friends, work, the arts, or recreation. Sometimes even going to church, synagogue, or temple brings no relief. We feel alone, separate, powerless, and frightened.

- BIG QUESTIONS. In the face of major crisis, we ask the big questions. Why are we here? Is this a moral, benevolent universe? If God's Love is Omnipotent, why is there so much suffering and evil in the world? Do good and justice ultimately triumph? Life on the physical plane does not give easy answers to these questions. Some believe in karma and reincarnation as the explanation for ultimate justice. Others remain mystified. In any case, we need something to hold on to as we go through our trials and face the abyss. We need something that can get us through these conditions, however long or severe, something more powerful than the worst scenarios life can bring. But what if brutal reality challenges and ultimately strips away our illusions and belief, leaving us in despair? Who can we turn to if we experience only turmoil and questioning? Does God's Love exist in the cave of darkness? Following are some suggestions.

- ACCEPTANCE. While we may not understand why there is so much suffering and evil, we can accept horror and tragedy as part of the mystery. We can accept our current condition as the next step in our spiritual development.

- FAITH. We can have faith in our ability to transform suffering into spiritual power.

- SCHOOL. We can accept pain as a teacher and stimulant for the growth of spiritual qualities.

- PRAYER. Though we are not sure where we are going, we can ask for help from a Higher Power with infinite compassion and wisdom; and we can trust that He knows what He is doing.

- LOVE. We can follow the path guided by Love.

- ROLL THE UNIVERSAL HEALING WHEEL. To work our way through extreme conditions, we will need to build an infrastructure of patience, courage, strength, and endurance. We can do this by developing and maintaining our spiritual practice. No matter how rough it gets, our job is to persist. We need to keep rolling the Universal Healing Wheel. If we do the work, eventually the Light of Spirit enters the cave of darkness bearing gifts of peace, wisdom, and strength.

- GRACE: In the cave of darkness, we lose our illusion of control and safety. We fall through the cracks in our belief system and hit what seems to be the bottom, a spiritual ground zero where we experience fear associated with the unknown. Although we may feel helpless, we persist in our spiritual practice. We yearn, work, search, and persevere. Because of our efforts, strength grows and grace follows. Omniscient Love, bearing gifts of protection and peace, comes to our rescue. Through our work and God's grace, we discover that the ground of all being is not the unknown and terror, but Omniscient Love and peace.

This is the way to humility through the cave of darkness. It cannot be taught. It must come from experiencing the transformation of suffering and powerlessness to serenity and security through grace. God comes to our rescue by resurrecting our feeling of safety. Then we know that our peace is a gift from the mysterious, wonderful power of God; we are nothing but for His grace. Jesus said, "Of myself I can do nothing. The Father who dwells in me, He does the work."

KNOWING OUR PLACE

- DELUSIONS OF COMPLETENESS. In humility, we know where we are on the spiritual path. We have a realistic view of our strengths, progress, limitations, and the work that remains. This may not be as easy as it sounds. All too often we use our spiritual belief system to provide all of the answers. Thinking we have discovered the truth, we elevate ourselves above others and become arrogant. Identifying ourselves as special, chosen, or children of God while others are excluded, we deny our problems and delude ourselves into thinking that we are already complete. We can invoke the image of God as our true self, but not at the expense of losing awareness of our limitations. We should not think that we are complete just because we have joined a religion or walk on a spiritual path.

- EMBRACE THE UNKNOWN. We do not have all the answers, and we do not need them. We embrace the unknown as a source of wisdom, strength, and peace. When we cannot know the answers; we can live the questions.

- PERSEVERE. Change is slow, difficult, and often painful. Do the work and be patient. Keep going, and you will be victorious.

- GRACE CANNOT FLOW WITHOUT HUMILITY. God cannot get into the body-temple when it is filled with junk products of the ego such as selfish desires, volatile emotions, fear, pride, or the denial of problems. In humility, we ask for help in becoming free of that ego which prevents us from knowing God. To create a channel for the flow of God's power, we need to reduce and ultimately eliminate the ego and replace it with soul qualities. Then, in the stillness and quiet of meditation, we can hear the sweet voice of Love whispering, "Welcome. You are at the brink of eternity. Become nothing and nobody. Then you will be one with Me, with everything, and everybody. This is the power of humility. Ask for help in all you do."

Grace cannot flow without humility. Know where you are on the spiritual path. We cannot move a finger, take a step, breathe, see, think, or digest food without Her power.

THE PRAYER OF AN UNKNOWN CONFEDERATE SOLDIER

I asked God for strength that I might achieve.
I was made weak that I might learn humbly to obey.

I asked for health that I might do greater things.
I was given infirmity that I might do better things.

I asked for riches that I might be happy.
I was given poverty that I might be wise.

I asked for power that I might have the praise of men.
I was given weakness that I might feel the need of God.

I asked for all things that I might enjoy life.
I was given life that I might enjoy all things.

I got nothing that I asked for but everything I hoped for.
Almost despite myself, my unspoken prayers were answered.

I am, among all men, most richly blessed.

POINTS TO REMEMBER

- God cannot get into the body-temple when it is filled with a restless mind, reactive emotions, and egotistical desires. We can experience the gentle sweetness of Her grace when we are soft and yielding, surrendered and meek. Bow down. Get low. Be still and empty where the grace of God can flow.

- We can counter pride, arrogance, and entitlement with humility and gratitude. We can endure injury with a patient, quiet heart. We can counter criticism and judgment with acceptance and support. We can counter condemnation with forgiveness. Soft is more powerful than hard.

- In spiritual reality, we do not actually own anything. All of our possessions are gifts on temporary loan from on high. Everything is a gift. We own nothing. Recognize the blessing and be grateful.

- The ego builds its empire on a foundation of control and power. The soul knows that the foundation of a spiritual life is Love and service. There is no place to go and nothing to do but Love and serve. The humble servant goes everywhere, helping everyone indiscriminately.

- Humility is patient and kind, tolerant and understanding, meek yet firm.

- The one you are with is the most important person in the world, the image of God, nay, God Herself.

- All of the lessons of life teach humility, but we must be awake. Otherwise, we miss the lesson.

- When you pass a test or conquer a barrier, you may go into a float pattern where you experience peace and joy. But just because you pass a test doesn't mean you pass the course, let alone go to the next grade, let alone graduate. When you are floating, it is just recess. Enjoy the recess but remember school is still in session. Expect classes to resume at any time. Beware the spiritual ego and spiritual swagger. Be humble. Know your place. The light is still dim.

- The quiet, lowly places are where we can find the peace of God. Most look for it in the high places. Spiritual experiences are possible there too; they can occur anywhere. However, if you graze in the lowland, stop and listen for a time, you will discover the peace and sweetness of humility, the mother of all virtue.

AFFIRMATIONS

- Humility is my temple, the cradle of wisdom.
- Equality brings peace and strength.
- I am nobody in particular.
- I let others discover my good qualities without my help.
- I find peace and contentment in humility and equality.
- I am a beginner every single moment.
- I progress because I know what I do not know.
- I ask to become a better person, not for more things.
- I ask for nothing more than inner contentment.
- I follow the lessons of life, all of which teach humility.

- Humility gives strength and serenity.
- Humility gives contentment and satisfaction.
- Humility brings me closer to God and humanity.
- Humility is Love.
- Humility is the path to Truth.
- I am learning humility under all conditions of life: success and failure, health and disease, wealth or poverty, the highs and the lows. This is the way to serenity.
- I am not high or low. I am equal.
- I am kind and gentle but not a doormat.
- I serve all equally.
- I serve the mighty and the meek with the same Love.
- I strive to remain humble at all times.
- I counter pride, arrogance, and entitlement with humility and gratitude.
- I endure injury with a patient, quiet heart.
- It is not about me. It is about service.
- I am nothing. God is everything.

EXERCISES

1. Describe the seven routes to humility.

2. Why is humility the mother of all virtue?

3. What is the connection between humility and other spiritual qualities?

4. Think of everything you know and compare it to what you don't know. You will see that your knowledge is infinitesimal, while the unknown always remains infinite. The more you know, the more you realize what you don't know.

5. What did Jesus mean when he said, "The meek shall inherit the

earth"? Think about the power of "soft over hard." Where is gentleness needed more in your life?

6. A middle-aged, developmentally disabled African American man dressed in old tattered clothes was waiting in the hall of my clinic. "How are you?" I asked. "Sad today," he said. "Why?" I asked. He replied, "I wish everybody good luck and happiness." From his sadness, he prays for others. This man teaches humility. Can you see how this applies to your life?

CHAPTER TWENTY-EIGHT

FAITH

Proof of Things Unseen

"Now faith is the assurance of things hoped for,
the conviction of things not seen."
— Hebrews 11.1

•   BELIEF VS. FAITH. A belief is an idea that remains untested. Faith is proof of things unseen. We may like an idea, but we cannot know if it is true until we prove it. Then we have faith. To test the reality of a belief, we need to develop a spiritual practice. Then, through direct personal experience, we can see for ourselves if it is true. In this way, we can discriminate spiritual law from fixed, untested belief.

•   SPIRITUAL LAW. Spiritual laws are universal truths that apply to all people, transcending history, culture, and conditions. These laws outline the nature of reality and the governance of the universe. Spiritual laws cannot fail. They operate with precise accuracy, just as surely as the laws that govern the physical universe.

•   PROOF OF THINGS UNSEEN. Saints and sages discover, live, master, and teach the workings of spiritual laws. They advise us to follow these laws to make our lives more effective. We can follow their lead, but we cannot have faith in metaphysical truths until we prove that they work in our lives. We must operate the laws ourselves. Then we have faith.

- FAITH IS AN INHERENT QUALITY OF THE SOUL. Faith, an eternal power that springs from the soul, cannot be touched or destroyed. Doubt and insecurity can temporarily overwhelm our faith, but it recovers. It is incomparably resilient. The magnificent power of faith does not come easily, however. Though it is an inherent quality of the soul, it lays dormant until exercised.

- TECHNIQUE. Following is a method for cultivating faith by converting belief to truth, through direct personal experience. This method helps us determine if a spiritual concept or method is empty or an immutable truth deserving of our faith:

  1. Test
  2. Hypothesis
  3. Practice
  4. Experience
  5. Faith

1. TEST:

- Faith cannot grow without tests. A test can be any pain or problem. We all experience loss, pain, and tragedy. Some of us have to face the darkness of barbaric crime or catastrophic violence. All of us must eventually leave our possessions, loved ones, and bodies behind. At death, each of us must face the abyss, the mysterious infinite unknown.

2. HYPOTHESIS:

- Religions and spiritual teachers give us advice on how to handle the painful problems of life. The advice is massive, complex, confusing, and contradictory. To decipher spiritual fiction from fact, we need to convert fixed beliefs or dogma to hypothesis requiring proof. To do this, we transfer authority from others to ourselves. We should not blindly follow religion, teachers, or masters. Our own experience is the ultimate criterion for determining truth.

- We can test any concept or method. Does the body-temple harbor the soul and the God of the universe? Are karma and reincarnation true? Is unconditional Love the key to the kingdom of heaven? Does meditation work? Does compassionate service to humanity give us peace of mind and strength? We can put these profoundly important questions to the test of direct personal experience in the laboratory of life. The experiment may take years. On the way, we stay receptive. We do not accept or reject the theory. We just do the work by developing a spiritual practice.

3. PRACTICE:

- We can practice any one or a combination of spiritual methods.

4. EXPERIENCE:

- Discovering truth through personal experience is called spiritual discrimination or discernment. Direct personal experience is the teacher and ultimate authority. If a method or concept works, we keep it. If not, we discard it. We trust our ability to tell the difference.

5. FAITH:

- We prove to ourselves that a concept or method works in our lives, thus converting untested belief to faith through experience.

- We can apply this five-step method to any spiritual practice or idea. Following is an example of how to apply the method to prove the existence of the soul and God.

PROVING THE EXISTENCE OF THE SOUL AND GOD

1. TEST:

-   A painful problem arrives. It disturbs our peace and indicates an area in need of work.

2. HYPOTHESIS:

-   We can test Steps 7–10 of this model: skillful pain management (Step 8) and spiritual practice (Step 9) lead to the discovery of the soul and Higher Power (Step 7) as the peace, Love, and joy we crave (Step 10). We have a soul made of Love qualities, which we will discover if we practice spiritual disciplines in response to life's problems. When we do the work, we experience a progressive growth of courage, peace, forgiveness, and other wonderful spiritual qualities. With continued practice, God reveals Himself as a loving Friend whose aid arrives in many forms, with reinforcements, on His schedule.

3. PRACTICE:

-   The arrival of a painful problem indicates we have homework in the school of life.

-   We can accept our current condition as the next step in our spiritual development.

-   We pick any one or a combination of spiritual methods that fit our problem, and we accept our pain as a teacher and stimulant for the growth of spiritual qualities. Pain is an intelligent teacher who will lead us to our greatest spiritual asset: Love.

-   Pain is the purifying agent that transforms negativity into spiritual power. When we enter the pain, it reveals the lessons we need to learn. The lessons always have to do with learning how to cultivate soul qualities.

- Through introspection, our pain informs us of the nature of our problems. Through transformation, we respond to our problems by cultivating Love, compassion, understanding, and forgiveness. This is the work of the spiritual path.

- When overwhelmed with difficult problems, we may be tempted to give up our spiritual practice. To avoid this, we need to be patient and persevere. There will be dry periods where we feel there is no progress. When we think we are not growing, remember that effort is progress and good results are accumulating. Faith does not come without tests and work. When we do the work, God responds in His way and on His schedule.

4. EXPERIENCE:

- We are in a relationship with God. Our job is to practice spiritual methods. When we do this, spiritual qualities slowly grow. To give us additional assistance, God enters our lives as Friend, Father, Mother, Guide, Protector, Teacher, Healer, or Counselor. We experience ego reduction, pain relief, healing, guidance, and protection.

- When we contact God, there may be an unmistakable change in consciousness. We experience changeless peace, ecstatic joy, pure Love, intuitive knowledge, or light of the soul.

- Whether we understand our suffering as karma or as part of God's mystery, we do our part to work on our problems. As we progress on the spiritual path, we become increasingly aware of how grace operates in our lives. We see how God appears and disappears in an apparent play of hide and seek. In the beginning, we cannot hold on to God all of the time. However, with practice, we are able to find and keep Him more and more. Each time He reappears, our faith grows. Faith is the knowledge that He is there and will be back. Then, even if we feel separate or empty, we know that we have not been abandoned.

• As we go through tests, we may continue to experience turbulence in the form of fear and doubt. Nevertheless, we learn through experience that when we do our part and wait with patience, grace comes in the form of direction, relief, inspiration, courage, forbearance, or protection.

• Gradually, we come to understand that God's grace is continuous, even during the most difficult times. He is always right here, right now, helping, and guiding. No matter what the world or our bodies are doing, God is present.

5. FAITH:

• As our experiential faith grows, it slowly replaces and finally eliminates doubt. Then we know that we have a Friend who is always with us, helping and guiding. We know the ground of all being is His Omniscient Love, greater than any pain. We know He will never fail us in our hour of need, and that we get what we need when we need it. We know our work and His grace combine to reduce our egos, melt our problems, expand our soul qualities, and get us through any barrier. At mastery, when we know the immutable peace of the soul, the fiercest conditions cannot shake our faith. When we know our soul is eternally safe and protected, we remain fearless even in the face of death. This is perfect faith and perfect surrender.

• To know the soul and God is to have the power that faith intends, a power that lights the way, moving us forward in the face of darkness. While earthly conditions may be fierce, faith directs us to our spiritual home, a place where there is no loss.

POINTS TO REMEMBER

- Faith arises when evidence is lacking. It starts with hope and possibility. It ends with experience.

- Faith is the bridge between the material world of limitation and insecurity and the spiritual world of immortality and peace.

- Blind belief is weaker than faith proved by direct experience.

- The brain has a pharmacy that can send healing chemicals to the cells of our body. Thoughts of faith have healing power. Send faithful thoughts to heal the body, mind, and soul through chemistry.

- Faith is a dynamic healing power that can get us through any trial.

- We can grow when life is smooth, but our greatest progress may come when we face difficult problems. It is at these times that we need faith the most. If we continue our spiritual practice, we gain strength and endurance. Eventually our burden lifts and peace comes. We prove to ourselves that we can get through any trial if we persevere.

- For those who believe in a God of Love: The answer to pain and evil would be Love even if God did not exist, but He does. There is a God of Love. Respond with Love, and you will see Him respond to you.

- We learn through experience that Love is greater than any problem. Moreover, each victory of Love over pain expands our faith.

- Faith is the knowledge of our inner connection to the river of Divinity, the infinite source of compassion.

- God's grace is continuous. She is Love, compassion, and peace no matter what the world is doing.

- A solution is forthcoming to any problem. When we do our part and wait with patience, grace comes. Never doubt the infinite grace of the Creator.

AFFIRMATIONS

- I get what I need when I need it.
- Every test is the next step in my spiritual development.
- I transform suffering into spiritual qualities.
- I do my part by cultivating strength and courage.
- God has set up His school of life. He knows what He is doing.
- I get help from the God of infinite compassion and wisdom.
- God is my Friend, Protector, Teacher, Counselor, and Healer.
- God is always right here, right now, helping, and guiding.
- God's great healing power knows how to transform my suffering into spiritual power.
- My work and God's grace get me through anything.
- Love is greater than any pain.
- Nothing can stop me.
- I never give up.
- Nothing can touch my faith.
- I am the immutable peace of the soul.
- I remain fearless even in the face of death.

EXERCISES

1. Following is a list of ideas that can serve as a basis of faith. Review the list to see if any of these ideas are already a part of your faith system. We can have faith in:

   a. Ourselves
   b. Our Higher Power

c. Other people

d. A connection to something larger than ourselves

e. Higher meaning and purpose

f. The meaning inherent in our story

g. The positives of life

h. Beauty, truth, goodness, and Love

i. Our own strength

j. Our ability to contribute

k. Each has a special gift to give

l. Our ability to respond to problems

m. The healing power of the soul

n. The power and intelligence that runs the universe

o. What comes to us is the next step in our spiritual development

p. Pain as the teacher and stimulant for the growth of spiritual qualities

q. All of our experiences teach us soul qualities

r. The existence of a plan for each of us and the world. The plan is good.

s. Our ability to respond to negative with positive

2. What is the basis of your faith?

3. What can you turn to when tested with loss, abandonment, rejection, disease, disability, poverty, sickness, trauma, or failure?

4. Is there a central organizing principle in your belief system that cannot be touched?

5. What is the definition of faith proposed in this chapter?

6. Describe the five-step method for cultivating faith by converting belief to truth through direct personal experience.

7. Review the following four categories. Where do you stand in this continuum?

   a. Atheists dogmatically assert the non-existence of Spirit. Their logic stems from their lack of spiritual experiences.
   b. Believers dogmatically assert the existence of Spirit often without spiritual experience to back up their beliefs.
   c. Agnostics do not know. They are willing to test truth and wait. The cosmos says, "Test me." Agnostics respond by asking the cosmos questions. This is the most scientific stance. It depends on direct experience. There is a transfer of authority from religion, leaders, and books to the body-temple. Ideas and methods are tested in the laboratory of human experience.
   d. Faith is proof of things unseen based on direct personal experience.

CHAPTER TWENTY-NINE

COURAGE

The Bridge Between Fear and Peace

- FEAR HAS A PURPOSE. Change and loss mark life on the physical plane. We will ultimately lose everything: loved ones, possessions, and ultimately, the body. At death, we face the abyss, the infinite unknown. Fear, a natural and intelligent response to these changes, has two key functions. It identifies the nature of the dangers we face, and it helps us fashion the best strategy for survival.

- FEAR BECOMES THE PROBLEM. Fear becomes a problem itself, however, if we avoid it. If we run, it takes on a life of its own. Although we may temporarily gain comfort by pushing fear into the subconscious, it does not remain dormant. Rather, it infuses the conscious mind with fearful fancy, chronic worry, and doubt. It may escalate to panic or terror. Irrational fear ties up energy, impairs judgment, adversely affects health, and obstructs psychological and spiritual growth.

- FEAR CAN BE DIFFICULT TO DETECT. We design all kinds of creative disguises to avoid fear. If we dig deep enough, however, we can find our fear hiding behind anger, jealousy, addiction, dependency, self-importance, and rigid beliefs. To master fear, we must first strip it of its many costumes, experience it directly, and face it with courage.

- COURAGE IS THE BRIDGE BETWEEN FEAR AND PEACE.

When we courageously work through our fears, new levels of peace and strength slowly emerge. If we face it until it is gone, we eventually reach the grand prize, the fearless peace of the soul.

- THE CHANGELESS PEACE OF THE SOUL. In ordinary consciousness, we feel insecure, knowing that we can lose what we have at any time. In spiritual consciousness, we feel safe, since there is nothing to lose. The soul is conscious, immortal peace.

- NOTHING CAN TOUCH THE SOUL. The soul is eternally protected and safe. With sustained spiritual practice, we can shift from the fear and insecurity of the material plane to the permanent peace of the soul.

- THE ROLE OF THE MIND. The key to maintaining peace is the mind. Everything that happens is perceived by the mind. The mind, in turn, determines the body's response. The mind is conditioned to respond to events with fear or tranquility. If the mind reacts with fearful thoughts, the body responds with an elevated heartbeat, sweat, shortness of breath, butterflies in the stomach, dry mouth, and a feeling of impending doom. If the mind stays calm, the body stays relaxed.

- RECONDITION THE MIND. By practicing the spiritual methods described in this work, we can recondition the mind to remain calm in frightening circumstances. Ordinarily we use a small percentage of our concentration, thus leaving our minds susceptible to thoughts of fear and insecurity. A concentrated mind maintains its focus on the peace of the soul, no matter what.

- CHANGE FEAR THOUGHTS TO PEACE THOUGHTS. In effect, our work is to change thoughts of fear to those of peace by practicing mindfulness, meditation, the Presence of God, affirmations, yoga, or any of the other techniques described in this book. With sustained practice, the mind remains calm, positive, strong, and focused under all conditions. Eventually, we can achieve the superconscious state of fearless peace.

- THREE STAGES. We go from fear to peace in three stages: fear to courage to peace.

  1. FEAR. In Stage 1, we try to avoid fear. This makes it grow.
  2. COURAGE. Fear is an enemy only if we run and hide. If we ride its waves until they dissipate, it will give us its power. In Stage 2, we face all of our fears with courage. Slowly, peace replaces fear.
  3. PEACE. In Stage 3, we reach the permanent peace of the soul.

The following process offers a way to help us achieve mastery over our fears:

TECHNIQUE

1. Introspection
2. Spiritual practice
3. Grace
4. Mastery

1. INTROSPECTION:

- To gain soul-peace, we need to identify our fear, whether it presents itself directly or in disguise. We may experience fear directly as an increase in heart rate, respiratory rate, tremors, butterflies in the stomach, dry mouth, or a feeling of impending doom.

- Fear can also manifest indirectly as anger, rigid beliefs, self-importance, domination, aggression, or addiction. To get to deeper states of peace, we need to face these hidden fears. We can start by unmasking our defenses through introspection. Then we are in direct contact with our fear.

- To unmask the defenses that cover your fear, retreat to a quiet place. Practice deep breathing and meditation to achieve stillness. Go deep. Ask your subconscious and Higher Power to guide you to your hidden fears. Be patient. Listen for the soft voice within. Let nothing stand in the way of the truth. Eventually, you will realize that fear is hiding behind your many defenses.

2. SPIRITUAL PRACTICE:

- Fear is a difficult emotion to master, but we can do it. We can master fear if we face it. We must stand our ground, step into the fear, and stare it down. This is difficult, painful, and requires long-term practice.

- With persistence and perseverance, we can slowly reduce our fears, expand our peace, and eventually reach the permanent peace of the soul. As soon as you become aware of fear, practice one or a combination of the following techniques:

  a. PEOPLE. We can get help from family, friends, and counselors.
  b. ACTIVITIES. We can distract ourselves by engaging in constructive meaningful activity: work, school, volunteering, recreation, socialization, sports, the arts, and hobbies.
  c. BELIEF SYSTEM. We can go to church, synagogue, or mosque.
  d. BREATHE. Practice deep abdominal breathing.
  e. PROGRESSIVE MUSCLE RELAXATION. We can tense and relax our muscles as described in Chapter Fourteen.
  f. AFFIRMATIONS. We can affirm the existence of the immutable peace of the soul even if we do not feel it. We might also practice affirmations related to strength, courage, heroism,

endurance, faith, trust, belief, confidence, power, and immortality.

g. VISUALIZE. We can picture ourselves in fearless peace even as we go through our trial.

h. MINDFULNESS. Mindfulness practice helps us surrender into the moment, take a stand, and hold our ground. We are awake, aware, and ready for anything. This is the stance of a spiritual warrior.

i. MEDITATION. In the stillness of deep meditation, peace dissolves fear.

We can practice these or other methods described in this book in any comfortable combination. We persevere, fight our battle with courage, and do our best. While we do our part, we can get additional help by turning to our Higher Power, a bottomless source of strength. To make contact with our Higher Power, practice the Presence of God, select an image, pray, and have faith.

j. THE PRESENCE. God is omnipresent peace. We can practice the Presence of God as the immutable peace within ourselves. It is there, just underneath the stormy weather.

k. SELECT AN IMAGE. We can choose an image such as Father, Mother, Buddha, Krishna, Christ, and so on. The image is symbolic of God's benevolence. We can make our attachment to the image stronger than the fear that confronts us. We can apply all of our will, thought, feeling, and concentration to our image. We hold on to the image as the waves of fear move through our being. If the image is swept away, we bring it back.

l. PRAYER. We can talk to God and ask for help. We can tell Her that we want to experience the changeless peace of the soul.

m. FAITH. We can have faith in the omnipotent healing power of God. She is there, helping and guiding. She cannot fail.

3. GRACE:

- When we do our part, grace flows. We realize God is present, helping, protecting, guiding, and caring. God's power is infinitely greater than our fear. On Her schedule, she comes to our rescue. The turbulent waves of fear subside. Peace comes.

4. MASTERY:

- When fear returns, we continue our spiritual practice. Slowly, we gain confidence and trust as we realize our effort, combined with God's grace, can get us through anything.

- At mastery, we move forward fearlessly because we know God is there, taking us to safety. Here nothing can touch us, nothing can harm us, and nothing can ruffle us. We are fearless peace.

POINTS TO REMEMBER

- We are afraid of what we cannot control. However, when we cannot change bad outer conditions, we can respond with courage. Courage is the bridge between fear and peace.

- Most worry focuses on the future. We can break the habit of worry by learning to focus our attention on the present, living one day or one moment at a time. Focus on the present by practicing mindfulness, breathing, and affirmations. The current moment is all you have to work with, and it is all you need.

- When you begin to worry, feel insecure, and become afraid, use your will and thoughts to bring yourself to a state of faith, trust, belief, and positive thinking. You can learn to respond to any event with even-minded courage.

- Despite the variety and excitement that the future offers, we resist and fear change and the unknown. But fear is the enemy only if we do not face it. Face your fear. Step into the middle of it. Stand your ground. Stare it down. Practice affirmations, breathing, the Presence of God, mindfulness, yoga, and other spiritual methods with will, intensity, and concentration. Persevere and endure. Practice these methods throughout your life.

- Continue your fight as long as you live. Work towards even-mindedness under all conditions. Hold on to your image of God no matter what the world or body throws at you.

- When afraid, affirm unconditional peace. Even if you do not feel reassured, continue your affirmation of peace with faith and concentration. Peace is inside, waiting to come out if you will only battle with courage and perseverance. Eventually you will reach the permanent peace of the soul.

AFFIRMATIONS

- I am fearless peace.
- I look fear in the face.
- I embrace fear with courage.
- I hold my ground in the face of fear.
- I am calm.
- Courage and faith dissolve my fears.
- I have lived through many difficult problems. I can take the next thing that comes along.
- I am steady and even-minded in the face of trouble.
- I rise up every time I fail.
- Love and faith give me courage.
- I endure. I persevere. I have courage.
- I stay in the fear one minute longer. My courage grows.
- I stay in the fear five minutes longer. My courage grows.
- I stay in the fear until it ends. My courage grows.
- I have grace under pressure.
- I will take whatever life gives.

- I face pain, the unknown, and death.
- God is peace. Wherever I am, God is. I am peace.
- I am shaking in my boots. I go forward anyway.
- Effort is progress.
- Peace consumes anxiety.
- Love is stronger than fear. I am willing to work for it.
- Peace is stronger than fear. I am willing to work for it.
- I stay deep in the ocean of peace, away from the turbulent surface waves that try to ruffle me.
- I am the fearless peace of the soul.

EXERCISES

1. Discuss fear as a natural and intelligent response to life on the physical plane.

2. What happens if we do not face our fears?

3. What disguise does fear wear in your life?

4. Describe the relationship between fear, courage, and peace.

5. Describe the peace of the soul.

6. Discuss the importance of the mind in dealing with fear.

7. Describe and practice the four steps of the fear management process.

CHAPTER THIRTY

FORGIVENESS

The Peace Medicine

The quality of mercy is not strain'd;
it droppeth as the gentle rain from heaven
upon the place beneath: it is twice bless'd:
it blesseth him that gives and him that takes.
Tis mightiest in the mightiest;
it becomes
the throned monarch better than his crown ...
It is an attribute to God Himself.
And earthly power doth then show likest God
when mercy seasons justice.
— Shakespeare, *The Merchant of Venice*

- UNCONDITIONAL FORGIVENESS. One of the greatest teaching acts in history is the crucified Jesus Christ forgiving his tormentors, "for they know not what they do." It was one thing for Christ to preach Love for all, including enemies, but quite another for him to demonstrate mercy while experiencing exquisite agony at the hand of those enemies. The forgiving Christ on the cross is the ultimate symbol of the healing power of compassion and understanding. While suffering unimaginable pain, he expressed selfless sympathy for his adversaries. This supreme act of unconditional forgiveness, arguably the most difficult aspect of unconditional Love, is beyond the reach of ordinary mortals. Nevertheless, we can learn how to forgive on a smaller scale and build from there.

- PROVOCATION. All of us suffer the provocations of other people, and each of us has acted poorly towards others. On a small scale, we are confronted daily with minor incidents: disagreement, misunderstanding, or frank rudeness. And most of us at one time or another experience major problems from physical, mental, or sexual violence, infidelity, betrayal, rejection, abandonment, and unjust treatment.

- FIGHT-FLIGHT. Our natural reaction when provoked is anger and fear. These emotions are part of the fight or flight response, a built-in survival mechanism. Anger and fear are good defenses, but difficult emotions to manage. They seem to have a life of their own. Instead of intelligently guiding us to protection and safety, these feelings often become the problem. They stick to us, feed on themselves, and infiltrate our identity in counterproductive ways.

- ESCALATION. Anger smolders as resentment or expands into all-consuming rage. Unresolved anger stays in the body, causing health problems, fatigue, and depression. When it becomes a tool for vengeance and punishment, it leads to escalating cycles of violence and the perpetuation of danger. Fear spirals into painful panic attacks or paranoia. In addition, painful memories and replays of traumatic events often dominate our thoughts. To rid ourselves of the pain, we may turn to self-destructive behaviors such as promiscuity or addiction. Some of us become abusive ourselves, passing our pain along to others. It seems like the wrongdoer injects us with a painful toxin, and we make it worse by responding with our own toxic thoughts, feelings, and behaviors. There appears to be no remedy.

- THE ANTIDOTE. At some point, however, we begin to realize that we are suffering not only from the original trauma, but also from our own reactions. Though we cannot control what has happened to us, we can control our response. Forgiveness, a spiritual practice taught by the great religious traditions, provides us with the antidote to the poisonous effects of the original trauma and our own toxic reactions.

- THE TRANSFORMING POWER OF FORGIVENESS. Forgiveness transforms anger and resentment into understanding, compassion, and loving-kindness. Forgiveness, an aspect of the higher self and an expression of unconditional Love, is itself unconditional. It is applicable to any degree of offense or abuse.

- PEACE OF MIND RETURNS. The main reason to forgive is to rid ourselves of recycled pain resulting from the original trauma, so that we can reclaim peace of mind and enjoy life. Without forgiveness, we may stay locked up in our own emotional prison indefinitely, thus perpetuating the original insult of the wrongdoer. Fortunately, we have the power to neutralize the toxins injected by others with the medication of forgiveness. When we choose forgiveness, we give ourselves a precious gift: the return of our peace of mind.

- CORRECTIVE ACTION OUTSIDE, FORGIVENESS IN-SIDE. Forgiveness does not imply weakness or passivity, nor do we deny or minimize what has happened. An evil action remains what it is: terrible, repulsive, or simply obnoxious. We do not tolerate or condone injustice, and we hold people accountable for their actions. We should not trust the wrongdoer or remain in dangerous situations. Forgiveness is managing our inner life while taking action for safety, protection, and justice in the outer world. While we heal and integrate traumatic memories inside, we take corrective action outside.

- FORGIVENESS IS NOT RECONCILIATION. Reconciliation is the repair of and return to relationship with the wrongdoer. Forgiveness is the healing of the self without involving the offender. We can gain the inner peace of forgiveness without reconciliation. We cannot reconcile without some degree of forgiveness. Just as forgiveness is a choice, so is reconciliation. We do not have to reconcile.

- THE PEACE-MEDICINE. Forgiveness is a powerful healer, greater than anger or even murderous rage. It soothes and quiets other emotions, including depression, anxiety, shame, and guilt. Forgiveness nullifies the noxious power of the offender and releases us from the prison of past trauma and our own toxic emotions. When we bathe our cells, tissues, and organs with the peace-medicine of forgiveness, we reap the benefits of the relaxation response, and our healing power expands. When we forgive, we gain strength, courage, compassion, and joy, our relationships improve, and we become more skillful at solving our problems.

- FORGIVENESS IS NOT FOR EVERYBODY. Despite these benefits, forgiveness is controversial. Religions and individuals vary in their approach; there is no one correct way to deal with it. Each person must choose to forgive or not, a choice involving complex, intimate questions. Some choose not to forgive. This decision should be respected. Forgiveness is not for everybody.

- WE NEED A METHOD. Those who choose to forgive will need a process; simply intending to forgive is not enough. We need to learn how to swim upstream, against the torrent of emotions that demand revenge. This very difficult task requires strength, courage, and skill, since it is much easier to respond in kind when mistreated. Following is a ten-step method designed to guide the reader through a process of forgiveness. This technique can help us manage small, daily challenges as well as major life crises.

- INFORMED CONSENT. Before beginning, please be aware that the forgiveness process is not without risk. The process may release intense emotions that become overwhelming. If this occurs, stop the process, take a break, and engage in pleasant, comforting activities alone or with friends. Then return to your forgiveness work.

If your pain is severe and unrelenting, you may need to consult with a mental health or spiritual counselor. Generally, the criteria for seeking professional consultation are a loss of sleep or appetite, an inability to complete daily tasks, thoughts of harming yourself or others, or any symptom of concern.

TECHNIQUE

1. Action
2. Let the story unfold
3. Spiritualize the story
4. Affirmation
5. Visualization
6. Meditation
7. Grace
8. Service
9. Self-forgiveness
10. The forgiving character

1. ACTION:

- When provoked or violated, we need to take the necessary external corrective action for self-defense and protection. The focus is on safety for our loved ones and ourselves. If the abuser is still present, we may need separation and an order of protection. If a crime is involved, we need to press charges and seek justice. When we are physically safe, we can retreat for the extended inner work of forgiving.

2. LET THE STORY UNFOLD:

- Review the chapter on the transformation of emotion. Remember, emotions are intelligent messengers carrying information about our problems and solutions. We can ride the waves of anger, depression, fear, guilt, and shame until they dissipate. If we surrender to the pain, we get the necessary lessons, solve our problems, cultivate spiritual qualities, and move on. Initially the process involves letting the story unfold.

- The first step is to remember the facts of the event. Then experience and feel the emotions associated with the event.

- We should not be surprised to find multiple layers of emotional pain requiring weeks, months, or years of work. There are deep pockets of hidden emotion that block the flow of healing energy.

- It takes time to remove all of the debris. We need to accept and absorb the pain as it comes. We must work our way through the many layers of anger, one at a time. The process may seem finished when more anger appears, years later. Process whatever emotions arise until there are none left. Because of intense pain, you may tend to avoid some, moving through the process too quickly. Take your time. Do not rush. Let the story unfold completely.

- To let the story unfold, let each emotion surface and speak its truth, whatever that might be. Emotions seek understanding and validation, not value judgments. If we allow our emotions to speak freely at this stage, we will often hear a story about injustice, unfairness, loss, humiliation, insecurity, and revenge. There may be questions about good and evil, why we suffer, and the role of God in the story.

- The value of letting the story unfold freely is that we get our emotions to move out of their hiding places in the body and the subconscious. However, if we stop at this stage, we recycle a story based on self-righteous anger, smoldering resentment, and vengeful fantasy. Unless we give the story higher meaning, we may remain locked up in the prison of our own painful emotions indefinitely.

- The transition to the next stage, spiritualizing the story, is difficult.

In the face of severe anger, the idea of adding anything positive to the story such as understanding or compassion for the wrongdoer seems ridiculous. When anger is very strong, we may have to wait before proceeding to the next stage.

- When you are ready, make a firm commitment to the process of forgiveness. Stop telling your story to other people, to reduce some of its momentum, and begin working Steps 3–7. As you work through these steps, you may experience additional turbulence, swimming as you are against the current of your raging emotions. Take your time and pace yourself. If your reaction is too disturbing, you may not be ready to proceed.

3. SPIRITUALIZE THE STORY:

- We can continue to tell ourselves a story driven by hate, pain, and despair, but then we remain victims of the abuser and suffer unnecessarily. To mobilize ourselves out of the position of victim, we transform anger into peace and strength by spiritualizing the story. Spiritualizing the story includes understanding the offender and separating the soul of the offender from their bad behavior.

- To understand the offender, we can look at the developmental causes and conditions that led to the hurtful act. Sometimes, it is not clear why the wrongdoer acted out. Often, however, we find offenders are deeply troubled victims of neglect, abandonment, and abuse themselves. There is a lack of Love, moral guidance, education, meaningful employment, and self-knowledge. Although this does not excuse wrongdoing, it helps us understand and respect the problems confronting the offender.

- Some actions are so barbaric, however, that no degree of understanding can neutralize our outrage and disgust. In these circumstances, we can still separate the soul from the evil action to realize our common humanity. On the spiritual plane, we are all the same:

431

human beings with a soul. We can maintain this vision by seeing the good in everyone, even when it is not immediately apparent.

- Looking at the perpetrator's history and separating the soul from the wrongful behavior lay the groundwork for a gradual shift from anger to respect and compassion. This transition takes time. It is a difficult part of the process. Anger, fear, and resentment are polar opposites of understanding, compassion, and forgiveness. These emotions fight with each other.

- The experience can be tumultuous and overwhelming. It is easy to get lost and quit. For additional help with this difficult process, we can affirm, visualize, and meditate. With these techniques, we gain access to a wider pool of healing energy.

4. AFFIRMATION:

- Forgiveness affirmations bring us into alignment with the healing power of unconditional Love. Practice the following or similar affirmations no matter what others do. Eventually, these thoughts become your reality:

  o Everyone is a child of the same Father-Mother God.
  o _____ is a child of God, equal in Her sight.
  o I see the humanity and soul of _____.
  o I drink the peace-medicine of forgiveness.
  o I drink at the fountain of understanding and compassion.
  o I establish myself as a center of understanding and compassion.
  o Understanding and compassion radiate throughout my entire being.
  o Love and kindness fill my body-temple and radiate to all beings.
  o I see the beauty and goodness of every soul.
  o I am concerned for others as I am for myself.

o   The soul remains uncorrupted behind our mistakes and flaws.
o   I am the soul, the image of God within, pure Love.
o   The Love I feel for all beings remains the same despite provocation.
o   I forgive others.
o   I forgive myself.
o   I am willing to forgive_____.
o   I make peace with family, friends, strangers, and enemies alike, for therein lays my peace.
o   I love family, friends, strangers, and enemies alike.

5.   VISUALIZATION. THE LOVE-LIGHT HEALING EXERCISE:

•   Sit in a comfortable chair in a quiet place. Close your eyes and take several slow, deep, abdominal breaths. Concentrate on your spiritual eye, at the center of the forehead just above the eyebrows. Relax and focus on the warmth and sense of well-being in your heart. Ask God for help in feeling Her Love for the soul of the wrongdoer.

•   Now visualize the one who has harmed you, immersed in the healing Love-light of God. Imagine the light dissolve and replace the imperfections of the wrongdoer with peace and harmony.

•   Then immerse yourself in the light. Visualize the healing light dissolving and replacing your anger with peace and harmony.

•   You might also visualize the forgiving Christ on the cross or another image that would help you dissolve the pain given to you by others.

6.   MEDITATION:

•   We can get additional help with forgiveness from meditation. In the stillness of meditation, we reach the deep healing power of Love and Her consort qualities. It is here, in stillness, that we slowly and subtly replace our problems with spiritual qualities. Spiritual qualities are the healing powers. They have more power than our problems.

- In the stillness of meditation, Love burns up hate, kindness dissolves cruelty, understanding breeds compassion, and compassion melts anger. Instead of remaining a victim of other people's problems and our own recycled painful emotions, we cultivate peace and strength. When we come out of meditation, we give Love and kindness to all whom we meet.

7. GRACE:

- We do the work as described in Steps 1–6 above, but we are not strong enough to do all of the work of forgiveness on our own. Fortunately, we have access to God's infinite ocean of all-forgiving Love. We can tap into Her vast powers of compassion and mercy by asking for Her help and grace.

- Retreat to a quiet place and make contact with your Higher Power. You might pray, "Divine Mother, You know I cannot forgive on my own. I need Your help. Bless me with Your grace. Help me build a story based on understanding, compassion, and forgiveness. Give me Your Love and forgiveness that I may give it to others."

- When we do the work and ask for Her help, on Her schedule and by Her grace, the gate to Her infinite healing power opens. She sweeps away anger, resentment, shame, guilt, humiliation, and other such emotions, replacing them with peace, forgiveness, and harmony.

8. SERVICE:

- With our work and God's grace, Love qualities replace harmful

434

emotions. We channel our expanded understanding, compassion, and peace into universal service. We can express our service to humanity as a quest for justice, human rights, or any action that benefits others.

9. SELF-FORGIVENESS:

*   All of us make mistakes that hurt others. We become aware of our mistakes when others give us feedback or from introspection. When we see that we have hurt someone, we feel guilt. This is good. Guilt is intelligent. It helps us become responsible for our flaws, and it deters us from repeating the same mistakes.

*   Guilt becomes a problem, however, when we are too hard on ourselves. Excessive guilt leads to low self-esteem, which can become self-hate. We lose our peace of mind. The flow of Love between our self and others is blocked. The antidote to excessive guilt is self-forgiveness.

*   To forgive ourselves, we can follow the same steps described here in the forgiveness process. By following these steps, we can learn to be gentle, patient, and understanding with ourselves even when we make mistakes. In addition, we must do what we can to change our behavior, apologize to the one we hurt, and make amends.

10. THE FORGIVING CHARACTER:

*   Forgiveness is a skill we can learn through study and practice. We can start with forgiving a small event or a single person and expand from there. The more we forgive, the easier it gets. We think forgiveness. We intend forgiveness. We tell forgiveness stories. We practice forgiveness until it becomes a habit, part of our character.

*   Eventually, when our forgiving muscles are very strong, we can forgive unconditionally and instantaneously. Then we have a great

gift to give to the world! Instead of revenge and retribution, we give understanding and compassion. Instead of transferring the pain others inflict on us, we return kindness. When we learn to give ourselves unconditional Love, we become our own best friend. When we absorb the pain of others and transform it to peace and harmony, we reduce the pain of the world.

GENERAL RULES FOR THE FORGIVENESS HEALING PROCESS

- The forgiveness healing process works, but it takes time. It is slow, painful, and difficult. It may take weeks, months, or years. There is no timetable. We cannot control the speed. The process must be allowed to unfold on its own time. We need to work with each step, however long it takes. We should not try to rush or force our way through the process. There are no short cuts.

- Although we all heal at different rates, forgiveness generally takes longer if the hurt was deep.

- There may be times when we experience pain without relief. This is part of the process. Do not give up. Forgiveness is a lifelong discipline. A breakthrough can occur at any time. With practice, it gets easier. Be gentle with yourself and persevere.

- We can only do a little bit of work at a time. When the pain is too intense, we need to take time away.

- If the forgiveness process becomes overwhelming, seek professional consultation with a mental health or spiritual counselor.

- Whenever we experience new waves of anger or resentment, we can rework the steps. Eventually, we completely transform our anger into peace and strength.

ADDITIONAL POINTS TO REMEMBER

- Forgiving helps us deal with major problems such as physical or sexual assault, infidelity, abandonment, injustice, and cruelty. It also helps us with smaller, daily challenges when we conflict with others. It is easy to judge others who are insensitive. However, even mild resentment infiltrates our consciousness, stealing our peace of mind. We must become more aware of the subtle, insidious forms of anger and resentment that occur in response to the provocations of daily life. Then we can refine our consciousness by responding with the healing power of forgiveness. We need a lot of forgiveness; the daily challenges are many.

- When we make mistakes, we want forgiveness. It helps to remember this when we are doing the difficult work of forgiving those who have harmed us. They want forgiveness, too.

- Anger is a poison. Forgiveness is the antidote. The karma of the criminal is between them and God. The attitude of the criminal is irrelevant to our healing process.

- Martin Luther King, Jr. said, "The chain reaction of evil—hate begetting hate, wars producing more wars—must be broken, or we shall be plunged into the dark abyss of annihilation. Love is the only force capable of transforming an enemy into a friend. By its very nature, hate destroys and tears down; by its very nature, Love creates and builds up. We love every man because God loves him. At this level, we love the person who does an evil deed, although we hate the deed that he does."

- We do not accept evil. We fight for safety and justice. This does not necessarily heal our inner being, however. For this, we need forgiveness.

- Forgiveness is a skill we can develop. It is a good tool to have. No one is immune to the daily challenges of life or to a major attack, but if we know how to forgive, we can maintain peace of mind and strength.

- Forgiveness heals individuals, families, religions, and nations. There is no end to the expansive power of Love. How great it is that we can reduce our pain, the pain of others, and the pain of the world with the healing power of forgiveness!

EXERCISES

1. Describe the ten-step forgiveness process.

2. Review how your belief system addresses forgiveness. What are some of the ways that it supports or inhibits forgiveness?

3. Forgiveness is a choice. Describe the pros and cons of forgiveness. This may help you decide if forgiveness is a good idea for you. If you are clear about the benefits of forgiveness, you will be more likely to persist when the process becomes difficult.

4. When a negative person causes us to react negatively, we get mired in negativity. The negativity inside is composed of two layers: the input of the offensive person, and our reaction to it. With gentle compassion, we can dissolve this complex. Try directing compassion to the offender and to yourself.

CHAPTER THIRTY-ONE

TRUTH

Four Pathways to Truth

- "THE TRUTH SHALL MAKE YOU FREE." Jesus said, "You shall know truth and the truth shall make you free." This chapter outlines what this truth might be and how to find it. Following is a discussion of how four dimensions of truth work together to help us expand healing power and improve our ability to manage suffering:

  1. Scientific truth
  2. Spiritual truth
  3. Personal truth
  4. Truth of the spoken word.

SCIENTIFIC TRUTH

- THE LAWS OF PHYSICAL SCIENCE. We want to know how the world works, and we want to get it right. We can do this on the physical plane through controlled experiments where scientific laws emerge as immutable facts of life: water freezes at thirty-two degrees every time. Such measurable certainty is not possible on the spiritual level. Here, too, there are absolute truths and laws, but no controlled experiments, blood tests, or X-rays to help us discover their precise nature. Nevertheless, recent advances in health care research reveal a relationship between spirituality and healing. We know people who have a spiritual practice have better outcomes in medicine, surgery, mental health, and in fighting addiction. From these and similar studies we can infer, but not prove, the nature of spiritual truths.

SPIRITUAL TRUTH

- THE LAWS OF METAPHYSICAL SCIENCE. Great religious traditions and their teachers attempt to outline for us the laws and principles that govern the universe beyond the physical plane; hence the term "metaphysical truth." We cannot measure metaphysical truths with precision. For example, there is no absolute proof by scientific means for the existence and nature of God. This leaves room for interpretation and disagreement. In the vast array of spiritual books and teachers, we find a variety of conflicting ideas and beliefs. How can we determine the nature of spiritual truth?

- THE SCIENTIFIC METHOD IN METAPHYSICS. To verify spiritual truth, we accept no idea on blind faith. Instead, we decide for ourselves via experimentation. The laboratory is human experience. The test tube is the body. Our tools are the built-in equipment of the body: consciousness, energy, reason, feeling, intuition, and direct personal experience. We use these tools when we practice any of the spiritual disciplines described in this work.

- TESTING A NEW IDEA IN THE LABORATORY OF DIRECT PERSONAL EXPERIENCE. Consider the method of spiritual study described in Chapter Sixteen. Contemplation is a powerful tool for determining truth. We can see which ideas work for us by realizing them through practice. In this lesson, we learned how to realize a spiritual idea through the following six steps:

  1. Choose a topic
  2. Study
  3. Affirm
  4. Act
  5. Introspect
  6. Mastery

For example, we might want to explore whether compassion and forgiveness heal anger and depression. By practicing the six-step method of contemplation, we can test this theory.

Testing a new idea is like trying on glasses to see which lens gives us the clearest vision. If an idea fits, we have better eyesight and can see life more clearly. However, some ideas will not prove plainly true or false for years. For example, the Hindus and Buddhists speak about karma and reincarnation. Christ recommended unconditional Love as the ticket into the kingdom of heaven. These are very powerful ideas that may or may not be true. Rather than accepting or rejecting them, we might put these ideas on as one would glasses, and over time see if they help us see more clearly or create blurred vision.

Each of the spiritual methods described in this work give us an opportunity to test new ideas in the laboratory of personal experience. We can prove or disprove a new idea by developing a spiritual practice.

PERSONAL TRUTH

- INTROSPECTION. In the chapter on transformation of emotion, we learned how to find personal truth or self-knowledge through introspection. As in the metaphysical realm, there is no blood test or X-ray to help us determine personal truth. Nevertheless, we can succeed in discovering the truth of our lives by learning how to introspect. In introspection, we learn to work with and through our painful problems. Pain is the teacher bearing the gift of truth and self-knowledge.

- TRANSFORMATION OF EMOTION. Please review Chapter Twenty-Three, the Transformation of Emotion. This chapter teaches us how to extract the important information hidden in our pain. Pain is the teacher of the lessons we need to learn and the spiritual qualities we need to develop. When we stay with our pain, we get to the truth.

- DENIAL AND SUPPRESSION. The greatest barrier to the discovery of personal truth is our desire to avoid suffering. The truth often hurts. When we deny or suppress the painful truths about our lives, we create distortion and self-deception.

- DISTORTION AND DELUSION. Although we think we know what is going on as the story of our lives evolves, all of us have distorted thinking. The mind, however marvelous and amazing, is not always precisely accurate. Bias, prejudice, and fixed false ideas result in our holding unrealistic ideas about ourselves, others, and life. Distorted thinking occurs especially during times of high emotion. All of us have had painful experiences with associated thinking patterns that color later experiences in negative, distorted ways. Some people have experiences that appear to be real but are actually delusions or hallucinations. We cling to irrational or frankly delusional ideas as though they were true to the point that they interfere with our functioning or safety.

TECHNIQUE

Following is a process that can help us use suffering to discover the deeper truths of our personal story. In this process, we go within to seek guidance from our Higher Power and soul, the center of truth within ourselves:

1. CREATE A SAFE HEALING SPACE:

- Sit quietly. Use your breathing and meditation techniques to bring in as much stillness as you can.

2. ASK FOR HELP FROM YOUR HIGHER POWER:

- Ask for guidance from the infinitely intelligent power that is truth itself. Open yourself to the wisdom of the Great Teacher. Ask the Teacher, "What is the meaning of my suffering? Direct me to the lessons I need to learn. What mistakes have I made that need correction? What flaws do I have?" Ask for elimination of all that is untrue and illumination of the truth.

3. LET THE STORY UNFOLD:

-   Bring your pain to awareness. Accept the pain as an honored guest and teacher. It carries valuable information about your life's meaning and purpose. Gently enter the center of the pain and let it tell its story. Let the story unfold in whatever direction it naturally takes. Do not resist, fight, repress, or deny anything. Observe your thoughts, feelings, and bodily sensations. Avoid nothing. Do not rush the process. Accept whatever shows up precisely as it is.

-   The purpose of this exercise is to find the truth about ourselves, no matter how uncomfortable we may be. This may be difficult at first because of the ego, which we have already learned resists change and clings to outmoded ideas.

-   The soul, on the other hand, is willing to go through a process of fearless introspection for the sake of the truth. It is not afraid to be wrong or to change. It wants to find and correct flaws and mistakes in order for us to become better people.

-   Acknowledge the ego's version of the story. Although incapable of introspection, it may give you some valuable information. For example, the ego may be right when it finds fault with others; however, the ego gets stuck in self-righteous anger. We become prisoner of our own emotions and miss opportunities for growth.

-   It is easy to find fault with others and hard to look within. However, we cannot correct our flaws unless we find them. To get to the truth about ourselves, we need to get past our ego and self-righteousness.

We can do this when we use our pain to find out the truth, not just about others but also about ourselves. Even as the ego tries to hide our faults by blaming others, the truth-seeking soul will guide us to the deeper truths within.

- Through a process of fearless introspection, we can use our pain to find our mistakes and flaws. As the ego and emotions tell their story and finally wind down, shift toward introspection. As you look inward, remain gentle and compassionate with yourself.

- Ask your soul and Higher Power to guide you to the truth, whatever it might be. In the light of soul truth, acknowledge your strengths and accomplishments as well as your problems.

- Create a list of problems including flaws, mistakes, bad habits, attachments, and distorted ideas.

4. SPIRITUALIZE THE STORY:

- When you finish letting the story unfold, you should have a good idea of your strengths and accomplishments, as well as your weaknesses.

- Now it is time to spiritualize the story. Here, we recognize the purpose of pain: *replacing flaws with spiritual qualities.* Guided by these qualities, the story unfolds in the direction of the Spirit.

- Consult your problem list and the spiritual alphabet. In response to each problem, choose one or a combination of spiritual qualities. If angry and self-righteous, you may need more understanding, compassion, and forgiveness. If anxious and insecure, you might need courage, strength, and perseverance. If guilty and ashamed, you may need acceptance and forgiveness for yourself.

- Remember not to focus on the problem, which will only strengthen its grip. Instead, place all of your attention on the chosen healing quality. Let these qualities be your guide.

- Bring all of your thoughts, feelings, and actions into alignment with healing qualities. As we replace our imperfections with spiritual qualities, the soul expands. Know that you are in the presence of truth when you experience peace, compassion, Love, patience, kindness, forgiveness, courage, and humility.

SPEAKING TRUTH

- THE GREAT POWER OF THE SPOKEN WORD. When we tell ourselves the truth, we gain self-knowledge. We also need to speak the truth in our relationships. The goal of communication is the welfare and benefit of all. This is difficult when there is conflict and emotions are running high. When distraught, our words may be true but are often unnecessarily forceful and destructive. We have great power to create harm or good with the spoken word.

- IMPECCABLE TRUTH GUIDED BY SWEETNESS OF SPEECH. To combat negative communications, we can align our intent with the truth of the spoken word. However, truth spoken without kindness may be destructive. Sweetness of speech buffers the potential harshness of truth. The spoken word laced with truth and tempered with kindness incites effective communication and skillful problem solving. Following is an exercise combining impeccable truth and sweetness of speech.

1. Avoid gossip, criticism, judgment, debate, and harsh words.
2. Align all of your thoughts and speech with the soul qualities listed in the spiritual alphabet.
3. Speak truth with compassion and kindness.
4. Practice opened-minded discussion.
5. Listen, listen, listen … and then listen some more.

6. Be aware that your word has the vibratory power to spread truth, healing, and Love.

- Our speech is a reflection of who we are. When we cultivate Love, our thoughts, words, and actions naturally follow suit.

TRUTH IS LOVE

- In this chapter, we reviewed four pathways to truth:

1. Scientific truth: using research methods to discover the immutable laws of nature with measurable certainty
2. Metaphysical truth: using the laboratory of human experience to discover higher laws through the practice of spiritual disciplines
3. Personal truth: using fearless introspection to gain self-knowledge
4. The truth of the spoken word: speaking truth guided by sweetness of speech

- These four distinct routes to truth are connected. They work together. In each of the four methods, we can study ourselves to learn about the ultimate nature of reality. We can do this because the design of a human being reflects the design of the universe. We are a microcosm of the macrocosm. Our mind is a reflection of the Universal Mind. Our soul is a droplet of the great ocean of Spirit. We are made of the same powerful intelligence that creates, operates, and sustains the universe.

- Whether we follow the path of science, metaphysics, our personal story, or the spoken word, we discover the same truth: pain management (Step 8) and spiritual practice (Step 9) lead to the realization of our soul and Spirit (Step 7) as the peace, Love, and joy we crave (Steps 1 and 10). When we manage our pain skillfully and practice spiritual discipline, we shall know the truth, and it shall make us free. That truth is Love.

- All paths lead to Love. Love is a fundamental solution to all of our problems. Physical science will prove it. Metaphysicians already know it. We can verify it in our personal story. We can demonstrate it with the power of our word. Love is the law, the answer to the cosmic puzzle, God Herself.

POINTS TO REMEMBER

- The universe operates by law. We can study ourselves to understand the laws that govern the universe.

- All of the spiritual methods described in this work lead to the discovery that our soul and Spirit are comprised of the unlimited peace, Love, and joy we crave. We can know this through direct personal experience. The pursuit of truth leads to the experience of these qualities.

- God is Love. We can know Love in silence and express it in words and deeds as service. Then we know the peace that surpasses understanding. This is the law. This is the truth.

- "Truth is not to be found by anybody who has not got an abundant sense of humility. If you would swim on the bosom of the ocean of Truth, you must reduce yourself to zero" (Mahatma Gandhi).

- Dishonesty is a barrier to spiritual growth. Telling the truth to ourselves, however difficult, is liberating.

- Personal truth reflects metaphysical truth. Our personal story fits into the cosmic story. In discovering meaning in our personal life, we can discover the meaning of life. Follow Love and keep your eyes open. Everything will fall into place.

AFFIRMATIONS

- I establish myself as a center of truth.
- Truth heals.
- I take time daily to reflect upon the power of my word.
- I am true to myself.
- I am true to others.
- My word has the power to carry the truth.
- My word is powerful, positive, and passionate.
- I speak truth guided by sweetness of speech.
- I only speak what is true, necessary, and kind.
- I perceive truth when I am equal to all others.
- I live in truth when I am in Love.
- I live in truth when I am compassionate.
- I live in truth when I am of service.
- I live in truth when I am at peace.
- I live in truth when I recognize beauty.
- I live in truth when I am good.
- The intentions of my words are Love qualities. Otherwise, I do not speak.
- The discovery of truth is the driving force of my life.

EXERCISES

1. Ultimately, it is up to you to decide what truth is at both the individual and cosmic levels. Describe the four methods for discovering truth identified in this chapter. How might these methods help you discern for yourself the nature of truth?

2. Discuss how the four types of truth help us expand healing power, become more skillful pain managers, and evolve spiritually.

3. What is the greatest barrier to self-knowledge?

4. How does the ego interfere with our ability to discover truth?

5. Can you think of a time when your thinking was incorrect and how you came to know the truth later?

6. Describe a time when you used denial to avoid a painful truth. What helped you discover the truth?

7. Describe the method for discovering personal truth through introspection.

8. How does the soul guide us to truth during introspection?

9. Describe how you can use the light of your soul qualities to discover and eliminate false or destructive thoughts.

10. In psychiatry, the question of healthy spirituality versus spiritual psychosis often comes up. How can you tell the difference? This is a complex question beyond the scope of this work. Having said that, here are three guidelines to help you decide. Focus on: (1) safety, (2) functioning, and (3) healing qualities. If a thought, feeling, desire, or action leads to safety, functioning, and the growth of healing qualities, it is good. On the other hand, if a thought, feeling, desire, or action leads to danger to self or others, reduced functioning, and a reduction in healing qualities, it is more likely psychotic or a distortion of the truth. Let peace, Love, joy, patience, kindness, gentleness, compassion, understanding, forgiveness, safety, and functioning be your guide. Roll the Universal Healing Wheel to stay spiritually healthy.

11. Describe the battle between the self-righteous ego and fearless introspection of the soul.

12. Describe how speaking truth guided by sweetness of speech helps us communicate and solve problems.

13. How do the four types of truth work together to help us discover the metaphysical laws that govern the universe?

CHAPTER THIRTY-TWO

INTUITION

A Higher Order of Intelligence

In this chapter, we will learn how to contact the Intelligence of the Universe, referred to as Omniscience, Wisdom, Wise Mind, or Infinite Intelligence. Wise Mind can help us solve problems, expand healing power, and manage our suffering skillfully.

- OMNISCIENCE. Omniscience is the intelligent power that creates, operates, and sustains the cosmos, from the tiniest particle to the grandest stellar system. Omniscience is Omnipresent. It occupies every millimeter of space. Omniscient Power organizes and expresses itself on Earth—not to mention in faraway galaxies and solar systems—in a seemingly endless parade of spectacular forms that often exceed the imagination. This power operates every particle, molecule, cell, tissue, organ, and system within our body so that we can hear, see, feel, think, and Love. We can use this Supreme Intelligence to help us solve our problems by cultivating the soul quality of intuition.

- INTUITION. In ordinary problem solving, we use reason to determine the best course of action. To get additional help, we can seek guidance from Omniscience through intuition. Intuition, a faculty of the soul, is a sixth sense. It is a higher order of intelligence beyond reason and the five senses.

- DIRECT KNOWLEDGE OF TRUTH. Intuition is the direct, infallible knowledge of the truth gleaned from our connection to

Omniscience. Omniscient Wisdom is pregnant with the will of the Universe: what needs to happen, the choices we need to make, the knowledge we need to get.

- WISDOM. Reason, associated with ordinary consciousness, works with the data collected through the five senses. Intuition works directly with Wise Mind within. Reason without intuition is unreliable since it is subject to the whims of desire, emotion, and the ego. Reason guided by intuition approaches wisdom, and pure intuition is wisdom itself.

- THE EGO. Reason is a marvelous tool that helps us solve problems and achieve goals. However, the mind, under the influence of the ego, is subject to bias, emotion, likes, and dislikes. Within the consciousness of the ego, we defend our current positions even if based on false convictions. We resist new ideas. We are afraid to be wrong and afraid to change.

- FALSE BELIEFS. Many seemingly spiritual people think they have intuition when in fact they are under the influence of ego, selfishness, and fixed false convictions. Unspeakable destruction occurs in the name of God, under the guise of intuition.

- WISDOM IS INSIDE. Intuition does not just happen. It does not come by being a member of a particular faith or following certain spiritual leaders. On the contrary, to be intuitive, we must transfer power from organized religion and its leaders to ourselves, for it is within each one of us that the direct connection to Omniscience exists.

- BEYOND ORDINARY CONSCIOUSNESS. Intuition is direct knowledge of the truth, beyond the information accessible to ordinary intellect and the senses. We cannot be intuitive in ordinary states of consciousness. We must go beyond reason, the senses, emotion, desires, and the ego.

- PREPARING THE SOIL OF CONSCIOUSNESS. The subtle and powerful ego needs to be right all of the time. To grow past it, we must not be afraid to change. We need to stop reacting, defending, and fighting for our current position when we are wrong. We must extricate ourselves from prejudice, bias, and false conviction. We need to reduce mental restlessness and high emotional reactivity. We need to eliminate bad habits, excessive material desire, and dependency on attachments. We must be fearlessly introspective to find our flaws and correct them. We must face all of our fears, including fear of the unknown and death. When we do this, we prepare the soil of our consciousness for the growth of intuition.

- HUMBLE, EMPTY, AND RECEPTIVE. Intuition manifests when we are still, humble, empty, and receptive. When we empty ourselves of mental and emotional restlessness, ego, selfish desires, and blind obedience to religious dogma, we can receive direction and guidance from the Divine Mind.

- STILLNESS. Stillness is the bridge between ordinary reason and intuition. We can get ideas and direction from Higher Intelligence when we are at peace with ourselves. When the mind is calm, we can receive guidance from the still small voice within. The more peace we have inside, the more guidance we receive from God through intuition.

TECHNIQUE FOR CULTIVATING INTUITION

- Following is an exercise in problem solving through intuition. We can use our reason, will, and common sense to work on our problems while using our intuitive connection to Omniscience to get additional help. We can do this by cultivating stillness in both meditation and activity.

1. Reason
2. Meditation

3. Guidance
4. Receptivity
5. Action
6. Blessing
7. Mastery

1. REASON:

- Work to solve your problem with reason, will, and common sense.

2. MEDITATION:

- To get additional help from your intuitive connection, reduce your restless thoughts, emotions, and desires by cultivating stillness in meditation.
- With eyes closed, focus on the point just above the eyebrows. This is the center of intuition and spiritual perception.
- Practice your routine meditation technique.
- Relax, surrender, and completely let go of thought.
- Be still and empty.
- Feel your heart center.

3. GUIDANCE:

- Invoke the presence of your Higher Power as the Infallible Intelligence that rules the universe.
- Present your problem to Wise Mind and ask for guidance.
- "What do I need to do in this situation?"
- "What do I need to know?"
- "Guide me to the right thing that I should do."
- "Guide me to the greater good for myself and others."
- "Your will my Lord, not mine."

4. RECEPTIVITY:

- Intuition can occur through thought, feeling, or visions.
- Be open and receptive to the whispers of counsel from within.
- Be aware of the feeling in your heart.
- Receive special guidance for your specific problems from the wisdom of your Confidante and Counselor.

5. ACTION:

- When you come out of meditation, try to remain inwardly calm so you can continuously receive guidance from Omniscience.
- Perform every act guided by that inner wisdom.
- When the mind becomes restless, take several slow, deep, abdominal breaths.
- Reaffirm the presence of your Higher Power as your Supreme Guide and Friend, taking you to the best course of action.
- Be prepared to change directions if necessary.

6. BLESSING:

- Recognize the blessing and the help that you are getting.
- Help comes in an endless variety of ways. Notice how events unfold, the arrival of key people teaching key lessons, the appearance of resources, and the expansion of positive thought, emotion, and healing qualities. You may experience guidance, protection, more skillful pain management, and a host of other solutions.

7. MASTERY:

- In the beginning, it is unreasonable to assume that our actions stem from pure intuition. We are all subject to ego, emotion, personal desire, and bias. We make mistakes. We cannot tell for sure if our actions result from ego, intuition, or a combination of both.

- However, Love and other spiritual qualities can always guide us to what is good for others and ourselves. Moreover, we are moving in the right direction when we learn how to cultivate progressively greater degrees of stillness in meditation and activity. Our intuition slowly grows as we become more still.

- As we approach mastery, when we are one with Supreme Wisdom, we can use our perfected intuition in the service of humanity.

POINTS TO REMEMBER

- To solve problems, we can work with ordinary reason, feeling, and the senses. We can use our good judgment and common sense. Simultaneously, we can ask for help from Wise Mind and receive it through our intuition.

- Intuition is direct knowledge of the truth, beyond the limited information given by ordinary intellect, emotion, the senses, and the ego.

- Intuition does not just happen. We have to work for it. It grows slowly. Intuition grows as we reduce our ego, calm the restless mind, eliminate emotional reactivity, and control excessive material desire.

- We can get to a higher order of intelligence in the stillness of meditation when we contact the intuition of the soul. When we calm our restless minds, emotions, and desires, we can receive guidance from this Higher Wisdom. Intuition is direct knowledge of the truth, which we can attain when we are completely still.

- We can commune with Infinite Intelligence in the stillness of deep meditation. Moreover, we can maintain contact with Omniscience in activity by remembering that this Intelligence occupies every millimeter of space. We live in the mind of God. That same Wisdom lives within us.

AFFIRMATIONS

- Omniscience = Wisdom = Infinite Intelligence = The Wise Mind
- I commune with Wisdom in the stillness of deep meditation.
- I bring Wisdom into the moments of my life.
- I ask Wise Mind for continuous guidance, direction, and support.
- I am in Wise Mind.
- Wise Mind is in me.
- Wisdom guides my thoughts.
- Wisdom guides my choices.
- Wisdom guides my relationships.
- Wisdom guides my work.
- I practice the presence of my Higher Power as the Infallible Intelligence that rules the universe.
- Omniscience continuously guides me to virtue and peace.
- I chant, "Omniscience, Omniscience, Omniscience."
- I affirm, "Wisdom, Wisdom, Wisdom."

EXERCISES

1. What is Omniscience?

2. Where is Omniscience?

3. What is intuition?

4. What is the relationship between intuition and Omniscience?

5. Have you had intuitive experiences such as thinking of a friend right before (s)he called or having a dream that came true?

6. What is the relationship between reason and intuition?

7. What are the barriers to intuition?

8. Describe how the ego can confuse ordinary consciousness with intuition. Has this happened to you?

9. How can intuition help you with your problems?

10. Describe the technique for cultivating intuition.

11. How can we maintain our connection to the Omniscience during activity?

12. Get out of your head, into your heart, and be still. There are secrets here. Test it. Go to silence and ask for help, guidance, and healing.

CHAPTER THIRTY-THREE

ONENESS

The Sacred Changeless One

*"In seemingly empty space there is one link, one life eternal,
one wave of life flowing through everything, animate and
inanimate, unifying everything in the universe, a oneness of life,
a unity and harmony so vast, so perfect, breathtakingly perfect,
that it automatically breeds reverence and humility."*
— Yogananda

- THE CHANGELESS ONE. The universe is one and changeless. In this chapter, we will learn how to contact the Changeless One, the One who creates, sustains, permeates, and connects all people and all space. We will explore this experience and its importance.

- A UNIFIED FIELD OF ENERGY. We live in an infinite ocean of conscious energy, a unified field of peaceful, joyful, loving energy that cannot be broken. When we immerse ourselves in this ocean, we experience unity with all of life. In the stillness of the ocean, we contact the pure, formless consciousness that is at once the source of everything and the link that connects all. This consciousness fills all space. It cannot be born, confined, limited, divided, or destroyed. When we experience this power, we know that we are immortal, indivisible, and connected to all.

- MAYA. We are always in the Changeless One, even as a wave is part of the ocean. However, because of maya, we experience ourselves as isolated waves, separate from the ocean.

Maya refers to the power inherent in ordinary consciousness that makes us think we are separate from the Creator, creation, and other creatures. Under the influence of maya, we experience the division, separation, limitation, impermanence, and suffering of ordinary or worldly consciousness.

Maya is powerful and seductive. It is responsible for our hook to the physical plane. It tricks us into thinking we can achieve peace, Love, and joy by focusing on the little wave of our life to the exclusion of the ocean. Under the spell of maya, we focus on our soap opera, possessions, and bodies while we exclude the Changeless One from our consciousness.

• FROM SEPARATION TO ONENESS. We love maya, the physical plane, despite the limitations, impermanence, and suffering it imposes. However, in order to contact the Changeless One, we must reduce the power of maya, since it and Oneness occupy the same space.

The Omnipresent Giver of peace and Love exists just behind the ever-changing world of people, events, and things. When we contact the Giver, we can draw from Her miraculous healing powers and qualities.

The shift from maya to Higher Consciousness is not easy. To find Her behind the veil of ordinary consciousness, we need help. This work describes a variety of methods designed to help us do this work. With persistent practice of these techniques, we can experience our little wave as a part of the Eternal Ocean. This results in a profound shift of consciousness from separation to oneness. Then we know that we are eternally safe and protected.

Following is a review of how two methods, meditation and practicing the Presence of Oneness, can help us experience the sacred unity of all creation.

MEDITATION

- RIDING THE SURFACE WAVES OF CHANGE. Think of life as an ocean. The waves represent the physical plane where all things are in a state of flux. At times, the waves of the ocean are calm. However, it is only a question of time before the waves become stormy. We spend most of our lives on the surface, riding the waves of change. Their power is great. They command our attention and dominate our consciousness. The waves of the ocean are akin to maya.

- THE VAST STILLNESS UNDERNEATH. Under the surface, the ocean is vast, still, one, and changeless. The goal of meditation is to shift our consciousness from the transient surface of the ocean to its depths; for it is only there that we can experience the eternal peace and safety of changelessness.

- STOP THE WORLD, BODY, SENSES, AND MIND. To get beneath the waves and benefit from the stillness, we must stop the world, body, senses, and mind. In meditation, we retreat from the world by sitting in a quiet place, closing our eyes, and keeping our body still. Then we discover the most difficult challenge: stopping the waves of the mind. Like the waves of the ocean, one thought after another pounds the shores of our consciousness. With practice, however, we can slowly reduce the intensity and frequency of our thoughts.

- THE DEEP HEALING POWER OF STILLNESS. As the mind slows, we become increasingly aware of the underlying ocean and its deep healing power of stillness. Immersed, we may still see the changing waves above. However, we care less about their variance, enjoying the peaceful gentle power of the ocean underneath.

- ALWAYS ONE WITH THE CHANGELESS ONE. With the consistent and regular practice of meditation, our identity slowly shifts. We are not the ever-changing surface waves. Rather, we are the changeless peace of the ocean below. Though the small waves, with a beginning, middle, and end, do define our lives, we are ever a part of the vast permanent ocean just underneath the wave. When we realize we are always one with the Changeless One, we are at peace no matter what the world or the body does.

PRACTICING THE PRESENCE OF ONENESS

- We can experience the Changeless One in activity as well as in meditation. Spirit and matter are two sides of the same coin. On the material side is maya, the physical world of change. On the spiritual side is the Giver, always offering peace, Love, wisdom, and safety. In ordinary consciousness, we focus on the physical world to the exclusion of the Spirit. This is unfortunate; the physical world, however entertaining, ultimately makes us feel separate, insecure, and afraid. When feeling this way, we can practice the Presence of our Higher Power as Oneness.

- Everything we do, even routine activity, can serve as a reminder that the Changeless One is always present. A student returns from a visit with her spiritual teacher, a master. A friend asked her what secrets she learned. She said, "I learned how to tie my shoes." For one who can see, even the most mundane routine is a window to, and a manifestation of, the Eternal One. Infinite peace, Love, wisdom, and safety are manifested through us at this very moment. We are one wave of the infinite ocean, made of the substance of that ocean. God is One and Changeless when we tie our shoes or experience an earthquake.

- To practice the presence of your Higher Power as such a unifying force, try the following exercise. You can practice this exercise whether you are involved in routine or stressful activities. The endgame is unity with the Great One underneath all, a unity that can never be severed.

1. Stop
2. Breathe
3. Present moment
4. Affirm
5. Act

1. STOP:

- When you become aware that your mind is unfocused or restless, stop and breathe.

2. BREATHE:

- Take several slow, deep abdominal breaths.

3. PRESENT MOMENT:

- Get into the present moment. This is where you can experience Oneness.

4. AFFIRM: Choose one or several of the affirmations below. Maintain thoughts of unity throughout the day:

- All opposing forces merge in the One.
- Unity and harmony permeate my thoughts and actions.
- The Changeless One is in every person, house, flower, and blade of grass.
- All in One and One in all.
- My awareness of unity creates unity.
- My yearning for unity creates unity.
- I keep the unity of the many worlds before me.
- My world is broken. I heal it with oneness.
- The world is broken. I heal it with oneness.
- Every person is part of one family.
- We are one.

- All of humanity is in the same boat.
- I am peace. I make peace. I am friend to all.
- I honor diversity.
- I am a part of one Great Body.
- I am a part of One Person.
- The infinite universe is One Being.
- One Omniscient Power permeates and governs all things.
- I see everything in Her, and Her in everything.
- I see everything in Him, and Him in everything.
- Spirit and matter exist in the same space. I focus on Spirit.
- God and maya exist in the same space. I focus on God.
- Division and unity exist in the same space. I focus on unity.
- Change and changelessness exist in the same space. I focus on changelessness.
- The Changeless One is in everything.
- Everything is in the Changeless One.
- The Changeless One is everywhere.
- Every moment is an aspect of and a window to the Infinite One.
- I live, move, and have my being in a unified field of peaceful, joyful, loving energy that cannot be broken.

5. ACT:

- The Sacred One is always right here, offering peace, Love, wisdom, and safety. Whether eating, driving, walking, sleeping, working, dressing, cleaning, socializing, exercising, sitting, thinking, feeling, or dreaming, know you are in the mind of God. Perform every action with the awareness that One Power connects all people, all objects, and all events.

- We can learn how to move from the surface of the ocean to its deeper waters. When we learn to be in that place of oneness in both meditation and in activity, we experience peace, safety, and unity with all beings. What a joy it is to experience even a sliver of this beauty within ourselves! What other response could there be but humility, gratitude, and awe? What other action could we take but gentle, compassionate service to humanity?

POINTS TO REMEMBER

- In higher consciousness, all of creation is one. All life is in One Life. All minds are in the One Mind. All hearts are in One Heart. All bodies are in One Body. When we feel our life, mind, heart, and body as separate, we suffer. When we experience unity with all life, we soar.

- The universe is one system through the law of interconnection. Everything is connected to everything else. Maya would have us believe we are isolated. We cannot separate any part from the whole, despite the delusive power of maya.

- Our problems stem from our feeling of separation. We can counter this by developing a spiritual practice. For example, when we practice unconditional Love and service to humanity, we see the unity and connection that rule the cosmic order. When we help one person, we help the universe.

- The Intelligent Power that runs the universe organizes every millimeter of space, from particle to galaxy. The human body is composed of atoms, cells, organs, and systems, each necessary for the body to work. Each of us is part of the greater system of family, city, nation, and Earth. The Earth is a member of the family of planets, which form solar systems, which form galaxies. Each part, from particle to galaxy, is necessary for the whole to function correctly. Our consciousness exists as part of a vastly complex universe. We are a part of the whole and have a rightful place in it. Every individual, group, and nation of this Earth has a unique, important, and necessary role to play in the stupendous human drama.

- The Teacher of Oneness presents life to us as a puzzle. Every circumstance we encounter reveals something. There are clues and lessons. We can put the pieces of the puzzle together to make a coherent whole. When we do the work, we discover how the pieces fit together in a unique way to create our personal story, which in turn fits into the grand story of life.

- Find the Changeless One in your own consciousness. Then even the simplest most mundane action holds the key to the universe. You can know Him when you do the laundry or brew a pot of tea. Intelligent Power is in every nook and cranny.

- When we know the Changeless One within, we need not fear any condition of the body or the world. It takes time to get to this advanced state. On the way, we need courage, faith, patience, and perseverance.

- The Changeless One unites everything, inside and outside, you and I, and all creation. Despite the apparent separation, we are all one.

EXERCISES

The following exercises help us achieve peace of mind and oneness with humanity:

1. The true test of religion, spirituality, or any belief system is Love. Does your path help you connect with others, or does it separate you?

2. Judgment of others creates separation. Acceptance and support bring us closer. What thoughts, feelings, and activities are you engaged in that separate you from others?

3. Finding the faults of others is easy. Instead, focus on their positive qualities. Give them support for their psychological and spiritual

growth. What thoughts, feelings, and activities are you engaged in that bring you closer to others?

4. The basis of all spirituality is morality and goodness. We must learn how to behave. First, do no harm to others in thought or word. Stop judging, criticizing, and gossiping. Then practice compassionate service. Notice the peace of mind and strength you kindle as a result. Keep going, and you will experience solidarity with humanity and creation.

5. In ordinary consciousness, under the direction of the ego, we often feel superior or inferior to others. In spiritual consciousness, we are equal and one. No matter what your ego tells you, practice equality and unity with all others. Notice the harmony and rhythm that come to you as a result.

6. We can use the consciousness of One to help us when we are in conflict with others. Think of someone who provokes you. Visualize the healing light of Love melting his or her imperfections. Visualize the healing light of Love melting your own imperfections. Picture yourself in harmony with this person.

CHAPTER THIRTY-FOUR

HEALING

The Infinite Intelligent Healing Power

- THE WISDOM OF THE BODY. Healing Power is part of the Omniscient Wisdom that runs the universe. We can trust the infinitely intelligent healing power to do its work as the process of life unfolds. Healing Power works without our awareness or assistance. It creates, operates, and sustains every cell, tissue, organ, and system in the body. It heals cuts, destroys foreign invaders, replaces worn-out cells, cleans up debris, regulates hormones, delivers food and oxygen to the cells, eliminates waste products and toxins, and much more.

With the practices described in this work, we can support and assist the healing power when it needs our help. Moreover, we can tap into this power to help us manage our suffering more skillfully. This chapter outlines two healing processes: "The Ocean" and "The House." In "The Ocean" we learn how to get help from the Great Healer in meditation for any pain or problem. In "The House" we learn how to expand our space to receive the problems of life with equanimity.

THE OCEAN

- THE GREAT HEALER. We live in an infinite Ocean of Love. The ocean has unlimited quantities of compassion, understanding, peace, forgiveness, courage, wisdom and other spiritual qualities. Each one of us is a drop of that ocean, made of the same qualities, but when we are separate from the ocean, these qualities remain limited. In ordinary states of consciousness, our droplet exists within but remains separate from the ocean. In advanced meditation, when separation dissolves, we join the ocean and absorb Her powers and qualities. This is contacting Higher Power in Her aspect as the Great Healer. In this role, She is the keeper of the Ocean of Love.

- LOVE IS MORE POWERFUL THAN ANY PAIN OR PROBLEM. We can bathe in the Ocean of Love. In meditation, when we calm the waves, we enter the deep part of the ocean and absorb Her nature. In the stillness and silence of meditation, Love and her sister qualities slowly expand and replace our ego and problems. Love is the great healing force in the universe. It is more powerful than any pain or problem. Armed with this knowledge, we can go to the Great Healer in meditation and ask for help.

- A SLOW PROCESS OF PURIFICATION, SOMETIMES BY FIRE. Healing is a slow process of purification, sometimes by fire. Although some problems dissolve easily, others are deeply embedded and take years of work. Often we think we have eliminated a problem, only to find additional layers later in life. Moreover, during crisis, we may experience immersion in the ocean of suffering rather than the Ocean of Love. Immersed in suffering, we feel as though we might drown in the pain waves. With long-term practice, however, we can learn how to ride out any wave of pain. When we stay with our pain, we come to the other side of the crisis where we find ourselves with more Love.

- LOVE BURNS UP PROBLEMS. Love burns up problems one layer at a time, until Love is all there is. At mastery, we are always deep in the Ocean of Love, no matter what the waves are doing. We come to know Love as the foundation of the universe. We feel safe, secure, and immortal. We are Love, and give only that.

We can expand any one or a combination of the qualities listed in the spiritual alphabet by entering the Ocean of Love in meditation. To get help with problems, try the following exercise:

1. Introspection
2. Spiritual Alphabet
3. Prayer
4. Meditation
5. Action
6. Repetition
7. Mastery

1. INTROSPECTION:

• Make a problem list. For example, your problem might be fear of dying.

2. SPIRITUAL ALPHABET:

• Consult the spiritual alphabet and decide which qualities you would like to expand in response to your problem. You might choose safety, security, and immortality.

3. PRAYER:

• Ask for help from the Keeper of the Ocean of Love. "Great Healer, I am drowning in waves of fear and pain. I need Your help. I need more of Your Love manifest as the safety, security, and immortality of my soul."

4. MEDITATION:

• With your will and concentration, eliminate all thoughts except those of safety, security, and immortality.

• In the increasing stillness of meditation, notice how the feeling of safety, security, and immortality permeates and saturates your whole being.

- As peace spreads throughout your body, feel your fear slowly dissolve.

- Bathe in the healing ocean as long as you can.

5. ACTION:

- When you come out of meditation, bring your expanded feeling of safety, deep peace, and immortality to all your experiences.

6. REPETITION:

- Repeat this process as often as possible.

7. MASTERY:

- In time, with your effort and God's grace, your little droplet of ocean completely merges with the Ocean of Love. Then you will know you are safe, secure, and immortal.

- Go to the healing ocean as often as possible. Bring all of your painful problems to the Great Healer. Consult the spiritual alphabet. Choose one or any combination of qualities you need in response to your problems. Focus on these qualities in the stillness of meditation. Repeat this process of purification until your Love is perfect. Give that Love to all whom you meet.

POINTS TO REMEMBER

- We can turn the tables on our pain and make it work for us. Bring any problem to the stillness of deep meditation. Invoke your Higher Power as the Great Healer. Ask for help. In the stillness of deep meditation, through the grace of the Keeper of the ocean, Love qualities slowly replace our ego and problems.

- Love is more powerful than even the most brutal reality. We can go to the Ocean of Love in deep meditation and absorb its unlimited supply of healing qualities as often as necessary until we achieve mastery. At mastery, we experience our consciousness as a part of the vast ocean below. Then we know we are safe, secure, and immortal. Then we can assist others in their journey toward the same.

THE HOUSE

- FIRST FLOOR: TESTS AND TRIALS. Imagine you live in a two-story house. On the first floor is the physical plane, with all its tests and trials. Here we often struggle with issues, problems, flaws, and symptoms. Sometimes we react well, other times, poorly. We need help.

- SECOND FLOOR: HEALING QUALITIES. On the second floor are soul qualities. The atmosphere on the second floor is still, silent, serene and spacious. Here there is unlimited Love and associated healing qualities. The goal is to bring these qualities to the first floor to help us manage our painful problems.

- STEPS TO THE SECOND FLOOR. The steps to the second floor are spiritual practices such as affirmations, mindfulness, meditation, and loving service. When we practice these and other spiritual disciplines, we climb to the second floor where we absorb the qualities needed to manage whatever difficulties we must face on the first floor.

- THE UNINVITED GUEST. All of us have problems that take up residence on the first floor of our home against our will. Some of these we can fix. Others do not respond so easily. We do everything we can to eliminate them. However, no matter what we try, some problems will not budge. We cannot fix them or evict them. On the contrary, the more we struggle, the more upset and agitated we become.

- THE INVITED GUEST: TEACHER IN THE SCHOOL OF LIFE. When we find ourselves in this dilemma, we can accept the problem in our home as a resident instructor. Until this time, the problem has been treated as an uninvited guest. When agitated, it is often because we have not created enough space for the problem. Now we give the guest a room with plenty of space and an atmosphere graced with healing and acceptance.

We turn the table on the problem by going up to the second floor, where there is unlimited space. We take a portion of this space to the first floor and create a guestroom for the problem. We can create as many rooms as we need; there is an infinite supply of space on the second floor of this magical house. We can do this with all of our problems so that on the first floor, all we have are invited guests, our teachers in the school of life.

TECHNIQUE

In this exercise, we transfer the magical healing powers of the qualities on the second floor to the first floor:

1. Introspection
2. Guest-teachers
3. Healing and purification
4. Action
5. Repetition
6. Mastery

1. INTROSPECTION:

- Make a list of problems that you are unable to eliminate from the first floor of your house (for example, highly reactive emotions).

2. CONVERT PROBLEMS TO INVITED GUEST-TEACHERS:

- Practice meditation, mindfulness, service to humanity, or any other set of spiritual practices that you enjoy. These disciplines will help you climb to the second floor where you can draw from an unlimited supply of space and healing qualities.

- With your expanded space from the second floor, create a room for your problem. Fill the atmosphere of the room with acceptance, thus making the uninvited problem a guest-teacher. This sets the stage for healing and purification.

3. HEALING AND PURIFICATION:

- When we respond to our painful problems with soul qualities, we heal and purify our consciousness.

- All our problems are teachers with the goal of helping us expand spiritual qualities until these qualities are unconditional. Go back up to the second floor to get whatever spiritual qualities you need to manage your problem. We have an army of one hundred qualities to choose from up there! You can cultivate these qualities by practicing any one or a combination of spiritual methods.

- For highly reactive emotions, you might choose peace, even-mindedness, and patience. Permeate all of the rooms in your house and all of your problems with these qualities.

4. ACTION:

- Bring your expanded peace, even-mindedness, and patience to all of your actions.

5. REPETITION:

- Repeat this process of healing and purification until the spiritual qualities become unconditional.

6. MASTERY:

- In the end, we become patient, peaceful, and even-minded under all conditions. Then we can give these qualities to all we meet.

POINTS TO REMEMBER

- An uninvited problem that we cannot eliminate creates agitation. We can reduce this agitation by giving the problem a spacious room filled with stillness, silence, and serenity.

- When life does not change, our response to it can. We can accept all problems with serenity. When we practice the spiritual methods described in this work, we create an increasingly serene space to hold our problems.

- We can bring the spiritual qualities down to the first floor in response to the tests and trials of our lives. When we focus on these qualities instead of our problems, we slowly spiritualize the entire first floor of our home. Eventually, Love, compassion, understanding, humor, cheerfulness, and strength permeate our atmosphere.

- In the beginning, in ordinary consciousness, a problem like a big fish creates many ripples in a small pond. In higher states of consciousness, the same fish has little or no effect, as our consciousness has expanded. We have the space inside to handle anything, including death.

- Whenever we have problems with difficult people, we can give each of them a room with plenty of space. We can then permeate that room with understanding, patience, tolerance, and kindness.

- Do not try to escape your problems. They are invited guest-teachers, but they do not own the house. Welcome these guests into your home but not as permanent residents. Remember, your problems are teachers, helping expand your spiritual qualities until these qualities are unconditional.

- Never forget: you have the help of an army of one hundred spiritual qualities!

AFFIRMATIONS

- I add Love to every moment.
- I entertain every guest-teacher.
- I accept all problems with serenity.
- I am serene no matter what happens.
- I manifest unflinching peace no matter what the world does.
- I manifest unflinching peace no matter what state my body is in.
- I stay deep in the Ocean of Love no matter what happens on the surface.
- I am safe, secure, and immortal.
- I hold all of my problems in a compassionate space.
- I hold all of your problems in a compassionate space.
- I burn karmic problems with Love.
- Love burns karma: mine, yours, and ours.
- I surround, feed, permeate, and saturate all of my problems with healing qualities.

EXERCISES

1. Describe the seven steps of the healing process called "The Ocean."

2. Do you use meditation to help you work with your pain and problems?

3. How might you use "The Ocean" to help you contain, reduce, or eliminate your pain and problems?

4. Describe the six steps of the healing process called "The House."

5. What happens if you do not have enough space in your house to hold your problems?

6. When you practice spiritual disciplines, you expand the space in your house so it will be big enough to hold your problems. When you have a lot of space, problems can show up with barely a ripple. Is your house big enough? What will you do to create more space?

7. Make a list of the people who provoke you. In a meditative state, visualize each one of them in a room with plenty of space. Then permeate the room with understanding, patience, tolerance, and kindness. Picture yourself with each of these people in harmony and peace.

8. When you feel ashamed because of your mistakes, visualize yourself in a spacious room filled with understanding, compassion, and forgiveness. Absorb these qualities.

You have completed your review of ten powerful healing qualities. In the next chapter, you will learn how to create a balanced healing program.

PART SEVEN
CONCLUSION

CHAPTER THIRTY-FIVE

A BALANCED HEALING PROGRAM

Putting It All Together

- In this chapter, you will learn how to create a personal, balanced healing program to use for any painful condition, including major life crises or longstanding problems.

- TESTS AND TRIALS. Our most basic instinct is to be happy and avoid suffering. Yet, physical, mental, and emotional pains frequently slip past our best defenses. Our natural impulse is to do whatever it takes to rid ourselves of the discomfort. However, there is no escape from the inevitable suffering of life.

- UNSKILLFUL PAIN MANAGEMENT. We lock all of the doors of our body-home, trying to keep the peace by warding off uninvited guests. All too often our attempts to avoid suffering compound our problems. When we persist in trying to escape our problems, our pain increases to the point of despair, physical and mental illness, disrupted relationships, reduced functioning, and potential danger to others and ourselves.

- SKILLFUL PAIN MANAGEMENT. On the other hand, stepping into the pain and managing our problems wisely leads to healing, peace of mind, strength, and ultimately, joy. Pain is a directional signal pointing the way to our internal powers. When we learn to use suffering as a stimulant for the growth of spiritual qualities, the result is a shift in the locus of control from outside to inside. From this position of inner peace and strength, we can handle whatever comes our way.

Following is a complete list of the pain management techniques described in this book. These techniques help us mobilize our resources so that we can work through our problems, realize our spiritual power, and avoid unnecessary suffering. In this chapter, we will review how these methods work together to help us meet challenges head-on. To help you manage problems and pain, you can choose any one or a combination of the following:

Horizontal Axis:

1. People
2. Activities
3. Belief system

Vertical Axis:

4. Affirmations
5. Habit transformation
6. Progressive muscle relaxation
7. Breathwork
8. Contemplation
9. Meditation
10. Prayer
11. Mindfulness
12. Practicing the Presence of God
13. Service
14. Yoga
15. Transformation of emotion

1. PEOPLE:

- When we suffer, we turn to trusted friends and family. We tell our story seeking understanding, support, and solace. At times, we seek advice, but more often, we just need to be heard and accepted. Just getting the story out brings relief and healing.

- Often, however, we experience emotional pain that does not go away after talking it out. And sometimes our relationships make things worse because we are misunderstood or poorly treated.

- Even if we have a strong, loving support network filled with understanding, humor, and forgiveness, we will have emotional pain requiring management by other methods. In fact, one of the mistakes many of us make is looking to others for emotional pain relief when it is not possible. This leads to codependency, which is, in effect, addiction to people. We become codependent when we look to others to solve problems that can only be solved by ourselves.

2. ACTIVITIES:

- Constructive, meaningful activities are powerful pain managers. School, work, training, volunteering, culture, sports, recreation, and hobbies provide us with opportunities for growth and healing. We need a list of activities to turn to when pain arrives. It is helpful to have activities performed alone and with others.

3. BELIEF SYSTEM:

- Belief systems help us manage our pain. We experience relief when we discover the meaning of life. When we find our metaphor or story, we can survive even the worst conditions.

- Many go to church, synagogue, or mosque for traditional worship, support of like-minded people, and service work. This may be enough for some people. Others need additional help. Spiritual belief systems give us twelve additional tools to help us manage our pain (Options 4–15 above.)

A PERSONAL HEALING PROGRAM

- HORIZONTAL AXIS. The first three options are practiced on the physical plane, here referred to as the horizontal axis. In our culture, most people try to manage their pain exclusively on the physical plane though relationships, activities, and external worship. This tendency can be a problem. Most of us need to do some internal work as well.

- VERTICAL AXIS. Options 4-15 are practiced internally, in a space referred to here as the vertical axis. In a balanced healing program, there will be a healthy balance between horizontal or external practices and vertical or internal practices. When this balance is achieved, we accomplish the ultimate goal: cultivation of spiritual qualities.

- BALANCE. Review the pain management options listed above. Through trial and error, we can discover which option or combination of options will work for any given problem. For some problems, good friends and activities will suffice. On other days, contemplation, reading sacred texts, and meditation are most effective.

Some techniques, such as meditation or the transformation of emotion, may be more difficult for some people. If a technique causes too much pain, you can turn to another less invasive method.

For example, if processing emotions causes you to feel frightened and you are tempted to turn to an unhealthy painkiller such as alcohol, you can turn to a different method, such as support from your friends or going to the gym, to restore your balance. When you feel stronger, you can return to the transformation of emotion.

You can move from emotional processing to being with a friend for dinner, to emotional processing, to watching television, to prayer and meditation, to physical exercise, to emotional processing, and so forth.

The combination of methods used on any particular day may vary.

As our experience grows, our ability to match techniques to problems improves. We become more effective pain managers. Eventually, we reach the point where we can handle anything, including the unknown and death.

CONCLUSION

- THE GREAT ONES. Buddha and Christ discovered the secret connection between skillful pain management and healing. Recognizing pain as a law of life, the Buddha teaches us how to transform personal suffering into compassion for others. Christ on the cross demonstrated masterful skill in pain management when he forgave his tormentors at a time of excruciating suffering. We can follow their lead if we experience our pain and learn from it.

- LOVE IS THE GOAL. The ultimate goal of pain management is Love. When we stop running and accept pain as our teacher, we learn the necessary lessons that inevitably have to do with expansion of Love. There is a powerful narrative embedded in our feelings having to do with unconditional Love, friendship, and service. When we understand and forgive others and ourselves, the way is opened for healing and purification.

- ELIMINATE ALL TRACES OF NEGATIVITY. With Love as your tool, dig deep. Eliminate all traces of negativity. Get rid of your bad habits. Practice affirmation, mindfulness, the Presence of God, and meditation. Contemplate the great sacred texts. Transform emotion to self-knowledge. Learn how to spiritualize your story. Serve all of humanity.

- DESIGN YOUR OWN PROGRAM. With people, activities, a strong belief system, and the twelve internal practices described in this work, you can field whatever life throws at you. Design a pain management program for yourself. Work with these practices for the rest of your life. Arrange and rearrange the methods to find the combinations that best suit you.

- HOMEWORK FIRST, THEN ENJOY THE SHOW. Accept pain as your teacher and allow the healing power to do its work. And remember, you can play hooky from school and go to the movies, but eventually you have to return to class. You need to do your homework first. You need to learn how to be a good pain manager. Then you can enjoy the show.

- THE GREAT PHYSICIAN. The Great Physician prescribes Love as the medication for all our ills. Follow Love and keep your eyes open. It will take you where you need to go. Even if you must pass through the cave of darkness, Love will light the way. Let your pain take you to the next level of higher consciousness. For every problem you navigate, you rise. When you complete all of your problems, you will rise above all of creation. Then you will know the foundation of the universe is eternal peace, Omniscient Love and ecstatic joy.

In my heart of hearts,
only the Love of God.
I scatter it everywhere,
to the good-God hidden in all forms.
Then I see Her unseen hand, everywhere.

POINTS TO REMEMBER

- As described in Step 5, Tools Become Barriers: The restless mind, highly reactive emotions, excessive material desires, the troubles of the body, hyperactivity, and the ego add untold difficulty to the already formidable inevitable suffering of life. To help manage this reactivity, we need an individualized balanced healing program with options on both the horizontal and vertical axis.

- Many of us have longstanding problems that may take years of work. We should not be discouraged if these problems do not respond immediately. Effort is progress. If we do the work, our problems slowly burn up. We stop attracting the same negative circumstances and people. The positive experiences in our lives increase. Peace, courage, strength, and wisdom grow.

- There are times in all of our lives when there are too many problems to handle at once. Problems compound. Our pain grows from moderate to severe. We go into crisis. There may be symptoms, impaired functioning, and danger. We can get discouraged or frightened. This may be a time to seek professional help. Some are reluctant to do this, thinking it to be failure. However, life is painful. At times, suffering is great. Getting help is a sign of strength and wisdom.

- We want to avoid pain and be happy. We have an aversion to suffering. We are afraid that our pain may cause us to lose control. We choose all kinds of behavior to avoid suffering, but pain is a part of reality. Eventually we must face it. If your life is focused only on feeling good, you are vulnerable to bad habits. Go deeper. Face your pain, fears, and problems. If you manage your pain wisely by practicing the spiritual disciplines described in this work, you will find out who you really are: peace, Love, joy, power, and wisdom.

AFFIRMATIONS

- I am a stronger and wiser because of my tests and challenges.
- Better to have pain than to remain the same.
- Every problem is an opportunity in disguise.
- Rather than seek pleasure and avoid pain, I accept both as having benefit.
- I develop spiritual muscles by working through my painful problems.
- I accept the difficulties of life as necessary for spiritual growth.

- I am strong and calm in any outer condition.
- Time and Love heal all of my wounds.
- I thank Spirit for providing me with opportunities to grow and transform.
- Suffering leads to compassion, strength, and wisdom.
- Suffering leads to peace, Love, and joy.

EXERCISES

1. Review the list of pain management options described in this lesson. Which of these methods are you currently using? Which of these methods might you add to your program?

2. Discuss how people, activities, a belief system, (horizontal axis) and the twelve spiritual methods (vertical axis) work together to help manage pain and suffering.

3. What is the nature of a balanced healing program?

"May you find the peace, Love, and joy that are your soul."

APPENDIX A

Group Guidelines

I use this book for teaching in a group setting. We follow these guidelines. If there is a new member in the group, we read these guidelines before we start.

* Introduction and names

* The model is a composite of universal healing principles from the great wisdom traditions. It does not push religion. It does try to equip persons of all persuasions with the essential healing principle embedded within the religions.

* While we do not promote a particular religion, we do promote the development of your individual approach to spirituality.

* We have respect and tolerance for the great variety of ways to understand and practice spirituality.

* The model is for any person: atheist, agnostic, spiritual, or religious.

* The model is for any problem: physical, mental, emotional, social, spiritual.

* The methods can be practiced anywhere and anytime: at home, at work, or at play.

- There is a cafeteria of options. You can add these options to your current belief system or build your own program.

- Take what you need and leave the rest.

- The term "Higher Power" is used to describe the God of your understanding, your higher self, higher states of consciousness, or your higher meaning and purpose.

- One person's traction device is the next person's gag reflex. Don't let language stop you. For some people, even the word spirituality is a problem. Nuke offensive language and substitute your own. For example, you might substitute Higher Power for God, higher self for soul, higher for spiritual, healing qualities for spiritual qualities, or cognitive-behavioral practice for spiritual practice.

- Some chapters in this book speak to those who believe in a God of Love. Other chapters are more universal. If you don't believe in God, let alone God as Love, substitute with words like spiritual qualities, healing qualities, qualities, The Tao, The Way, the Great Spirit, compassion, or any other term that gives you traction. The universal goal is to become a more skillful pain manager, expand healing power, and evolve. As you proceed, use whatever term is most acceptable to you.

- Stay in your own lane.

- Reform yourself and not others. We are not here to change others. We are here to change ourselves.

- We do not proselytize (convert others to our point of view.)

- We engage in discussion without debate.

- We are here to listen and share, learn and grow, study and practice.

- Although active participation is encouraged, it is perfectly okay to remain silent throughout the meeting.

- During the class, we take turns reading. If you don't wish to read, you are welcome to pass.

- The group is 60-90 minutes. Each person reads a paragraph followed by a discussion and contemplation of the material.

- We avoid giving advice or trying to fix other people's problems. We focus on our personal experience using the spiritual methods for cultivating soul qualities in response to life's problems.

- When we finish the book, we return to the beginning and read it again.

- This is an open group. You can come and go as you please.

- We begin and end each class with a period of silent meditation for two minutes. The best meditation position is with the eyes closed, focused on the point just above the eyebrows, feet flat on the floor, hands resting in your lap with palms upward, spine straight, and slightly bent as a bow. You may repeat your focus word, mantra, or a favorite affirmation. You might also just focus on your breath.

APPENDIX B

Definitions

- **Brutal reality:** Death, pain and suffering, and the unknown. Referred to as reality because on the physical plane, suffering is unavoidable and death wins in the end. Brutal reality ultimately replaces the illusion of safety, security, and immortality defined below.

- **Ego:** What keeps us separate from others, the creation, and the Creator. Selfishness. I, me, my, mine. Territorial and self-important.

- **Healing Power:** The magnificently intelligent Healing Power that operates every cell in the body. It knows what to do. It is incomparably brilliant.

- **Healing Qualities:** a list of one hundred qualities also referred to as the spiritual alphabet. These qualities are the attributes of Love and reflect the character of the higher self, true self, or soul.

- **Higher Power:** The God of your understanding, Higher Consciousness, higher meaning and purpose or higher self.

- **Higher Self:** true self, soul, a composite of the one hundred qualities listed in the spiritual alphabet.

- **Horizontal axis:** External action on the physical plane involving people, activities, things, events, and places. Used in conjunction with vertical axis which is internal action involving the practice of the spiritual methods described in this work. A balanced healing program includes work in both domains.

- **Illusion of safety, security, and immortality:** There is no such thing as permanent or absolute safety on the physical plane. The best we can do on the physical plane is create a feeling of safety based on the sense that we have more time. Referred to as an illusion as it is temporary, limited, and ultimately replaced by brutal reality.

- **Inevitable suffering of life:** Life is difficult and painful for everyone. There is no way around it. All of us have to face the minor irritations of routine daily living and major life problems such as disease, disability, the unknown and death. This is the inevitable suffering of life. Reactivity is the suffering we add to the inevitable suffering of life. Reactivity is reversible. The inevitable suffering of life is not reversible.

- **Love:** A combination of one hundred qualities defined in Step 7. For our purposes, each time you read the word Love, you can consider that as one or a combination of these qualities. If you don't favor the word Love, you are encouraged to use one of the following names or any label that gives you inspiration; you can call it Truth, Power, Wisdom, Self-Knowledge, higher self, true self, soul, the Buddha, Atman, the Image of God, Spiritual Qualities, Spiritual Alphabet, Healing Alphabet, Spiritual Properties, Qualities, Healing Qualities, or the Attributes of Love. It doesn't matter what you call it. What does matter is the recognition that at the very core of your being exists a host of healing qualities that can help you manage any painful problem.

- **Mental health:** The mind is calm, positive, focused, strong, and resilient. It is awake, alert, and ready for problem solving, creative

494

intelligence, shaping meaning, goal accomplishment, pain management, and the creation of health, success, harmony, and joy.

- **Reactivity:** Step 5 is called Tools Become Barriers. There are six tools we use to achieve the core drive: thought, feeling, desire, body, activity, and ego. When the six tools are in alignment, they are powerful assets. When they go out of alignment, they become liabilities. The restless mind, high emotional reactivity, excessive material desire, the body, hyperactivity, and egotism add an additional layer of suffering to the inevitable suffering of life. This is called reactivity. Reactivity is reversible.

- **Recovery:** Getting your life back no matter your disease or disability.

- **Skillful pain management:** There are two layers of pain: the inevitable suffering of life, and our reaction to it. We cannot control the former but we can control the latter. When you practice the techniques described in this book, you reduce reactivity, the add-ons to the inevitable suffering of life. You cultivate strength and peace no matter what your body or the world throws at you. You become a more skillful pain manager, and your quality of life improves accordingly.

- **Spiritual alphabet:** The one hundred qualities defined in Step 7 also referred to as healing qualities, qualities, the attributes of Love, or Love.

- **Spiritual evolution:** When the qualities listed in the spiritual alphabet such as peace, strength, courage, Love, compassion, understanding and forgiveness grow. You will feel better, become a better person, and experience higher states of consciousness.

- **Spirituality:** Religious elements include story, metaphor, parable, concepts, images, aspects, sacred texts, rituals, traditional worship, social gatherings, committee work, attending services, music, architecture, and listening to sermons. Spirituality is the healing qualities and higher states of consciousness that permeate these elements.

- **Spiritual practice:** Practicing any one or a combination of the fifteen methods described in this work.

- **Superconsciousness:** an unmistakable shift in consciousness sometimes described as the peace that surpasses understanding, pure Love, ecstatic joy, unfathomable stillness, intuitive wisdom, a feeling of oneness with everything and other wonderful expressions of Spirit. These experiences may last from a few minutes or hours to several days but there is inevitably a return to ordinary consciousness unless one is a spiritual master.

- **Traction device:** What gives the inspiration to do the work. Traction devices for the Universal Healing Wheel are any of the elements from the great wisdom traditions: concepts, images, aspects, rituals, story, sermons, music, art, or metaphor. May include God, the God of Love, the masters, mystery, karma, reincarnation, and much more.

- **Universal Healing Wheel:** problem-method-quality or PMQ.

  1. Problem: any problem of body, mind, or soul
  2. Method: any one or a combination of fifteen practice methods described in this work
  3. Quality: any one or a combination of one hundred healing qualities

  PMQ is the essential healing principle of any wisdom tradition. It is necessary and sufficient for psychosocial and spiritual healing. This is all you need.

- **USA (unconditional, spontaneous, automatic):** At mastery, when a spiritual quality is fully developed, it is USA, or unconditional, spontaneous, and automatic. The greatest example of this is Jesus on the cross proclaiming, "Forgive them for they know not what they do." Jesus expressed unconditional, spontaneous, and automatic forgiveness, signaling his status as a grand spiritual master.

- **Vertical axis:** Internal action involving the practice of spiritual methods described in this work. It is used in conjunction with horizontal axis, which is external action on the physical plane involving people, activities, things, events, and places. A balanced healing program includes work in both domains.

- **Wisdom Tradition:** All of the great religions, spiritual teachings, and other psychosocial healing models such as the 12-steps, DBT, mindfulness based cognitive-behavioral therapy, mindfulness based stress reduction, and many more.

APPENDIX C

Staging Disease and Recovery

For Low Income Persons with Chronic Severe Illness

- We can use the models described in this work, "Brutal Reality and the Illusion of Safety, Security and Immortality" (1980) and "Healing Power: Ten Steps to Pain Management and Spiritual Evolution" (2005) for staging disease and recovery. Following is an example of staging for low-income persons who suffer from chronic severe illness.

SPIN → FLOAT → INTEGRATE

- SPIN. This is high acuity requiring multiple visits to the emergency room, hospital, and clinics. Those in the spin zone have one or more of the following: active physical illness, mental illness, and addiction, low or no income, unemployment, and homelessness. These individuals often spin between the hospital, jail, and street. There may be danger to self or others.

- FLOAT. With medication, housing, and financial support, mental illness, physical illness, and substance use improve. Symptoms if present are more manageable. People isolate in their rooms, watch TV, smoke, hang out, and wander aimlessly. There may be some social contact but little or no connection to meaningful social, recreational, vocational or spiritual activity. There is often no meaning and purpose.

- INTEGRATE. This is community integration involving people, activities, and belief systems. People get their social, recreational, vocational, and spiritual lives back.

- FLOAT → INTEGRATE. To move from float to integrate, we need positive action on the horizontal axis of people, activities, and belief system. For deepest healing, we need to move from fixed to opened belief systems, and add vertical axis healing options including self-knowledge. See Figure 1 and Figure 2. This requires managing that gap between fixed and opened belief systems where even a little anxiety is perceived as the uninvited guest in the living room. (the cheeseburger effect)

- GAP MANAGEMENT. To manage the anxiety in the gap, roll the Universal Healing Wheel. For any pain or problem, there are 15 methods: 3 on the external horizontal axis and 12 on the internal vertical axis. Some will chose none of these. Others will apply all fifteen. Following is an example of a way to stage recovery using the 15 methods.

STAGING RECOVERY USING THE 15 METHODS

Horizontal Axis:

1. People
2. Activities
3. Belief system
    a. Fixed
    b. Opened

Vertical Axis:

4. Affirmations
5. Habit transformation
6. Progressive muscle relaxation

7. Breathwork
8. Contemplation
9. Meditation
10. Prayer
11. Mindfulness
12. Practicing the Presence of God
13. Service
14. Yoga
15. Transformation of emotion

1. LEVEL 1: No Options. This individual chooses none of the 15 methods. There is an inability or lack of motivation for community integration. Some people are overwhelmed by stimulation and need to stay alone to remain stable. Others may lack initiative or energy. The illness may be too acute. There may be too much pain. This individual will remain in spin and float.

2. LEVEL 2: People and or activities. This individual chooses people and or activities. There is social and recreational recovery but an inability to engage in cognitive-behavioral work (belief systems) or vocational recovery. This person profits from day programs and drop-in centers.

3. LEVEL 3: People, activities, and belief system. This individual engages with people and activities and has a belief system: traditional religion, 12-step program, or other healing models. This includes social, vocational, recreational, and spiritual recovery. This individual remains primarily on the horizontal axis and has an external locus of control.

4. LEVEL 4: People, activities, and belief system with any one or combination of vertical axis options. There may be a need to move from a fixed to an opened belief system. The locus of control begins to shift from outside to inside.

5. LEVEL 5: As with Level 4 but add transformation of emotion and meditation, the two most difficult and advanced vertical axis techniques. With the addition of these two powerful digging tools, one can remove all traces of negativity, leading to the recovery of the higher self and Higher Power as the *unlimited* peace, joy, Love, and safety we crave. The locus of control is primarily inside.

• These are not rigid categories and this is not the only way to stage recovery.

Figure 1

| Spin | ⟷ | Float | ⟷ | Integrate |

People:

Community, family, friends, us: all of us need a support network filled with Love, compassion, understanding, courage, forgiveness, and humor.

Who do you have to talk to? Who do you trust?

Activities:

Constructive meaningful activities: work, school, training, volunteer, library, walking, reading, sports, TV, exercise, computer, Internet, culture, music, all of the arts.

What is your day like?

Float

Belief Systems:

Core beliefs, religious/secular/spiritual, the story, the lens by which you understand the world around you; traditional worship, 12 steps, other healing models, the 12 internal vertical axis methods: Do you have a spiritual, religious, or secular program?

Self Knowledge:

Developed self, deeper understanding, insight. This is equivalent to Transformation of Emotion, one of the 12 vertical axis methods.

How do you handle emotions like anger, depression, guilt, fear, etc?"

Figure 2

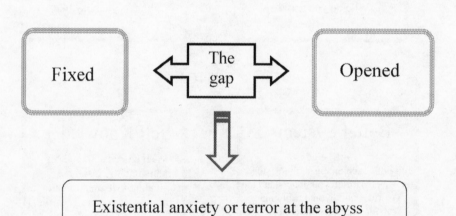

Belief Systems:

Core beliefs, religious/secular/spiritual, the story,
the lens by which you understand the world
around you; traditional worship, 12 steps, other
healing models

Fixed ⟵ The gap ⟶ Opened

Existential anxiety or terror at the abyss
reluctance/resistance

PERMISSIONS

I gratefully acknowledge permission from these sources to reprint the following:

"The Guest House" from *The Essential Rumi*, translations by Coleman Barks, 1995, reprinted by permission of Coleman Barks

"Two Frogs in Trouble," from the teachings of Paramahansa Yogananda, reprinted with permission of Self-Realization Fellowship.

REFERENCES

Alter, R. 2000. *The transformative power of crisis.* New York: Harper-Collins.

Anandamoy. 2001. Converting what you read into personal realization. *Self-Realization Magazine* Spring: 44-50.

Benson, H. 1996. *Timeless healing: The power and biology of belief.* New York: Fireside.

Benson, H. 1975. *The relaxation response.* New York: Morrow.

Birkedahl, N. 1990. *The habit control workbook.* Oakland: New Harbinger Publications.

Bloch, D. 1998. *Words that heal: Affirmations for daily living.* New York: Bantam Books.

Bloch, D. 1992. *I am with you always.* New York: Bantam Books.

Cooper, D. 1999. *A heart of stillness.* Woodstock: Skylight Paths Publishing.

Cooper, D. 1999. *Silence, simplicity, and solitude.* Woodstock: Skylight Paths Publishing.

Courage to change. 1992. New York: Al-Anon Family Group Headquarters.

Dass, R. and B. Mirabai. 1992. *Compassion in action.* New York: Bell Tower.

Dass, R. and P. Gorman. 1985. *How can I help?* New York: Alfred A. Knopf.

Dossey, L. 1992. *Healing words: The power of prayer and the practice of medicine.* New York: Harper-Collins.

Enright, R. 2001. *Forgiveness is a choice.* Washington D.C.: American Psychological Association.

Firestone, T. 1998. *With roots in heaven.* New York: Penguin.

Frankl, V. 1984. *Man's search for meaning.* New York: Washington Square Press.

Gibran, K. 1955. *The prophet.* New York: Alfred A. Knopf.

Hanh, T. N. 1992. *Peace is every step.* New York: Bantam.

Hendricks, G. 1995. *Conscious breathing.* New York: Bantam.

Herrmann, R. 2000. *God, science, and humility.* Philadelphia: Templeton Foundation Press.

Jackson, E. 1974. *Progressive relaxation.* Chicago: University of Chicago Press.

Kabat-Zinn, J. 1994. *Wherever you go, there you are.* New York: Hyperion.

Kabat-Zinn, J. 1990. *Full catastrophe living.* New York: Delta.

Kamala. 1969. *Priceless precepts.* Oakland: Kamala.

Keating, T. 2002. *Intimacy with God*. New York: The Crossroad Publishing Company.

Keating, T. 2001. *Open mind, open heart*. New York: Continuum.

Keating, T. 1997. *Active meditations for contemplative prayer*. New York: Continuum.

Khalsa, G. S. and Bhajan. 2000. *Breathwalk*. New York: Broadway Books.

Kornfield, J. 2000. *After the ecstasy, the laundry*. New York: Bantam Books.

Kushner, L. 1995. *Honey from the rock*. Woodstock: Jewish Lights Publishing.

Lawrence, B. and Laubach, F. 1973. *Practicing His presence*. Beaumont, Texas: The SeedSowers.

Lawrence, B. 1982. *The practice of the Presence of God*. Springdale, Pennsylvania: Whitaker House.

Luskin, F. 2002. *Forgive for good*. San Francisco: Harper.

Mata, D. 2003. *Intuition: Soul-guidance for life's decisions*. Los Angeles: Self-Realization Fellowship.

Mata, D. 1990. *Finding the joy within you*. Los Angeles: Self-Realization Fellowship.

Mata, D. 1971. *Only love*. Los Angeles: Self-Realization Fellowship.

May, G. 1991. *The awakened heart*. San Francisco: Harper.

May, G. 1982. *Care of mind, care of spirit*. San Francisco: Harper.

Moffit, P. 2002. Forgiving the unforgivable. *Yoga Journal* February.

Mosley, G. and J. Hill. 2000. *The power of prayer around the world.* Philadelphia: Templeton Foundation Press.

Prabhavananda, S. 1953. *How to know God.* Hollywood: Vedanta Press.

Rinpoche, S. 1993. *The Tibetan book of living and dying.* San Francisco: Harper.

Ruiz, D. M. 2001. *Prayers: Communions with our creator.* San Rafael: Amber-Allen Publishing.

Ruiz, D. M. 2000. *The four agreements companion book.* San Rafael: Amber-Allen Publishing.

Ruiz, D. M. 1997. *The four agreements: A Toltec wisdom book.* San Rafael: Amber-Allen Publishing.

Ruskan, J. 2000. *Emotional clearing.* New York: Broadway Books.

Salzberg, S. 2002. *Faith.* New York: Riverhead Books.

Schroeder, Gerald. 2001. *The hidden face of God.* New York: Touchstone

Segal, Z. 2002. *Mindfulness-based cognitive therapy for depression.* New York: Guilford Press.

Smith, H. 1999. *The world's religions.* San Francisco: Harper.

Sobel, D. and R. Ornstein. 1996. *The healthy mind, healthy body handbook.* New York: Patient Education Media.

Sorokin, P. 2002. *The ways and power of love*. Philadelphia: Templeton Foundation Press.

Templeton, J. 2002. *Wisdom from world religions*. Philadelphia: Templeton Foundation Press.

Templeton, J. 1999. *Agape love: A tradition found in eight world religions*. Philadelphia: Templeton Foundation Press.

Templeton, J. 1997. *Worldwide laws of life*. Philadelphia: Templeton Foundation Press.

The big book. 1983. New York: Alcoholics Anonymous World Services.

Vanzant, I. 1998. *One day my soul just opened up*. New York: Simon and Schuster.

Walsh, R. 1999. *Essential spirituality*. New York: John Wiley and Sons.

Walter, D. 1990. *The essence of self-realization*. Nevada City: Crystal Clarity Publishers.

Weil, A. 1999. *Breathing, the master key to self-healing*. Boulder: Sounds True, Inc.

Yogananda, P. 2003. Faith. *Self-Realization Magazine* Spring, 4-15.

Yogananda, P. 2003. *Living fearlessly*. Los Angeles: Self-Realization Fellowship.

Yogananda, P. 1999. *Inner peace*. Los Angeles: Self-Realization Fellowship.

Yogananda, P. 1997. *Journey to self-realization.* Los Angeles: Self-Realization Fellowship.

Yogananda, P. 1997. *Autobiography of a yogi.* Los Angeles: Self-Realization Fellowship.

Yogananda, P. 1995. *The Bhagavad Gita.* Los Angeles: Self-Realization Fellowship.

Yogananda, P. 1986. *The divine romance.* Los Angeles: Self-Realization Fellowship.

Yogananda, P. 1984. *Worldwide prayer circle.* Los Angeles: Self-Realization Fellowship.

Yogananda, P. 1982. *Man's eternal quest.* Los Angeles: Self-Realization Fellowship.

Yogananda, P. 1981. *Scientific healing affirmations.* Los Angeles: Self-Realization Fellowship.

Yogananda, P. 1968. *Spiritual diary.* Los Angeles: Self-Realization Fellowship.

Zubko, A. 1998. *Treasury of spiritual wisdom.* San Diego: Blue Dove Press.

INDEX

126, 127, 131, 132, 138, 140, 141,
147, 148, 149, 155, 158, 167, 171,
172, 174, 177, 179, 183, 184, 185,
186, 187, 188, 189, 190, 191, 192,
193, 194, 196, 197, 198, 199, 200,
202, 203, 204, 210, 213, 217, 218,
223, 227, 229, 230, 231, 232, 233,
234, 235, 238, 239, 240, 241, 245,
246, 247, 248, 249, 250, 251, 252,
253, 254, 256, 257, 258, 259, 260,
261, 262, 263, 264, 265, 266, 268,
271, 278, 279, 280, 281, 282, 283,
284, 287, 288, 289, 290, 291, 292,
293, 294, 295, 298, 304, 309, 310,
313, 315, 316, 317, 323, 326, 330,
331, 336, 337, 338, 340, 341, 342,
350, 353, 363, 369, 372, 374, 376,
378, 383, 384, 386, 387, 388, 392,
397, 402, 409, 413, 417, 418, 424,
427, 435, 437, 438, 442, 446, 451,
452, 453, 454, 455, 456, 457, 461,
463, 464, 465, 466, 467, 481, 486,
494, 495, 496, 509, 510
mind-body medicine 16, 17, 20, 21, 24,
25, 110
mindfulness 8, 12, 18, 36, 59, 74, 75,
84, 85, 87, 97, 98, 99, 103, 104,
112, 122, 131, 134, 140, 162, 173,
174, 175, 180, 214, 223, 268, 272,
273, 277, 279, 283, 284, 287, 288,
289, 292, 293, 294, 295, 296, 298,
299, 303, 304, 317, 322, 323, 326,
328, 346, 366, 375, 376, 379,
384, 386, 388, 390, 391, 418, 421,
422, 423, 473, 475, 482, 485, 497,
501, 510
mystery 6, 73, 75, 86, 99, 107, 113, 136,
139, 267, 270, 290, 399, 411, 496

N

non-attachment 75, 99, 336

non-injury 75, 99

O

ocean 62, 81, 115, 134, 139, 149, 253,
254, 257, 308, 312, 315, 334, 368,
370, 386, 387, 389, 390, 395, 424,
434, 446, 447, 459, 460, 461, 462,
464, 469, 470, 471, 472, 473, 477,
478
omnipresence 303, 308, 309, 310
omnipresent 107, 113, 128, 137, 253,
268, 269, 272, 302, 306, 315, 331,
334, 366, 368, 388, 389, 421, 451,
460
omniscience 134, 289, 290, 308, 393,
394, 395, 396, 451, 452, 453, 455,
456, 457, 458
omniscient 23, 31, 80, 107, 113, 128,
253, 269, 272, 289, 290, 301, 303,
310, 341, 380, 395, 400, 412, 451,
452, 464, 469, 486
Omniscient Love 128, 341, 380, 400,
412, 486
oneness 75, 88, 99, 133, 134, 268, 339,
359, 377, 459, 460, 462, 463, 464,
466, 496
openness 59, 75, 99, 355
order 15, 59, 75, 99, 101, 121, 133, 151,
159, 170, 215, 217, 231, 238, 255,
259, 261, 270, 284, 301, 320, 330,
346, 349, 354, 385, 386, 387, 429,
443, 451, 456, 460, 465

P

pain is the teacher 47, 84, 90, 101, 105,
130, 136, 151, 152, 197, 203, 284,
298, 361, 441
pain management 12, 13, 16, 22, 25,
26, 28, 29, 31, 35, 36, 42, 45, 47,
60, 69, 82, 83, 89, 90, 98, 101,
117, 118, 122, 144, 154, 163, 177,
209, 229, 233, 238, 293, 298, 347,

364, 369, 377, 410, 446, 455, 481, 482, 484, 485, 488, 495

Patanjali 336, 337, 343

patience xvi, 11, 27, 49, 75, 85, 99, 103, 104, 105, 112, 114, 122, 130, 138, 167, 170, 173, 188, 190, 196, 197, 198, 210, 216, 241, 260, 263, 313, 340, 341, 352, 354, 355, 361, 397, 398, 399, 412, 414, 445, 449, 466, 475, 476, 478

peace viii, ix, x, 3, 8, 11, 13, 15, 16, 18, 19, 21, 27, 29, 36, 38, 39, 40, 43, 45, 46, 47, 48, 49, 51, 52, 54, 58, 59, 60, 61, 62, 63, 64, 65, 67, 69, 71, 73, 75, 77, 81, 83, 85, 87, 88, 89, 90, 97, 98, 99, 100, 101, 103, 104, 105, 106, 109, 110, 112, 115, 116, 117, 120, 121, 122, 126, 130, 133, 134, 135, 137, 138, 140, 141, 144, 145, 148, 149, 151, 152, 153, 155, 157, 158, 159, 161, 162, 164, 166, 170, 171, 172, 173, 176, 177, 179, 180, 183, 184, 188, 192, 194, 196, 197, 198, 199, 200, 201, 203, 207, 210, 214, 216, 218, 226, 227, 232, 233, 234, 235, 239, 242, 243, 245, 246, 247, 249, 251, 252, 254, 255, 257, 258, 259, 260, 261, 262, 263, 264, 265, 270, 271, 272, 273, 278, 279, 282, 283, 284, 285, 290, 291, 292, 294, 295, 296, 298, 302, 305, 306, 310, 311, 313, 314, 321, 324, 326, 329, 330, 332, 333, 334, 337, 338, 340, 341, 350, 354, 355, 356, 359, 361, 362, 367, 371, 372, 375, 383, 384, 385, 386, 387, 388, 389, 390, 391, 392, 396, 399, 400, 401, 403, 409, 410, 411, 412, 413, 414, 417, 418, 419, 420, 421, 422, 423, 424, 425, 427, 428, 431, 432, 433, 434, 435, 436, 437, 438, 445,

446, 447, 448, 449, 453, 457, 460, 461, 462, 464, 466, 467, 469, 472, 475, 477, 478, 481, 482, 486, 487, 488, 495, 496, 502, 508, 511

perfection 75, 99, 175, 304, 365

perseverance 47, 75, 77, 99, 132, 138, 170, 173, 190, 198, 212, 242, 341, 355, 420, 423, 444, 466

play 23, 28, 31, 35, 53, 55, 61, 63, 73, 75, 76, 84, 99, 172, 183, 208, 209, 213, 252, 261, 285, 287, 311, 312, 320, 335, 336, 394, 411, 465, 486, 489

positive thinking 75, 99, 200, 422

power viii, ix, x, 3, 7, 10, 12, 14, 15, 19, 21, 22, 23, 24, 25, 26, 27, 28, 29, 30, 31, 33, 34, 35, 38, 40, 41, 42, 43, 45, 47, 48, 49, 52, 53, 54, 55, 59, 61, 62, 63, 64, 65, 69, 71, 73, 75, 76, 78, 79, 80, 81, 82, 83, 87, 88, 89, 97, 98, 99, 101, 102, 104, 107, 108, 109, 110, 113, 115, 118, 119, 123, 125, 126, 127, 128, 129, 132, 137, 138, 139, 142, 143, 144, 145, 146, 147, 148, 149, 150, 151, 152, 154, 155, 156, 158, 159, 161, 162, 164, 168, 169, 171, 173, 179, 183, 184, 185, 186, 187, 189, 190, 191, 195, 197, 198, 199, 200, 201, 202, 203, 204, 208, 209, 210, 211, 212, 213, 214, 216, 217, 218, 237, 239, 241, 242, 246, 247, 251, 253, 254, 255, 258, 259, 262, 263, 264, 265, 267, 268, 269, 270, 271, 272, 285, 290, 291, 294, 301, 302, 303, 305, 306, 308, 309, 310, 312, 314, 317, 323, 325, 327, 329, 330, 333, 335, 338, 340, 341, 350, 351, 352, 355, 356, 364, 368, 372, 380, 385, 388, 389, 391, 392, 394, 395, 396, 399, 400, 401, 402, 405, 408, 410,

ABOUT THE AUTHOR

Dr. Phil Shapiro is a psychiatrist and devotee of yoga-meditation with an interest in the magnificent intelligent healing power as an antidote to the brutal realities of life. He has had a 40-year career as a clinician, teacher, and administrator in public psychiatry. Work has taken him from the inner city to the Alaska bush, from holistic to addiction medicine, and from the boardroom to the streets. In 1974, he worked in one of the first interdisciplinary holistic clinics in New York City.

In l983, he became the Director of Mental Health and Developmental Disabilities for the State of Alaska. Following that, he was the Chief Medical Officer at Oregon State Hospital and then Clinical Director of Forensic Psychiatry at Western State Hospital. He has been a surveyor, reviewing quality of care in hospitals and clinics throughout the country. For the past eighteen years, he has worked in community mental health centers.

Dr. Shapiro received his medical degree in l969 from the University of Illinois Medical School, where he was a member of the medical honorary society, Alpha Omega Alpha.

He trained in psychiatry at Albert Einstein College of Medicine, Downstate and Kings County Hospital in New York City and received a masters degree in public health from Columbia University. Dr. Shapiro has been on the faculty of the Department of Psychiatry at Columbia University and is currently an Associate Clinical Professor in the Department of Psychiatry at Oregon Health and Sciences University.

While he has studied the nature of disease and healing with many of the masters of psychiatry, psychology, and spirituality, his greatest teachers have been his patients who carry the devastating aspects of life: racism, poverty, mental and physical illness, homelessness, child sex abuse, rape, domestic violence, and addiction. These courageous people and the mean streets they walk continue to be his teachers of the brutal realities of life.

Dr. Shapiro lives in Portland, Oregon happily married to Sharon Whitney, author and playwright. They have two sons and five grand-children. He works for a community mental health center where his understanding of suffering and the magnificence of the healing power continue to evolve.